ning

ADVANCE PRAISE FOR *THE ETHNIC CLEANSING OF PALESTINE*

'Ilan Pappe is Israel's bravest, most principled, most incisive historian.'

—John Pilger

'Ilan Pappe has written an extraordinary book of profound relevance to the past, present, and future of Israel/Palestine relations.'

—Richard Falk, Professor of International Law and Practice, Princeton University

'If there is to be real peace in Palestine/Israel, the moral vigour and intellectual clarity of The Ethnic Cleansing of Palestine will have been a major contributor to it.'

—Ahdaf Soueif, author of The Map of Love

'This is an extraordinary book - a dazzling feat of scholarly synthesis and Biblical moral clarity and humaneness.'

—Walid Khalidi, Former Senior Research Fellow, Center for Middle Eastern Studies, Harvard University

'Fresh insights into a world historic tragedy, related by a historian of genius.'

—George Galloway MP

'Groundbreaking research into a well-kept Israeli secret. A classic of historical scholarship on a taboo subject by one of Israel's foremost New Historians.'

—Ghada Karmi, author of In Search of Fatima

'Ilan Pappe is out to fight against Zionism, whose power of deletion has driven a whole nation not only out of its homeland but out of historic memory as well. A detailed, documented record of the true history of that crime, *The Ethnic Cleansing of Palestine* puts an end to the Palestinian "Nakbah" and the Israeli "War of Independence" by so compellingly shifting both paradigms.'

—Anton Shammas, Professor of Modern Middle Eastern Literature, University of Michigan

'An instant classic. Finally we have the authoritative account of an historic event, which continues to shape our world today, and drives the conflict in the Middle East. Pappe is the only historian who could have told it, and he has done so with supreme command of the facts, elegance, and compassion. The publication of this book is a landmark event.'

—Karma Nabulsi, research fellow at Nuffield College, Oxford University

'The first book to so clearly document the ethnic cleansing of Palestine in 1948, of which the massacre at Deir Yassin was emblematic. A masterful achievement.'

—Daniel McGowan, Executive Director, Deir Yassin Remembered, Hobart and William Smith Colleges

THE ETHNIC CLEANSING
OF PALESTINE

ILAN PAPPE

ONEWORLD

OXFORD

THE ETHNIC CLEANSING OF PALESTINE

First published by Oneworld Publications Limited 2006
Copyright © Ilan Pappe 2006
Reprinted 2007 (three times)

ISBN-13: 978-1-85168-467-0

Typeset by Jayvee, Trivandrum, India
Cover design by Jon Gray
Printed and bound by TJ International Ltd, Padstow, Cornwall

Oneworld Publications Limited
185 Banbury Road
Oxford OX2 7AR
England
www.oneworld-publications.com

The publishers would like to thank the United Nations Relief and Works Agency for
permission to reproduce the photographs on plates 8, 10–12, 18, 19, copyright © UNRWA.
The publishers would also like to thank the Institute of Palestine Studies, Beirut, for
permission to publish the photographs on plates 14-17, all from the book
All That Remains (ed. Walid Khalidi) and for generously providing maps 3, 4, and 7;
and would like to express their sincere gratitude to Abu al-Sous of
www.palestineremembered.com, whose assistance in locating images has been invaluable.
The photographs on plates 4 & 13 copyright © Bettmann/Corbis; the photograph on
plate 1 copyright © Hulton-Deutsch Collection/Corbis; the photograph on
plate 6 copyright © Getty Images; the facsimile article on
plate 7 copyright © *New York Times*.

Photograph on the front endpapers shows the village of Saffuriyya prior to its destruction
Photograph on the back endpapers shows the Nahr al-Barid refugee camp in northern Lebanon
(copyright © UNRWA)

Contents

List of Illustrations, Maps, and Tables

ILLUSTRATIONS: PLATE SECTION

1. Irgun troops marching through Tel-Aviv, 14 May 1948
2. Jewish forces occupy a village near Safad
3. Jewish forces enter Malkiyya
4. Arab men of military age are marched to holding camps
5. The Red House in Tel-Aviv, headquarters of the Hagana
6. Refugee women, children and the elderly are evacuated
7. The *New York Times* report on the Deir Yassin massacre
8. Palestinian refugees flock to the sea to escape
9. Refugees on the move
10. Loading belongings into trucks for the journey
11. Elderly refugees
12. Palestinian refugees flee on fishing boats
13. Jewish immigrants arrive at the port in Haifa
14. The village of Iqrit before its destruction
15. The village of Iqrit, 1990
16. A theme park on the site of Tantura
17. The cemetery of Salama
18. Nahr al-Barid refugee camp in northern Lebanon
19. Baqa'a refugee camp, Jordan

MAPS AND TABLES

Acknowledgements

Over the years, the theme of this book was discussed with many friends, all of whom, in one way or another, have contributed to this book with their encouragement and support; many also provided me with documents, testimonies and evidence. There were so many of them that I do not dare compose a list, but wish to thank them collectively. The military material was collected by Oshri Neta-Av, and I thank him for what was, in hindsight, a very difficult task, not only because of the voluminous material, but also due to a murky political atmosphere.

Uri Davis, Nur Masalha and Charles Smith read the manuscript, and I hope that, at least in part, the end result reflects their industrious work. Needless to say, the final version is mine and they share no responsibility for the text. Nonetheless, I owe them a great deal and wish to thank them very much for their cooperation.

Walid Khalidi and Anton Shamas, who read the manuscript, provided moral support and empowerment, which made the writing of the book a valuable and meaningful project, even prior to publication.

My dear old friend Dick Bruggeman, as always, was there editing meticulously and painstakingly. This project could not have been completed without him.

Novin Doostdar, Drummond Moir, Kate Kirkpatrick, and above all Juliet Mabey at Oneworld lost sleep and time over this manuscript. I hope the end result is a fine reward for their immense efforts.

Revital, Ido and Yonatan, as always, suffered for the fact that their husband and father did not choose a far-away country in the distant past as a specialist subject, hobby and obsession. This book is another attempt to tell them, as much as anyone else, why our beloved country is devastated, hopeless and torn by hatred and bloodshed.

And finally, this book is not formally dedicated to anyone, but it is written first and foremost for the Palestinian victims of the 1948 ethnic

cleansing. Many of them are friends and comrades, many others are name-
less to me, and yet ever since I learned about the Nakba I have carried with
me their suffering, their loss and their hopes. Only when they return will I
feel that this chapter of the catastrophe has finally reached the closure we all
covet, enabling all of us to live in peace and harmony in Palestine.

Preface

THE RED HOUSE

> We are not mourning the farewell
> We do not have the time nor the tears
> We do not grasp the moment of farewell
> Why, it is the Farewell
> And we are left with the tears
>
> Muhammad Ali Taha (1988), a refugee
> from the village of Saffuriyya

> 'I am for compulsory transfer; I do not see anything immoral in it.'
> David Ben-Gurion to the Jewish Agency Executive, June 1938[1]

The 'Red House' was a typical early Tel-Avivian building. The pride of the
Jewish builders and craftsmen who toiled over it in the 1920s, it had been
designed to house the head office of the local workers' council. It remained
such until, towards the end of 1947, it became the headquarters of the
Hagana, the main Zionist underground militia in Palestine. Located near
the sea on Yarkon Street in the northern part of Tel-Aviv, the building
formed another fine addition to the first 'Hebrew' city on the
Mediterranean, the 'White City' as its literati and pundits affectionately
called it. For in those days, unlike today, the immaculate whiteness of its
houses still bathed the town as a whole in the opulent brightness so typical
of Mediterranean port cities of the era and the region. It was a sight for sore
eyes, elegantly fusing Bauhaus motifs with native Palestinian architecture in
an admixture that was called Levantine, in the least derogatory sense of the
term. Such, too, was the 'Red House', its simple rectangular features graced
with frontal arches that framed the entrance and supported the balconies on
its two upper storeys. It was either its association with a workers' movement

that had inspired the adjective 'red', or a pinkish tinge it acquired during sunset that had given the house its name.[2] The former was more fitting, as the building continued to be associated with the Zionist version of socialism when, in the 1970s, it became the main office for Israel's kibbutzim movement. Houses like this, important historical remnants of the Mandatory period, prompted UNESCO in 2003 to designate Tel-Aviv as a World Heritage site.

Today the house is no longer there, a victim of development, which has razed this architectural relic to the ground to make room for a car park next to the new Sheraton Hotel. Thus, in this street, too, no trace is left of the 'White City', which it has slowly transmogrified into the sprawling, polluted, extravagant metropolis that is modern Tel-Aviv.

In this building, on a cold Wednesday afternoon, 10 March 1948, a group of eleven men, veteran Zionist leaders together with young military Jewish officers, put the final touches to a plan for the ethnic cleansing of Palestine. That same evening, military orders were dispatched to the units on the ground to prepare for the systematic expulsion of the Palestinians from vast areas of the country.[3] The orders came with a detailed description of the methods to be employed to forcibly evict the people: large-scale intimidation; laying siege to and bombarding villages and population centres; setting fire to homes, properties and goods; expulsion; demolition; and, finally, planting mines among the rubble to prevent any of the expelled inhabitants from returning. Each unit was issued with its own list of villages and neighbourhoods as the targets of this master plan. Codenamed Plan D (*Dalet* in Hebrew), this was the fourth and final version of less substantial plans that outlined the fate the Zionists had in store for Palestine and consequently for its native population. The previous three schemes had articulated only obscurely how the Zionist leadership contemplated dealing with the presence of so many Palestinians living in the land the Jewish national movement coveted as its own. This fourth and last blueprint spelled it out clearly and unambiguously: the Palestinians had to go.[4] In the words of one of the first historians to note the significance of that plan, Simcha Flapan, 'The military campaign against the Arabs, including the "conquest and destruction of the rural areas" was set forth in the Hagana's Plan Dalet.' The aim of the plan was in fact the destruction of both the rural and urban areas of Palestine.

As the first chapters of this book will attempt to show, this plan was both the inevitable product of the Zionist ideological impulse to have an exclusively Jewish presence in Palestine, and a response to developments on the ground once the British cabinet had decided to end the mandate. Clashes with local Palestinian militias provided the perfect context and pretext for implementing the ideological vision of an ethnically cleansed Palestine. The Zionist policy was first based on retaliation against Palestinian attacks in February 1947, and it transformed into an initiative to ethnically cleanse the country as a whole in March 1948.[6]

Once the decision was taken, it took six months to complete the mission. When it was over, more than half of Palestine's native population, close to 800,000 people, had been uprooted, 531 villages had been destroyed, and eleven urban neighbourhoods emptied of their inhabitants. The plan decided upon on 10 March 1948, and above all its systematic implementation in the following months, was a clear-cut case of an ethnic cleansing operation, regarded under international law today as a crime against humanity.

After the Holocaust, it has become almost impossible to conceal large-scale crimes against humanity. Our modern communication-driven world, especially since the upsurge of electronic media, no longer allows human-made catastrophes to remain hidden from the public eye or to be denied. And yet, one such crime has been erased almost totally from the global public memory: the dispossession of the Palestinians in 1948 by Israel. This, the most formative event in the modern history of the land of Palestine, has ever since been systematically denied, and is still today not recognised as an historical fact, let alone acknowledged as a crime that needs to be confronted politically as well as morally.

Ethnic cleansing is a crime against humanity, and the people who perpetrate it today are considered criminals to be brought before special tribunals. It may be difficult to decide how one ought to refer to or deal with, in the legal sphere, those who initiated and perpetrated ethnic cleansing in Palestine in 1948, but it is possible to reconstruct their crimes and to arrive at both an historiographical account that will prove more accurate than the ones achieved so far, and a moral position of greater integrity.

We know the names of the people who sat in that room on the top floor of the Red House, beneath Marxist-style posters that carried such slogans as 'Brothers in Arms' and 'The Fist of Steel', and showed 'new' Jews – muscular, healthy and tanned – aiming their rifles from behind protective barriers in the 'brave fight' against 'hostile Arab invaders'. We also know the names

of the senior officers who executed the orders on the ground. All are familiar figures in the pantheon of Israeli heroism.[7] Not so long ago many of them
were still alive, playing major roles in Israeli politics and society; very few are
still with us today.

For Palestinians, and anyone else who refused to buy into the Zionist
narrative, it was clear long before this book was written that these people
were perpetrators of crimes, but that they had successfully evaded justice
and would probably never be brought to trial for what they had done.
Besides their trauma, the deepest form of frustration for Palestinians has
been that the criminal act these men were responsible for has been so thor-
oughly denied, and that Palestinian suffering has been so totally ignored,
ever since 1948.

Approximately thirty years ago, the victims of the ethnic cleansing
started reassembling the historical picture that the official Israeli narrative
of 1948 had done everything to conceal and distort. The tale Israeli historiography had concocted spoke of a massive 'voluntary transfer' of hundreds
of thousands of Palestinians who had decided temporarily to leave their
homes and villages so as to make way for the invading Arab armies bent on
destroying the fledgling Jewish state. By collecting authentic memories and
documents about what had happened to their people, Palestinian historians
in the 1970s, Walid Khalidi foremost among them, were able to retrieve a
significant part of the picture Israel had tried to erase. But they were quickly
overshadowed by publications such as Dan Kurzman's *Genesis 1948* which
appeared in 1970 and again in 1992 (now with an introduction by one of the
executors of the ethnic cleansing of Palestine, Yitzhak Rabin, then Israel's
prime minister). However, there were also some who came out in support of
the Palestinian endeavour, like Michael Palumbo whose *The Palestinian
Catastrophe*, published in 1987, validated the Palestinian version of the 1948
events with the help of UN documents and interviews with Palestinian
refugees and exiles, whose memories of what they had gone through during
the Nakba still proved to be hauntingly vivid.[8]

We could have had a political breakthrough in the battle over memory
in Palestine with the appearance on the scene in the 1980s of the so-called
'new history' in Israel. This was an attempt by a small group of Israeli historians to revise the Zionist narrative of the 1948 war.[9] I was one of them. But
we, the new historians, never contributed significantly to the struggle
against the Nakba denial as we sidestepped the question of ethnic cleansing

and, typically of diplomatic historians, focused on details. Nonetheless, using primarily Israeli military archives, the revisionist Israeli historians did succeed in showing how false and absurd was the Israeli claim that the Palestinians had left 'of their own accord'. They were able to confirm many cases of massive expulsions from villages and towns and revealed that the Jewish forces had committed a considerable number of atrocities, including massacres.

One of the best-known figures writing on the subject was the Israeli historian Benny Morris.[10] As he exclusively relied on documents from Israeli military archives, Morris ended up with a very partial picture of what happened on the ground. Still, this was enough for some of his Israeli readers to realise that the 'voluntary flight' of the Palestinians had been a myth and that the Israeli self-image of having waged a 'moral' war in 1948 against a 'primitive' and hostile Arab world was considerably flawed and possibly already bankrupt.

The picture was partial because Morris took the Israeli military reports he found in the archives at face value or even as absolute truth. Thus, he ignored such atrocities as the poisoning of the water supply into Acre with typhoid, numerous cases of rape and the dozens of massacres the Jews perpetrated. He also kept insisting – wrongly – that before 15 May 1948 there had been no forced evictions.[11] Palestinian sources show clearly how months before the entry of Arab forces into Palestine, and while the British were still responsible for law and order in the country – namely before 15 May – the Jewish forces had already succeeded in forcibly expelling almost a quarter of a million Palestinians.[12] Had Morris and others used Arab sources or turned to oral history, they might have been able to get a better grasp of the systematic planning behind the expulsion of the Palestinians in 1948 and provide a more truthful description of the enormity of the crimes the Israeli soldiers committed.

There was then, and there is still now, a need, both historical and political, to go beyond descriptions such as the one we find in Morris, not only in order to complete the picture (in fact, provide the second half of it), but also – and far more importantly – because there is no other way for us to fully understand the roots of the contemporary Israeli-Palestinian conflict. But above all, of course, there is a moral imperative to continue the struggle against the denial of the crime. The endeavour to go further has already been started by others. The most important work, to be expected given his previous significant contributions to the struggle against denial, was Walid Khalidi's seminal book *All That Remains*. This is an almanac of the destroyed villages, which is still an essential guide for anyone wishing to comprehend the enormity of the 1948 catastrophe.[13]

One might suggest that the history already exposed should have been enough to raise troubling questions. Yet, the 'new history' narrative and recent Palestinian historiographical inputs somehow failed to enter the public realm of moral conscience and action. In this book, I want to explore both the mechanism of the 1948 ethnic cleansing, and the cognitive system that allowed the world to forget, and enabled the perpetrators to deny, the crime the Zionist movement committed against the Palestinian people in 1948.

In other words, I want to make the case for the paradigm of ethnic cleansing and use it to replace the paradigm of war as the basis for the scholarly research of, and the public debate about, 1948. I have no doubt that the absence so far of the paradigm of ethnic cleansing is part of the reason why the denial of the catastrophe has been able to go on for so long. When it created its nation-state, the Zionist movement did not wage a war that 'tragically but inevitably' led to the expulsion of 'parts of' the indigenous population, but the other way round: the main goal was the ethnic cleansing of all of Palestine, which the movement coveted for its new state. A few weeks after the ethnic cleansing operations began, the neighbouring Arab states sent a small army – small in comparison to their overall military might – to try, in vain, to prevent the ethnic cleansing. The war with the regular Arab armies did not bring the ethnic cleansing operations to a halt until their successful completion in the autumn of 1948.

To some, this approach – adopting the paradigm of ethnic cleansing as the a priori basis for the narrative of 1948 – may from the outset look as an indictment. In many ways it is indeed my own *J'Accuse* against the politicians who devised, and the generals who perpetrated, the ethnic cleansing. Still, when I mention their names, I do so not because I want to see them posthumously brought to trial, but in order to humanise the victimisers as well as the victims: I want to prevent the crimes Israel committed from being attributed to such elusive factors as 'the circumstances', 'the army' or, as Morris has it, '*à la guerre comme à la guerre*', and similar vague references that let sovereign states off the hook and enable individuals to escape justice. I accuse, but I am also part of the society that stands condemned in this book. I feel both responsible for and part of the story and, like others in my own society, I am convinced, as my final pages show, that such a painful journey into the past is the only way forward if we want to create a better future for us all, Palestinians and Israelis alike. Because, at heart, that is what this book is about.

I am not aware that anyone has ever tried this approach before. The two official historical narratives that compete over the story of what happened in Palestine in 1948 both ignore the concept of ethnic cleansing. While the Zionist/Israeli version claims that the local population left 'voluntarily', the Palestinians talk about the 'catastrophe', the Nakba, that befell them, which in some ways is also an elusive term as it refers more to the disaster itself rather than to who or what caused it. The term Nakba was adopted, for understandable reasons, as an attempt to counter the moral weight of the Jewish Holocaust (Shoa), but in leaving out the actor, it may in a sense have contributed to the continuing denial by the world of the ethnic cleansing of Palestine in 1948 and after.

The book opens with a definition of ethnic cleansing that I hope is transparent enough to be acceptable to all, one that has served as the basis for legal actions against perpetrators of such crimes in the past and in our own days. Quite surprisingly, the usual complex and (for most normal human beings) impenetrable legal discourse is here replaced by clear, jargon-free language. This simplicity does not minimise the hideousness of the deed nor does it belie the crime's gravity. On the contrary: the result is a straightforward description of an atrocious policy that the international community today refuses to condone.

The general definition of what ethnic cleansing consists of applies almost verbatim to the case of Palestine. As such, the story of what occurred in 1948 emerges as an uncomplicated, but by no means a consequently simplified, or secondary, chapter in the history of Palestine's dispossession. Indeed, adopting the prism of ethnic cleansing easily enables one to penetrate the cloak of complexity that Israeli diplomats trot out almost instinctively and Israeli academics routinely hide behind when fending off outside attempts to criticise Zionism or the Jewish state for its policies and behaviour. 'Foreigners', they say in my country, 'do not and cannot understand this perplexing story' and there is therefore no need even to try to explain it to them. Nor should we allow them to be involved in the attempts to solve the conflict – unless they accept the Israeli point of view. All one can do, as

Israeli governments have been good at telling the world for years, is to allow 'us', the Israelis, as representatives of the 'civilised' and 'rational' side in the conflict, to find an equitable solution for 'ourselves' and for the other side, the Palestinians, who after all epitomise the 'uncivilised' and 'emotional' Arab world to which Palestine belongs. The moment the United States proved ready to adopt this warped approach and endorse the arrogance that underpins it, we had a 'peace process' that has led, and could only lead, nowhere, because it so totally ignores the heart of the matter.

But the story of 1948, of course, is not complicated at all, and therefore this book is written as much for newcomers to the field as it is aimed at those who already, for many years and various reasons, have been involved with the question of Palestine and how to bring us closer to a solution. It is the simple but horrific story of the ethnic cleansing of Palestine, a crime against humanity that Israel has wanted to deny and cause the world to forget. Retrieving it from oblivion is incumbent upon us, not just as a greatly over-due act of historiographical reconstruction or professional duty; it is, as I see it, a moral decision, the very first step we must take if we ever want reconcil-iation to have a chance, and peace to take root, in the torn lands of Palestine and Israel.

Chapter 1

An 'Alleged' Ethnic Cleansing?

It is the present writer's view that ethnic cleansing is a well-defined policy of a particular group of persons to systematically eliminate another group from a given territory on the basis of religious, ethnic or national origin. Such a policy involves violence and is very often connected with military operations. It is to be achieved by all possible means, from discrimination to extermination, and entails violations of human rights and international humanitarian law ... Most ethnic cleansing methods are grave breaches of the 1949 Geneva Conventions and 1977 Additional Protocols.

> Drazen Petrovic, 'Ethnic Cleansing – An Attempt at Methodology', *European Journal of International Law*, 5/3 (1994), pp. 342–60.

DEFINITIONS OF ETHNIC CLEANSING

Ethnic cleansing is today a well-defined concept. From an abstraction associated almost exclusively with the events in the former Yugoslavia, 'ethnic cleansing' has come to be defined as a crime against humanity, punishable by international law. The particular way some of the Serbian generals and politicians were using the term 'ethnic cleansing' reminded scholars they had heard it before. It was used in the Second World War by the Nazis and their allies, such as the Croat militias in Yugoslavia. The roots of collective dispossession are, of course, more ancient: foreign invaders have used the

term (or its equivalents) and practised the concept regularly against indigenous populations, from Biblical times to the height of colonialism.

The Hutchinson encyclopedia defines ethnic cleansing as expulsion by
force in order to homogenise the ethnically mixed population of a particular region or territory. The purpose of expulsion is to cause the evacuation
of as many residences as possible, by all means at the expeller's disposal,
including non-violent ones, as happened with the Muslims in Croatia,
expelled after the Dayton agreement of November 1995.

This definition is also accepted by the US State Department. Its experts
add that part of the essence of ethnic cleansing is the eradication, by all
means available, of a region's history. The most common method is that of
depopulation within 'an atmosphere that legitimises acts of retribution and
revenge'. The end result of such acts is the creation of a refugee problem. The
State Department looked in particular at what happened around May 1999
in the town of Peck in Western Kosovo. Peck was depopulated within
twenty-four hours, a result that could only have been achieved through
advance planning followed by systematic execution. There had also been
sporadic massacres, intended to speed up the operation. What happened in
Peck in 1999 took place in almost the same manner in hundreds of
Palestinian villages in 1948.[1]

When we turn to the United Nations, we find it employs similar definitions. The organisation discussed the concept seriously in 1993. The UN's
Council for Human Rights (UNCHR) links a state's or a regime's desire to
impose ethnic rule on a mixed area – such as the making of Greater Serbia –
with the use of acts of expulsion and other violent means. The report the
UNCHR published defined acts of ethnic cleansing as including separation
of men from women, detention of men, explosion of houses' and subsequently repopulating the remaining houses with another ethnic group. In
certain places in Kosovo, the report noted, Muslim militias had put up
resistance: where this resistance had been stubborn, the expulsion entailed
massacres.[2]

Israel's 1948 Plan D, mentioned in the preface, contains a repertoire of
cleansing methods that one by one fit the means the UN describes in its definition of ethnic cleansing, and sets the background for the massacres that
accompanied the massive expulsion.

Such references to ethnic cleansing are also the rule within the scholarly
and academic worlds. Drazen Petrovic has published one of the most

comprehensive studies on definitions of ethnic cleansing. He associates ethnic cleansing with nationalism, the making of new nation states, and national struggle. From this perspective he exposes the close connection between politicians and the army in the perpetration of the crime and comments on the place of massacres within it. That is, the political leadership delegates the implementation of the ethnic cleansing to the military level without necessarily furnishing any systematic plans or providing explicit instructions, but with no doubt as to the overall objective.[3]

Thus, at one point – and this again mirrors exactly what happened in Palestine – the political leadership ceases to take an active part as the machinery of expulsion comes into action and rolls on, like a huge bulldozer propelled by its own inertia, only to come to a halt when it has completed its task. The people it crushes underneath and kills are of no concern to the politicians who set it in motion. Petrovic and others draw our attention to the distinction between massacres that are part of genocide, where they are premeditated, and the 'unplanned' massacres that are a direct result of the hatred and vengeance whipped up against the background of a general directive from higher up to carry out an ethnic cleansing.

Thus, the encyclopedia definition outlined above appears to be consonant with the more scholarly attempt to conceptualise the crime of ethnic cleansing. In both views, ethnic cleansing is an effort to render an ethnically mixed country homogenous by expelling a particular group of people and turning them into refugees while demolishing the homes they were driven out from. There may well be a master plan, but most of the troops engaged in ethnic cleansing do not need direct orders: they know beforehand what is expected of them. Massacres accompany the operations, but where they occur they are not part of a genocidal plan: they are a key tactic to accelerate the flight of the population earmarked for expulsion. Later on, the expelled are then erased from the country's official and popular history and excised from its collective memory. From planning stage to final execution, what occurred in Palestine in 1948 forms a clear-cut case, according to these informed and scholarly definitions, of ethnic cleansing.

Popular Definitions

The electronic encyclopedia Wikipedia is an accessible reservoir of knowledge and information. Anyone can enter it and add to or change existing definitions, so that it reflects – by no means empirically but rather intuitively – a wide public perception of a certain idea or concept. Like the scholarly and encyclopedic definitions mentioned above, Wikipedia characterises ethnic cleansing as massive expulsion and also as a crime. I quote:

> At the most general level, ethnic cleansing can be understood as the forced expulsion of an 'undesirable' population from a given territory as a result of religious or ethnic discrimination, political, strategic or ideological considerations, or a combination of these.[4]

The entry lists several cases of ethnic cleansing in the twentieth century, beginning with the expulsion of the Bulgarians from Turkey in 1913 all the way up to the Israeli pullout of Jewish settlers from Gaza in 2005. The list may strike us as a bit bizarre in the way it incorporates within the same category Nazi ethnic cleansing and the removal by a sovereign state of its own people after it declared them illegal settlers. But this classification becomes possible because of the rationale the editors – in this case, everyone with access to the site – adopted for their policy, which is that they make sure the adjective 'alleged' precedes each of the historical cases on their list.

Wikipedia also includes the Palestinian Nakba of 1948. But one cannot tell whether the editors regard the Nakba as a case of ethnic cleansing that leaves no room for ambivalence, as in the examples of Nazi Germany or the former Yugoslavia, or whether they consider this a more doubtful case, perhaps similar to that of the Jewish settlers whom Israel removed from the Gaza Strip. One criterion this and other sources generally accept in order to gauge the seriousness of the allegation is whether anyone has been indicted before an international tribunal. In other words, where the perpetrators were brought to justice, i.e., were tried by an international judicial system, all ambiguity is removed and the crime of ethnic cleansing is no longer 'alleged'. But upon reflection, this criterion must also be extended to cases that should have been brought before such tribunals but never were. This is admittedly more open-ended, and some clear-cut crimes against humanity require a long struggle before the world recognises them as historical facts. The Armenians learned this in the case of their genocide: in 1915, the Ottoman government embarked on a systematic decimation of the Armenian people. An estimated one million perished by 1918, but no individual or group of individuals has been brought to trial.

ETHNIC CLEANSING AS A CRIME

Ethnic cleansing is designated as a crime against humanity in international treaties, such as that which created the International Criminal Court (ICC), and whether 'alleged' or fully recognised, it is subject to adjudication under international law. A special International Criminal Tribunal was set up in The Hague in the case of the former Yugoslavia to prosecute the perpetrators and criminals and, similarly, in Arusha, Tanzania, in the case of Rwanda. In other instances, ethnic cleansing was defined as a war crime even when no legal process was instigated as such (for example, the actions committed by the Sudanese government in Darfur).

This book is written with the deep conviction that the ethnic cleansing of Palestine must become rooted in our memory and consciousness as a crime against humanity and that it should be excluded from the list of *alleged* crimes. The perpetrators here are not obscure – they are a very specific group of people: the heroes of the Jewish war of independence, whose names will be quite familiar to most readers. The list begins with the indisputable leader of the Zionist movement, David Ben-Gurion, in whose private home all early and later chapters in the ethnic cleansing story were discussed and finalised. He was aided by a small group of people I refer to in this book as the 'Consultancy', an ad-hoc cabal assembled solely for the purpose of plotting and designing the dispossession of the Palestinians.[5] In one of the rare documents that records the meeting of the Consultancy, it is referred to as the Consultant Committee – *Haveadah Hamyeazet*. In another document the eleven names of the committee members appear, although they are all erased by the censor (nonetheless, as will transpire, I have managed to reconstruct all the names).[6]

This caucus prepared the plans for the ethnic cleansing and supervised its execution until the job of uprooting half of Palestine's native population had been completed. It included first and foremost the top-ranking officers of the future Jewish State's army, such as the legendary Yigael Yadin and Moshe Dayan. They were joined by figures unknown outside Israel but well grounded in the local ethos, such as Yigal Allon and Yitzhak Sadeh. These military men co-mingled with what nowadays we would call the 'Orientalists': experts on the Arab world at large and the Palestinians in particular, either because they themselves came from Arab countries or because they were scholars in the field of Middle Eastern studies. We will encounter some of their names later on as well.

Both the officers and the experts were assisted by regional commanders, such as Moshe Kalman, who cleansed the Safad area, and Moshe Carmel, who uprooted most of the Galilee. Yitzhak Rabin operated both in Lyyd and Ramla as well as in the Greater Jerusalem area. Remember their names, but begin to think of them not just as Israeli war heroes. They did take part in founding a state for Jews, and many of their actions are understandably revered by their own people for helping to save them from outside attacks, seeing them through crises, and above all offering them a safe haven from religious persecution in different parts of the world. But history will judge how these achievements will ultimately weigh in the balance when the opposite scale holds the crimes they committed against the indigenous people of Palestine. Other regional commanders included Shimon Avidan, who cleansed the south and of whom his colleague, Rehavam Zeevi, who fought with him, said many years later, 'Commanders like Shimon Avidan, the commander of the Givati Brigade, cleansed his front from tens of villages and towns'.[7] He was assisted by Yitzhak Pundak, who told Ha'aretz in 2004, 'There were two hundred villages [in the front] and these are gone. We had to destroy them, otherwise we would have had Arabs here [namely in the southern part of Palestine] as we have in Galilee. We would have had another million Palestinians'.[8]

And then there were the intelligence officers on the ground. Far from being mere collectors of data on the 'enemy', they not only played a major role in the cleansing but also took part in some of the worst atrocities that accompanied the systematic dispossession of the Palestinians. They were given the final authority to decide which villages would be destroyed and who among the villagers would be executed.[9] In the memories of Palestinian survivors they were the ones who, after a village or neighbourhood had been occupied, decided the fate of its occupants, which could mean the difference between imprisonment and freedom, or life and death. Their operations in 1948 were supervised by Issar Harel, later the first person to head the Mossad and the Shabak, Israel's secret services. His image is familiar to many Israelis. A short bulky figure, Harel had the modest rank of colonel in 1948, but was nonetheless the most senior officer overseeing all the operations of interrogation, blacklisting and the other oppressive features of Palestinian life under the Israeli occupation.

Finally, it bears repeating that from whatever angle you look at it – the legal, the scholarly, and up to the most populist – ethnic cleansing

is indisputably identified today as a crime against humanity and as involving war crimes, with special international tribunals judging those indicted
of having planned and executed acts of ethnic cleansing. However, I should
now add that, in hindsight, we might think of applying – and, quite frankly,
for peace to have a chance in Palestine we ought to apply – a rule of obsoles-
cence in this case, but on one condition: that the one political solution normally regarded as essential for reconciliation by both the United States and
the United Nations is enforced here too, namely the unconditional return of
the refugees to their homes. The US supported such a UN decision for
Palestine, that of 11 December 1948 (Resolution 194), for a short – all too
short – while. By the spring of 1949 American policy had already been reoriented onto a conspicuously pro-Israeli track, turning Washington's
mediators into the opposite of honest brokers as they largely ignored the
Palestinian point of view in general, and disregarded in particu-lar the
Palestinian refugees' right of return.

RECONSTRUCTING AN ETHNIC CLEANSING

By adhering to the definition of ethnic cleansing as given above, we absolve
ourselves from the need to go deeply into the origins of Zionism as the ideological cause of the ethnic cleansing. Not that the subject is not important,
but it has been dealt with successfully by a number of Palestinian and Israeli
scholars such as Walid Khalidi, Nur Masalha, Gershon Shafir and Baruch
Kimmerling, among others.[10] Although I would like to focus on the immediate background preceding the operations, it would be valuable for readers
to recap the major arguments of these scholars.

A good book to begin with is Nur Masalha's *Expulsion of the
Palestinians*,[11] which shows clearly how deeply rooted the concept of transfer was, and is, in Zionist political thought. From the founder of the Zionist
movement, Theodor Herzl, to the main leaders of the Zionist enterprise in
Palestine, cleansing the land was a valid option. As one of the movement's
most liberal thinkers, Leo Motzkin, put it in 1917:

> Our thought is that the colonization of Palestine has to go in two direc-
> tions: Jewish settlement in Eretz Israel and the resettlement of the
> Arabs of Eretz Israel in areas outside the country. The transfer of so
> many Arabs may seem at first unacceptable economically, but is

nonetheless practical. It does not require too much money to resettle a Palestinian village on another land.[12]

The fact that the expellers were newcomers to the country, and part of a colonization project, relates the case of Palestine to the colonialist history of ethnic cleansing in North and South America, Africa and Australia, where white settlers routinely committed such crimes. This intriguing aspect of the historical instance Israel offers was the subject of several recent and excellent studies. Gershon Shafir and Baruch Kimmerling informed us about the connection between Zionism and Colonialism, a nexus that can bring us at first to exploitation rather than expulsion, but once the idea of an exclusive Jewish economy became a central part of the vision, there was no room for Arab workers or peasants.[13] Walid Khalidi and Samih Farsoun connected the centrality of the transfer ideology more closely to the end of the mandate, and they ask why the UN entrusted the fate of so many Palestinians to a movement that had clearly included transfer in its ideology.[14]

I will seek less to expose the ideological inclination of those involved than to highlight the systematic planning with which they turned an ethnically mixed area into a pure ethnic space. This is the purpose of my opening chapters. I will return to the ideological connection towards the end of the book when I analyze it as the only adequate explanation we have for the ethnic cleansing by Israel of the Palestinians that started in 1948 but continues, in a variety of means, to today.

A second, more unpleasant task will be to reconstruct the methods Israel used for executing its master plan of expulsion and destruction, and examine how and to what extent these were typically affiliated with acts of ethnic cleansing. As I argued above, it seems to me that, had we never heard of the events in the former Yugoslavia but had been aware only of the case of Palestine, we would be forgiven for thinking that the US and UN definitions were inspired by the Nakba, down to almost their last minute detail.

Before we delve into the history of the ethnic cleansing in Palestine and try to contemplate the implications it has had up to the present day, we should pause for a moment and think about relative numbers. The figure of three-quarters of a million uprooted Palestinians can seem to be 'modest' when set in the context of the transfer of millions of people in Europe that was an outcome of the Second World War, or the dispossessions occurring in Africa in the beginning of the twenty-first century. But sometimes one needs to relativise numbers and think in percentages to begin to understand the magnitude of a tragedy that engulfed the population of an entire country. Half of the indigenous people living in Palestine were driven out, half of their villages and towns were destroyed, and only very few among them ever managed to return.

But beyond numbers, it is the deep chasm between reality and representation that is most bewildering in the case of Palestine. It is indeed hard to understand, and for that matter to explain, why a crime that was perpetrated in modern times and at a juncture in history that called for foreign reporters and UN observers to be present, should have been so totally ignored. And yet, there is no denying that the ethnic cleansing of 1948 has been eradicated almost totally from the collective global memory and erased from the world's conscience. Imagine that not so long ago, in any given country you are familiar with, half of the entire population had been forcibly expelled within a year, half of its villages and towns wiped out, leaving behind only rubble and stones. Imagine now the possibility that somehow this act will never make it into the history books and that all diplomatic efforts to solve the conflict that erupted in that country will totally sideline, if not ignore, this catastrophic event. I, for one, have searched in vain through the history of the world as we know it in the aftermath of the Second World War for a case of this nature and a fate of this kind. There are other, earlier, cases that have fared similarly, such as the ethnic cleansing of the non-Hungarians at the end of the nineteenth century, the genocide of the Armenians, and the holocaust perpetrated by the Nazi occupation against travelling people (the Roma, also known as Sinti) in the 1940s. I hope in the future that Palestine will no longer be included in this list.

Chapter 2

The Drive for an
Exclusively Jewish State

The United Nations General Assembly strongly rejects polices and
ideologies aimed at promoting ethnic cleansing in any form
Resolution 47/80 16 December 1992

ZIONISM'S IDEOLOGICAL MOTIVATION

Zionism emerged in the late 1880s in central and eastern Europe as a national
revival movement, prompted by the growing pressure on Jews in those
regions either to assimilate totally or risk continuing persecution (though, as
we know, even complete assimilation was no safeguard against annihilation
in the case of Nazi Germany). By the beginning of the twentieth century,
most of the leaders of the Zionist movement associated this national revival
with the colonization of Palestine. Others, especially the founder of the
movement, Theodor Herzl, were more ambivalent, but after his death, in
1904, the orientation towards Palestine was fixed and consensual.

Eretz Israel, the name for Palestine in the Jewish religion, had been
revered throughout the centuries by generations of Jews as a place for holy pilgrimage, never as a future secular state. Jewish tradition and religion clearly
instruct Jews to await the coming of the promised Messiah at 'the end of times'
before they can return to Eretz Israel as a sovereign people in a Jewish theoc-
racy, that is, as the obedient servants of God (this is why today several streams
of Ultra-Orthodox Jews are either non or anti-Zionist). In other words,

Zionism secularised and nationalised Judaism. To bring their project to fruition, the Zionist thinkers claimed the biblical territory and recreated, indeed reinvented, it as the cradle of their new nationalist movement. As they saw it, Palestine was occupied by 'strangers' and had to be repossessed. 'Strangers' here meant everyone not Jewish who had been living in Palestine since the Roman period.[1] In fact, for many Zionists Palestine was not even an 'occupied' land when they first arrived there in 1882, but rather an 'empty' one: the native Palestinians who lived there were largely invisible to them or, if not, were part of nature's hardship and as such were to be conquered and removed. Nothing, neither rocks nor Palestinians, was to stand in the way of the national 'redemption' of the land the Zionist movement coveted.[2]

Until the occupation of Palestine by Britain in 1918, Zionism was a blend of nationalist ideology and colonialist practice. It was limited in scope: Zionists made up no more than five per cent of the country's overall population at that time. Living in colonies, they did not affect, nor were they particularly noticed by, the local population. The potential for a future Jewish takeover of the country and the expulsion of the indigenous Palestinian people, which historians have so clearly recognised in retrospect in the writings of the founding fathers of Zionism, became evident to some Palestinian leaders even before the First World War; others were less interested in the movement.

Historical evidence shows that at some time between 1905 and 1910, several Palestinian leaders discussed Zionism as a political movement aiming to purchase land, assets and power in Palestine, although the destructive potential was not fully comprehended at that period. Many members of the local elite saw it as part of the European missionary and colonialist drive – which in part it was, but of course it had an additional edge to it that turned into a dangerous enterprise for the native population.[3]

This potential was not often discussed or articulated by the Zionist leaders themselves, but some Palestinian notables and intellectuals must have sensed the looming danger, since we find them trying to convince the Ottoman government in Istanbul to limit, if not totally prohibit, Jewish immigration and settlement into Palestine, which was under Turkish rule until 1918.[4]

The Palestinian member of the Ottoman Parliament, Said al-Husayni, claimed on 6 May 1911 that 'the Jews intend to create a state in the area that will include Palestine, Syria and Iraq'.[5] However, Al-Husayni belonged to a family, and a group of local notables, who until the 1930s preached against the Zionist colonization while selling lands to the newcomers. As the Mandatory years went by, the sense of a looming danger, indeed a catastrophe, settled in among the more intellectual sections of the elite,[6] but it was never translated into proper preparations for the existential danger awaiting their society.

Others around Palestine, such as the leading Egyptian literati, saw the movement of Jews into Palestine as an irresponsible attempt on the part of Europe to transfer its poorest and often stateless people into the country, not as part of a master plan aimed at the dispossession of the local people. To them, this movement of wretched people seemed but a minor threat compared with the far more conspicuous attempt European colonial powers and churches were making to take over the 'Holy Land' through their missionaries, diplomats and colonies.[7] Indeed, prior to the British occupation of Palestine at the end of 1917, the Zionists were vague where their actual plans were concerned, not so much for lack of orientation, but more because of the need to prioritise the concerns of the as yet small Jewish immigrant community: there was always the threat of being thrown out again by the government in Istanbul.

However, when a clearer vision for the future needed to be spelled out for internal consumption, we find no ambiguity whatsoever. What the Zionists anticipated was the creation of a Jewish state in Palestine in order to escape a history of persecutions and pogroms in the West, invoking the religious 'redemption' of an 'ancient homeland' as their means. This was the official narrative, and it no doubt genuinely expressed the motivation of most of the Zionist leadership's members. But the more critical view today sees the Zionist drive to settle in Palestine, instead of other possible locations, as closely interwoven with nineteenth-century Christian millenarianism and European colonialism. The various Protestant missionary societies and the governments in the European Concert competed among themselves over the future of a 'Christian' Palestine that they wanted to pry away from the Ottoman Empire. The more religious among the aspirants in the West regarded the return of the Jews to Palestine as a chapter in the divine scheme, precipitating the second coming of Christ and the creation of a pietist state there. This religious zeal inspired pious politicians, such as Lloyd George, the British prime minister during the First World War, to act with even greater commitment for the success of the Zionist project. This did not prevent him from supplying his government at the same time with a host of 'strategic', rather than messianic, considerations for why Palestine should be colonised by the Zionist movement, which were mostly infused by his own overriding distrust of, and disdain for, 'Arabs' and 'Mohammedans', as he called the Palestinians.[8]

Recent scholarship also tends to question the more Marxist flavour that the official Israeli historiography has claimed for the early colonization of Palestine by portraying Zionism as a positive endeavour to carry the socialist and Marxist revolutions beyond their less successful attempts in Russia.[9] The more critical view depicts this aspiration as doubtful at best and as manipulative at worst. Indeed, much like today's more liberal-minded Israeli Jews who are ready to drop the principles of democracy when faced with the prospect of a demographic majority of non-Jews in the country, so, it seems, did the socialist Zionists quickly substitute their more universal dreams with the powerful allure of nationalism. And when the main objective became making Palestine exclusively Jewish rather than socialist, it was significantly the Labour movement within Zionism that instituted and implemented the ethnic cleansing of the local population.

The early Zionist settlers directed most of their energy and resources towards buying up plots of land in an attempt to enter the local labour market and create social and communal networks that could sustain their as yet small and economically vulnerable group of newcomers. The more precise strategies of how best to take over Palestine as a whole and create a nation-state in the country, or in part of it, were a later development, closely associated with British ideas of how best to solve the conflict Britain itself had done so much to exacerbate.

The moment British Foreign Secretary Lord Balfour gave the Zionist movement his promise in 1917 to establish a national home for the Jews in Palestine,[10] he opened the door to the endless conflict that would soon engulf the country and its people. In the pledge he made in his government's name, Balfour promised to protect the aspirations of the non-Jewish population – a strange reference to the vast native majority – but the declaration clashed precipitately with both the aspirations and natural rights of the Palestinians for nationhood and independence.

By the end of the 1920s, it was clear that this proposal had a potentially violent core, as it had already claimed the lives of hundreds of Palestinians and Jews. This now prompted the British to make a serious, albeit reluctant, attempt to solve the smouldering conflict.

Until 1928, the British government had treated Palestine as a state within the British sphere of influence, not as a colony; a state in which, under British tutelage, the promise to the Jews and the aspirations of the Palestinians could both be fulfilled. They tried to put in place a political structure that would represent both communities on an equal footing in the state's parliament as well as in government. In practice, when the offer was made it was less equitable; it advantaged the Zionist colonies and discriminated against the Palestinian majority. The balance within the new proposed legislative council was in favour of the Jewish community who were to be allied with members appointed by the British administration.[11]

As the Palestinians made up the majority of between eighty and ninety per cent of the total population in the 1920s, they understandably refused at first to accept the British suggestion of parity, let alone one that disadvantaged them in practice – a position that encouraged the Zionist leaders to endorse it. A pattern now emerges: when, in 1928, the Palestinian leadership, apprehensive of the growing Jewish immigration into the country and the expansion of their settlements, agreed to accept the formula as a basis for negotiations, the Zionist leadership quickly rejected it. The Palestinian uprising in 1929 was the direct result of Britain's refusal to implement at least their promise of parity after the Palestinians had been willing to set aside the democratic principal of majoritarian politics, which Britain had championed as the basis for negotiations in all the other Arab states within its sphere of influence.[12]

After the 1929 uprising, the Labour government in London appeared inclined to embrace the Palestinian demands, but the Zionist lobby succeeded in reorienting the British government comfortably back onto the Balfourian track. This made another uprising inevitable. It duly erupted in 1936 in the form of a popular rebellion fought with such determination that it forced the British government to station more troops in Palestine than there were in the Indian subcontinent. After three years, with brutal and ruthless attacks on the Palestinian countryside, the British military subdued the revolt. The Palestinian leadership was exiled, and the paramilitary units that had sustained the guerilla warfare against the Mandatory forces were disbanded. During this process many of the villagers involved were arrested, wounded or killed. The absence of most of the Palestinian leadership and of viable Palestinian fighting units gave the Jewish forces in 1947 an easy ride into the Palestinian countryside.

In between the two uprisings, the Zionist leadership had wasted no time in working out their plans for an exclusively Jewish presence in Palestine: first, in 1937, by accepting a modest portion of the land, when they responded favourably to a recommendation by the British Royal Peel commission to partition Palestine into two states;[13] and second, in 1942, by attempting a more maximalist strategy, demanding all of Palestine for itself. The geographical space it coveted may have changed with time and according to circumstances and opportunities, but the principal objective remained the same. The Zionist project could only be realised through the creation in Palestine of a purely Jewish state, both as a safe haven for Jews from persecution and a cradle for a new Jewish nationalism. And such a state had to be exclusively Jewish not only in its socio-political structure but also in its ethnic composition.

MILITARY PREPARATIONS

From the outset, the British Mandatory authorities had allowed the Zionist movement to carve out an independent enclave for itself in Palestine as the infrastructure for a future state, and in the late 1930s the movement's leaders were able to translate the abstract vision of Jewish exclusivity into more concrete plans. Zionist preparations for the eventuality of taking the land by force, should it fail to be granted to them through diplomacy, included the building of an efficient military organisation – with the help of sympathetic British officers – and the search for ample financial resources (for which they could tap the Jewish Diaspora). In many ways the creation of an embryonic diplomatic corps was also an integral part of the same general preparations that were aimed at snatching, by force, a state in Palestine.[14]

It was one British officer in particular, Orde Charles Wingate, who made the Zionist leaders realise more fully that the idea of Jewish statehood had to be closely associated with militarism and an army, first of all to protect the growing number of Jewish enclaves and colonies inside Palestine but also – more crucially – because acts of armed aggression were an effective deterrent against the possible resistance of the local Palestinians. From there, the road to contemplating the enforced transfer of the entire indigenous population would prove to be very short indeed.[15]

Orde Wingate was born in India in the early twentieth century to a military family and received a very religious upbringing. He began an Arabophile career in the Sudan, where he gained prestige with a particularly effective ambush policy against slave traders. In 1936, he was assigned to Palestine where he quickly became enchanted by the Zionist dream. He decided actively to encourage the Jewish settlers and started teaching their troops more effective combat tactics and retaliation methods against the local population. It is no wonder that his Zionist associates greatly admired him.

Wingate transformed the principal paramilitary organisation of the Jewish community in Palestine, the Hagana. Established in 1920, its name literally means 'defence' in Hebrew, ostensibly to indicate that its main purpose was protecting the Jewish colonies. Under the influence of Wingate, and the militant mood he inspired among its commanders, the Hagana quickly became the military arm of the Jewish Agency, the Zionist governing body in Palestine that in the end developed and then implemented plans for the Zionist military takeover of Palestine as a whole, and the ethnic cleansing of its native population.[16]

The Arab revolt gave the Hagana members a chance to practise the military tactics Wingate had taught them in the Palestinian rural areas, mostly in the form of retaliatory operations against such targets as roadside snipers or thieves taking goods from a kibbutz. The main objective, however, seems to have been to intimidate Palestinian communities who happened to live in proximity to Jewish settlements.

Wingate succeeded in attaching Hagana troops to the British forces during the Arab revolt so that they could learn even better what a 'punitive mission' to an Arab village ought to entail. For example, in June 1938 Jewish troops got their first taste of what it meant to occupy a Palestinian village: a Hagana unit and a British company jointly attacked a village on the border between Israel and Lebanon, and held it for a few hours.[17]

Amatziya Cohen, who took part in the operation, remembered the British sergeant who showed them how to use bayonets in attacking defenseless villagers: 'I think you are all totally ignorant in your Ramat Yochanan [the training base for the Hagana] since you do not even know the elementary use of bayonets when attacking dirty Arabs: how can you put your left foot in front!' he shouted at Amatziya and his friends after they had returned to base.[18] Had this sergeant been around in 1948, he would have been proud to see how quickly Jewish troops were mastering the art of attacking villages.

The Hagana also gained valuable military experience in the Second World War, when many of its members volunteered for the British war effort. Others who remained behind in Palestine continued to monitor and infiltrate the 1200 or so Palestinian villages that had dotted the countryside for hundreds of years.

THE VILLAGE FILES

More was needed than just savouring the excitement of attacking a Palestinian village: systematic planning was called for. The suggestion came from a young bespectacled historian from the Hebrew University by the name of Ben-Zion Luria, at the time an employee of the educational department of the Jewish Agency. Luria pointed out how useful it would be to have a detailed registry of all Arab villages, and proposed that the Jewish National Fund (JNF) conduct such an inventory. 'This would greatly help the redemption of the land,' he wrote to the JNF.[19] He could not have chosen a better audience: his initiative to involve the JNF in the prospective ethnic cleansing was to generate added impetus and zeal to the expulsion plans that followed.

Founded in 1901, the JNF was the principal Zionist tool for the colonization of Palestine. It served as the agency the Zionist movement used to buy Palestinian land upon which it then settled Jewish immigrants. Inaugurated by the fifth Zionist Congress, it spearheaded the Zionization of Palestine throughout the Mandatory years. From the onset it was designed to become the 'custodian', on behalf of the Jewish people, of the land the Zionists gained possession of in Palestine. The JNF maintained this role after the creation of the State of Israel, with other missions being added to its primary role over time.[20]

Most of the JNF's activities during the Mandatory period and surrounding the Nakba were closely associated with the name of Yossef Weitz, the head of its settlement department. Weitz was the quintessential Zionist colonialist. His main priority at the time was facilitating the eviction of Palestinian tenants from land bought from absentee landlords who were likely to live at some distance from their land or even outside the country, the Mandate system having created borders where before there were none.

Traditionally, when ownership of a plot of land, or even a whole village, changed hands, this did not mean that the farmers or villagers themselves had to move;[21] Palestine was an agricultural society, and the new landlord would need the tenants to continue cultivating his lands. But with the advent of Zionism all this changed. Weitz personally visited the newly purchased plot of land often accompanied by his closest aides, and encouraged the new Jewish owners to throw out the local tenants, even if the owner had no use for the entire piece of land. One of Weitz's closest aides, Yossef Nachmani, at one point reported to him that 'unfortunately' tenants refused to leave and some of the new Jewish land owners displayed, as he put it, 'cowardice by pondering the option of allowing them to stay.'[22] It was the job of Nachmani and other aides to make sure that such 'weaknesses' did not persist: under their supervision these evictions quickly became more comprehensive and effective.

The impact of such activities at the time remained limited because Zionist resources after all were scarce, Palestinian resistance fierce, and the British policies restrictive. By the end of the Mandate in 1948, the Jewish community owned around 5.8% of the land in Palestine. But the appetite was for more, if only for the available resources to expand and new opportunities open up; this is why Weitz waxed lyrical when he heard about the village files, immediately suggesting turning them into a 'national project.'[23]

All involved became fervent supporters of the idea. Yitzhak Ben-Zvi, a prominent member of the Zionist leadership, a historian and later the second president of Israel, explained in a letter to Moshe Shertock (Sharett), the head of the political department of the Jewish Agency (and later one of Israel's prime ministers), that apart from topographically recording the layout of the villages, the project should also include exposing the 'Hebraic origins' of each village. Furthermore, it was important for the Hagana to know which of the villages were relatively new, as some of them had been built 'only' during the Egyptian occupation of Palestine in the 1830s.[24]

The main endeavour, however, was mapping the villages, and therefore a topographer from the Hebrew University working in the Mandatory cartography department was recruited to the enterprise. He suggested conducting an aerial photographic surveys, and proudly showed Ben-Gurion two such aerial maps for the villages of Sindiyana and Sabbarin (these maps, now in the Israeli State Archives, are all that remains of these villages after 1948).

The best professional photographers in the country were now invited to join the initiative. Yitzhak Shefer, from Tel-Aviv, and Margot Sadeh, the wife of Yitzhak Sadeh, the chief of the Palmach (the commando units of the Hagana), were recruited too. [The film laboratory operated in Margot's house with an irrigation company serving as a front: the lab had to be hidden from the British authorities who could have regarded it as an illegal intelligence effort directed against them. The British did have prior knowledge of it, but never succeeded in spotting the secret hideout. In 1947, this whole cartographic department was moved to the Red House.[25]

The end results of both the topographic and Orientalist efforts were the detailed files the Zionist experts gradually built up for each of Palestine's villages. By the late 1930s, this 'archive' was almost complete. Precise details were recorded about the topographic location of each village, its access roads, quality of land, water springs, main sources of income, its socio-political composition, religious affiliations, names of its muhktars, its relationship with other villages, the age of individual men (sixteen to fifty) and many more. An important category was an index of 'hostility' (towards the Zionist project, that is), decided by the level of the village's participation in the revolt of 1936. There was a list of everyone who had been involved in the revolt and the families of those who had lost someone in the fight against the British. Particular attention was given to people who had allegedly killed Jews. As we shall see, in 1948 these last bits of information fuelled the worst atrocities in the villages, leading to mass executions and torture.

Regular members of the Hagana who were entrusted with collecting the data on 'reconnaissance' journeys into the villages realised, from the start, that this was not a mere academic exercise in geography. One of these was Moshe Pasternak, who joined one of the early excursions and data collection operations in 1940. He recalled many years later:

> We had to study the basic structure of the Arab village. This means the structure and how best to attack it. In the military schools, I had been taught how to attack a modern European city, not a primitive village in the Near East. We could not compare it [an Arab village] to a Polish, or an Austrian one. The Arab village, unlike the European ones, was built topographically on hills. That meant we had to find out how best to approach the village from above or enter it from below. We had to train our 'Arabists' [the Orientalists who operated a network of collaborators] how best to work with informants.[26]

Indeed the problem noted in many of the villages' files was how to create a collaborationist system with the people Pasternak and his friends regarded as primitive and barbaric: 'People who like to drink coffee and eat rice with their hands, which made it very difficult to use them as informants.' In 1943, he remembered, there was a growing sense that finally they had a proper network of informants in place. That same year the village files were re-arranged to become even more systematic. This was mainly the work of one man, Ezra Danin, who would play a leading role in the ethnic cleansing of Palestine.[27]

In many ways, it was the recruitment of Ezra Danin, who had been taken out of his successful citrus grove business, that injected the intelligence work and the organisation of the village files with a new level of efficiency. Files in the post-1943 era included detailed descriptions of the husbandry, the cultivated land, the number of trees in plantations, the quality of each fruit grove (even of each single tree), the average amount of land per family, the number of cars, shop owners, members of workshops and the names of the artisans in each village and their skills.[28] Later, meticulous detail was added about each clan and its political affiliation, the social stratification between notables and common peasants, and the names of the civil servants in the Mandatory government.

And as the data collection created its own momentum, one finds additional details popping up around 1945, such as descriptions of village mosques and the names of their imams, together with such characterisations as 'he is an ordinary man', and even precise accounts of the living rooms inside the homes of these dignitaries. Towards the end of the Mandatory period the information becomes more explicitly military orientated: the number of guards (most villages had none) and the quantity and quality of the arms at the villagers' disposal (generally antiquated or even non-existent).[29]

Danin recruited a German Jew named Yaacov Shimoni, later to become one of Israel's leading Orientalists, and put him in charge of special projects inside the villages, in particular supervising the work of the informants.[30] One of these Danin and Shimoni nicknamed the 'treasurer' (ha-gizbar). This man, who proved a fountain of information for the files' collectors, supervised the network of collaboration for them between 1941–1945. He was exposed in 1945 and killed by Palestinian militants.[31]

Danin and Shimoni were soon joined by two other people, Yehoshua Palmon and Tuvia Lishanski. These, too, are names to remember as they took an active part in preparing for the ethnic cleansing of Palestine. Lishanski was already busy in the 1940s with orchestrating campaigns against the tenants who lived on plots of lands the JNF had bought from present or absentee landlords, and he directed all his energy towards intimidating and then forcibly evicting these people from the lands their families had been cultivating for centuries.

Not far away from the village of Furaydis and the 'veteran' Jewish settlement Zikhron Yaacov, where today a road connects the coastal highway with Marj Ibn Amir (Emeq Izrael) through Wadi Milk, lies a youth village (a kind of boarding school for Zionist youth) called Shefeya. It was here that in 1944 special units in the service of the village files project received their training and it was from here that they went out on their reconnaissance missions. Shefeya looked very much like a spy village in the Cold War: Jews walking around speaking Arabic and trying to emulate what they believed were the customary ways of life and behaviour of rural Palestinians.[32]

In 2002, one of the first recruits to this special training base recalled his first reconnaissance mission to the nearby village of Umm al-Zinat in 1944. Their aim had been to survey the village and bring back information such as where the mukhtar lived, where the mosque was located, where the rich people of the village resided and who had been active in the 1936 revolt. This was not a very dangerous mission as the infiltrators knew they could exploit the traditional Arab hospitality code, and were even guests at the home of the mukhtar himself. As they failed to collect in one day all the data they were seeking, they asked to be invited back. For their second visit they had been instructed to get information about the fertility of the land, the quality of which seemed to have impressed them greatly. In 1948, Umm al-Zinat was destroyed and all its inhabitants expelled without any provocation on their part whatsoever.[33]

The final update of the village files took place in 1947. It focused on creating lists of 'wanted' persons in each village. In 1948 Jewish troops used these lists for the search-and-arrest operations they carried out as soon as they had occupied a village. That is, the men in the village would be lined up and those appearing on the lists would then be identified, often by the same person who had informed on them in the first place but who would now be wearing a cloth sack over his head with two holes cut out for his eyes so as not to be recognised. The men who were picked out were often shot on the spot. Criteria for inclusion in these lists were involvement in the Palestinian national movement, having close ties to the leader of the movement, the Mufti al-Hajj Amin al-Husayni, and, as mentioned, having participated in actions against the British and the Zionists.[34] Other reasons for being included in the lists were a variety of allegations, such as 'known to have travelled to Lebanon' or 'arrested by the British authorities for being a member of a national committee in the village'.[35]

The first category, involvement in the Palestinian national movement, was very liberally defined and could include whole villages. Affiliation with the Mufti or to the political party he headed was very common. After all, his party had dominated local Palestinian politics ever since the British Mandate was officially established in 1923. The party's members went on to win national and municipal elections and hold the prominent positions in the Arab Higher Committee that became the embryonic government of the Palestinians. In the eyes of the Zionist experts this constituted a crime. If we look at the 1947 files, we find that villages with about 1500 inhabitants usually had between twenty and thirty such suspects (for instance, around the southern Carmel mountains, south of Haifa, Umm al-Zinat had thirty such suspects and the nearby village of Damun had twenty-five).[36]

Yigael Yadin recalled that it was this minute and detailed knowledge of what was happening in each single Palestinian village that enabled the Zionist military command in November 1947 to conclude 'that the Palestine Arabs had nobody to organise them properly.' The only serious problem was the British: 'If not for the British, we could have quelled the Arab riot [the opposition to the UN Partition Resolution in 1947] in one month.'[37]

FACING THE BRITISH: 1945–1947

Beyond carefully charting rural Palestine in preparation for the future takeover of the country, the Zionist movement had by now also obtained a much clearer sense of how best to get the new state off the ground after the Second World War. A crucial factor in this was that the British had already destroyed the Palestinian leadership and its defence capabilities when they suppressed the 1936 Revolt, thus allowing the Zionist leadership ample time and space to set out their next moves. Once the danger of a Nazi invasion into Palestine was removed in 1942, the Zionist leaders became more keenly aware that the sole obstacle that stood in their way of successfully seizing the land was the British presence, not any Palestinian resistance. This explains why, for example, in a meeting in the Biltmore Hotel in New York in 1942, we find Ben-Gurion putting demands on the table for a Jewish common-wealth over the whole of Mandatory Palestine.[38]

As the Second World War drew to a close, the Jewish leadership in Palestine embarked on a campaign to push the British out of the country. Simultaneously, they continued to map out their plans for the Palestinian population, the country's seventy-five per cent majority. Leading Zionist figures did not air their views in public, but confided their thoughts only to their close associates or entered them into their diaries. One of them, Yossef Weitz, wrote in 1940: 'it is our right to transfer the Arabs' and 'The Arabs should go!'[39] Ben-Gurion himself, writing to his son in 1937, appeared con-vinced that this was the only course of action open to Zionism: 'The Arabs will have to go', but one needs an opportune moment for making it happen, such as a war.[40] The opportune moment came in 1948. Ben-Gurion is in many ways the founder of the State of Israel and was its first prime minister. He also masterminded the ethnic cleansing of Palestine.

DAVID BEN-GURION: THE ARCHITECT

David Ben-Gurion led the Zionist movement from the mid 1920s until well into the 1960s. Born David Gruen in 1886 in Plonsk, Poland (then part of Czarist Russia), he had come to Palestine in 1906, already an ardent Zionist. Short of stature, with a large shock of white hair swept backwards and invariably dressed in khaki uniform, his figure is by now familiar to many around the world. When the ethnic cleansing operations began, he added a pistol to his military gear and a kufiyya around his neck, imitating the way his elite units were fitted out. He was by then approximately sixty years old and, although suffering from serious backaches, he was the Zionist move-ment's highly energetic and hard-working leader.

His central role in deciding the fate of the Palestinians stemmed from the complete control he exercised over all issues of security and defence in the Jewish community in Palestine. He had risen to power as a union leader, but was soon busy engineering the Jewish State in-the-making. When the British offered the Jewish community a state in 1937, but over a much smaller por-tion of Palestine than they had in mind, Ben-Gurion accepted the proposal as a good start, but he aspired to Jewish sovereignty over as much of Palestine as possible. He then swayed the Zionist leadership into accepting both his supreme authority and the fundamental notion that future statehood meant absolute Jewish domination. How to achieve such a purely Jewish state was also discussed under his guidance around 1937. Two magic words now emerged: Force and Opportunity. The Jewish state could only be won by force, but one had to wait for the opportune historical moment to come along in order to be able to deal 'militarily' with the demographic reality on the ground: the presence of a non-Jewish native majority population.

Ben-Gurion's focus on long-term processes and comprehensive solutions was atypical of most of his colleagues in the Zionist leadership. They still hoped that by purchasing a piece of land here and a few houses there they would be able to establish the envisaged new reality. Ben-Gurion understood early on that this would never be enough – and of course he was right: by the end of the Mandate, as we have already seen, the Zionist movement had only been able to purchase around six per cent of the land.[41]

But even the more cautious Zionist leaders, such as Ben-Gurion's second-in-command, Moshe Sharett, the 'foreign minister' of the Jewish community in Mandatory Palestine, associated the settlement of Jews in Palestine with the dispossession of the indigenous Palestinians. For example, on 13 December 1938, when giving a lecture to the employees of the Zionist organisations in Jerusalem, Sharett could report to them on a particularly satisfying achievement: the purchase of 2500 dunam in the Baysan Valley in eastern Palestine (one dunam equals 1000 square metres, or 0.1 hectares). He added a telling detail:

> This purchase was accompanied, interestingly, by transfer of population [unsure of his audience's familiarity with the term, he repeated it in English]. There is a tribe that resides west of the Jordan river and the purchase will include paying the tribe to move east of the river; by this [act] we will reduce the number of Arabs [in Palestine].[42]

In 1942, as we saw above, Ben-Gurion was already aiming much higher when he publicly staked out the Zionist claim for the whole of Palestine. As in the days of the Balfour declaration, Zionist leaders understood the promise to include the country as a whole. But he was a pragmatic colonialist as well as a state-builder. He knew that maximalist schemes such as the Biltmore programme, which clamoured for the whole of Mandatory Palestine, would not be deemed realistic. It was also, of course, impossible to pressure Britain while it was holding the fort against Nazi Germany in Europe. Consequently he lowered his ambitions during the Second World War. But the post-war British Labour government under Clement Atlee had different plans for Palestine. Now that Jews in Europe were no longer facing the danger of annihilation, and most of them preferred to leave for the other side of the Atlantic rather than head towards the Middle East, the new British cabinet and its energetic foreign secretary, Ernest Bevin, were looking for a solution that would be based on the wishes and interests of the people actually living in Palestine, and not of those the Zionist leaders claimed might want to move there – in other words, a democratic solution.

Armed, but especially terrorist, attacks by the Jewish underground militias failed to change that policy. Against the bombing of bridges, military bases and the British headquarters in Jerusalem (the King David Hotel), the British reacted mildly – especially in comparison with the brutal treatment they had meted out to Palestinian rebels in the 1930s. Retaliation took the form of a disarmament campaign of Jewish troops, a large number of whom they themselves had armed and recruited, first in the war against the Palestinian rebellion in 1937, and then against the Axis powers in 1939. Disarmament was very partial, but arrests were relatively numerous, enough for the Zionist leaders to realise they needed to pursue a more adaptive policy as long as the British were still responsible for law and order in the land. As we have already seen, in the immediate aftermath of the Second World War Britain held a disproportionately large number of troops – 100,000 – in a country of less than two million people. This definitely served as a deterrent, even when in the wake of the Jewish terrorist attack on the King David Hotel this force was somewhat reduced. It was these considerations that prompted Ben-Gurion to conclude that a somewhat more 'reduced' state, over eighty per cent of Palestine, would be sufficient to allow the Zionist movement to fulfill its dreams and ambitions.[43]

In the final days of August 1946, Ben-Gurion gathered together the leadership of the Zionist movement in a hotel in Paris, the Royal Monsue, to help him find an alternative to the Biltmore plan that had aimed to take over all of Palestine. An 'old-new' idea of the Zionist movement now resurfaced: partitioning Palestine. 'Give us independence, even on a small part of the land,' pleaded Nachum Goldman with the British government in London while his colleagues in Paris were deliberating their next move. Goldman was the most 'dovish' member of the Zionist leadership at the time, and his call for only a 'small' part of Palestine did not reflect Ben-Gurion's ambitions: he accepted the principle but not the dimensions. 'We will demand a large chunk of Palestine' Ben-Gurion told those he had summoned to the French capital. Like generations of Israeli leaders after him, up to Ariel Sharon in 2005, Ben-Gurion found he had to hold back the more extremist Zionist members, and he told them that eighty to ninety per cent of Mandatory Palestine was enough to create a viable state, provided they were able to ensure Jewish predominance. Neither the concept nor the percentage would change over the next sixty years. A few months later the Jewish Agency translated Ben-Gurion's 'large chunk of Palestine' into a map which it distributed to everyone relevant to the future of Palestine. This 1947 map envisaged a Jewish state that anticipated almost to the last dot pre-1967 Israel, i.e., Palestine without the West Bank and the Gaza Strip.[44]

During all these deliberations, the Zionist leaders never discussed the possibility of any resistance from the local population: their chief concern was the British and, maybe, the international response. This is not accidental. The Zionist leadership was aware of the total collapse of the Palestinian leadership after the Second World War and of the hesitant position the Arab states as a whole were displaying on the Palestine question. The desperate situation of the indigenous population of Palestine becomes poignantly clear the moment we realise that those who had crushed their liberation movement, the British Mandatory authorities, were now the only ones standing between them and a coolly determined and highly motivated Zionist movement that coveted most of their homeland. But worse was to come as Europe prepared to compensate the Jewish people for the Holocaust that had raged on its soil with a state in Palestine, ignoring at the same time that this could only come about at the expense of the indigenous Palestinians.

Given the power vacuum on the Palestinian side, it is not surprising to see the Zionist decision-makers act as though the Palestinians were not a factor to be considered. But, of course, they still formed the vast majority in the land, and as such they were a 'problem'. Moreover, the Arab world, potentially at least, could come to their rescue and send in armies and provide arms. David Ben-Gurion was fully aware of this possible scenario, and therefore preoccupied himself and his closest associates with the issue of security, *bitachon* in Hebrew. This became an obsession Ben-Gurion nourished so carefully and successfully that it came to overshadow all other social and political issues on the agenda of the Jewish community in Palestine and later, of course, in Israel.[45]

Bitachon was then and remains until today a meta-term used by Zionist and, later, Israeli leaders to cover a wide range of issues and justify numerous core policies, from arms purchases abroad, internal struggle with other political parties, preparations for the future state, and the policy adopted against the local Palestinian population. The latter was retaliatory in nature and in discourse, but quite often provocative in action. From 1946 onwards, a more comprehensive set of strategic objectives emerged, aimed at consolidating the future scenarios and plans. David Ben-Gurion played a crucial role in shaping Israel's *bitachon* outlook because of the structural changes he introduced into the Zionist decision-making mechanism that placed him at the top of what before had been a rather cumbersome and ineffective pyramid. When in 1946 the 22nd Zionist Congress entrusted Ben-Gurion with the defence portfolio, he had total control over all security issues of the Jewish community in Palestine.[46]

Though as yet without a state, Ben-Gurion already now functioned as defence minister and as a prime minister of sorts (given his authority to pass resolutions within a government). In many aspects he shared responsibility, and most issues on the agenda of the Jewish community were discussed in a democratic way within institutions that represented the composition of the major political groups among the Jews in Palestine. But as the time came nearer when crucial decisions needed to be made with regards to the fate of the Palestinians, Ben-Gurion began to ignore the official structure and started relying on more clandestine formations.

The major topic on the Zionist agenda in 1946 and 1947, the struggle against the British, resolved itself with the British decision, in February 1947, to quit Palestine and to transfer the Palestine question to the UN. In fact, the British had little choice: after the Holocaust they would never be able to deal with the looming Jewish rebellion as they had with the Arab one in the 1930s and, as the Labour party made up its mind to leave India, Palestine lost much of its attraction. A particularly cold winter in 1947 drove the message home to London that the Empire was on its way to become a second-rate power, its global influence dwarfed by the two new superpowers and its economy crippled by a capitalist system that caused Sterling to drop precipitously. Rather than hold on to remote places such as

Palestine, the Labour party saw as its priority the building of a welfare state at home. In the end, Britain left in a hurry and with no regrets.[47]

Ben-Gurion had already realised by the end of 1946 that the British were on their way out, and with his aides began working on a general strategy that could be implemented against the Palestinian population the moment the British were gone. This strategy became Plan C, or *Gimel* in Hebrew.

Plan C was a revised version of two earlier plans, A and B. Plan A was also named the 'Elimelech plan', after Elimelech Avnir, the Hagana commander in Tel-Aviv who in 1937, at Ben-Gurion's request, had already set out possible guidelines for the takeover of Palestine in the event of a British withdrawal. Plan B had been devised in 1946 and both plans were now fused into one to form Plan C.

Like Plans A and B, Plan C aimed to prepare the military forces of the Jewish community in Palestine for the offensive campaigns they would be engaged in against rural and urban Palestine the moment the British were gone. The purpose of such actions would be to 'deter' the Palestinian population from attacking Jewish settlements, and to retaliate for assaults on Jewish houses, roads and traffic. Plan C spelled out clearly what punitive actions of this kind would entail:

> Killing the Palestinian political leadership.
> Killing Palestinian inciters and their financial supporters.
> Killing Palestinians who acted against Jews.
> Killing senior Palestinian officers and officials [in the Mandatory system].
> Damaging Palestinian transportation.
> Damaging the sources of Palestinian livelihoods: water wells, mills, etc.
> Attacking nearby Palestinian villages likely to assist in future attacks.
> Attacking Palestinian clubs, coffee houses, meeting places, etc.

Plan C added that all data required for the performance of these actions could be found in the village files: lists of leaders, activists, 'potential human targets', the precise layout of villages, and so on.[48]

However, within a few months, yet another plan was drawn up: Plan D (*Dalet*).[49] It was this plan that sealed the fate of the Palestinians within the territory the Zionist Leaders had set their eyes on for their future Jewish State. Indifferent as to whether these Palestinians might decide to collaborate with or oppose their Jewish State, Plan Dalet called for their systematic and total expulsion from their homeland.

Chapter 3

Partition and Destruction: UN Resolution 181 and its Impact

The most brutal element of the conflict in the former Yugoslavia was the 'ethnic cleansing', designed to force minority groups out of areas occupied by a different majority.

Previously, different peoples had lived together in the same village and there had been no division into ethnic groups and no ethnic cleansing. Thus, the causes of the situation were clearly political.

Summary record of the UN Committee on the
Elimination of Racial Discrimination, 6 March 1995
with regard to the former Yugoslavia.

PALESTINE'S POPULATION

When the Zionist movement started its ethnic cleansing operations in Palestine, in early December 1947, the country had a 'mixed' population of Palestinians and Jews. The indigenous Palestinians made up the two-third majority, down from ninety per cent at the start of the Mandate. One third were Jewish newcomers, i.e., Zionist settlers and refugees from war torn

Europe, most of whom had arrived in Palestine since the 1920s.[1] As of the late nineteenth century, the indigenous Palestinians had been seeking the right of self-determination, at first within a pan-Arab identity, but then, soon after the First World War, through the Mandate system that promised to lead the new nation-states it had created in the Middle East to independence and towards a future based on principles of democracy. But Britain's Mandate charter for Palestine also incorporated, wholesale, the 1917 Balfour Declaration and, with it, Britain's promise to the Zionist movement to secure a 'homeland' for the Jews in Palestine.

Despite Britain's pro-Zionist policies and the presence of a growing Jewish minority, Palestine was still very much an Arab country by the end of the Mandate. Almost all of the cultivated land in Palestine was held by the indigenous population – only 5.8% was in Jewish ownership in 1947 – which makes the use here of the adjective 'mixed' somewhat misleading, to say the least. Although the Zionist leaders had tried to persuade Jewish immigrants, ever since the movement had set foot in Palestine, to settle in the countryside, they had failed to do so: Jewish newcomers overwhelmingly preferred the cities and towns. As a result, most of the Zionist settler colonies in the rural areas lay far apart from each other; in some areas, such as the Galilee in the north and the Naqab (the Negev) in the south, they were effectively isolated islands amidst the surrounding Palestinian countryside.

This isolation meant these colonies were built like military garrisons rather than villages: what inspired their layout and design were security considerations rather than human habitation. Their introverted seclusion contrasted bizarrely with the open spaces of the traditional Palestinian villages with their natural stone houses and their accessible, unhindered, approaches to the nearby fields and the orchards and olive groves around them.

That so few Jews had settled in the Palestinian countryside proved to be a serious problem for those who wanted to base their solution to the growing conflict between the two communities on the principle of partition. On the one hand, logic and common sense dictated that the countryside as a whole – more than three quarters of the territory – should remain Palestinian. The towns, on the other hand, were almost equally inhabited. The question was, how to devise two distinct Palestinian and Jewish entities with homogenous populations when this was the reality on the ground? Partitioning Palestine was originally a British solution, but it became a centrepiece of Zionist policy from 1937. Earlier, the British had put forward several others options, notably the creation of a bi-national state, which the Jews had rejected, and a cantonised Palestine (following the Swiss model), which both sides had refused to consider. In the end, London gave up the attempt to find a solution for the looming conflict and, in February 1947, transferred the question of Palestine to the United Nations. Favoured by the Zionist leadership, and now backed by Britain, partition became the name of the game. The interests of the Palestinians were soon almost totally excised from the process.

THE UN'S PARTITION PLAN

An inexperienced UN, just two years old in 1947, entrusted the question of the future of Palestine's fate into the hands of a Special Committee for Palestine, UNSCOP, none of whose members turned out to have any prior experience in solving conflicts or knew much about Palestine's history.

UNSCOP too decided to sponsor partition as the guiding principle for a future solution. True, its members deliberated for a while over the possibility of making all of Palestine one democratic state – whose future would then be decided by the majority vote of the population – but they eventually abandoned the idea. Instead, UNSCOP recommended to the UN General Assembly to partition Palestine into two states, bound together federation-like by economic unity. It further recommended that the City of Jerusalem would be established as *corpus separatum* under an international regime administered by the UN. The report UNSCOP came up with in the end envisaged that the two future states would be identical except for their internal demographic balance, and it therefore stressed the need for both entities to adhere to liberal democratic precepts. On 29 November 1947 this became General Assembly Resolution 181.[2]

It is clear that by accepting the Partition Resolution, the UN totally ignored the ethnic composition of the country's population. Had the UN decided to make the territory the Jews had settled on in Palestine correspond with the size of their future state, they would have entitled them to no more than ten per cent of the land. But the UN accepted the nationalist claims the Zionist movement was making for Palestine and, furthermore, sought to compensate the Jews for the Nazi Holocaust in Europe.

As a result, the Zionist movement was 'given' a state that stretched over more than half of the country. That the members of UNSCOP veered towards the Zionist point of view was also because the Palestinian leadership had been opposed since 1918 to the partitioning of their land. Throughout its history this leadership, made up mainly of urban notables, quite often failed to truly represent the native population of Palestine; however, this time they got it right and fully backed the popular resentment among Palestine's society towards the idea of 'sharing' their homeland with European settlers who had come to colonise it.

The Arab League, the regional inter-Arab Organisation, and the Arab Higher Committee (the embryonic Palestinian government) decided to boycott the negotiations with UNSCOP prior to the UN resolution, and did not take part in the deliberations on how best to implement it after November 1947. Into this vacuum the Zionist leadership stepped with ease and confidence, quickly setting up a bilateral dialogue with the UN on how to work out a scheme for the future of Palestine. This is a pattern we will see recur frequently in the history of peacemaking in Palestine, especially after the Americans became involved in 1967: up to the present day, 'bringing peace to Palestine' has always meant following a concept exclusively worked out between the US and Israel, without any serious consultation with, let alone regard for, the Palestinians.

The Zionist movement so quickly dominated the diplomatic game in 1947 that the leadership of the Jewish community felt confident enough to demand UNSCOP allocate them a state comprising over eighty per cent of the land. The Zionist emissaries to the negotiations with the UN actually produced a map showing the state they wanted, which incorporated all the land Israel would occupy a year later, that is, Mandatory Palestine without the West Bank. However, most of the UNSCOP members felt this was a bit too much, and convinced the Jews to be satisfied with fifty-six per cent of the land. Moreover, Catholic countries persuaded the UN to make Jerusalem an international city given its religious significance, and therefore UNSCOP also rejected the Zionist claim for the Holy City to be part of the future Jewish State.[3]

Partitioning the country – overwhelmingly Palestinian – into two equal parts has proven so disastrous because it was carried out against the will of the indigenous majority population. By broadcasting its intent to create equal Jewish and Arab political entities in Palestine, the UN violated the basic rights of the Palestinians, and totally ignored the concern for Palestine in the wider Arab world at the very height of the anti-colonialist struggle in the Middle East.

Far worse was the impact the decision had on the country itself and its people. Instead of calming the atmosphere, as it was meant to do, the resolution only heightened tensions and directly caused the country to deteriorate into one of the most violent phases in its history. Already in February 1947, when the British first announced their intention to leave Palestine, the two communities had seemed closer to a total clash than ever before. Although no significant outbursts of violence were reported before the UN adopted its Partition Resolution on 29 November 1947, anxiety was particularly high in the mixed towns. So long as it was unclear which way the UN would go, life continued more or less as normal, but the moment the die was cast and people learned that the UN had voted overwhelmingly in favour of partitioning Palestine, law and order collapsed and a sense of foreboding descended of the final showdown that partition spelled. The chaos that followed produced the first Arab-Israeli war: the ethnic cleansing of the Palestinians had started.

THE ARAB AND PALESTINIAN POSITIONS

As I explained above, the Palestinian leadership decided from the start to boycott the UN proceedings. This decision features often in contemporary Israeli propaganda as proof that the Palestinians themselves – not Israel – should be held responsible for the fate that befell them in 1948. Palestinian historiography has successfully fended off such accusations by exposing the extent to which the procedures the UN opted to follow were unjust and illegal, and by exploring the raison d'être behind the establishment of UNSCOP. Before we proceed I want to summarise these arguments and examine them in more detail.

By opting for partition as its primary objective, the UN ignored a basic principled objection the Palestinians were voicing against the plan, with which mediators had been familiar since Britain made the Balfour Declaration thirty years earlier. Walid Khalidi succinctly articulated the Palestinian position as follows: 'The native people of Palestine, like the native people of every other country in the Arab world, Asia,

Africa, America and Europe, refused to divide the land with a settler community.'⁴

Within a few weeks of UNSCOP starting its work, the Palestinians realised the cards had been stacked against them: the final result of this process would be a UN resolution on partitioning the country between the Palestinians, as the indigenous population, and a settler colony of newcomers, many of whom had arrived only recently. When Resolution 181 was adopted in November 1947, their worst nightmare began to unfold in front of their eyes: nine months after the British had announced their decision to leave, the Palestinians were at the mercy of an international organisation that appeared ready to ignore all the rules of international mediation, which its own Charter endorsed, and was willing to declare a solution that in Palestinian eyes was both illegal and immoral. Several leading Palestinians at the time demanded that its legality be tested in the International Court of Justice (founded in 1946), but this was never to happen.⁵ One does not have to be a great jurist or legal mind to predict how the international court would have ruled on forcing a solution on a country to which the majority of its people were vehemently opposed.

The injustice was as striking then as it appears now, and yet it was hardly commented on at the time by any of the leading Western newspapers then covering Palestine: the Jews, who owned less than six per cent of the total land area of Palestine and constituted no more than one third of the population, were handed more than half of its overall territory. Within the borders of their UN-proposed state, they owned only eleven per cent of the land, and were the minority in every district. In the Negev – admittedly an arid land but still with a considerable rural and Bedouin population, which made up a major chunk of the Jewish state – they constituted one per cent of the total population.

Other aspects that undermined the legal and moral credibility of the resolution quickly emerged. The Partition Resolution incorporated the most fertile land in the proposed Jewish state as well as almost all the Jewish urban and rural space in Palestine. But it also included 400 (out of more than 1000) Palestinian villages within the designated Jewish state. In hindsight, it may be argued in UNSCOP's defence that Resolution 181 was based on the assumption that the two new political entities would peacefully coexist and therefore not much attention needed to be paid to balances of demography and geography. If this were the case, as some UNSCOP members were to argue later, then they were guilty of totally misreading Zionism and grossly underestimating its ambitions. Again in the words of Walid Khalidi, Resolution 181 was 'a hasty act of granting half of Palestine to an ideological movement that declared openly already in the 1930s its wish to de-Arabise Palestine.'[6] And thus Resolution 181's most immoral aspect is that it included no mechanism to prevent the ethnic cleansing of Palestine.

Let us look more closely at the final map that the UN proposed in November 1947 (see Map 5). Palestine was actually to be divided into three parts. On forty-two per cent of the land, 818,000 Palestinians were to have a state that included 10,000 Jews, while the state for the Jews was to stretch over almost fifty-six per cent of the land which 499,000 Jews were to share with 438,000 Palestinians. The third part was a small enclave around the city of Jerusalem which was to be internationally governed and whose population of 200,000 was equally divided between Palestinians and Jews.[7]

The almost equal demographic balance within the allocated Jewish state was such that, had the map actually been implemented, it would have created a political nightmare for the Zionist leadership: Zionism would never have attained any of its principal goals. As Simcha Flapan, one of the first Israeli Jews to challenge the conventional Zionist version of the 1948 events, put it, had the Arabs or the Palestinians decided to go along with the Partition Resolution, the Jewish leadership would have been sure to reject the map UNSCOP offered them.[8]

Actually, the UN map was an assured recipe for the tragedy that began to unfold the day after Resolution 181 was adopted. As theoreticians of ethnic cleansing acknowledged later, where an ideology of exclusivity is adopted in a highly charged ethnic reality, there can be only one result: ethnic cleansing. By drawing the map as they did, the UN members who voted in favour of the Partition Resolution contributed directly to the crime that was about to take place.

THE JEWISH REACTION

By 1947, David Ben-Gurion presided over a political structure of decision-making that probably constitutes the only complex aspect of the history related in this book, but this is dealt with in depth elsewhere,[9] and is beyond the remit of this book. Briefly, it allowed him to determine almost single-handedly the main policies of the Jewish community vis-à-vis the world, the Arab neighbours and the Palestinians. It was Ben-Gurion who now led his associates simultaneously to accept and ignore the UN Partition Resolution on 29 November 1947.

The categorical rejection of the scheme by the Arab governments and the Palestinian leadership made it undoubtedly easier for Ben-Gurion to believe that he could both accept the plan and work against it. Already in October 1947, before the resolution was adopted, Ben-Gurion clarified to his friends in the leadership that if the map of the partition plan were not satisfactory, the Jewish state would not be obliged to accept it.[10]

It is clear, therefore, that the rejection or acceptance of the plan by the Palestinians would not have changed Ben-Gurion's assessment of the plan's deficiencies where he was concerned. For him and his friends at the top of the Zionist hierarchy, a valid Jewish state meant a state that stretched over most of Palestine and allowed for no more than a tiny number of Palestinians, if any at all, to be included.[11] Similarly, Ben-Gurion was unfazed by the resolution's call that Jerusalem be turned into an international city. He was determined to make the entire city his Jewish capital. That in the end he failed to do so was only because of complications and disagreements arising in the Jordanian-Jewish negotiations over the future of the country and the city, of which more is said later.

As unhappy as he was with the UN map, Ben-Gurion realised that under the circumstances – the total rejection of the map by the Arab world and the Palestinians – the delineation of final borders would remain an open question. What mattered was international recognition of the right of the Jews to have a state of their own in Palestine. An observant British official in Jerusalem wrote to his government that the Zionist acceptance of the partition resolution was selective: the Zionists rejoiced in the international recognition of the Jewish State, but then claimed that the UN had offered 'non-Zionist conditions for maintaining it'.[12]

The expected Arab and Palestinian rejection of the plan[13] allowed Ben-Gurion and the Zionist leadership to claim that the UN plan was a dead letter the day it was accepted – apart, of course, from the clauses that recognised the legality of the Jewish state in Palestine. Its borders, given the Palestinian and Arab rejection, said Ben-Gurion, 'will be determined by force and not by the partition resolution.'[14] As would be the fate of the Arabs living in it.

THE CONSULTANCY BEGINS ITS WORK

A formula now emerges. The less important the body Ben-Gurion appeared in front of, the more supportive the leader was of the Partition Resolution; the more significant the forum, the more adamant he proved in his scornful rejection of it. In the special body that advised him on security issues, the Defence Committee, he dismissed the Partition Resolution out of hand, and already on 7 October 1947 – before UN Resolution 181 was even adopted – we find him telling the inner circle of his colleagues in the Consultancy that in the light of the Arab refusal to cooperate with the UN, there 'are no territorial boundaries for the future Jewish State.'[15]

In October and November 1947 the Consultancy became Ben-Gurion's most important reference group. It was only among them that he discussed openly what the implications would be of his decision to disregard the partition map and to use force in order to ensure Jewish majority and exclusivity in the country. In such 'sensitive' matters he could confide only in this highly select coterie of politicians and military men.

It was precisely because he understood that these questions could not be aired in public that Ben-Gurion had created the 'Consultancy' in the first place. As explained above, this was not an official outfit, and we have no proper minutes from most of their meetings.[16] It is doubtful whether notes were taken at all – apart from at one or two very crucial meetings that did get transcribed and to which I will come back later. However, Ben-Gurion recorded summaries of many of the meetings in his diary, an important historical source for those years. Moreover, some of the Consultancy's members would be interviewed in later years, and others wrote autobiographies and memoirs. In the following pages I take my cues from Ben-Gurion's diary, archival correspondence and the private archive of Israel Galili, who was present in all the meetings (all sources included in the Ben-Gurion Archives in Sdeh Boker). In addition, an intensive correspondence surrounded these meetings, which can be found in various Israeli archives. The meetings took place partly in Ben-Gurion's house in Tel-Aviv and partly in the Red House. As on 10 March 1948, some meetings were

convened on Wednesdays in the Red House, within the official weekly meeting of the High Command, the *Matkal* (the formal parts of these meetings
are recorded in the IDF archives). Other, more private, consultations took
place in Ben-Gurion's house, a day after the more formal Wednesday meeting. The latter meetings were referred to, very cautiously, in Ben-Gurion's
diary, but can be reconstructed with the help of sources such as Yossef
Weitz's diary, Israel Galili's archives and the letters of Ben-Gurion to various
colleagues, most notable of whom was his second in command, Moshe
Sharett (who was abroad for most of this period).[17] On 15 May 1948, the
meetings moved to a new place east of Tel-Aviv, which became the headquarters of the Israeli Army.

The Consultancy, as we saw, was a combination of security figures and
specialists on 'Arab affairs', a formula that was to serve as the core for most of
the bodies entrusted with advising future governments of Israel throughout
the years on issues of state security, strategies and policy planning towards
the Arab world in general and the Palestinians in particular.[18] This
entourage around Ben-Gurion began to hold regular meetings in February
1947, from the moment the British decided to leave Palestine, and more frequently in October 1947, when it transpired that the Palestinians would
reject the UN Partition Plan. Once the Palestinian and general Arab positions were clear, the members of the Consultancy knew not only that they
were to decide the fate of the Palestinians in the UN-designated Jewish state,
but that their policies were also about to affect the Palestinians living in areas
the UN had accorded to the Arab state in Palestine. In the next chapter we
shall see how the thinking of the Consultancy evolved until it devised a final
plan for the dispossession of one million Palestinians, no matter where they
happened to be in the country.

The first documented meeting of the Consultancy is that of 18 June
1947, during the regular Wednesday afternoon meeting of the High
Command. Ben-Gurion reported the meeting both in his diary and in his
published memoirs. He told those present that the Jewish community
would need to 'defend not only our settlements, but the country as a whole
and Our National Future'. Later on, in a speech he gave on 3 December 1947,
he would repeat the term 'our national future' and use it as a code for the
demographic balance in the country.[19]

Chapter 4

Finalising a Master Plan

NATO Spokesman Jamie Shea said all reports reaching NATO indicated that what was happening in Kosovo was a well-organized master plan by Belgrade. He said the reported pattern of violence was that Serb tanks were surrounding villages, then paramilitaries are going in rounding up civilians at gunpoint, separating young men from women and children. The women and children are then expelled from their homes and then sent forward towards the border. After they have left the villages, the homes are looted and then systematically torched.

CNN, 30 March 1999

These operations can be carried out in the following manner: either by destroying villages (by setting fire to them, by blowing them up, and by planting mines in their debris) and especially of those population centers which are difficult to control continuously; or by mounting combing and control operations according to the following guidelines: encirclement of the villages, conducting a search inside them. In case of resistance, the armed forces must be wiped out and the population expelled outside the borders of the state.

Plan Dalet, 10 March, 1948

THE METHODOLOGY OF CLEANSING

The chronology of key events between February 1947 and May 1948 is worth recapping at this point. Hence, I will present an initial overview of the period I wish to focus on in detail in this chapter. First, in February 1947, the decision was made by the British Cabinet to pull out of Mandatory Palestine and leave it to the UN to solve the question of its future. The UN took nine months to deliberate the issue, and then adopted the idea of partitioning the country. This was accepted by the Zionist leadership who, after all, championed partition, but was rejected by the Arab world and the Palestinian leadership, who instead suggested keeping Palestine a unitary state and who wanted to solve the situation through a much longer process of negotiation. The Partition Resolution was adopted on 29 November 1947, and the ethnic cleansing of Palestine began in early December 1947 with a series of Jewish attacks on Palestinian villages and neighbourhoods in retaliation for the buses and shopping centres that had been vandalised in the Palestinian protest against the UN resolution during the first few days after its adoption.[1] Though sporadic, these early Jewish assaults were severe enough to cause the exodus of a substantial number of people (almost 75,000).

On 9 January, units of the first all-Arab volunteer army entered Palestine and engaged with the Jewish forces in small battles over routes and isolated Jewish settlements. Easily winning the upper hand in these skirmishes, the Jewish leadership officially shifted its tactics from acts of retaliation to cleansing operations. Coerced expulsions followed in the middle of February 1948 when Jewish troops succeeded in emptying five Palestinian villages in one day. On 10 March 1948, Plan Dalet was adopted. The first targets were the urban centres of Palestine, which had all been occupied by the end of April. About 250,000 Palestinians were uprooted in this phase, which was accompanied by several massacres, most notable of which was the Deir Yassin massacre. Aware of these developments, the Arab League took the decision, on the last day of April, to intervene militarily, but not until the British Mandate had come to an end.

The British left on 15 May 1948, and the Jewish Agency immediately declared the establishment of a Jewish state in Palestine, officially recognised by the two superpowers of the day, the USA and the USSR. That same day, regular Arab forces entered Palestine.

By February 1948, the American administration had already concluded that the UN Partition Resolution, far from being a peace plan, was proving a recipe for continued bloodshed and hostility. Therefore, it twice offered alternative schemes to halt the escalation of the conflict: a trusteeship plan for five years, in February 1948, and a three-month cease-fire, on 12 May. The Zionist leadership rejected both peace proposals out of hand.[2]

The official Zionist strategy was fed throughout this period by two impulses. The first consisted of ad-hoc reactions to two startling developments on the ground. One was the fragmentation, if not total disintegration, of the Palestinian political and military power systems, and the other the growing disarray and confusion within the Arab world in the face of the aggressive Jewish initiatives and the simultaneous international endorsement of the Zionist project and the future Jewish state.

The second impulse to propel Zionist strategic thinking was the drive to exploit to the full the unique historical opportunity they saw opening up to make their dream of an exclusively Jewish state come true. As we saw in the previous chapters, this vision of a purely Jewish nation-state had been at the heart of Zionist ideology from the moment the movement emerged in the late nineteenth century. By the mid 1930s, a handful of Zionist leaders recognised the clear link between the end of British rule and the possibility of the de-Arabisation of Palestine, i.e., making Palestine free of Arabs. By the end of November 1947, most of those in the inner circle of the leadership appeared to have grasped this nexus as well, and under Ben-Gurion's guidance they now turned all their attention to the question of how to make the most of the opportunity that this connection appeared to have given them.

Before 1947, there had been other, more urgent, agendas: the primary mission had been to build a political, economic and cultural Zionist enclave within the country, and to ensure Jewish immigration to the area. As mentioned previously, ideas of how best to deal with the local Palestinian population had remained vague. But the impending end of the British Mandate, the Arab rejection of the partition resolution, and Ben-Gurion's keen realization of how much of Palestine he would need to the make the Jewish state viable now helped translate past ideologies and nebulous scenarios into a specific master plan.

Prior to March 1948, the activities the Zionist leadership carried out to implement their vision could still be portrayed as retaliation for hostile Palestinian or Arab actions. However, after March this was no longer the case: the Zionist leadership openly declared – two months *before* the end of the Mandate – it would seek to take over the land and expel the indigenous population by force: Plan Dalet.

Defining the Space

The first step towards the Zionist goal of obtaining as much of Palestine as possible with as few Palestinians in it as feasible was to decide what constituted a viable state in geographical terms. The UN Partition Plan, formalised in Resolution 181, designated the Negev, the coast, the eastern valleys (Marj Ibn Amir and the Baysan Valley) and lower Galilee for the Jews, but this was not enough. Ben-Gurion had the habit of regularly meeting with, what he called his 'war cabinet', which was an ad-hoc group of Jewish officers who had served in the British army (under pressure from other Hagana members, he later had to disband it). He now set out to impress on these officers the idea that they should start preparing for the occupation of the country as a whole. In October 1947, Ben-Gurion wrote to General Ephraim Ben-Artzi, the most senior officer among them, explaining that he wanted to create a military force able both to repel a potential attack from neighbouring Arab states and to occupy as much of the country as possible, and hopefully all of it.[3]

For the time being the Zionist leadership decided to determine the territory of their future state according to the location of the most remote and isolated Jewish settlements. All the land between these colonies, isolated at the extreme ends of the Mandatory state, had to become Jewish, and preferably enveloped by additional 'security zones' as buffer areas between them and Palestinian habitations.[4]

Since they were privy to the ongoing negotiations with the Hashemites in Transjordan, several members of the leadership allowed only one constraint to influence the shape of their future map, and that was the possibility that certain areas in the east of Palestine, in today's West Bank, could become part of a future Greater Jordan rather than a Greater Israel. In late 1946 the Jewish Agency had embarked on intensive negotiations with King Abdullah of Jordan. Abdullah was a scion of the Hashemite royal family from the Hejaz – the seat of the holy Muslim cities of Mecca and Medina – that had fought alongside the British in the First World War. In reward for their services to the crown, the Hashemites had been granted the kingdoms of Iraq and Jordan that the Mandate system had created. Initially (in the Husayn-McMahon correspondence of 1915/1916) the Hashemites had also been promised Syria, according to their understanding at least, in a British attempt to block a French take-over of that part of the Middle East.

However, when the French ousted Abdullah's brother, Faysal, from Syria, the British compensated him, instead of Abdullah, with Iraq.[5]

As the eldest son of the dynasty, Abdullah was unhappy with his share in the deal, all the more so because in 1924 the Hejaz, the Hashemites' home base, was wrested from them by the Saudis. Transjordan was little more than an arid desert princedom east of the River Jordan, full of Bedouin tribes and some Circassian villages. No wonder he wished to expand into fertile, cultural and populated Palestine, and all means justified the goal. The best way to achieve this, he soon found out, was to cultivate a good relationship with the Zionist leadership. After the Second World War he reached an agreement in principle with the Jewish Agency over how to divide post-mandatory Palestine between them. Vague ideas of sharing the land became a basis for serious negotiations that started after UN Resolution 181 was adopted on 29 November 1947. As there were very few Jewish colonies in the area the king wanted to acquire (today's West Bank), most of the leaders of the Jewish community were 'willing' to give up this part of Palestine, even though it included some biblical Jewish sites, such as the city of Hebron (al-Khalil). Many of them would later regret this decision and back the push to occupy the West Bank in the June 1967 war, but at the time the Jordanian quid pro quo was very tempting indeed: Abdullah promised not to join any all-Arab military operations against the Jewish state. There were ups and downs in these negotiations as the Mandate drew to an end, but they remained intact not just because there were so few Jews in the West Bank but also because the Jordanians, with the help of an Iraqi contingent, successfully repelled repeated Jewish attempts to occupy parts of the West Bank throughout the second half of 1948 (one of the few triumphant chapters in the Arab military history of 1948).[6]

This decided the geographical territory the Zionist movement coveted, in other words, Palestine as a whole, the same territory they had demanded in the Biltmore programme of 1942, but with this one qualification, if one accepts – as most historians do today – that the Zionist leadership was committed to their collusion with the Jordanians. This meant that the Jewish leadership anticipated their future state to stretch over eighty per cent of Mandatory Palestine: the fifty-six per cent promised to the Jews by the UN, with an additional twenty-four per cent taken from the Arab state the UN had allocated to the Palestinians. The remaining twenty per cent would be picked up by the Jordanians.[7]

This tacit agreement with Jordan in many ways constituted the second step towards ensuring the ethnic cleansing operation could go ahead unhindered: crucially it neutralised the strongest army in the Arab world, and confined it to battle with the Jewish forces solely in a very small part of Palestine. Without the Jordanian Army, the Arab Legion, the Arab world lacked all serious capacity to defend the Palestinians or foil the Zionist plan to establish a Jewish state in Palestine at the expense of the indigenous population.

Creating the Means

The third and possibly most decisive step towards ensuring a successful ethnic cleansing was building an adequate military capability. The Consultancy wanted to be left in no doubt that the military force the Jewish community possessed would be strong enough to implement successfully their two-pronged plan to take over most of Palestine and dislocate the Palestinians living there. In addition to taking over the Mandatory state once the last British troops had left, it would need to halt all attempts by Arab forces to invade the Jewish state in the making, while simultaneously carrying out the ethnic cleansing of all the parts of Palestine it would occupy. A highly competent professional army thus became a vital tool in the construction of a solidly Jewish state in ex-Mandatory Palestine.

All in all, on the eve of the 1948 war, the Jewish fighting force stood at around 50,000 troops, out of which 30,000 were fighting troops and the rest auxiliaries who lived in the various settlements. In May 1948, these troops could count on the assistance of a small air force and navy, and on the units of tanks, armoured cars and heavy artillery that accompanied them. Facing them were irregular para-military Palestinian outfits that numbered no more than 7000 troops: a fighting force that lacked all structure or hierarchy and was poorly equipped when compared with the Jewish forces.[8] In addition, in February 1948, about 1000 volunteers had entered from the Arab world, reaching 3000 over the next few months.[9]

Until May 1946, the two sides were poorly equipped. Then the newly founded Israeli army, with the help of the country's Communist party, received a large shipment of heavy arms from Czechoslovakia and the Soviet Union,[10] while the regular Arab armies brought some heavy weaponry of their own. A few weeks into the war, the Israeli recruitment was so efficient that by the end of the summer their army stood at 80,000 troops. The Arab regular force never crossed the 50,000 threshold, and in addition had stopped receiving arms from Britain, which was its main arms supplier.[11]

In other words, during the early stages of the ethnic cleansing (until May 1948), a few thousand irregular Palestinians and Arabs were facing tens of thousands of well-trained Jewish troops. As the next stages evolved, a Jewish force of almost double the number of all the Arab armies combined had little trouble completing the job.

On the margins of the main Jewish military power operated two more extreme groups: the Irgun (commonly referred to as *Etzel* in Hebrew) and the Stern Gang (*Lehi*). The Irgun had split from the Hagana in 1931 and in the 1940s was led by Menachem Begin. It had developed its own aggressive policies towards both the British presence and the local population. The Stern Gang was an offshoot of the Irgun, which it left in 1940. Together with the Hagana, these three organisations were united into one military army during the days of the Nakba (although as we shall see, they did not always act in unison and coordination).

An important part of the Zionists' military effort was the training of special commando units, the Palmach, founded in 1941. Originally these were created to assist the British army in the war against the Nazis in case the latter reached Palestine. Soon, the Palmach's zeal and activities were directed against the Palestinian rural areas. From 1944 onwards, it was also the main pioneering force in building new Jewish settlements. Before being dismantled in the autumn of 1948, its members were highly active and carried out some of the main cleansing operations in the north and the centre of the country.

In the ethnic cleansing operations that followed, the Hagana, the Palmach and the Irgun were the forces that actually occupied the villages. Soon after their occupation, villages were transferred into the hands of less combatant troops, the Field Guard (*Hish* in Hebrew). This was the logistics arm of the Jewish forces, established in 1939. Some of the atrocities that accompanied the cleansing operations were committed by these auxiliary units.

The Hagana also had an intelligence unit, founded in 1933, whose main function was to eavesdrop on the British authorities and intercept communications between the Arab political institutions inside and outside the country. It is this unit that I mentioned earlier as supervising the preparation of the village files and setting up the network of spies and collaborators inside the rural hinterland that helped identify the thousands of Palestinians who were later executed on the spot or imprisoned for long periods once the ethnic cleansing had started.[12]

Together these troops formed a military might strong enough to reinforce Ben-Gurion's conviction in the ability of the Jewish community both to become the heir to the Mandatory state and to take over most of the Palestinian territory and the properties and assets it contained.[13]

Immediately upon the adoption of UN Resolution 181 the Arab leaders officially declared they would dispatch troops to defend Palestine. And yet, not once between the end of November 1947 and May 1948 did Ben-Gurion and, one should add, the small group of leading Zionist figures around him sense that their future state was in any danger, or that the list of military operations was so overwhelming that they would impinge on the proper expulsion of the Palestinians. In public, the leaders of the Jewish community portrayed doomsday scenarios and warned their audiences of an imminent 'second Holocaust'. In private, however, they never used this discourse. They were fully aware that the Arab war rhetoric was in no way matched by any serious preparation on the ground. As we saw, they were well informed about the poor equipment of these armies and their lack of battlefield experience and, for that matter, training, and thus knew they had only a limited capability to wage any kind of war. The Zionist leaders were confident they had the upper hand militarily and could drive through most of their ambitious plans. And they were right.

Moshe Sharett, the Jewish state's foreign minister 'designate', was out of the country during the months leading up to the declaration of the state. Every now and then he would receive letters from Ben-Gurion directing him how best to navigate between the need to recruit global and Jewish support for a future state in danger of being annihilated, and at the same time keeping him abreast of the true reality on the ground. When, on 18 February 1948, Sharett wrote to Ben-Gurion: 'We will have only enough troops to defend ourselves, not to take over the country,' Ben-Gurion replied:

> If we will receive in time the arms we have already purchased, and maybe even receive some of that promised to us by the UN, we will be able not only to defend [ourselves] but also to inflict death blows on the Syrians in their own country – and take over Palestine as a whole. I am in no doubt of this. We can face all the Arab forces. This is not a mystical belief but a cold and rational calculation based on practical examination.[14]

This letter was wholly consistent with other letters the two had been exchanging ever since Sharett had been dispatched abroad. It began with a letter in December 1947 in which Ben-Gurion sought to convince his political correspondent of the Jews' military supremacy in Palestine: 'We can starve the Arabs of Haifa and Jaffa [if we wish to do so].'[15] This confident posture regarding the Hagana's ability to take Palestine as a whole, and even beyond, would be maintained for the duration of the fighting, inhibited only by the promises they had made to the Jordanians.

There were, of course, moments of crisis, as I will describe later, in implementing the policies. These occurred when it proved impossible to defend all the isolated Jewish settlements and to secure free access of supply to the Jewish parts of Jerusalem. But most of the time the troops the Zionist leaders had at their disposal were sufficient to allow the Jewish community to prepare for both a possible confrontation with the Arab world and for the cleansing of the local population. Moreover, the Arab intervention only materialised on 15 May 1948, five and a half months after the UN partition resolution had been adopted. During that long period most of the Palestinians – apart from a few enclaves where paramilitary groups were trying to organise some sort of resistance – remained defenseless in the face of Jewish operations already underway.

When it comes to reconstructing that part of an historical process where intangible ideology becomes tangible reality, there are two options that we, as historians, can choose. In the case of 1948 Palestine, the first would be to draw the reader's attention to how consistent the Zionist leaders – from Herzl down to Ben-Gurion – were in their desire to empty the future Jewish state of as many Palestinians as possible, and then describe how this links up with the actual expulsions perpetrated in 1948. This approach is preeminently represented by the work of the historian Nur Masalha, who has meticulously charted for us the genealogy of the expulsionist dreams and plans of the Zionist 'founding fathers'.[16] He shows how the wish to de-Arabise Palestine formed a crucial pillar in Zionist thinking from the very first moment the movement entered onto the political stage in the form of Theodor Herzl. As we have seen, Ben-Gurion's thoughts on the issue were clearly articulated by 1937. His biographer Michael Bar-Zohar explains, 'In internal discussions, in instructions to his people, the "Old Man" demonstrated a clear stand: it was better that the smallest possible number of Arabs remain within the area of the state.'[17] The other option would be to concentrate on the incremental development of policy-making and try to show how, meeting by meeting, decisions about strategy and methods gradually coalesced into a systematic and comprehensive ethnic cleansing plan. I will make use of both options.

The question of what to do with the Palestinian population in the future Jewish state was being discussed intensively in the months leading up to the end of the Mandate, and a new notion kept popping up in the Zionist corridors of power: 'the Balance'. This term refers to the 'demographic balance' between Arabs and Jews in Palestine: when it tilts against Jewish majority or exclusivity in the land, the situation is described as disastrous. And the demographic balance, both within the borders the UN offered the Jews and within those as defined by the Zionist leadership itself, was exactly that in the eyes of the Jewish leadership: a looming disaster.

The Zionist leadership came up with two kinds of response to this predicament: one for public consumption, the other for the limited corps of intimates Ben-Gurion had collected around himself. The overt policy he and his colleagues started voicing publicly in forums such as the local People's Assembly (the Jewish 'parliament' in Palestine) was the need to encourage massive Jewish immigration into the country. In smaller venues the leaders admitted that increased immigration would never be enough to counterbalance the Palestinian majority: immigration needed to be combined with other means. Ben-Gurion had described these means already in 1937 when discussing with friends the absence of a solid Jewish majority in a future state. He told them that such a 'reality' – the Palestinian majority in the land – would compel the Jewish settlers to use force to bring about the 'dream' – a purely Jewish Palestine.[18] Ten years later, on 3 December 1947 in a speech in front of senior members of his Mapai party (the Eretz Israel Workers Party), he outlined more explicitly how to deal with unacceptable realities such as the one envisaged by the UN partition resolution:

> There are 40% non-Jews in the areas allocated to the Jewish state. This composition is not a solid basis for a Jewish state. And we have to face this new reality with all its severity and distinctness. Such a demographic balance questions our ability to maintain Jewish sovereignty ... Only a state with at least 80% Jews is a viable and stable state.[19]

On 2 November, i.e., almost a month before the UN General Assembly Resolution was adopted, and in a different venue, the Executive of the Jewish Agency, Ben-Gurion spelled out for the first time in the clearest possible terms that ethnic cleansing formed the alternative, or complementary, means of ensuring that the new state would be an exclusively Jewish one. The Palestinians inside the Jewish state, he told his audience, could become a fifth column, and if so 'they can either be mass arrested or expelled; it is better to expel them.'[20]

But how to implement this strategic goal? Simcha Flapan asserts that the majority of the Zionist leaders at the time would have stopped short of mass expulsion. In other words, had the Palestinians refrained from attacking Jewish targets after the partition resolution was adopted, and had the Palestinian elite not left the towns, it would have been difficult for the Zionist movement to implement its vision of an ethnically cleansed Palestine.[21] And yet, Flapan also accepted that Plan Dalet was a master plan for the ethnic cleansing of Palestine. Unlike, for instance, the analysis Benny Morris offers in the first edition of his book on the making of the refugee problem, but very much in line with the shift he gave that analysis in the second edition, the clear blueprint for Palestine's ethnic cleansing, Plan Dalet, was not created in a vacuum.[22] It emerged as the ultimate scheme in response to the way events gradually unfolded on the ground, through a kind of ad-hoc policy that crystallised with time. But that response was always inexorably grounded in the Zionist ideology and the purely Jewish state that was its goal. Thus, the main objective was clear from the beginning – the de-Arabisation of Palestine – whereas the means to achieve this most effectively evolved in tandem with the actual military occupation of the Palestinian territories that were to become the new Jewish state of Israel.

Now that the territory had been defined and military supremacy assured, the fourth step for the Zionist leadership towards completing the dispossession of Palestine was to put in place the actual concrete means that would enable them to remove such a large population. In the territory of their future greater Jewish state there lived, in early December 1947, one million Palestinians, out of an overall Palestinian population of 1.3 million, while the Jewish community itself was a minority of 600,000.

Choosing the Means: Worrisome Normality (December 1947)

The Arab Higher Committee declared a three-day strike and organised a public demonstration in protest against the UN decision to adopt the Partition Resolution. There was nothing new in this type of response: it was the usual Palestinian reaction to policies they deemed harmful and dangerous–short and ineffective. Some of the demonstrations got out of hand and spilled over into Jewish business areas, as happened in Jerusalem where demonstrators attacked Jewish shops and a market. But other incidents were attacks that, according to Jewish intelligence, had nothing to do with the UN decision. For example, there was the ambushing of a Jewish bus, an incident that almost all Israeli history books identify as the beginning of the 1948 war. Staged by the Abu Qishq gang, the action was motivated more by clannish and criminal impulses than by any national agenda.[23] In any case, after three days, foreign reporters observing the demonstrations and strikes detected a growing reluctance among common Palestinians to continue the protest, and noted a clear desire to return to normalcy. After all, for most Palestinians Resolution 181 meant a dismal, but not new, chapter in their history. Over the centuries, the country had been passed from one hand to another, sometimes belonging to European or Asian invaders and sometimes to parts of Muslim empires. However, the peoples' lives had continued more or less unchanged: they toiled the land or conducted their trade wherever they were, and quickly resigned themselves to the new situation until it changed once again. Hence, villagers and city dwellers alike waited patiently to see what it would mean to be part of either a Jewish state or any other new regime that might replace British rule. Most of them had no idea what was in store for them, that what was about to happen would constitute an unprecedented chapter in Palestine's history: not a mere transition from one ruler to another, but the actual dispossession of the people living on the land.

The eyes of the Palestinian community now turned towards Cairo, the seat of the Arab League and the temporary residence of their leader, al-Hajj Amin al-Husayni, in exile ever since the British had expelled him in 1937. The first days after the resolution found the Arab leaders in total disarray, but gradually during December 1947 some sort of a policy began to take shape. Arab leaders, especially of the countries neighbouring Palestine, preferred not to take individual or drastic decisions on the subject. They were perfectly aware that public opinion in their countries wanted to see urgent action taken against the UN decision. Consequently, the Arab League Council, made up of the Arab states' foreign ministers, recommended the dispatch of arms to the Palestinians and the establishment of an all-Arab volunteer force, to be called the Arab Liberation Army (*Jaish al-Inqath*, literally 'Rescue Army', from the verb *anqatha*, 'to rescue from imminent danger'). The League appointed a Syrian general at its head. Later that month, small groups of this army began trickling into Palestine, thereby providing a welcome pretext for the Consultancy to discuss the further escalation of the Hagana operations already underway.

The pattern was set, and from this perspective the month of December 1947 is perhaps the most intriguing chapter in the history of Palestine's ethnic cleansing. The mild reaction in the Arab capitals surrounding Palestine was welcomed by Ben-Gurion's Consultancy – while the indifferent, almost lethargic Palestinian response *disturbed* them. In the first three days after the Partition Resolution was adopted, a small select group within the Consultancy met every day,[24] but they then relaxed somewhat and the format returned to the weekly Wednesday afternoon meetings of the High Command, with additional get-togethers of the smaller group a day after (usually at Ben-Gurion's home). The first meetings in December were devoted to assessing the Palestinian mood and intention. The 'experts' reported that, despite the early trickling of volunteers into the Palestinian villages and towns, the people themselves seemed eager to continue life as normal.[25] This craving for normality remained typical of the Palestinians inside Palestine in the years to come, even in their worst crises and at the nadir of their struggle; and normality is what they have been denied ever since 1948.

But the swift return to normality and the Palestinians' wish not to become embroiled in a civil war posed a problem for a Zionist leadership determined to reduce drastically, if not totally, the number of Arabs within their future Jewish state. They needed a pretext, and this of course would be more difficult to create if the moderate Palestinian reaction continued. 'Fortunately' for them, at one point the army of Arab volunteers expanded their acts of hostility against Jewish convoys and settlements, thus making it easier for the Consultancy to frame the occupation and expulsion policy as a form of justified 'retaliation', *tagmul* in Hebrew. But already in December 1947, the Consultancy had begun to use the Hebrew word *yotzma* ('initiative') to describe the strategy it intended to follow with respect to the Palestinians in the territory of their coveted Jewish state. 'Initiative' meant taking action against the Palestinian population without waiting for a pretext for *tagmul* to come along. Increasingly, pretexts for retaliation would be conspicuously missing.

Palti Sela was a member of the intelligence units that would play a crucial role in implementing the ethnic cleansing operations. One of their tasks was to report daily on the mood among, and trends within, the rural population of Palestine. Stationed in the north-eastern valleys of the country, Sela was astonished by the apparent difference in the way the communities on either side reacted to the new political reality unfolding around them. The Jewish farmers in the kibbutzim and in the collective or private settlements turned their residences into military outposts – reinforcing their fortifications, mending fences, laying mines, etc. – ready to defend and attack; each member was issued with a gun and integrated into the Jewish military force. The Palestinian villages, to Sela's surprise, 'continued life as usual'. In fact in the three villages he visited – Ayndur, Dabburiyya and Ayn Mahel – people received him as they had always done, greeting him as a potential customer for bartering, trading and exchanging pleasantries or news. These villages were near the British hospital of Afula, where units of the Arab Legion were stationed as part of the British police force in the country. The Jordanian soldiers, too, seemed to regard the situation as normal and were not engaged in any special preparations. Throughout December 1947, Sela summed up in his monthly report: normalcy is the rule and agitation the exception.[26] If these people were to be expelled, it could not be done as 'retaliation' for any aggression on their part.

THE CHANGING MOOD IN THE CONSULTANCY: FROM RETALIATION TO INTIMIDATION

On the top floor of the Red House, on Wednesday afternoon, 10 December 1947, a disappointed Consultancy met to assess the situation. Two speakers were leading the conversation, Ezra Danin and Yehoshua Palmon.[27]

Ezra Danin, as already mentioned, was a citrus grove businessman who had been invited into the intelligence corps because of his knowledge of Arabic (he was born in Syria). Danin was in his mid-forties when he joined the Hagana in 1940; in 1947 he became the head of its 'Arab section', which supervised the work of Arab Jews and indigenous Arab collaborators who spied for the High Command within the Palestinian community as well as in neighbouring Arab countries. In May 1948 he assumed a new role: supervising the post-occupation activities of the Jewish forces when the ethnic cleansing operation began in earnest. His people were responsible for the procedures that were followed after a Palestinian village or neighbourhood had been occupied. This meant that, with the help of informants, they detected and identified men who were suspected of having attacked Jews in the past, or of belonging to the Palestinian national movement, or who simply were disliked by the local informants who exploited the opportunity to settle old scores. The men thus selected were usually executed on the spot. Danin quite often came to inspect these operations at first hand. His unit was also responsible, as soon as a village or town had been occupied, for separating all men of 'military age', namely between ten and fifty, from the rest of the villagers, who were then 'just' expelled or imprisoned for long periods in POW camps.[28]

Yehoshua ('Josh') Palmon was in many ways Danin's second-in-command and also took a great personal interest in the implementation of the policy of selection, interrogation and sometimes execution. Younger than Danin and born in Palestine itself, Palmon already had an impressive military career behind him. As a recruit to a British commando unit he had participated in the occupation of Syria and Lebanon in 1941 that brought French Vichy rule there to an end. The officers under Danin and Palmon's command were known to and feared by many Palestinians, who quickly learned to spot them despite their attempts to dress anonymously in dull khaki uniform. They acted behind the scenes in hundreds of villages, and the oral history of the Nakba is full of references to these men and the atrocities they committed.[29]

But on 10 December 1947, Danin and Palmon were still hidden from the public eye. They opened the meeting by reporting that members of the Palestinian urban elite were leaving their houses and moving to their winter residences in Syria, Lebanon and Egypt. This was a typical reaction from the urbanites in moments of stress – moving to safety until the situation calmed down. And yet Israeli historians, including revisionist ones such as Benny Morris, have interpreted these traditional temporary sorties as 'voluntary flight', in order to tell us that Israel was not responsible for them. But they left with the full intention of returning to their homes again later, only to be prevented by the Israelis from doing so: not allowing people to return to their homes after a short stay abroad is as much expulsion as any other act directed against the local people with the aim of depopulation.

Danin reported that this was the only instance they had been able to detect of Palestinians moving towards areas outside the UN-designated borders of the Jewish state, apart from several Bedouin tribes who had relocated closer to Arab villages out of fear of Jewish attacks. Danin seems to have been disappointed by this, because almost in the same breath he called for a far more aggressive policy – despite the fact that there were no offensive initiatives or tendencies on the Palestinian side – and went on to explain to the Consultancy the benefits it would have: his informants had told him that violent actions against Palestinians would terrify them, 'which will render help from the Arab world useless,' implying that the Jewish forces could do whatever they want with them.

'What do you mean by violent action?' inquired Ben-Gurion.

'Destroying the traffic (buses, lorries that carry agricultural products and private cars) ... sinking their fishing boats in Jaffa, closing their shops and preventing raw materials from reaching their factories.'

'How will they react?' asked Ben-Gurion.

'The initial reaction may be riots, but eventually they will understand the message.' The main goal was thus to assure that the population would be at the Zionists' mercy, so their fate could be sealed. Ben-Gurion seemed to like this suggestion, and wrote to Sharett three days later to explain that the general idea: the Palestinian community in the Jewish area would be 'at our mercy' and anything the Jews wanted could be done to them, including 'starving them to death'.[30]

It was another Syrian Jew, Eliyahu Sasson, who tried to some extent to play the devil's advocate in the Consultancy; he seemed doubtful about the new aggressive approach Danin and Palmon were outlining. He had emigrated to Palestine in 1927, and was perhaps the most intriguing and also ambivalent member of the Consultancy. In 1919, before becoming a Zionist, he had joined the Arab national movement in Syria. In the 1940s, his main role was to instigate a policy of 'divide and rule' inside the Palestinian community but also in the neighbouring Arab countries. He was thus instrumental in strengthening the alliance with the Jordanian Hashemite king over the future of Palestine, but his attempts to pit one

Palestinian group against another would become obsolete now that the Zionist leadership was moving towards a comprehensive ethnic cleansing of the country as a whole. However, his legacy of 'divide and rule' had its inevitable impact on Israeli policy in the years to come, as we can see, for instance, in the efforts Ariel Sharon made in 1981 when, as defence minister and on the advice of the Arabist Professor Menahem Milson, he attempted to undermine the Palestinian resistance movement by setting up so-called 'Village Leagues' as part of a pro-Israeli outfit in the occupied West Bank. This was a short-term and abortive endeavour. A more successful one was the incorporation, as early as 1948, of the Druze minority into the Israeli army within units that later became the principal tool for oppressing the Palestinians in the Occupied Territories.

The 10 December meeting would be the last in which Sasson tried to persuade his colleagues that despite the need for 'a comprehensive plan', as he called it – namely the uprooting of the local population – it was still prudent not to regard the whole Arab population as enemies, and to continue employing 'divide-and-rule' tactics. He was very proud of his role in the 1930s in arming Palestinian groups, the so-called 'peace gangs', that were made up of rivals of the Palestinian leader al-Hajj Amin al-Husayni. These units fought against the national Palestinian formations during the Arab Revolt. Sasson now wanted to bring these divide and rule tactics to target some loyal Bedouin tribes.

DECEMBER 1947: EARLY ACTIONS

The Consultancy not only rejected the idea of incorporating more collaborative 'Arabs', but they also went so far as to suggest putting behind them the whole notion of 'retaliation', as adopted at the time on the advice of Orde Wingate. Most of the participants in the meeting favoured 'engagement' in a systematic campaign of intimidation. Ben-Gurion approved, and the new policy was implemented the day after the meeting.

The first step was a well-orchestrated campaign of threats. Special units of the Hagana would enter villages looking for 'infiltrators' (read 'Arab volunteers') and distribute leaflets warning the local people against cooperating with the Arab Liberation Army. Any resistance to such an incursion usually ended with the Jewish troops firing at random and killing several villagers. The Hagana called these incursions 'violent reconnaissance' (*hasiyur ha-alim*). This, too, was part of the legacy of Orde Wingate, who had instructed the Hagana in the use of this terrorist method against Palestinian villagers in the 1930s. In essence the idea was to enter a defenceless village close to midnight, stay there for a few hours, shoot at anyone who dared leave his or her house, and then depart. Even in Wingate's day this was already intended more as a show of force than a punitive action or retaliatory attack.

In December 1947, two such defenseless villages were chosen for the revival of Wingate's tactics: Deir Ayyub and Beit Affa. When today you drive south-east of the city of Ramla for about 15 kilometres, especially on a wintry day when the typical thorny, yellow gorse bushes of the inner plains of Palestine turn green, you come upon a bizarre view: long lines of rubble and stones stretching out on an open field surrounding a relatively large imaginary square area. These were the stone fences of Deir Ayyub. In 1947, the rubble was a low stone wall that had been built more for aesthetic reasons than for the protection of the village, which had about 500 inhabitants. Named after Ayyub – Job in Arabic – most of its people were Muslim, living in stone and mud houses typical of the area. Just before the Jewish attack, the village had been celebrating the opening of a new school, which already had the gratifying number of fifty-one pupils enrolled in it, all made possible by money the villagers had collected among themselves and from which they could also pay the teacher's salary. But their joy was instantly obliterated when at ten o'clock at night a company of twenty Jewish troops entered the village – which, like so many villages in December, had no defence mechanism of any kind – and began firing randomly at several houses. The village was later attacked three more times before being evacuated by force in April 1948, when it was completely destroyed. Jewish forces made a similar attack in December against Beit Affa in the Gaza Strip, but here the raiders were successfully repelled.[31]

Threatening leaflets were also distributed in Syrian and Lebanese villages on Palestine's border, warning the population:

> If the war will be taken to your place, it will cause massive expulsion of the villagers, with their wives and their children. Those of you who do not wish to come to such a fate, I will tell them: in this war there will be merciless killing, no compassion. If you are not participating in this war, you will not have to leave your houses and villages.[32]

There now followed a number of operations of destruction in limited areas throughout rural and urban Palestine. Actions in the countryside were at first hesitant. Three villages in the upper eastern Galilee were selected: Khisas, Na'ima and Jahula, but the operation was cancelled, perhaps because the High Command deemed them as yet too ambitious. The cancellation, however, was partly ignored by the commander of the Palmach in the north, Yigal Allon. Allon wanted to experience an attack on at least one village, and decided to assault Khisas.

Khisas was a small village with a few hundred Muslims and one hundred Christians, who lived peacefully together in a unique topographical location in the northern part of Hula Plain, on a natural terrace that was about 100 metres wide. This terrace had been formed thousands of years before by the gradual shrinking of Lake Hula. Foreign travellers used to single this village out for the natural beauty of its location on the banks of the lake, and its proximity to the Hasbani River.[33] Jewish troops attacked the village on 18 December 1947, and randomly started blowing up houses at the dead of night while the occupants were still fast asleep. Fifteen villagers, including five children, were killed in the attack. The incident shocked *The New York Times*' correspondent, who closely followed the unfolding events. He went and demanded an explanation from the Hagana, which at first denied the operation. When the inquisitive reporter did not let go, they eventually admitted it. Ben-Gurion issued a dramatic public apology, claiming the action had been unauthorised but, a few months later, in April, he included it in a list of successful operations.[34]

When the Consultancy had met again on Wednesday, 17 December, they were joined by Yohanan Ratner and Fritz Eisenshtater (Eshet), two officers who had been designated by Ben-Gurion to formulate a 'national strategy' before he devised the Consultancy body. The meeting expanded on the implications of the successful Khisas operation, with some members calling for additional 'retaliatory' operations that were to include the destruction of villages, expulsion of people, and resettlement in their stead by Jewish settlers. The following day, in front of the formal larger body of the Jewish community that was responsible for defence affairs, 'The Defence Committee', Ben-Gurion summarized the earlier meeting. The operation seemed to thrill everyone, including the representative of the ultra Orthodox Jews, *Agudat Israel*, who said: 'We were told that the army had the ability of destroying a whole village and taking out all its inhabitants; indeed, let's do it!'

The committee also approved the appointment of intelligence officers for each such operation. They would play a crucial role in executing the next stages of the ethnic cleansing.[35]

The new policy was also aimed at the urban spaces of Palestine, and Haifa was chosen as the first target. Interestingly, this city is singled out by mainstream Israeli historians and the revisionist historian Benny Morris as an example of genuine Zionist goodwill towards the local population. The reality was very different by the end of 1947. From the morning after the UN Partition Resolution was adopted, the 75,000 Palestinians in the city were subjected to a campaign of terror jointly instigated by the Irgun and the Hagana. As they had only arrived in recent decades, the Jewish settlers had built their houses higher up the mountain. Thus, they lived topographically above the Arab neighbourhoods and could easily shell and snipe at them. They had started doing this frequently since early December. They used other methods of intimidation as well: the Jewish troops rolled barrels full of explosives, and huge steel balls, down into the Arab residential areas, and poured oil mixed with fuel down the roads, which they then ignited. The moment panic-stricken Palestinian residents came running out of their homes to try to extinguish these rivers of fire, they were sprayed by machine-gun fire. In areas where the two communities still interacted, the Hagana brought cars to Palestinian garages to be repaired, loaded with explosives and detonating devices, and so wreaked death and chaos. A special unit of the Hagana, *Hashahar* ('Dawn'), made up of *mistarvim* – literally Hebrew for 'becoming Arab', that is Jews who disguised themselves as Palestinians – was behind this kind of assault. The mastermind of these operations was someone called Dani Agmon, who headed the 'Dawn' units. On its website, the official historian of the Palmach puts it as follows: 'The Palestinians [in Haifa] were from December onwards under siege and intimidation.'[36] But worse was to come.

The early eruption of violence put a sad end to a relatively long history of workers' cooperation and solidarity in the mixed city of Haifa. This class consciousness was curbed in the 1920s and 1930s by both national leaderships, in particular by the Jewish Trade Union movement, but it continued to motivate joint industrial action against employers of all kinds, and inspired mutual help at times of recession and scarcity.

The Jewish attacks in the city heightened tensions in one of the major areas where Jews and Arabs worked shoulder to shoulder: the refinery plant of the Iraqi Petroleum Company in the bay area. This began with a gang from the Irgun throwing a bomb into a large group of Palestinians who were waiting to enter the plant. The Irgun claimed it was in retaliation for an earlier attack by Arab workers on their Jewish co-workers, a new phenomenon in an industrial site where Arab and Jewish workers had usually joined forces in trying to secure better labour conditions from their British employers. But the UN Partition Resolution seriously dented that class solidarity and tensions grew high. Throwing bombs into Arab crowds was the specialty of the Irgun, who had already done so before 1947. However, this particular attack in the refineries was undertaken in coordination with the Hagana forces as part of the new scheme to terrorise the Palestinians out of Haifa. Within hours, Palestinian workers reacted and rioted, killing a large number of Jewish workers – thirty-nine – in one of the worst but also last Palestinian counterattacks; the last, because there the usual chain of retaliatory skirmishes stopped.

The next stage introduced a new chapter in the history of Palestine. Eager to test, among other things, British vigilance in the face of their actions, the Hagana's High Command, as part of the Consultancy, decided to ransack a whole village and massacre a large number of its inhabitants. At the time the British authorities were still responsible for maintaining law and order and were very much present in Palestine. The village the High Command selected was Balad al-Shaykh, the burial place of Shaykh Izz al-Din al-Qassam, one of Palestine's most revered and charismatic leaders of the 1930s, who was killed by the British in 1935. His grave is one of the few remains of this village, about ten kilometres east of Haifa, still extant today.[37]

A local commander, Haim Avinoam, was ordered to 'encircle the village, kill the largest possible number of men, damage property, but refrain from attacking women and children.'[38] The attack took place on 31 December and lasted three hours. It left over sixty Palestinians dead, not all of them men. But note the distinction still made here between men and women: in their next meeting, the Consultancy decided that such a separation was an unnecessary complication for future operations. At the same time as the attack on Balad al-Shaykh, the Hagana units in Haifa tested the ground with a more drastic action: they went into one of the city's Arab neigbourhoods, Wadi Rushmiyya, expelled its people and blew up its houses. This act could be regarded as the official beginning of the ethnic cleansing operation in urban Palestine. The British looked the other way while these atrocities were being committed.

Two weeks later, in January 1948, the Palmach 'used' the momentum that had been created to attack and expel the relatively isolated Haifa neighbourhood of Hawassa. This was the poorest quarter of town, originally made up of huts and inhabited by impoverished villagers who had come to seek work there in the 1920s, all living in dismal conditions. At the time there were about 5000 Palestinians in this eastern part of the city. Huts were blown up, and so was the local school, while the ensuing panic caused many people to flee. The school was rebuilt on the ruins of Hawassa, now part of the Tel-Amal neighbourhood, but this building too was recently destroyed to make room for a new Jewish school.[39]

JANUARY 1948: FAREWELL TO RETALIATION

These operations were accompanied by acts of terrorism by the Irgun and the Stern Gang. Their ability to sow fear in Haifa's Arab neighbourhoods, and in other cities as well, was directly influenced by the gradual but obvious British withdrawal from any responsibility for law and order. In the first week of January alone the Irgun executed more terrorist attacks than in any period before. These included detonating a bomb in the Sarraya house in Jaffa, the seat of the local national committee,[40] which collapsed leaving twenty-six people dead. It continued with the bombing of the Samiramis Hotel in Qatamon, in western Jerusalem, in which many people died, including the Spanish consul. This last fact seems to have prompted Sir Alan Cunningham, the last British High Commissioner, to issue a feeble complaint to Ben-Gurion, who refused to condemn the action, either in private or in public. In Haifa such actions were now a daily occurrence.[41]

Cunningham appealed again to Ben-Gurion when in the weeks that followed he noticed the shift in the Hagana's policy from retaliation to offensive initiatives, but his protestations were ignored. In the last meeting he had with Ben-Gurion in March 1948, he told the Zionist leader that to his mind, while the Palestinians were trying to maintain calm in the country, the Hagana did all it could to escalate the situation.[42] This did not contradict Ben-Gurion's assessment. He told the Jewish Agency Executive, shortly after he met Cunningham: 'I believe the majority of the Palestinian masses accept the partition as a fait accompli and do not believe it is possible to overcome or reject it ... The decisive majority of them do not want to fight us.'[43] From Paris, the Jewish Agency representative there, Emile Najjar, wondered how he could pursue an effective propaganda policy given the present reality.[44]

The national committee of the Palestinians in Haifa appealed again and again to the British, assuming, wrongly, that since Haifa was to be the last station in the British evacuation, they would be able to rely on their protection at least until then. When this failed to materialise, they started sending numerous desperate letters to members of the Arab Higher Committee inside and outside Palestine asking for guidance and help. A small group of volunteers reached the city in January, but by then some of the notables and community leaders had realised that the moment the UN had adopted the Partition Resolution, they were doomed to be dispossessed by their Jewish neighbours. These were people whom they themselves had first invited to come and stay with them back in the late Ottoman period, who had arrived wretched and penniless from Europe, and with whom they had shared a thriving cosmopolitan city – until that fateful decision by the UN.

Against this background one should recall the exodus at this time of about 15,000 of Haifa's Palestinian elite – many of them prosperous merchants whose departure ruined local trade and commerce, thus putting an extra burden on the more impoverished parts of the city.

The picture would not be complete without mentioning here the overall nature of the Arab activity up to the beginning of January 1948. During December 1947, Arab irregulars had attacked Jewish convoys but refrained from attacking Jewish settlements.[45] In November the Consultancy had already defined its policy of retaliating for each such attack. But the feeling among the Zionist leaders was that they needed to move on to more drastic actions.

THE LONG SEMINAR: 31 DECEMBER–2 JANUARY[46]

'This is not enough,' exclaimed Yossef Weitz when the Consultancy met on Wednesday, 31 December 1947, only a few hours before the people of Balad al-Shaykh were massacred. And he now suggested openly what he had been privately writing in his diary back in the early 1940s: 'Is it not now the time to get rid of them? Why continue to keep in our midst those thorns at a time when they pose a danger to us?'[47] Retaliation seemed to him an old-fashioned way of doing things, as it missed the main purpose of attacks on and subsequent occupation of villages. Weitz had been added to the Consultancy because he was the head of the settlement department of the Jewish National Fund, having already played a crucial role in translating for his friends the vague notions of transfer into a concrete policy. He felt the present discussion of what lay ahead lacked a sense of purpose, an orientation he had outlined in the 1930s and '40s.

'Transfer', he had written in 1940, 'does not serve only one aim – to reduce the Arab population – it also serves a second purpose by no means less important, which is: to evict land now cultivated by Arabs and to free it for Jewish settlement.' Therefore, he concluded: 'The only solution is to transfer the Arabs from here to neighbouring countries. Not a single village or a single tribe must be let off.'[48]

Weitz was a particularly valuable addition to the Consultancy because of his prior involvement in the village files project. Now, more than any other member of the Consultancy, Weitz deeply involved himself in the practicalities of the ethnic cleansing, jotting down details about every location and village for future reference, and entering his own surveys into those of the village files. His most trusted colleague in those days was Yossef Nachmani, a kindred soul, who shared Weitz's dismay at what they both saw as the lacklustre performance of the Jewish leadership on this issue. Weitz wrote to Nachmani that the takeover of all Arab land was a 'sacred duty'. Nachmani concurred and added that a kind of jihad (he used the term 'mil-hement kibush', a war of occupation) was required, but that the Jewish leadership failed to see its necessity. Weitz's alter ego wrote: 'The current leadership is characterised by impotent and weak people.' Weitz was equally disappointed by the leadership's inability, as he saw it, to rise to the historical occasion. His invitation to the Consultancy, and especially to their first meeting in January, made Weitz privy for the first time to the plans for ethnic cleansing as they evolved at the leadership level.[49]

Weitz's chance to display his ideas more widely came immediately, as that first Wednesday in January was turned into a long seminar, for which the participants moved into Ben-Gurion's home nearby. It was Ben-Gurion's idea to have a longer meeting as he sensed opportunities were opening up to make his dream of a Greater Israel come true. In this more comfortable setting, Weitz and others could make extended speeches and elaborate their views at leisure. This was also the only meeting of the Consultancy for which we have a protocol, found in the archives of the Hagana. For this 'Long Seminar' Weitz had prepared a memo, personally addressed to Ben-Gurion, in which he urged the leader to endorse his plans for transferring the Palestinian population out of areas the Jews wanted to occupy, and to make such actions the 'cornerstone of Zionist policy'. He obviously felt that the 'theoretical' stage of transfer plans was over. The time to start implementing the ideas had come. In fact, Weitz left the Long Seminar with a permit to create his own small cabal under the title of a 'transfer committee', and by the next meeting showed up with concrete plans, about which more will be said below.

Even the most liberal participant invited to the Long Seminar, Dr Yaacov Tahon, seemed to concur, dropping the more hesitant position he had previously taken. Tahon was a German Jew who, together with Arthur Rupin, had developed the first plans for the Jewish colonization of Palestine in the early decades of the twentieth century. As a true colonialist, at first he saw no need to expel the 'natives'; all he wanted was to exploit them. But in the Long Seminar he also appeared taken by Weitz's notion that 'without transfer there will be no Jewish State'.

Indeed, there was hardly a dissenting voice, which is why the Long Seminar is such a pivotal meeting in this story. Its departure point, accepted by all, was that ethnic cleansing was necessary; the remaining questions, or rather problems, were more of a psychological and logistical nature. Ideologues such as Weitz, Orientalists such as Machnes, and army generals such as Allon complained that their troops had not yet properly absorbed the previous orders they had been given to expand operations beyond the usual selective actions. The main problem, as they saw it, was that they seemed unable to put behind them the old methods of retaliation. 'They are still blowing up a house here and house there,' complained Gad Machnes, a colleague of Danin and Palmon, who ironically was to become the director general of the Israeli ministry for minorities in 1949 (where at least, one might add in his favour, he appeared to have shown some remorse about his conduct in 1948, admitting candidly in the 1960s that: 'If it had not been for the open [Zionist military] preparations which had a provocative nature, the drift into war [in 1948] could have been averted.'). But back then, in January 1948, he seemed impatient that the Jewish troops were still engaged in searching for 'guilty individuals' in each location, instead of actively inflicting damage.

Allon and Palmon now set out to explain the new orientation to their colleagues: there was a need for a more aggressive policy in areas that had been 'quiet for too long'.[50] There was no need to persuade Ben-Gurion. By the end of the Long Seminar he had given the green light to a whole series of provocative and lethal attacks on Arab villages, some as retaliation, some not, the intention of which was to cause optimal damage and kill as many villagers as possible. And when he heard that the first targets proposed for the new policy were all in the north, he demanded a trial action in the south as well, but it had to be specific, not general. In this he suddenly revealed himself as a vindictive book-keeper. He pushed for an attack on the town of Beersheba (Beer Sheva today), particularly targeting the heads of al-Hajj Salameh Ibn Said, the deputy mayor and his brother, who in the past had both refused to collaborate with the Zionist plans for settlement in the area. There was no need, stressed Ben-Gurion, to distinguish any more between the 'innocent' and the 'guilty' – the time had come for inflicting collateral damage. Danin recalled years later that Ben-Gurion spelled out what collateral damage meant: 'Every attack has to end with occupation, destruction and expulsion.'[51] Danin even claimed that some specific villages were discussed.[52]

As for the 'conservative' mood among the Hagana troops, and Wingate's training of them as a retaliatory force, Yigael Yadin, the acting chief of staff of the Hagana – and as of 15 May 1948 of the Israeli army – suggested that the way forward lay in adopting a new, more straightforward terminology and a tougher form of indoctrination. He recommended abandoning the term 'retaliation': 'This is not what we are doing; this is an offensive and we need to initiate preemptive strikes, no need for a village to attack us [first]. We have not used properly our ability to strangulate the economy of the Palestinians.' The, for many Israelis, legendary head of the Palmach, Yitzhak Sadeh, agreed with Yadin and added, 'We were wrong to initiate only retaliations.' What was needed was instilling in the troops that aggression 'is the mood and mode now'.

His second in command, Yigal Allon, was even more critical. He criticised the Consultancy indirectly for not having issued explicit orders for a comprehensive attack at the beginning of December. 'We could have taken Jaffa by now easily and should have attacked the villages around Tel-Aviv. We have to go for a series of "collective punishments" even if there are children living in the [attacked] houses'. When Eliyahu Sasson, helped by Reuven Shiloah, one of his aides (later a leading figure in Israeli Orientalism), tried to draw attention to the fact that provocation was liable to alienate friendly or peaceful Palestinians, as he would throughout the seminar, Allon impatiently sidelined him by declaring: 'A call for peace will be weakness!' Moshe Dayan expressed similar views, and Ben-Gurion ruled out any attempt to reach an agreement in Jaffa or anywhere else.

That there was still a psychological problem among the troops was indeed evident in the case of Jaffa. In the weekly meeting of 7 January, officials of Tel-Aviv's municipality wondered why the Hagana, and not just the Irgun, was provoking the Arabs of Jaffa, when they themselves had been successful in ensuring an atmosphere of peace between the two neighbouring cities.[53] On 25 January 1948, a delegation of these senior officials came to see Ben-Gurion at home, complaining that they had detected a distinct change in the Hagana's behaviour towards Jaffa. There was an unwritten agreement between Jaffa and Tel-Aviv that the two towns would be divided by a strip of no-man's land along the coast, which enabled an uneasy coexistence. Without consulting them, the Hagana troops had entered this area, covered by citrus groves, and had upset this delicate balance. And this was done at a time, remonstrated one of the participants, that the two municipalities were trying to reach a new modus vivendi. He complained that the Hagana seemed to be doing its best to foil such attempts and spoke of them attacking randomly: killing people without provocation, near the water wells, within the no man's land, robbing the Arabs, abusing them, dismantling wells, confiscating assets, and shooting for the sake of intimidation.[54]

Similar complaints, Ben-Gurion noted in his diary, were coming from members of other Jewish municipalities located in proximity to Arab towns or villages. Protests had come in from Rehovot, Nes Ziona, Rishon Le-Zion, and Petah Tikva, the oldest Jewish settlements in the greater Tel-Aviv area, whose members, like their Palestinian neighbours, failed to grasp that the Hagana had adopted a 'new approach' against the Palestinian population.

A month later, however, we already find these very same officials sucked into the more general atmosphere of intransigence as they tell Ben-Gurion: 'We have to hit Jaffa in every possible way.' The temptation was indeed great: in February the picking season of the oranges for which Jaffa was famous was in full swing and a greedy Tel-Aviv municipality quickly set aside its earlier inclination to maintain a modus vivendi with the neighbouring Palestinian town.[55] There was in fact no need for their pleas: a few days before, the High Command had already decided to attack the citrus groves and picking stations of the Palestinians in Jaffa.[56]

In the weekend that followed the Long Seminar, in a meeting with six out of the eleven members of his Consultancy,[57] Ben-Gurion hinted to them why he thought the policy of the military High Command had not at first struck a chord with the civilian heads of the municipality, and he suggested to the smaller cabal they start using a new term: 'aggressive defense'. Yadin liked the idea and said: 'We have to explain to our commanders that we have the upper hand . . . we should paralyse the Arab transport and their economy, harass them in their villages and the cities and demoralise them.' Galili concurred but warned: 'We still cannot destroy places as we do not have the equipment' and he was also worried about the British reaction.[58]

But it was Yigal Allon, and not Tel-Aviv's senior city clerks, who carried the day. He wanted a clear directive from above to the troops who, he now reported, were full of enthusiasm and eager at any moment to go and assault Arab villages and neighbourhoods. The absence of a clear coordinating hand also troubled the rest of the military men in the Consultancy. Zealous troops, it was reported, sometimes attacked villages in areas where the High Command currently wished to avoid any provocation. One particular case discussed in the Long Seminar was an incident in the western Jerusalemite neighbourhood of Romema. That area of the city had been particularly quiet until a local Hagana commander decided to intimidate the Palestinians in the neighbourhood under the pretext that the owner of a petrol station there encouraged villagers to strike out at passing Jewish traffic. When the troops killed the station owner, his village, Lifta, retaliated by striking at a Jewish bus. Sasson added that the allegation had proved to be false. But the Hagana attack signalled the onset of a series of offensives against Palestinian villages on the western slopes of the Jerusalem mountains, especially directed at the village of Lifta that, even according to Hagana intelligence, had never attacked any convoys at all.

Until five years ago, when a new road connected the main Jerusalem–Tel-Aviv highway to the northern Jewish neighbourhoods of Jerusalem was built – illegally on occupied territory after 1967 – upon entering the city you could see on your left a number of attractive old houses, still almost wholly intact, clinging to the mountain. They are gone now, but for many years these were the remnants of the picturesque village of Lifta, one of the very first to be ethnically cleansed in Palestine. It had been the residence of Qasim Ahmad, the leader of the 1834 rebellion against the Egyptian rule of Ibrahim Pasha, which some historians view as the first national revolt in Palestine. The village was a fine example of rural architecture, with its narrow street running parallel to the slopes of the mountains. The relative prosperity it enjoyed, like many other villages, especially during and after the Second World War, manifested itself in the construction of new houses, the improvement of roads and pavements, as well as in an overall higher standard of living. Lifta was a large village, home to 2500 people, most of them Muslims with a small number of Christians. Another sign of the recent prosperity was the girls' school a number of the villages had combined forces to build in 1945, investing their joint capital.

Social life in Lifta revolved around a small shopping centre, which included a club and two coffee houses. It attracted Jerusalemites as well, as no doubt it would today were it still there. One of the coffee houses was the target of the Hagana when it attacked on 28 December 1947. Armed with machine guns the Jews sprayed the coffee house, while members of the Stern Gang stopped a bus nearby and began firing into it randomly. This was the first Stern Gang operation in rural Palestine; prior to the attack, the gang had issued pamphlets to its activists: 'Destroy Arab neighbourhoods and punish Arab villages.'[59]

The involvement of the Stern Gang in the attack on Lifta may have been outside the overall scheme of the Hagana in Jerusalem, according to the Consultancy, but once it had occurred it was incorporated into the plan. In a pattern that would repeat itself, creating faits accomplis became part of the overall strategy. The Hagana High Command at first condemned the Stern Gang attack at the end of December, but when they realised that the assault had caused villagers to flee, they ordered another operation against the same village on 11 January in order to complete the expulsion. The Hagana blew up most of the houses in the village and drove out all the people who were still there.

This was the ultimate outcome of the Long Seminar: although the Zionist leadership acknowledged the need for a coordinated and supervised campaign, they decided to turn every unauthorised initiative into an integral part of the plan, giving it their blessing retrospectively. Such was the case in Jerusalem, where sporadic retaliatory actions were systemised into an offensive initiative of occupation and expulsion. On 31 January, Ben-Gurion gave direct orders to David Shaltiel, the city's military commander, to assure Jewish contiguity and expansion through the destruction of Shaykh Jarrah, the occupation of other neighborhoods, and the immediate settlement of Jews in the evicted places. His mission was 'to settle Jews in every house of an evicted semi-Arab neighbourhood, such as Romema.'[60]

The mission was successfully accomplished. On 7 February 1948, which happened to fall on a Saturday, the Jewish Sabbath, Ben-Gurion came up from Tel-Aviv to see the emptied and destroyed village of Lifta with his own eyes. That same evening he reported jubilantly to the Mapai Council in Jerusalem what he had seen:

> When I come now to Jerusalem, I feel I am in a Jewish (*Ivrit*) city. This is a feeling I only had in Tel-Aviv or in an agricultural farm. It is true that not all of Jerusalem is Jewish, but it has in it already a huge Jewish bloc: when you enter the city through Lifta and Romema, through Mahaneh Yehuda, King George Street and Mea Shearim – there are no Arabs. One hundred percent Jews. Ever since Jerusalem was destroyed by the Romans – the city was not as Jewish as it is now. In many Arab neighbourhoods in the West you do not see even one Arab. I do not suppose it will change. And what happened in Jerusalem and in Haifa – can happen in large parts of the country. If we persist it is quite possible that in the next six or eight months there will be considerable changes in the country, very considerable, and to our advantage. There will certainly be considerable changes in the demographic composition of the country.[61]

Ben-Gurion's diary also reveals how eager he was in January to move ahead with building a more effective assault force. He was particularly worried that the Irgun and the Stern Gang continued their terror attacks against the Palestinian population without any coordination from the Hagana command. David Shaltiel, the Jerusalem Hagana commander, reported to him that in his city, and actually all over the country, the Irgun often acted in areas where the other forces were not yet fully prepared. For example, troops belonging to the Irgun had murdered Arab drivers in Tiberias and were torturing captured villagers everywhere. Shaltiel was mainly fretting about the repercussions for the isolated Jewish quarter in Jerusalem's Old City. All the Jewish attempts then and later to occupy that part of the city failed because of the resistance the Jordanian Legion put up to ensure it remained part of Jordan. In the end, the people of the Jewish quarter themselves decided to surrender.

Allon, Yadin, Sadeh and Dayan, the military professionals in the Consultancy, understood the 'Old Man', as they affectionately called Ben-Gurion, better than anyone else. Any military action, authorised or not, helped contribute to the expulsion of the 'strangers'. When he confided his thoughts to them privately, he added another reason for simultaneously encouraging an official coordinated policy and local 'unauthorised' initiatives: the new intimidation policy had to be connected to the question of Jewish settlements. There happened to be thirty settlements in the UN-designated Arab state. One of the most effective ways to incorporate them into the Jewish state was to build new settlement belts between them and the Jewish designated areas. These were the same tactics Israel would use again in the occupied West Bank during the years of the Oslo accord and again in the early years of the twenty-first century.

The person who understood Ben-Gurion the least was Eliahu Sasson. He reported to the Long Seminar another case of what he thought was an unprovoked and 'barbaric' Jewish attack on peaceful villagers. This was the case of Khisas, mentioned earlier. He complained in the seminar: 'Actions such as the one in Khisas will prompt quiet Arabs to act against us. In all the areas where we committed no provocative actions – in the coastal plain and the Negev – the atmosphere is calm, but not in the Galilee.' As before, no one listened to him. All participants concurred with Moshe Dayan when he told Sasson: 'Our action against Khisas ignited the Galilee and this was a good thing.' There appears to be no trace of Ben-Gurion's earlier reaction to the Khisas operation, when he had gone so far as to publish an apology. In the Long Seminar he sided with those who welcomed the act, but suggested that actions like this should not be done officially in the name of the Hagana: 'We need to involve the Mossad [the special branch that would become Israel's secret service] in such actions.' In his diary he laconically summarised the meeting by repeating Allon's words:

> There is a need now for strong and brutal reaction. We need to be accurate about timing, place and those we hit. If we accuse a family – we need to harm them without mercy, women and children included. Otherwise, this is not an effective reaction. During the operation there is no need to distinguish between guilty and not guilty.[62]

Eliahu Sasson left the Long Seminar still believing that he had persuaded Ben-Gurion to continue with a selective policy directed against 'hostile'

Arabs that would allow 'friendly' areas, most of the country in fact, to remain calm and peaceful. But in the following meetings, we soon find him toeing the general line, and he no longer mentions the divide-and-rule tactics he had championed before, realising that none of his associates was interested any longer in exploiting distinctions between political forces, but only in expelling as many Palestinians as possible.

Yigal Allon and Israel Galili, on the other hand, left the meeting with the impression that they had been given a free rein to start massive attacks against the Palestinian towns and villages within the coveted Jewish state. The military men appeared to grasp Ben-Gurion's wishes better, or at least assumed that he would not object to more aggressive initiatives on their part. They were right.

Ben-Gurion's shift at this point to systematic operations of take-over, occupation and expulsion had much to do with his keen understanding of the fluctuations in the global mood. In the Long Seminar we find him stressing the need for further swift operations as he sensed a possible change in the international political will regarding the Palestine crisis. UN officials had begun to realise that the peace resolution their organisation had adopted was not a solution at all, but actually fostered war, as had American diplomats and British officials. True, the presence of the ALA on the whole served to restrain Palestinian actions and postponed any significant general Arab invasion, but the danger of a shift in UN and American policies remained, and establishing facts, Ben-Gurion believed, was the best means to thwart any such potential change of policy.

Moreover, the sense that an opportune moment for action towards cleansing the country was developing was reinforced by the fact that the Zionist leadership knew how weak the Palestinian and Arab military opposition actually was. The intelligence unit of the Hagana was well aware, through telegrams it intercepted, that the ALA failed to cooperate with the paramilitary groups led by Abd al-Qadir al-Husayni in Jerusalem and Hassan Salameh in Jaffa. This lack of cooperation resulted in the ALA deciding, in January 1948, not to operate in the cities but rather to try and attack isolated Jewish settlements.[63] The acting commander of the ALA was Fawzi Al-Qawqji, a Syrian officer, who had led a group of volunteers, mainly from Iraq, into Palestine in the 1936 Revolt. Ever since then he had been at loggerheads with the Husayni family, and gave his loyalty instead to the governments of Syria and Iraq, who had authorised his move into Palestine both in 1936 and in 1948. The Iraqi government saw al-Hajj Amin al-Husayni as a rival to its Hashemite sister-country Jordan, while the Syrian government of the time was apprehensive of his pan-Arabist ambitions. Hence, an Arab League decision to divide Palestine between the three commanders, al-Qawqji in the north, Abd al-Qadir in Jerusalem and Salameh in Jaffa, was a farce, and what little military power the Palestinians themselves possessed was made wholly ineffective by the way it was being employed.

In a way, the hesitations in the global community about the way things were going and the highly limited nature of the pan-Arab military activity could have restored calm to Palestine and opened the way for a renewed attempt to solve the problem. However, the new Zionist policy of an aggressive offensive that the Consultancy hastened to adopt blocked all possible moves towards a more reconciliatory reality.

On 9 January 1948, the first significant unit of the ALA volunteer army crossed into Palestine, mainly into the areas the UN had allotted to the future Arab state; quite often they camped along the boundaries of this imaginary state. In general, they adopted a defensive policy and focused on organising the people's fortification lines in cooperation with the national committees – bodies of local notables that had been established in 1937, which acted as an emergency leadership in the cities – and with the village mukhtars. However, in several limited cases, especially after just crossing the border, they assaulted Jewish convoys and settlements. The first settlements that came under attack were Kefar Sold (9 January 1948) and Kefar Etzion (14 January 1948). Thirty-five Jewish troops, who were part of a convoy that was sent to help Kefar Etzion (south west of Jerusalem), were ambushed and killed. Long after these Hagana troops were killed, '35', '*Lamed-Heh*' in Hebrew (which substitutes letters for numbers), continued to serve as a codename for operations carried out supposedly in retaliation for this attack. Ben-Gurion's biographer, Michael Bar-Zohar, commented rightly that these operations had already been contemplated during the Long Seminar and all were aimed at inflicting the kind of collateral damage Ben-Gurion had envisaged there as desirable. The attack on the *Lamed-Heh* convoy proved to be just one more pretext for the new offensive initiative, the final plan for which would be implemented in March 1948.[64]

After the Long Seminar, Jewish military operations began more systematically to transcend retaliation and punitive action, moving to cleansing initiatives within the UN-designated area of the Jewish state. The word cleansing, 'tihur', was used economically in the Consultancy's meetings, but appears on every order the High Command passed down to the units on the ground. It means in Hebrew what it means in any other language: the expulsion of entire populations from their villages and towns. This determination overshadowed all other political consideration. There were crossroads ahead where the Zionist leadership was offered a chance to take a different course of action, both by the United States and by Arab actors on the scene. Ben-Gurion and his Consultancy had decided to blaze a clear road ahead, and they rejected these offers one after the other.

FEBRUARY 1948: SHOCK AND AWE

Nothing of the atmosphere that pervaded the first meetings of the Consultancy was reflected in the fiery speeches Ben-Gurion delivered to the wider public. Melodramatic and full of pathos, he told his audience: 'This is a war aimed at destroying and eliminating the Jewish community,' never referring to the passivity of the Palestinians or the provocative nature of Zionist actions.

These speeches, one should add, were not just rhetoric. The Jewish forces did suffer casualties in their attempts to keep the lines open to all the isolated settlements the Zionists had planted in the heart of the Palestinian areas. By the end of January, 400 Jewish settlers had died in these attacks – a high number for a community of 660,000 (but still a much lower number than the 1500 Palestinians who had so far been killed by the random bombardment and shelling of their villages and neighbourhoods). These casualties Ben-Gurion now depicted as 'victims of a second Holocaust'.

The attempt to portray Palestinians, and Arabs in general, as Nazis was a deliberate public relations ploy to ensure that, three years after the Holocaust, Jewish soldiers would not lose heart when ordered to cleanse, kill and destroy other human beings. Already in 1945, Natan Alterman, the national poet of the Jewish community, had identified the impending confrontation with the Palestinians with the war against the Nazis in Europe:

Like you the brave English nation
that stood with its back
to the wall when Europe and France
were covered black

and you fought on the beaches, in the houses and the streets,
so will we fight in the beaches, in the houses and the streets.
The triumphant English people greet us on our last battle.

In some of his public appearances, Ben-Gurion even went so far as to describe the Jewish war effort as an attempt to protect the honour of the UN and its Charter. This discrepancy between a destructive and violent Zionist policy on the one hand and an overt discourse of peace on the other will reoccur at various junctures in the history of the conflict, but the deceitfulness in 1948 seems to have been particularly startling.

In February 1948, David Ben-Gurion decided to enlarge the Consultancy and absorb into it members of the Zionist organisations responsible for recruitment and arms purchase. Again, this brings to the fore how closely interconnected the issues of ethnic cleansing and military capability were. While still appearing outside with doomsday scenarios of a second Holocaust, the enlarged Consultancy heard Ben-Gurion outline amazing achievements in the compulsory recruitment the Zionist leadership had imposed on the Jewish community and in the arms purchases it had made, especially in the sphere of heavy weaponry and aircraft.

It was these new procurements of arms that by February 1948 had enabled the forces on the ground to extend their operations and act with greater efficiency in the Palestinian hinterland. A principal result of the upgraded weaponry were the heavy bombardments, especially from new mortars, that were now carried out on densely populated villages and neighbourhoods.

The confidence of the military can be gauged from the fact that the Jewish army was now able to develop its own weapons of destruction. Ben-Gurion followed personally the purchase of a particularly lethal weapon that would soon be used to set fire to the fields and houses of Palestinians: a flame-thrower. An Anglo-Jewish professor of chemistry, Sasha Goldberg, headed the project of purchasing and then manufacturing this weapon, first in a laboratory in London and later in Rehovot, south of Tel-Aviv, in what was to become the Weizmann Institute in the 1950s.[65] The oral history of the Nakba is full of evidence of the terrible effect this weapon had on people and properties.

The flame-thrower project was part of a larger unit engaged in developing biological warfare under the directorship of a physical chemist called Ephraim Katzir (later the president of Israel who in the 1980s, through a slip of the tongue, revealed to the world that the Jewish state possessed nuclear weapons). The biological unit he led together with his brother Aharon, started working seriously in February. Its main objective was to create a weapon that could blind people. Katzir reported to Ben-Gurion: 'We are experimenting with animals. Our researchers were wearing gas masks and adequate outfit. Good results. The animals did not die (they were just blinded). We can produce 20 kilos a day of this stuff.' In June, Katzir suggested using it on human beings.[66]

More military might was also needed since the Arab Liberation Army units had now positioned themselves in some of the villages, and greater effort would be required to occupy them. In some places the arrival of the ALA was more important psychologically than materially. They had no time to turn the villagers into fighting men, nor did they have the equipment to defend the villages. All in all, the ALA had only reached a few villages by February, which meant that most of the Palestinians remained unaware of how dramatically and crucially their life was about to change. Neither their leaders nor the Palestinian press had any inkling of what was being contemplated behind closed doors in the Red House, close to the northern outskirts of Jaffa. February 1948 saw major cleansing operations, and it was only then, in certain parts of the country, that the meaning of the imminent catastrophe began to dawn on people.

In the middle of February 1948, the Consultancy met to discuss the implications of the growing presence of Arab volunteers inside Palestine. Eliyahu Sasson reported that no more than 3000 volunteers in total had so far entered as part of the ALA (Ben-Gurion's diary cites a smaller number). He described all of them as 'poorly trained' and added that if 'we do not provoke them, they will remain idle and the Arab states will send no more volunteers'. This prompted Yigal Allon once more to speak out vociferously in favour of large-scale cleansing operations, but he was opposed by Yaacov Drori, the designated Chief of Staff, who insisted they adopt a more cautious approach. However, Drori fell ill soon thereafter and ceased to play a role. He was replaced by the more bellicose Yigael Yadin.[67]

On 9 February, Yadin had already shown his true intentions by calling for 'deep invasions' into the Palestinian areas. He specified heavily populated villages such as Fassuta, Tarbikha, and Aylut in the northern Galilee as targets for such invasions, with the aim of totally destroying the villages. The Consultancy rejected the plan as too far-reaching and Ben-Gurion suggested shelving it for the time being. Yadin's codename for his plan had been '*Lamed-Heh*'; he had meant it as retaliation for the assault on the Gush Etzion convoy.[68] A few days later, the Consultancy did approve other similar plans – with the same codename – inside Palestine's rural areas, but still insisted they should be related, at least loosely, to Arab acts of hostility. These operations were also Yigael Yadin's brainchild. They began on 13 February 1948 and focused on several areas. In Jaffa, houses were randomly selected and then dynamited with people still in them, the village of Sa'sa was attacked, as well as three villages around Qisarya (Caesarea today).

The February operations, carefully planned by the Consultancy, differed from the actions that took place in December: no longer sporadic, they formed part of a first attempt to link the concept of unhampered Jewish transport on Palestine's main routes with the ethnic cleansing of villages. But unlike the following month, when operations would be given codenames and clearly defined territories and targets, directives were still vague.

The first targets were three villages around the ancient Roman city of Caesarea, a town whose impressive history went all the way back to the Phoenicians. Established as a trading colony, Herod the Great later named it Caesarea in honour of his patron in Rome, Augustus Caesar. The largest of these villages was Qisarya, where 1500 people lived within the ancient walls of the old city. Among them, as was quite common in the Palestinian villages on the coast, were several Jewish families who had bought land there and lived practically inside the village. Most of the villagers lived in stone houses next to Bedouin families, who were part of the village but still lived in tents. The village wells provided enough water for both the semi-sedentary and the peasant communities, and allowed them to cultivate extensive tracts of land and grow a wide range of agricultural produce, including citrus fruit and bananas. Thus, Qisarya was a typical model of the live-and-let-live attitude that pervaded coastal rural life in Palestine.

The three villages were chosen because they were easy prey: they had no defence force of any kind, neither local nor volunteers from the outside. The order came on 5 February to occupy, expel and destroy them.[69]

Qisarya was the first village to be expelled in its entirety, on 15 February 1948. The expulsion took only a few hours and was carried out so systematically that the Jewish troops were able to evacuate and destroy another four villages on the same day, all under the watchful eyes of the British troops stationed in police stations nearby.[70]

The second village was Barrat Qisarya ('outside Qaysariyya'), which had a population of about 1000. There are a number of photographs from the 1930s of this village showing its picturesque location on the sandy beach close to the ruins of the Roman city. It was wiped out in February in an attack so sudden and fierce that both Israeli and Palestinian historians refer to its disappearance as quite enigmatic. Today a Jewish development town, Or Akiva, stretches out over every square metre of this destroyed village. Some old houses were still standing in the town in the 1970s, but they were quickly demolished when Palestinian research teams tried to document them as part of an overall attempt to reconstruct the Palestinian heritage in this part of the country.

Similarly, only vague information exists about the nearby village of Khirbat al-Burj. This village was smaller than the other two and its remains are still visible to the observant eye if one travels through the area east of the veteran Jewish settlement of Binyamina (relatively 'veteran', as it dates from 1922). The major building in the village was an Ottoman inn, a khan, and it is the only building still standing. Called the Burj, the plaque nearby will tell you that once this was a historic castle – not a word is said about the village. Today the building is a popular Israeli venue for exhibitions, fairs and family celebrations.[71]

North of these three villages, but not very far away, lies another ancient monument, the Crusader's castle of Atlit. This castle had impressively withstood both the passage of time and the various invading armies that had come down upon the region since the medieval era. The village of Atlit was built next to it and was unique for the rare example it presented of Arab-Jewish cooperation in Mandatory Palestine in the salt industry along its beaches. For ages, the village's topography had made it a source of salt extraction from the sea, and Jews and Palestinians jointly worked in the evaporation pans southwest of the village that produced quality sea salt. A Palestinian employer, the Atlit Salt company, had invited 500 Jews to live and work alongside the 1000 Arab inhabitants of the village. However, in the 1940s the Hagana turned the Jewish part of the village into a training ground for its members, whose intimidating presence soon reduced the number of Palestinians to 200. No wonder that with the operation in nearby Qisariya, the Jewish troops in the training base did not hesitate to expel their Palestinian co-workers from the joint village. Today the castle is closed to the public as it is now a major training base for Israel's Naval Commando elite units.

In February, the Jewish troops also reached the village of Daliyat al-Rawha, on the plain overlooking the Milq valley connecting the coast with the Marj Ibn Amir in northeast Palestine. In Arabic the name means 'the fragrant vine', a testimony to the scents and sights that still characterise this scenic part of the country. This, too, was a village where Jews lived among Arabs and owned land. The initiative for the attack had come from Yossef Weitz, who wanted to use the new phase of operations to get rid of the village. He had set his eyes on the rich soil, generously supplied by an extremely abundant source of natural water, which was responsible for the village's fertile fields and vineyards.[72]

Then came the raid on Sa'sa, on the night between 14 and 15 February. You cannot miss Sa'sa today. The Arabic pronunciation uses two laryngeal 'A's, but the sign to the entrance of the kibbutz built on the ruins of the Palestinian village points to 'Sasa', Hebraization having done away with the throaty pronunciation of the Arabic (difficult for Europeans to master) in favour of the obviously more European soft-sounding 'A's. Some of the original Palestinian houses have survived and now lie inside the kibbutz, on the way to Palestine's highest mountain, Jabel Jermak (Har Meron in Hebrew), 1208 metres above sea level. Beautifully located in the only evergreen part of the country, with its hewn-stone houses, Sa'sa is one of those Palestinian villages that appears quite often in Israeli official tourist guides.

The order to attack Sa'sa came from Yigal Allon, the commander of the Palmach in the north, and was entrusted to Moshe Kalman, the deputy commander of the third battalion that had committed the atrocities in Khisas. Allon explained that the village had to be attacked because of its location. 'We have to prove to ourselves that we can take the initiative,' he wrote to Kalman. The order was very clear: 'You have to blow up twenty houses and kill as many "warriors" [read: "villagers"] as possible'. Sa'sa was attacked at midnight – all the villages attacked under the '*Lamed-Heh*' order were assaulted around midnight, recalled Moshe Kalman. The *New York Times* (16 April 1948) reported that the large unit of Jewish troops encountered no resistance from the residents as they entered the village and began attaching TNT to the houses. 'We ran into an Arab guard,' Kalman recounted later. 'He was so surprised that he did not ask "*min hada?*", "who is it?", but "*eish hada?*", "what is it?" One of our troops who knew Arabic responded humorously [*sic*] "*hada esh!*" ("this is [in Arabic] fire [in

Hebrew]") and shot a volley into him.' Kalman's troops took the main street of the village and systematically blew up one house after another while families were still sleeping inside. 'In the end the sky prised open,' recalled Kalman poetically, as a third of the village was blasted into the air. 'We left behind 35 demolished houses and 60–80 dead bodies' (quite a few of them were children).[73] He commended the British army for helping the troops to transfer the two wounded soldiers – hurt by debris flying through the air – to the Safad hospital.[74]

The Long Seminar participants were called in for another meeting on 19 February 1948, four days after the attack on Sa'sa. It was a Thursday morning, they met once again in Ben-Gurion's home, and the Zionist leader recorded the discussion almost verbatim in his diary. The purpose was to examine the impact of the *Lamed Heh* operations on the Palestinians.

Josh Palmon brought the 'Orientalist' point of view: the Palestinians still showed no inclination to fight. He was supported by Ezra Danin who reported: 'The villagers show no wish to fight.' Moreover, the ALA was clearly confining its activities to the areas the UN resolution had allocated to a future Palestinian state. Ben-Gurion was unimpressed. His thoughts were already somewhere else. He was unhappy with the limited scope of the operations: 'A small reaction [to Arab hostility] does not impress anyone. A destroyed house – nothing. Destroy a neighborhood, and you begin to make an impression!' He liked the Sa'sa operation for the way it had 'caused the Arabs to flee'.

Danin thought the operation had sent shock waves through the nearby villages, which would serve to dissuade other villagers from taking part in the fighting. The conclusion was therefore to retaliate with force for every single Arab act, and not pay too much attention to whether particular villages or Arabs were neutral. [75] This feedback process between response and further planning would continue until March 1948. After that, ethnic cleansing stopped being part of retaliation, but was codifed into a well-defined plan that aimed to uproot the Palestinians en masse from their homeland.

Allon continued to expand on the lessons learned from the *Lamed-Heh* operations in the Consultancy's mid-February meeting: 'If we destroy whole neighbourhoods or many houses in the village, as we did in Sa'sa, we make an impression.' More people than usual were invited to this particular meeting. 'Experts' on Arab affairs from all over the country had been summoned, among them Giyora Zayd, from the western Galilee, and David Qaron from the Negev. The meeting spelled out the wish to prepare for an all-out operation. All of those present, without exception, reported that rural Palestine showed no desire to fight or attack, and was defenseless. Ben-Gurion concluded by saying he preferred to move more cautiously for the time being and see how events developed. In the meantime, the best thing to do was 'to continue to terrorize the rural areas ... through a series of offensives ... so that the same mood of passivity reported ... would prevail.'[76] Passivity, on the one hand, prevented actions in some areas, but led to many others elsewhere, on the other.

The month ended with the occupation and the expulsion of another village in the district of Haifa, the village of Qira. It too had a mixed Jewish and Arab population, and here, too, as in Daliyat al-Rawha, the presence of Jewish settlers on the village's land essentially sealed its fate. Again it was Yossef Weitz who urged the army commanders not to delay the operation in the village too long. 'Get rid of them now,'[77] he suggested. Qira was close to another village, Qamun, and Jewish settlers had built their homes strategically between the two.

Qira is very close to where I live today. Now called Yoqneam, Dutch Jews had bought some land here in 1935 before 'incorporating' the two evicted Palestinian villages into their settlement in 1948. Nearby Kibbutz Hazorea took over some of the land as well. Yoqneam is an attractive spot because it has one of the last clean water rivers in the Marj Ibn Amir area. In spring, the water gushes through a beautiful canyon down to the valley, as it did in the early days when it reached the stone houses of the village. The inhabitants of Qira called it the Muqata River; Israelis call it 'the river of peace'. Like so many other scenic sites in this area set aside for recreation and tourism, this one too hides the ruins of a 1948 village. To my shame it took me years to discover this.

Qira and Qamun were not the only places where Weitz could vent his expulsion impulses. He was eager to act wherever he could. In January, soon after he had been invited to join the Consultancy, his diary shows how he contemplated using the 'retaliation' policy for getting rid of Palestinian tenants on land already bought by Jews: 'Is it not time to get rid of them? Why should we continue to keep these thorns in our flesh?'[78] In another entry, for 20 January, he recommended that these tenants be treated according to 'our original plan', i.e., the ideas he had put forward in the 1930s for trans-ferring the Palestinians.[79]

Benny Morris lists a number of operations that Weitz directed in February and March for which, Morris adds, no authorization had been given by what Morris euphemistically calls 'the political leadership'. This is impossible. The centralised Hagana command authorised all actions of expulsion; it is true that, before 10 March 1948, it did not always want to know about them in advance, but it always granted authorization in retrospect. Weitz was never rebuked for the expulsions he was responsible for in Qamun and Qira, Arab al-Ghawarina in the Naman valley, Qumya, Mansurat al-Khayt, Husayniyya, Ulmaniyya, Kirad al-Ghannama and Ubaydiyya, all villages he had selected either for the quality of their land or because Jewish settlers resided in or nearby them.[80]

MARCH: PUTTING THE FINISHING TOUCHES TO THE BLUEPRINT

The Consultancy had first discussed a draft of Plan Dalet in the second half of February 1948. According to Ben-Gurion's diary this was on Sunday, 29 February, though one Israeli military historian put the date as 14 February.[81] Plan Dalet was finalised in the early days of March. Based on the recollections of the army generals from that period, Israeli historiography generally claims that March 1948 was the most difficult month in the history of the war. But this assessment is only based on one aspect of the unfolding conflict: the ALA attacks on the Jewish convoys to the isolated Jewish settlements that in early March briefly proved relatively effective. Moreover, some of the ALA officers at the time tried to fend off or retaliate for the ongoing Jewish offensives in the mixed cities by terrorizing the Jewish areas through a series of mini raids. Two such attacks gave the public the (false) impression that the ALA might after all be able to show some resistance in the face of a Jewish takeover.

In fact, March 1948 began with this final and short-lived Palestinian military effort to protect its community. The Jewish forces were not yet sufficiently well organised to be able to react immediately and successfully to every counterattack, which explains the sense of distress in some sections of the Jewish community. However, the Consultancy did not lose its grip on reality for a moment. When they met again at the beginning of March, they did not even discuss the ALA counterattack, nor did they seem to regard the overall situation as particularly troubling. Instead, under the guidance of Ben-Gurion, they were busy preparing a final master plan.

Some members of the Consultancy proposed to continue with the ethnic cleansing operations as the most effective means of protecting the routes to isolated settlements. Their main concern was the Tel-Aviv road to Jerusalem, but Ben-Gurion had already set his mind on something more comprehensive. The conclusion he had drawn from the period between late November 1947 and early March 1948 was that, despite all the efforts from above, a competent guiding hand on the ground was still missing. He also felt that three previous plans the Hagana had prepared for the takeover of the Mandatory state – one in 1937 and two more in 1946 – now needed updating. He therefore ordered a revision of these plans, the two recent ones being code-named Plans B and C.

We have no record of what Ben-Gurion said about ethnic cleansing to the team that made up the Consultancy on their regular Wednesday afternoon meeting on 10 March 1948, but we do have the plan they authored and which, after they had put the final touches to it, was approved by the Hagana High Command and then sent out as military orders to the troops in the field.

The official name of Plan Dalet was the Yehoshua plan. Born in Bellarus in 1905, Yehoshua Globerman had been sent to prison in the 1920s for anti-communist activity, but was released after three years in a Soviet jail after Maxim Gorki, a friend of his parents, had intervened on his behalf. Globerman was the commander of the Hagana in various parts of Palestine and was killed by unknown assailants in December 1947, who had fired at him while he was driving his car. He had been destined to become one of the future chiefs of staff of the Israeli army, but his untimely death meant that his name would be associated not with military prowess but rather with the Zionist master plan for the ethnic cleansing of Palestine. He was so revered by his peers that he was posthumously given the rank of general after the Jewish state was established.

A few days after Globerman was killed, the intelligence unit of the Hagana drafted the blueprint for the coming months. Codenamed Plan D, it contained direct references both to the geographical parameters of the

future Jewish state (the seventy-eight per cent coveted by Ben-Gurion) and
to the fate of the one million Palestinians living within that space:

> These operations can be carried out in the following manner: either by
> destroying villages (by setting fire to them, by blowing them up, and by
> planting mines in their rubble), and especially those population cen-
> tres that are difficult to control permanently; or by mounting combing
> and control operations according to the following guidelines: encir-
> clement of the villages, conducting a search inside them. In case of
> resistance, the armed forces must be wiped out and the population
> expelled outside the borders of the state.[82]

Villages were to be expelled in their entirety either because they were located
in strategic spots or because they were expected to put up some sort of resistance. These orders were issued when it was clear that occupation would
always provoke some resistance and that therefore no village would be
immune, either because of its location or because it would not allow itself to
be occupied. This was the master plan for the expulsion of all the villages in
rural Palestine. Similar instructions were given, with much the same word-
ing, for actions directed at Palestine's urban centres.

The orders coming through to the units in the field were more specific.
The country was divided into zones according to the number of brigades,
whereby the four original brigades of the Hagana were turned into twelve so
as to facilitate the implementation of the plan. Each brigade commander
received a list of the villages or neighbourhoods that had to be occupied,
destroyed and their inhabitants expelled, with exact dates. Some of the commanders were over-ambitious in executing their orders, and added additional locations in the momentum their zeal had created. Some of the
orders, on the other hand, proved too far-fetched and could not be implemented within the expected timeframe. This meant that several villages on
the coast that had been scheduled to be occupied in May were not destroyed
until July. And the villages in the Wadi Ara area – a valley connecting the
coast near Hadera with Marj Ibn Amir (Emeq Izrael) and Afula (today's
Route 65) – managed to survive repeated Jewish attacks throughout the war.
But they were the exception: the rule was the 531 villages and eleven urban
neighbourhoods and towns that were destroyed and their inhabitants
expelled under the direct orders the Consultancy put out in March 1948. By
then, thirty villages were already gone.

A few days after Plan D was typed up, it was distributed among the commanders of the dozen brigades the Hagana now incorporated. With the list each commander received came a detailed description of the villages in his realm of operation, and their imminent fate: occupation, destruction and expulsion. The Israeli documents released from the IDF archives in the late 1990s show clearly that, contrary to claims historians such as Benny Morris have made, Plan Dalet was handed down to the brigade commanders not as vague guidelines, but as clear-cut operational orders for action.[83]

Unlike the general draft that was sent to the political leaders, the list of villages the military commanders received did not detail how the action of destruction or expulsion should be carried out. There was no specification here for how villages could save themselves, for instance by surrendering unconditionally as promised in the general document. There was another difference between the draft handed to the politicians and the one the military commanders were given: the official draft stated that the plan would only be activated after the end of the Mandate; the officers on the ground were ordered to start executing it within a few days after its adoption. This dichotomy is typical of the relationship that exists in Israel between the army and politicians up to the present day – the army quite often misinforms the politicians as to its real intentions: Moshe Dayan did so in 1956, Ariel Sharon in 1982, and Shaul Mofaz in 2000.

What the political version of Plan Dalet and the military directives had in common was the overall purpose of the scheme. In other words, even before the direct orders had reached the field, the troops already knew exactly what was expected of them. That venerable and courageous Israeli campaigner for civil rights, Shulamit Aloni, who was a woman officer in those days, recalled how special political officers would come down and actively incite the troops by demonizing the Palestinians and invoking the Holocaust as the point of reference for the operations ahead, quite often the day after the indoctrinating event had taken place.[84]

After the Consultancy had approved Plan Dalet, the Acting Chief of Staff, Yigael Yadin, summoned all the intelligence officers of the Hagana to a building that housed the headquarters of the Jewish public health service, Kupat Holim, in Tel-Aviv's Zamenhof Street (still functioning as such opposite a popular Indian restaurant). Hundreds of officers filled what was normally a reception hall for patients.

Yadin did not tell them about Plan Dalet: the orders had gone out that week to their brigade commanders, but he provided them with a general idea that was meant to leave no doubt in their minds as to the troops' ability to carry out the plan. Intelligence officers were also Politruk (political commissars) of a kind, and Yadin realised he needed to account for the gap between the public declarations the leadership was making of an imminent 'second Holocaust' and the reality that the Jewish forces clearly faced no real challenge in the scheduled depopulation of the territory they wished to turn into their Jewish state. Yadin, dramatic as ever, set out to impress upon his listeners that since they were going to be issued with orders to occupy, conquer and dispossess a population, they deserved an explanation of how they could afford to do so when, as they read in their newspapers and heard from their politicians, they themselves were facing the 'danger of annihilation'. The officer, whose tall and lean figure would soon become familiar to all Israelis, then proudly told his audience: 'Today we have all the arms we need; they are already aboard ships, and the British are leaving and then we bring in the weapons, and the whole situation at the fronts will change.'[85]

In other words, when we find Yigael Yadin's narrative depicting the last weeks of March 1948 as the toughest period of the war as a whole, we might instead conclude that the Jewish community in Palestine was not in any danger of annihilation: it was facing some obstacles on the way to completing its ethnic cleansing plan. These difficulties were the relative lack of arms and the isolated Jewish colonies within the designated Arab state. Especially vulnerable seemed to be the few settlements inside the West Bank and those on the north-western parts of the Negev (Negba, Yad Mordechai, Nizanim and Gat). These four would still be left isolated even during the Egyptian forces' entry into Palestine that overtook them for a short while. Similarly, some settlements in the upper Galilee were not easily reached or defended as they were surrounded by scores of Palestinian villages that were lucky enough to have the protection of several hundreds of volunteers from the ALA. Finally, the road to Jerusalem was subjected to Palestinian sniper attacks, serious enough for a sense of siege to descend over the Jewish parts of the city that month.

Official Israeli historiography describes the next month, April 1948, as a turning point. According to this version, an isolated and threatened Jewish community in Palestine was moving from defence to offence, after its near defeat. The reality of the situation could not have been more different: the overall military, political and economic balance between the two communities was such that not only were the majority of Jews in no danger at all, but in addition, between the beginning of December 1947 and the end of March 1948, their army had been able to complete the first stage of the cleansing of Palestine, even before the master plan had been put into effect. If there were a turning point in April, it was the shift from sporadic attacks and counter-attacks on the Palestinian civilian population towards the systematic mega-operation of ethnic cleansing that now followed.

Chapter 5

The Blueprint for Ethnic Cleansing: Plan Dalet

The Serbs were interested in creating an ethnically pure Republika Srpska for the Serbs, but large Muslim minorities, especially in the cities, made it difficult for the Serbs to carve out homogenous ethnic entities. As a result, the army of the Republika Srpska under the leadership of General Ratko Mladic began a policy of 'ethnic cleansing' against Muslims in what they considered to be Serb lands.

GlobalSecurity.org, 2000–2005

The editors of Ben-Gurion's diary were surprised to discover that between 1 April and 15 May 1948, the leader of the Jewish community in Palestine seemed rather oblivious to the military side of events.[1]

Instead, he appeared much more preoccupied with domestic Zionist politics and was dealing intensively with organisational topics such as transforming the Diasporic bodies into organs of the new state of Israel. His diary certainly does not betray any sense of a looming catastrophe or a 'second Holocaust', as he proclaimed with pathos in his public appearances.

To his inner circles he spoke a different language. To members of his party Mapai, early in April, he proudly listed the names of the Arab villages Jewish troops had recently occupied. On another occasion, on 6 April, we find him rebuking socialist-leaning members of the Histadrut's executive who questioned the wisdom of attacking peasants instead of confronting their landlords, the effendis, telling one of its central figures: 'I do not agree with you that we are facing effendis and not peasants: our enemies are the Arab peasants!'[2]

His diary does indeed offer a stark contrast to the fear he planted in his audiences during public gatherings and, consequently, the Israeli collective memory. It suggests that by then he had realised Palestine was already in his hands. He was not, however, over-confident and did not join in the celebrations on 15 May 1948, aware of the enormity of the task ahead of him: cleansing Palestine and making sure Arab attempts would not stop the Jewish takeover. Like the Consultancy, he feared the outcome of developments in places where there was an obvious imbalance between isolated Jewish settlements and a potential Arab army – as was the case in remote parts of the Galilee and the Negev, as well as in some parts of Jerusalem. Ben-Gurion and his close associates nonetheless understood perfectly well that these local disadvantages could not change the overall picture: the ability of the Jewish forces to seize, even before the British had left, many of the areas the UN Partition Resolution had allocated to the Jewish state. 'Seizing' meaning only one thing: the massive expulsion of the Palestinians living there from their homes, businesses and land in both the cities and the rural areas.

Ben-Gurion may not have publicly rejoiced with the Jewish masses who danced in the streets on the day the British Mandate officially ended, but he was well aware that the power of the Jewish military forces had already begun to show on the ground. When Plan Dalet was put into effect, the Hagana had more than 50,000 troops at its disposal, half of which had been trained by the British army during the Second World War. The time had come to put the plan into effect.

OPERATION NACHSHON: THE FIRST PLAN DALET OPERATION

The Zionist strategy of building isolated settlements in the midst of densely populated Arab areas, approved retroactively by the British Mandatory authorities, proved a liability at times of tension. Attempts to bring supplies and troops to these faraway posts could not always be guaranteed, and once the country was in flames, the western approach road to Jerusalem, which passed through numerous Palestinian villages, was particularly difficult to safeguard, creating a sense of siege amongst the small Jewish population in the city. The Zionist leaders were also worried about the Jews in Jerusalem, for a different reason: they were made up mainly of Orthodox and Mizrahi communities whose commitment to Zionism and its aspirations was quite tenuous or even questionable. Thus, the first area chosen for putting Plan Dalet into action was the rural hills on the western slopes of the Jerusalem mountains, half way along the road to Tel-Aviv. This was Operation *Nachshon*, which would serve as a model for future campaigns: the sudden massive expulsions it employed were to prove the most effective means for maintaining isolated Jewish settlements or unblocking routes that were under enemy threat, such as the one leading to Jerusalem.

Every brigade assigned to the operation was asked to prepare to move into *Mazav Dalet*, State D, that is to ready themselves to implement the orders of Plan D: 'You will move to State Dalet, for an operative implementation of Plan Dalet,' was the opening sentence to each unit. And then 'the villages which you will capture, cleanse or destroy will be decided according to consultation with your advisors on Arab affairs and the intelligence officers.'[3] Judging by the end result of this stage, namely April–May 1948, this advice was not to spare a single village. Whereas the official Plan Dalet gave the villages the option to surrender, the operational orders did not exempt any village for any reason. With this the blueprint was converted into military order to begin destroying villages. The dates differed according to the geography: the Alexandroni Brigade, which would storm the coast with its tens of villages, leaving only two behind them, received its orders towards the end of April; the instruction to cleanse the Eastern Galilee arrived at the Golani Brigade headquarters on 6 May 1948, and the next day the first village in their 'area', Shajara, was cleansed.[4]

The Palmach units received their orders for Nachson on the very first day of April 1948. The night before, the Consultancy had met at Ben-Gurion's house to finalise the directives to the units. Their orders were clear: 'the principal objective of the operation is the destruction of Arab villages ... [and] the eviction of the villagers so that they would become an economic liability for the general Arab forces.'[5]

Operation Nachshon was also a novelty in other respects. It was the first operation in which all the various Jewish military organisations endeavoured to act together as a single army – providing the basis for the future Israeli Defence Forces (IDF). And it was the first operation in which the veteran East European Jews, who naturally dominated the military scene, were incorporated into the campaign alongside other ethnic groups such as newcomers the Arab world and from post-Holocaust Europe.

The commander of one battalion who participated in this operation, Uri Ben-Ari, mentioned in his memoirs that 'melting the Diasporas' was one of the important goals of Nachshon. Ben-Ari was a young German Jew who had arrived in Palestine a few years earlier. His unit made its final preparations for Nachshon on the Mediterranean coast, near Hadera. He recalled likening himself to Russian generals fighting the Nazis in the Second World War. The 'Nazis' in his case were a large number of defenceless Palestinian villages in proximity to the Jaffa–Jerusalem road and the para-military groups of Abd al-Qadir al-Husayni who had come to their rescue. Al-Husayni's units had been retaliating for earlier Jewish attacks by firing randomly at Jewish traffic on the road, wounding and killing passengers. But the villagers themselves, as elsewhere in Palestine, were trying to continue life as normal, unaware of the demonised image attributed to them by Ben-Ari and his comrades. Within a few days most of them would be expelled forever from the homes and fields where they and their ancestors had lived and worked for centuries. The para-military Palestinian groups under the command of Abd al-Qadir al-Husayni put up more resistance than Ben-Ari's battalion had expected, which meant that the Nachshon operation did not at first go as planned. By 9 April, however, the campaign was over.

This was the day that the first of the many villages around Jerusalem fell into Jewish hands, despite its auspicious name – Qastal (the Castle). It did have ancient fortifications, but these could not protect it from the superior Jewish forces. The Qastal was located on the last western peak before the final ascent to Jerusalem. The monument to the Hagana that Israel has put up at the site fails to mention that there was once on this very spot a Palestinian village. The plaque commemorating the battle is a typical example of how deeply rooted the language of Plan Dalet is in today's popular Israeli historiography. As in the plan, so on the plaque, the Qastal appears not as a village but as an 'enemy base': Palestinian villagers are dehumanised in order to turn them into 'legitimate targets' of destruction and expulsion. All over Israel many new settlements and national parks have become part of the country's collective memory without any reference to the Palestinian villages that once stood there, even where there are vestiges, such as an isolated house or a mosque, which visibly attest to the fact that people used to live there as recently as 1948.

On 9 April, while defending Qastal, Abd al-Qadir al-Husayni was killed in battle. His death so demoralised his troops that all the other villages in the Greater Jerusalem area swiftly fell into the hands of the Jewish forces. One by one, they were surrounded, attacked and occupied, their people expelled and their homes and buildings demolished. In some of them, the expulsion was accompanied by massacres, the most notorious of which is the one Jewish troops perpetrated, on the same day Qastal fell, in Deir Yassin.

Deir Yassin

The systematic nature of Plan Dalet is manifested in Deir Yassin, a pastoral and cordial village that had reached a non-aggression pact with the Hagana in Jerusalem, but was doomed to be wiped out because it was within the areas designated in Plan Dalet to be cleansed. Because of the prior agreement they had signed with the village, the Hagana decided to send the Irgun and Stern Gang troops, so as to absolve themselves from any official accountability. In the subsequent cleansings of 'friendly' villages even this ploy would no longer be deemed necessary.

On 9 April 1948, Jewish forces occupied the village of Deir Yassin. It lay on a hill west of Jerusalem, eight hundred metres above sea level and close to the Jewish neighbourhood of Givat Shaul. The old village school serves today as a mental hospital for the western Jewish neighbourhood that expanded over the destroyed village.

As they burst into the village, the Jewish soldiers sprayed the houses with machine-gun fire, killing many of the inhabitants. The remaining villagers were then gathered in one place and murdered in cold blood, their bodies abused while a number of the women were raped and then killed.[6]

Fahim Zaydan, who was twelve years old at the time, recalled how he saw his family murdered in front of his eyes:

> They took us out one after the other; shot an old man and when one of his daughters cried, she was shot too. Then they called my brother Muhammad, and shot him in front us, and when my mother yelled, bending over him – carrying my little sister Hudra in her hands, still breastfeeding her – they shot her too.[7]

Zaydan himself was shot, too, while standing in a row of children the Jewish soldiers had lined up against a wall, which they had then sprayed with bullets, 'just for the fun of it', before they left. He was lucky to survive his wounds.

Recent research has brought down the accepted number of people massacred at Deir Yassin from 170 to ninety-three. Of course, apart from the victims of the massacre itself, dozens of others were killed in the fighting, and hence were not included in the official list of victims. However, as the Jewish forces regarded any Palestinian village as an enemy military base, the distinction between massacring people and killing them 'in battle' was slight. One only has to be told that thirty babies were among the slaughtered in Deir Yassin to understand why the whole 'quantitative' exercise – which the Israelis repeated as recently as April 2002 in the massacre in Jenin – is insignificant. At the time, the Jewish leadership proudly announced a high number of victims so as to make Deir Yassin the epicentre of the catastrophe – a warning to all Palestinians that a similar fate awaited them if they refused to abandon their homes and take flight.[8]

Four nearby villages were next – Qalunya, Saris, Beit Surik and Biddu. Taking only an hour or so in each village, the Hagana units blew up the houses and expelled the people. Interestingly (or ironically, if you wish) Hagana officers claimed they had to struggle with their subordinates in order to prevent a frenzy of looting at the end of each occupation. Ben-Ari, who supervised the sappers unit that blew up the houses, recounts in his memoirs how he had single-handedly stopped the plunder of these villages, but this claim seems exaggerated to say the least, given that the peasants ran away with nothing while their possessions found their way into the living rooms and farms of both soldiers and officers as wartime mementos.[9]

Two villages in the same area were spared: Abu Ghawsh and Nabi Samuil. This was because their mukhtars had developed a relatively cordial relationship with the local commanders of the Stern Gang. Ironically, this saved them from destruction and expulsion: as the Hagana wanted to demolish them, the more extremist group, the Stern Gang, now came to their rescue. This was, however, a rare exception, and hundreds of villages suffered the same fate as Qalunya and the Qastal.[10]

THE URBICIDE OF PALESTINE

The confidence the Jewish command in early April had in their capacity not only to take over, but also to cleanse the areas the UN had granted to the Jewish state, can be gauged from the way, immediately after operation

Nachshon, they turned their attention to the major urban centres of Palestine. These were systematically attacked throughout the rest of the month, as UN agents and British officials stood by and watched indifferently.

The offensive against the urban centres began with Tiberias. As soon as news of Deir Yassin and the massacre three days later (12 April) in the nearby village of Khirbat Nasr al-Din reached the large Palestinian population in the city, many fled.[11] The people were also petrified by the daily heavy bombardments by the Jewish forces situated in the hills overlooking this historic, ancient capital on the Sea of Galilee, where 6000 Jews and 5000 Arabs and their forbears had for centuries co-existed peacefully. British obstruction meant that the ALA had only managed to supply the city with a force of about thirty volunteers. These were no match for the Hagana forces, who rolled barrel bombs down from the hills and used loudspeakers to broadcast terrifying noises to frighten the population – an early version of the supersonic flights over Beirut in 1983 and Gaza in 2005, which human rights organisations have decried as criminal acts. Tiberias fell on 18 April.[12]

The British played a questionable role in the attack on Tiberias. At first they offered to protect the Palestinian residents, but soon urged them to negotiate a general evacuation of the town with the Jewish forces. King Abdullah of Jordan was more 'practical': he sent thirty trucks to help move women and children. In his memoirs he claimed he was convinced another Deir Yassin was about to occur.[13] British officers later professed to having had similar apprehensions, but documents showing heavy British pressure on the community's leaders to leave do not reveal any great concern about an impending massacre. Some would say that the British thereby prevented Tiberias' Arab residents from being massacred; others would argue that they collaborated with the expellers. The role of the British is much clearer, and far more negative, in the next chapters of Palestine's urbicide, when Haifa and Jaffa were occupied.

The De-Arabisation of Haifa

As mentioned previously, operations in Haifa were retroactively approved and welcomed by the Consultancy, although not necessarily initiated by it. The early terrorization of the city's Arab population the previous December had prompted many among the Palestinian elite to leave for their residences in Lebanon and Egypt until calm returned to their city. It is hard to estimate how many fell within this category: most historians put the figure at around 15,000 to 20,000.[14]

On 12 January 1948, a local leader called Farid Sa'ad, the manager of the Arab Bank in Haifa, and a member of the local national committee, telegraphed Dr. Husayn Khalidi, the secretary of the Arab Higher Committee, in despair: 'It is good the Jews do not know the truth.'[15] The 'truth' was that the urban elite in Palestine had collapsed after a month of heavy Jewish shelling and aggression. However, the Jews knew exactly what was going on. Indeed, the Consultancy was well aware that the rich and well-to-do had already left in December, that the Arab arms were not arriving, and the Arab governments did little beyond airing their inflammatory war rhetoric in all directions so as to hide their inaction and unwillingness to intervene on behalf of the Palestinians.

The departure of the affluent meant that between 55,000 and 60,000 Palestinians in Haifa were leaderless and, given the relatively small number of armed Arab volunteers in the town, at the mercy of the Jewish forces in April 1948. This was despite the presence of British troops in the city, who were theoretically responsible for the locals' safety and well-being.

This phase of the Jewish operation around the city was given the ominous name of 'Scissors' (*Misparayim*), indicating both the idea of a pincer movement and of cutting the city off from its Palestinian hinterland. Haifa, like Tiberias, had been allocated in the UN plan to the Jewish state: leaving the only major port in the country in Jewish control was yet another manifestation of the unfair deal the Palestinians were offered in the UN peace proposal. The Jews wanted the port city but without the 75,000 Palestinians who lived there, and in April 1948, they achieved their objective.

As Palestine's main port, Haifa was also the last station on the trail of the British pull-out. The British had been expected to stay until August, but in February 1948 they decided to bring the date of departure forward to May. Their troops were consequently present in great numbers and they still had the legal and, one could argue, moral authority to impose law and order in the city. Their conduct, as many British politicians were later to admit, forms one of the most shameful chapters in the history of the British Empire in the Middle East.[16] The Jewish campaign of terrorization, begun in December, included heavy shelling, sniper fire, rivers of ignited oil and fuel sent down the mountain-side, and detonated barrels of explosives, and went on for the first months of 1948, but it intensified in early April. On 18 April, the day the Palestinians of Tiberias were put to flight, Major General Hugh Stockwell, the British commander of the Northern Sector seated in Haifa, summoned the Jewish authorities in the city to his office and informed them that in two days the British forces would be removed from locations in which they had been serving as a buffer zone between the two communities. This 'buffer' was the only obstacle preventing Jewish forces from a direct assault on, and takeover of, the Palestinian areas, where more than 50,000 people still resided. The road was wide open for the de-Arabisation of Haifa.

This task was given to the Carmeli Brigade, one of the top units of the Jewish army (there were brigades of 'lesser quality' such as Qiryati, made up of Arab Jews who were sent only on looting or less attractive 'missions'; the definition of Qiryati as possessing a 'lesser human quality' can be found in the Israeli documents).[17] The 2000 Carmeli Brigade troops faced a poorly equipped army of 500 local and mainly Lebanese volunteers, who had inferior arms and limited ammunition, and certainly nothing to match the armoured cars and mortars on the Jewish side.

The removal of the British barrier meant Operation Scissors could be replaced by Operation 'Cleansing the Leaven' (*bi'ur hametz*). The Hebrew term stands for total cleansing and refers to the Jewish religious practice of eliminating all traces of bread or flour from people's homes on the eve of the Passover, since as these are forbidden during the days of the feast. Brutally appropriate, the cleansing of Haifa, in which the Palestinians were the bread and the flour, began on Passover's eve, 21 April.

Stockwell, the British commander, knew in advance about the impending Jewish attack, and earlier that same day invited the 'Palestinian leadership' in the city for a consultation. He met with a group of four exhausted men, who became the Arab community's leaders for the hour, as none of the positions they held officially prepared them for the crucial historic moment that unfolded in Stockwell's office on that morning. Previous correspondence between them and Stockwell shows they trusted him as the keeper of law and order in the city. The British officer now advised them that it would be better for their people to leave the city, where they and most of their families had lived and worked ever since the mid-eighteenth century, when Haifa came to prominence as a modern town. Gradually, as they listened to Stockwell and their confidence in him faded, they realised that they would be unable to safeguard their community, and so they prepared for the worst: as the British would not protect them, they were doomed to be expelled. They told Stockwell they wanted to leave in an organised manner. The Carmeli Brigade made sure they would leave in the midst of carnage and havoc.[18]

On their way to meet the British commander, the four men could already hear the Jewish loudspeakers urging the Palestinian women and children to leave before it was too late. In other parts of the town, loudspeakers delivered a diametrically opposing message from the town's Jewish mayor, Shabtai Levi, a decent person by all accounts, who beseeched the people to stay and promised no harm would befall them. But it was Mordechai Maklef, the operation officer of the Carmeli Brigade, not Levi who called the shots. Maklef orchestrated the cleansing campaign, and the orders he issued to his troops were plain and simple: 'Kill any Arab you encounter; torch all inflammable objects and force doors open with explosives.' (He later became the Israeli army Chief of Staff.)[19]

When these orders were executed promptly within the 1.5 square kilometres where thousands of Haifa's defenceless Palestinians were still residing, the shock and terror were such that, without packing any of their belongings or even knowing what they were doing, people began leaving en masse. In panic they headed towards the port where they hoped to find a ship or a boat to take them away from the city. As soon as they had fled, Jewish troops broke into and looted their houses.

When Golda Meir, one of the senior Zionist leaders, visited Haifa a few days later, she at first found it hard to suppress a feeling of horror when she entered homes where cooked food still stood on the tables, children had left toys and books on the floor, and life appeared to have frozen in an instant. Meir had come to Palestine from the US, where her family had fled in the wake of pogroms in Russia, and the sights she witnessed that day reminded her of the worst stories her family had told her about the Russian brutality against Jews decades earlier.[20] But this apparently left no lasting mark on her or her associates' determination to continue with the ethnic cleansing of Palestine.

In the early hours of dawn on 22 April, the people began streaming to the harbour. As the streets in that part of the city were already overcrowded with people seeking escape, the Arab community's self-appointed leadership tried to instil some order into the chaotic scene. Loudspeakers could be heard, urging people to gather in the old marketplace next to the port, and seek shelter there until an orderly evacuation by sea could be organised. 'The Jews have occupied Stanton road and are on their way', the loudspeakers blared.

The Carmeli Brigade's war book, chronicling its actions in the war, shows little compunction about what followed thereafter. The brigade's officers, aware that people had been advised to gather near the port's gate, ordered their men to station three-inch mortars on the mountain slopes overlooking the market and the port – where the Rothschild Hospital stands today – and to bombard the gathering crowds below. The plan was to make sure people would have no second thoughts, and to guarantee that the flight would be in one direction only. Once the Palestinians were gathered in the marketplace – an architectural gem that dated back to the Ottoman period, covered with white arched canopies, but destroyed beyond recognition after the creation of the State of Israel – they were an easy target for the Jewish marksmen.[21]

Haifa's market was less than one hundred yards from what was then the main gate to the port. When the shelling began, this was the natural destination for the panic-stricken Palestinians. The crowd now broke into the port, pushing aside the policemen who guarded the gate. Scores of people stormed the boats that were moored there, and began to flee the city. We can learn what happened next from the horrifying recollections of some of the survivors, published recently. Here is one of them:

> Men stepped on their friends and women on their own children. The boats in the port were soon filled with living cargo. The overcrowding in them was horrible. Many turned over and sank with all their passengers.[22]

The scenes were so horrendous that when reports reached London, they spurred the British government into action as some officials, probably for the first time, began to realise the enormity of the disaster their inaction was creating in Palestine. The British foreign secretary, Ernest Bevin, was furious with Stockwell's behaviour, but Field-Marshal Montgomery, the chief of the imperial staff and thus Stockwell's boss, defended him.[23] The last communication between Haifa's Palestinian leaders and Stockwell took the form of a letter that speaks volumes:

> We feel distressed and profoundly aggrieved by the lack of sympathy on the part of the British Authorities to render aid to the wounded although they have been requested to do so.[24]

Safad is Next[25]

By the time Haifa fell, only a few towns in Palestine were still free, among them Acre, Nazareth and Safad. The battle over Safad began in the middle of April and lasted until 1 May. This was not due to any stubborn resistance from the Palestinians or the ALA volunteers, although they did make a more serious effort here than elsewhere. Rather, tactical considerations directed the Jewish campaign first to the rural hinterland around Safad, and only then did they move on the town itself.

In Safad there were 9500 Arabs and 2400 Jews. Most of the Jews were Ultra-Orthodox and had no interest at all in Zionism, let alone in fighting their Arab neighbours. This, and the relatively gradual way the Jewish takeover developed, may have given the eleven members of the local national committee the illusion that they would fare better than other urban centres. The committee was a fairly representative body that included the town's notables, ulama (religious dignitaries), merchants, landowners and ex-activists from the 1936 Revolt, of which Safad had been a major centre.[26] The false sense of security was reinforced by the relatively large presence of Arab volunteers in Safad, totaling more than 400, although only half of them were armed with rifles. Skirmishes in the town had begun in early January, triggered by an aggressive reconnaissance incursion by some Hagana members into the Palestinian neighbourhoods and market. A charismatic Syrian officer, Ihasn Qam Ulmaz, held the defences against repeated attacks by the Hagana's commando unit, the Palmach.

At first, these Palmach attacks were sporadic and ineffective, as its units focused their actions on the rural area around the town. But once they were through with the villages in Safad's vicinity (described later in this chapter) they could concentrate fully on the town itself, on 29 April 1948. Unfortunately for the people of Safad, at precisely the moment they needed him most, they lost the able Ulmaz. The volunteers army's new commander in the Galilee, Adib Shishakly (to become one of Syria's rulers in the 1950s) replaced him with one of the ALA's more incompetent officers. However, it is doubtful whether even Ulmaz would have fared better in view of the imbalance of power: 1000 well-trained Palmach troops confronting 400 Arab volunteers, one of many local imbalances that show the falsity of the myth of a Jewish David facing an Arab Goliath in 1948.[27]

The Palmach troops drove most of the people out, only allowing 100 old people to stay on, though not for long. On 5 June, Ben-Gurion noted dryly in his dairy: 'Abraham Hanuki, from [Kibbutz] Ayelet Hashahar, told me that since there were only 100 old people left in Safad they were expelled to Lebanon.'[28]

The Phantom City of Jerusalem

The urbicide did not skip Jerusalem, which quickly changed from the 'Eternal City', as a recent book by Salim Tamari puts it, into a 'Phantom City'.[29] Jewish troops shelled, attacked and occupied the western Arab neighbourhoods in April 1948. Some of the richer Palestinian inhabitants of these more affluent sections had left town a few weeks before. The rest were expelled from houses that still testify to the architectural beauty of the neighbourhoods the Palestinian elite had started building outside the walls of the Old City by the end of the nineteenth century. In recent years some of these masterpieces have begun to disappear: real estate fervour, architectural eccentricism and constructors' greed have combined to transform these elegant residential areas into streets of monstrous villas and extravagant palaces for rich American Jews who tend to flock to the city in their old age.

The British troops were still in Palestine when these areas were cleansed and occupied, but they remained aloof and did not intervene. Only in one area, Shaykh Jarrah – the first Palestinian neighborhood built outside the Old City's walls, where the leading notable families such as the Husaynis, the Nashashibis and the Khalidis had their domicile – did a local British commander decide to step in.

The instruction to the Jewish forces was very clear in April 1948. 'Occupy the neighbourhood and destroy all its houses.'[30] The cleansing attack began on 24 April 1948 but was halted by the British before it could be fully implemented. We have vital testimony of what happened in Shaykh Jarrah from the secretary of the Arab Higher Committee, Dr Husayn Khalidi, who lived there: his desperate telegrams to the Mufti were often intercepted by the Israeli intelligence and are kept in the Israeli archives.[31] Khalidi reports how the British commander's troops saved the neighbourhood, with the exception of the 20 houses the Hagana succeeded in blowing up. This confrontational British stance here indicates how very different the fate of many Palestinians would have been had British troops elsewhere intervened, as both the imperatives of the Mandatory charter and the terms of the UN partition resolution required them to do.

British inaction was the rule, however, as Khalidi's frantic appeals highlight as regards the rest of the Jerusalemite neighbourhoods, especially in the western part of the city. These areas had come under repeated shelling from the first day of January and here, unlike in Shaykh Jarrah, the British played a truly diabolical role, as they disarmed the few Palestinian residents who had weapons, promising to protect the people against Jewish attacks, but then instantly reneged on that promise.

In one of his telegraphs in early January, Dr Khalidi reported to Al-Hajj Amin, in Cairo, how almost every day a crowd of angry citizens would demonstrate in front of his house seeking leadership and calling for help. Doctors in the crowd told Khalidi that the hospitals were overcrowded with the injured and that they were running out of shrouds to cover the dead bodies. There was total anarchy and people were in a state of panic.

But worse was to come.[32] A few days after the aborted attack on Shaykh Jarrah, with the help of the same three-inch mortar bombs used in Haifa, Palestinian Northern and Western Jerusalem were hammered by endless shelling. Only Shu'fat held on and refused to surrender. Qatamon fell in the last days of April. Itzhak Levy, the head of the Hagana intelligence in Jerusalem, recalls: 'While the cleansing of Qatamon went on, pillage and robbery began. Soldiers and citizens took part in it. They broke into the houses and took from them furniture, clothing, electric equipment and food.'[33]

The entry of the Jordanian Arab Legion into the fighting changed the picture, and the cleansing operations were halted in the middle of May 1948. Some Jordanians were involved in the fighting before, as volunteers, and their contribution had helped slow down the Jewish advance, especially during the takeover of Qatamon, which involved intensive fighting with Jewish troops in the monastery of San Simon. But despite their heroic – in the description of Levy and his friends – attempt to defend the Palestinian neighbourhoods of the west, they failed. All in all, eight Palestinian neighbourhoods and thirty-nine villages were ethnically cleansed in the Greater Jerusalem area, their population transferred to the eastern part of the city. The villages are all gone today, but some of Jerusalem's most beautiful houses are still standing, now inhabited by Jewish families who took them over immediately after their eviction – silent reminders of the tragic fate of the people who used to own them.

Acre and Baysan

The urbicide continued into May with the occupation of Acre on the coast and Baysan in the east on 6 May 1948. In the beginning of May, Acre proved once again that it was not only Napoleon who found it hard to defeat it: despite severe overcrowding due to the huge influx of refugees from the neighbouring city of Haifa, heavy daily shelling by the Jewish forces failed to subdue the Crusader city. However, its exposed water supply ten kilometres to the north, from the Kabri springs, via an almost 200-year old aqueduct, proved its Achilles' heel. During the siege typhoid germs were apparently injected into the water. Local emissaries of the International Red Cross reported this to their headquarters and left very little room for guessing whom they suspected: the Hagana. The Red Cross reports describe a sudden typhoid epidemic and, even with their guarded language, point to outside poisoning as the sole explanation for this outbreak.[34]

On 6 May 1948, in Acre's Lebanese hospital, which belonged to the Red Cross, an emergency meeting was convened. Brigadier Beveridge, chief of the British medical services, Colonel Bonnet of the British army, Dr Maclean of the Medical Services, and Mr de Meuron, the Red Cross delegate in Palestine, met with city officials to discuss the seventy casualties the epidemic had already claimed. They concluded that the infection was undoubtedly water-borne, not due to crowded or unhygienic conditions, as the Hagana claimed. Tellingly, it had affected fifty-five British soldiers who were transferred to Port Said hospital in Egypt. 'Nothing like that ever happened in Palestine,' Brigadier Beveridge told de Meuron. The minute they had identified the aqueduct as the source, they switched to artesian wells and water from the agricultural station north of Acre. The refugees from Acre already in camps in the north were also examined in order to prevent the epidemic from spreading.

With their morale weakened by both the typhoid epidemic and the intensive shelling, residents heeded the call from loudspeakers that shouted at them: 'Surrender or commit suicide. We will destroy you to the last man.'[35] Lieutenant Petite, a French UN observer, reported that after the city fell into Jewish hands, there was widespread and systematic looting by the army, including furniture, clothes, and anything that might be useful to the new Jewish immigrants, and the removal of which might discourage the refugees' return.

A similar attempt to poison the water supply in Gaza on 27 May was foiled. The Egyptians caught two Jews, David Horin and David Mizrachi, trying to inject typhoid and dysentery viruses into Gaza's wells. General Yadin reported the incident to Ben-Gurion, then Israel's Prime Minister, who duly entered it in his diary, without comment. The two were later executed by the Egyptians without any official Israeli protestations.[36]

Ernest David Bergman, together with the Katzir brothers mentioned earlier, was part of a team working on Israel's biological warfare capability set up by Ben-Gurion in the 1940s, euphemistically called the Science Corps of the Hagana. Ephraim Katzir was appointed its director in May 1948, when the outfit was renamed 'HEMED' (Sweetness, the acronym of Hayl Mada – the Science corps). It did not contribute in any major way to the 1948 campaigns but its early input was indicative of the unconventional aspirations the state of Israel would pursue in the future.[37]

Roughly at the same time that Acre was occupied, the Golani Brigade seized the town of Baysan in Operation Gideon. As in Safad, after occupying several villages in the vicinity, they moved in on the town. The Jewish forces, with the successful takeovers of Haifa, Tiberias and Safad behind them, were confident and highly effective. Experienced now in mass evictions, they tried to force a swift departure in Baysan by issuing an ultimatum to the people to leave their homes within ten hours. The ultimatum was delivered to the 'city notables', namely a fraction of the local national committee. These notables declined and hastily tried to accumulate food stocks for a long siege; they organised some weapons, mainly two cannons brought in by volunteers, in order to repel the impending assault. Nahum Spigel, the commander of the Golani Brigade, wanted a swift offensive and to take a number of prisoners of war in order to exchange them for some Jewish prisoners the Jordanian forces had captured earlier in their successful bid for both the Jewish quarter in the Old City and the Zionist settlement of Gush Etzion. In fact, the Legion rescued the Gush Etzion settlers from the hands of angry Palestinian paramilitary groups that had attacked the isolated Jewish colony and the convoy that had come to save it.[38] (Today, Gush Etzion is a large Jewish settlement in the West Bank.) These settlers, together with the residents of the old Jewish quarter, were among the few Jewish POWs captured during the war. They were treated fairly and released soon after, unlike the thousands of Palestinians who were now, according to international law, citizens of the State of Israel, but on becoming prisoners were caged in pens.

After heavy daily bombardments, including from the air, the local committee in Baysan decided to surrender. The body that took the decision consisted of the *qadi*, the local priest, the municipal secretary and the richest merchant in town. They met Palti Sela and his colleagues to discuss the terms of surrender (before the meeting, the members asked permission to travel to Nablus to discuss capitulation, but this was refused). On 11 May, the town passed into Jewish hands. Palti Sela remembered particularly the two pathetic old artillery guns that had been meant to protect Baysan: two French anti-air cannon from the First World War, antiquated weaponry representative of the overall level of the arms the Palestinians and the volunteers possessed, on the eve of the regular Arab armies' entrance into Palestine.

Immediately after, Palti Sela and his colleagues were able to oversee the 'orderly expulsion' of the town's people. Some were transferred to Nazareth – still a free Palestinian city in May, but not for much longer – some to Jenin, but the majority were driven across the nearby Jordan River onto the opposite bank.[39] Eyewitnesses remember the hordes of people from Baysan as particularly panic-stricken and cowed, hurriedly making their way in the direction of the Jordan River and from there inland to makeshift camps. While the Jewish troops were busy with other operations nearby, however, quite a few of them succeeded in returning; Baysan is very close to both the West Bank and the River Jordan and therefore slipping back unnoticed was relatively easy. They succeeded in staying on until mid-June when the Israeli army loaded the people at gunpoint onto trucks and drove them across the river once again.

The Ruination of Jaffa

Jaffa was the last city to be taken, on 13 May, two days before the end of the Mandate. Like so many of Palestine's cities, it had a long history going back as far as the Bronze age, with an impressive Roman and Byzantine heritage. It was the Muslim commander, Umar Ibn al-'Aas, who took the town in 632 and imbued it with its Arab character. The Greater Jaffa area included twenty-four villages and seventeen mosques; today one mosque survives, but not one of the villages is left standing.

On 13 May, 5000 Irgun and Hagana troops attacked the city as Arab volunteers headed by Michael al-Issa, a local Christian, tried to defend it.

Among them was an extraordinary unit of fifty Muslims from Bosnia as well as members of the second generation of the Templars, German colonists who had come in the mid-nineteenth century as religious missionaries and now decided to try and defend their colonies (other Templars in the Galilee surrendered without a fight, and were swiftly driven out of their two pretty colonies, Waldheim and Beit Lehem, west of Nazareth).

All in all, Jaffa enjoyed the largest defense force available to the Palestinians in any given locality: a total of 1500 volunteers confronted the 5000 Jewish troops. They survived a three-week siege and attack that began in the middle of April and ended in the middle of May. When Jaffa fell, its entire population of 50,000 was expelled with the 'help' of British mediation, meaning that their flight was less chaotic than in Haifa. Still, there were scenes reminiscent of the horrors that took place in the northern harbour of Haifa: people were literally pushed into the sea when the crowds tried to board the far-too-small fishing boats that would take them to Gaza, while Jewish troops shot over their heads to hasten their expulsion.

With the fall of Jaffa, the occupying Jewish forces had emptied and depopulated all the major cities and towns of Palestine. The vast majority of their inhabitants – of all classes, denominations and occupations – never saw their cities again, while the more politicised among them would come to play a formative role in the re-emergence of the Palestinian national movement in the form of the PLO, demanding first and foremost their right to return.

THE CLEANSING CONTINUES

Already towards the end of March the Jewish operations had destroyed much of the rural hinterland of Jaffa and Tel-Aviv. There was an apparent division of labour between the Hagana forces and the Irgun. While the Hagana moved in an orderly fashion from one place to the next according to plan, the Irgun was allowed sporadic actions in villages beyond the scope of the original list. This is how the Irgun arrived in the village of Shaykh Muwannis (or Munis, as it is known today) on 30 March and expelled its inhabitants by force. Today you will find the elegant campus of Tel-Aviv University sprawling over the ruins of this village, while one of the village's few remaining houses has become the university's faculty club.[40]

Had there not been the tacit understanding between the Hagana and the Irgun, Shaykh Muwannis might have been saved. The heads of the village had made a serious effort to cultivate a cordial relationship with the Hagana in order to prevent their expulsion, but the 'Arabists' who had concluded the treaty were nowhere to be found on the day the Irgun showed up and expelled the entire village.[41]

In April the operations in the countryside were more closely connected to the urbicide. Villages near urban centres were taken and expelled, and sometimes subjected to massacres, in a campaign of terror designed to prepare the ground for a more successful takeover of the cities.

The Consultancy met again on a Wednesday, 7 April 1948. It was decided to destroy, and expel the inhabitants from, all the villages on the Tel-Aviv–Haifa road, Jenin–Haifa road and the Jerusalam–Jaffa road. At the end of the day, apart from a tiny handful of villages, no one was spared.[42]

Thus, on the day the Irgun wiped out Shaykh Muwannis, the Hagana occupied six villages in the same area within a week: Khirbat Azzun was the first, on 2 April, followed by Khirbat Lid, Arab al-Fuqara, Arab al-Nufay'at and Damira, all cleansed by 10 April, and Cherqis on the 15th. By the end of the month another three villages in the vicinity of Jaffa and Tel-Aviv – Khirbat al-Manshiyya, Biyar 'Adas and the large village of Miska – had all been taken and destroyed.[43]

All of this took place before a single regular Arab soldier had entered Palestine, and the pace now becomes hard to follow, for contemporary as well as for later historians. Between 30 March and 15 May, 200 villages were occupied and their inhabitants expelled. This is a fact that must be repeated, as it undermines the Israeli myth that the 'Arabs' ran away once the 'Arab invasion' began. Almost half of the Arab villages had already been attacked by the time the Arab governments eventually and, as we know, reluctantly decided to send in their troops. Another ninety villages would be wiped out between 15 May and 11 June 1948, when the first of two truces finally came into effect.[44]

Eyewitnesses on the Jewish side recall clearly thinking throughout April that the army could strive for more. In his recent interview with official historians, Palti Sela, whose testimony can be found in the Hagana Archives in Tel-Aviv, used colourful language to reconstruct that atmosphere of extra zeal. Palti Sela was a member of the Jewish forces that occupied and cleansed the town of Baysan, and who were ordered to push out the large Bedouin tribes that had for centuries seasonally resided in the area. He later remarked:

> After we cleansed the area from the Bedouin tribes the pus [he used the Yiddish word for a purulent wound: farunkel] of the Baysan are still infected with two villages, Faruna and Samariyya. They did not seem to be afraid and were still cultivating their fields and continued using the roads.[45]

One of the many villages captured during these attacks in the east was that of Sirin. Its story epitomises the fate that befell scores of villages depopulated by Jewish forces in Marj Ibn Amir and the Baysan Valley, where today one searches in vain for any trace of the Palestinian life that once flourished there.

The Village of Sirin

Sirin was occupied on 12 May 1948. It lay near Baysan on one of the Jiftiliq's lands: historically these lands, at times referred to as 'mudawar' lands, were nominally under the Ottoman Sultan's title but were cultivated by Palestinian farmers. Sirin grew into a thriving community around the burial place (maqam) of a Muslim holy man named Shaykh Ibn Sirin. The terrain in that part of Palestine is tough and the summers are unbearably hot. And yet the habitation that developed around the maqam and the nearby springs, three kilomotres away, resembled that of villages endowed with a much better climate and an endless flow of fresh water. Animals carried the water from the wells and diligent farmers used it to turn the rugged land into a small Garden of Eden. Sirin was an isolated community as it was unreachable by car, but outsiders who did frequent the village single out the particular style of the buildings there: Sirin's houses were made of volcanic black stones mixed with clay, and the roofs were covered with intertwined layers of wood and bamboo.

Sirin was noted as a fine example of the collective system of land-sharing to which the villagers adhered, dating back to the Ottoman period, and here had survived both the capitalization of the local agriculture and the Zionist drive for land. It boasted three rich bustans (gardens with fruit trees) and olive groves, which spread out over 9000 cultivated dunam of land (out of 17,000). The land belonged to the village as a whole and the size of the family determined its share in the crops and territory.

Sirin was also a village that had all the right connections. The main family, the Zu'bi, had been promised immunity by the Jewish Agency because they belonged to a collaborative clan. Mubarak al-Haj al-Zu'bi, the mukhtar, a young well-educated man, with close connections to the opposition parties, was a friend of the Jewish mayor of Haifa, Shabtai Levi, from the time they had both worked in Baron Rothschild's company. He was sure his 700 villagers would be exempt from the fate of the nearby villages. But there was another clan in the village, the hamulla of Abu al-Hija, who were more loyal to the ex-Mufti, al-Hajj Amin al-Husayni, and his national party. According to the 1943 Hagana village file on Sirin, it was the presence of this clan that doomed the village. The file noted that in Sirin ten members of the Abu al-Hija had participated in the 1936 Revolt and that 'none of them was arrested or killed and kept their ten rifles'.

The village suffered from time to time from the animosity between the two main hamullas, but, as everywhere in Palestine, matters improved after the Great Revolt, and by the end of the Mandate the village had put behind it the rift that tore it apart during the rebellious days of the 1930s.

Sirin's mukhtar hoped that the village's immunity would be further ensured by the presence of a small Christian clan that had an excellent relationship with the rest of the people. One of them was the village teacher who, in his class of 40 children, educated the next generation without any prejudice to politics or clannish affiliations. His best friend was Shaykh Muhammad al-Mustafa, the imam in the local mosque and the guardian of the Christian church and monastery that were also located inside the village.

Within a few short hours, this microcosm of religious coexistence and harmony was laid waste. The villagers did not put up a fight. The Jewish troops gathered the Muslims – of both clans – and Christians together and ordered them to start crossing the River Jordan to the other side. They then demolished the mosque, the church and the monastery, together with all the houses. Soon, all the trees in the bustans had withered away and died.

Today, a cactus hedge surrounds the rubble that was Sirin. Jews never succeeded in repeating the success of the Palestinians in holding on to the tough soil in the valley, but the springs in the vicinity are still there – an eerie sight as they serve no one.[46]

The ALA in Marj Ibn Amir

West of Sirin, in the Marj Ibn Amir (Izrael Valley), Fawzi al-Qawqji did what he could to limit the Jewish takeover, and carried out a few abortive attacks on the main Jewish kibbutz in the area, Mishmar Ha-Emek. In one of the bombardments of the kibbutz by the one cannon he had available, a direct hit killed three children. This awful tragedy is the only hostile event you will find mentioned in official Israeli history books as having taken place in this area.

The villages nearby did not contribute much to the ALA's efforts to bring good news back from the front to the Arab League that had sent them. In fact, many of them had signed non-aggression pacts with the kibbutzim in their vicinity. But as the ALA attack on Mishmar Ha-Emek fuelled the vengeful rage of the kibbutzniks, these villages were no longer immune from the growing aggression in the valley. The kibbutzniks urged the troops to continue the ethnic cleansing they had started to the east of the area. Many of the kibbutzim in this part of the Galilee belonged to the Zionist socialist party, Hashomer Ha-Tza'ir, some of whose members tried to adopt a more humane position. In July, some prominent Mapam members complained to Ben-Gurion about what they saw as an 'unnecessary' expansion of the cleansing operation. Ben-Gurion was quick to remind these conscientious kibbutzniks that they themselves had been glad to see the first phase initiated in the area back in April.[47] Indeed, if you were a Zionist Jew in 1948, this meant one thing and one thing only: full commitment to the de-Arabisation of Palestine.

Al-Qawqji's attack on Kibbutz Mishmar Ha-Emek on 4 April was in direct response to the Jewish mass expulsions that had started around 15 March. The first villages to go on that day had been Ghubayya al-Tahta and Ghubayya al-Fawqa, each with more than 1000 inhabitants. Later the same day it was the turn of the smaller village of Khirbat al-Ras. Occupation here, too, carried the by now familiar features of ethnic cleansing: expulsion of the people and destruction of their houses.

After the Mishmar Ha-Emek incident it was the turn of even larger villages: Abu Shusha, Kafrayn, Abu Zurayq, Mansi, and Naghnaghiyya (pronounced Narnariya): the roads east to Jenin soon filled with thousands of Palestinians whom the Jewish troops had expelled and sent walking, not far from where the bastion of Zionist socialism had its kibbutzim. The smaller village of Wadi Ara, with 250 people, was the last to be wiped out in April.[48]

Here, too, the Irgun contributed its share of the continued destruction of Palestine's countryside. They completed the vengeful attack on the remaining villages in Marj Ibn Amir, while the British Mandate troops were still there: Sabbarin, Sindiyana, Barieka, Khubbeiza and Umm al-Shauf. Some of the people in these villages fled under the heavy mortar fire of the attacking forces, while others who waved white flags signaling surrender were instantly exiled. In Sabbarin, the Irgun bandits, angered by the fact that they encountered some armed resistance, as punishment kept the women, old men and children confined for a few days within barbed wire – very much like the cages in which Palestinians today are kept for hours at checkpoints in the West Bank when they fail to present the right permits. Seven young Palestinian men found carrying arms were executed on the spot by Jewish troops, who then expelled the rest of the villagers to Umm al-Fahm, then not yet in Jewish hands.[49]

Each phase or operation in the various geographical locations produced new patterns of behaviour that were later adopted by the rest of the troops. A few days after the village of Kafrayn had been occupied and its people expelled, the army practised its skills on the now empty village, wiping it off the face of the earth.[50] This type of manoeuvre was used again and again, long after the war of 1948 had ended, well into the 1950s.

The operation in Safad's hinterland was already motivated less by rage than by efficient planning, and had been given the ominous codename of 'Broom' (*matateh*). It began with the cleansing of the villages along the Tiberias–Safad highway. The first village to go was Ghuwayr. After Tiberias fell, the mukhtar immediately realised what was in store for his village, as it was the nearest to the city. He asked Adib Shishakly, the head of the ALA volunteers, to help, and suggested distributing arms to the villagers, but Shishakly refused. The news demoralised the villagers, and women and children began fleeing to Rama on the road to Acre on the other side of the Galilee mountains. The mukhtar proceeded to recruit fifty peasants who, armed with their *hartoosh* (old hunting guns from the First World War) awaited the Jewish assault. On 22 April, the Jews, as was to become their custom, first sent a delegation proposing a collective evacuation of the men without fighting. In this case, however, the delegation was unusual: it was made up of people who in the past had maintained friendly ties with the village, and the Palestinians who were present at the meeting later recalled their apologetic tone when they explained that all the villages on the road between Tiberias and Safad were scheduled to be expelled. The mukhtar did not reveal the fact that the village was almost deserted and avowed that the people 'will defend their homes'.[51]

After the swift occupation of the village, another pattern emerged. A Jewish soldier went out on the roof of one of the houses and inquired whether among the men captured there were any Druze. 'If so', he shouted, 'they can stay. The rest have to go to Lebanon.' But even that option was not open to all, as the occupying force decided to conduct a selection process before 'allowing' the villagers to leave for Lebanon. Such selection operations were to become the model for the following expulsions, and one that has remained deeply engraved in the collective memory of Palestinians from the Nakba years, haunting them to this very day. Young men between the age of ten and thirty were taken aside and sent to prison camps. Forty men of Ghuwayr were thus separated from their families for eighteen months, languishing in pens.

The village of Ghuwayr was frequently visited by UN observers checking first-hand how the partition resolution was being implemented. They witnessed the expulsions. Representatives of the western media, including a *New York Times* reporter, were still filing stories about individual villages, although the public interest in their fate was by this time diminishing; in any case, western readers were never given the full picture of events.[52] Furthermore, it seems that none of the foreign correspondents dared openly to criticise the actions of the Jewish nation just three years after the Holocaust.

It was in and around Haifa that the ethnic cleansing operation gathered momentum, its deadly pace heralding the destruction to come. Fifteen villages – some of them small, that is with less than 300 people, some of them huge, with around 5000 – were expelled in quick succession. Abu Shusha, Abu Zurayq, Arab al-Fuqara, Arab al-Nufay'at, Arab Zahrat al-Dumayri, Balad Al-Shaykh, Damun, Khirbat al-Kasayir, Khirbat al-Manshiyya, Rihaniyya, Khirbat al-Sarkas, Khirbat Sa'sa, Wa'rat al-Sarris and Yajur were wiped off Palestine's map within a sub-district full of British soldiers, UN emissaries and foreign reporters.

Expulsion and flight were not enough to save the villagers. Many of them were hunted down by the Marxist kibbutzniks of Hashomer Ha-Tza'ir, who swiftly and efficiently looted their houses before detonating them. We have records of the verbal condemnation by concerned Zionist politicians from this period – which provided 'new historians' in Israel with material on the atrocities they had not encountered in other archival sources.[53] Today, these documents of complaint read more as an attempt by 'sensitive' Jewish politicians and soldiers to absolve their consciences. They form part of an Israeli ethos that can best be described as 'shoot and cry', the title of a collection of expressions of supposedly moral remorse by Israeli soldiers who had participated in a small-scale ethnic cleansing operation in the June 1967 war. These concerned soldiers and officers were then invited by the popular Israeli writer Amoz Oz and his friends to perform a 'rite of exoneration' in the Red House before it was demolished. Back in 1948, three years after the Holocaust, similar remonstrations served to ease the troubled consciences of Jewish soldiers involved in atrocities and war crimes against a largely defenseless civilian population.

Crying aloud while killing and expelling innocent people was one tactic for dealing with the moral implications of Plan D. The other one was dehumanizing the Palestinians who, as the Jewish Agency had promised the UN, were to become full citizens of the State of Israel. Instead, they were expelled, imprisoned or killed: 'Our army marches forward and conquers Arab villages and their inhabitants flee like mice,' wrote Yossef Weitz.[54]

The spectrum of military activity was still quite wide in April. Unlike in later months when vast areas were to be cleansed, in April some villages were still left intact; other villagers suffered a worse fate than expulsion and were subjected to massacres. The military orders reflected this spectrum when they distinguished between two kinds of action to be taken against Palestinian villages: cleansing (le-taher) and harassing (le-hatrid). Harassment was never specified. It consisted of the random shelling of cities, towns and villages and hit-or-miss fire on civilian traffic.[55] On 14 April, Ben-Gurion wrote to Sharett: 'From day to day we expand our occupation. We occupy new villages and we have just begun.'[56]

In some of the villages that were close to urban centres, the Jewish troops followed a policy of massacres in order to precipitate the flight of the people in the cities and towns nearby. This was the case of Nasr al-Din near Tiberias, Ayn al-Zaytun near Safad, and Tirat Haifa near Haifa. In all three of these villages, groups of men that were, in the parlance of the Hagana, 'males between the age of 10 and 50', were executed in order to intimidate and terrorise the village population and those living in the nearby towns.[57]

Out of the three massacres, historians do not yet have the full picture for Nasr al-Din, but the other two are well documented, the most well-known of which is Ayn al-Zaytun.

Ayn al-Zaytun

Ayn al-Zaytun is the best known of the three massacres because its story formed the basis for the only epic novel on the Palestinian catastrophe we have so far, *Bab al-Shams* by Elias Khoury. The events in the village were also chronicled in a semi-fictional Israeli novella on the period, Netiva Ben-Yehuda's *Between the Knots*.[58] *Bab al-Shams* was made into a film, a French-Egyptian co-production.[59] The scenes on the screen closely resemble the descriptions we find in *Between the Knots*, which Ben-Yehuda largely based on reports in the military archives and on oral recollections. The film also faithfully represents the beauty of the village, which lay in a low-lying canyon bisecting the high mountains of the Galilee on the road between Mayrun and Safad, and was graced by a stream of fresh water surrounded by hot mineral pools.

The village's strategic location, a mile west of Safad, made it an ideal target for occupation. It was also coveted by local Jewish settlers, who had started buying land nearby and who maintained an uneasy relationship with the villagers towards the end of the Mandate. Operation 'Broom' provided a chance for the Hagana's elite unit, the Palmach, not only to cleanse the village in accordance with Plan Dalet on 2 May 1948, but also to settle 'old accounts', namely the hostility with which the Palestinian villagers had viewed and received the settlers.

The operation was entrusted to Moshe Kalman, who had already successfully supervised savage attacks on Khisas, Sa'sa and Husayniyya in the same distinct. His troops encountered very little resistance, as the Syrian volunteers positioned there left hurriedly once the shelling of the village started at dawn: heavy mortar bombardment followed by the systematic throwing of hand grenades. Kalman's forces entered the village towards noon. Women, children, old people and a few younger men who had not left with the Syrian volunteers came out of hiding waving a white flag. They were immediately herded into the village centre.[60]

The film then re-enacts the search-and-arrest – in this case the search-and-execute – routine as performed by the special intelligence units of the Hagana. First, they brought in a hooded informer who scrutinised the men lined up in the village square; those whose names appeared on a pre-prepared list the intelligence officers had brought with them were identified. The men selected were then taken to another location and shot dead. When other men rebelled or protested, they were killed as well. In one incident, which the film captured extremely well, one of the villagers, Yusuf Ahmad Hajjar, told his captors that he, like the others, had surrendered and thus 'expected to be treated humanely'. The Palmach commander slapped him in the face and then ordered him, by way of punishment, to pick thirty-seven teenagers at random. While the rest of the villagers were forced into the storage room of the village mosque, the teenagers were shot with their hands tied behind their backs.

In his book, Hans Lebrecht offers another glimpse of the atrocities, and explains that 'at the end of May 1948, I was ordered by the military unit in which I served to build a temporary pump station, and to divert the "deserted" village's stream, Ayn Zaytun, to supply water to the battalion. The village had been totally destroyed, and among the debris there were many bodies. In particular, we found many bodies of women, children and babies near the local mosque. I convinced the army to burn the bodies'.[61]

These graphic descriptions are also found in the Hagana military reports,[62] but how many of Ayn al-Zaytun's villagers were actually executed is hard to tell. The military documents reported that all in all, including the executions, seventy people had been shot; other sources give a much higher number. Netiva Ben-Yehuda was a member of the Palmach and was in the village when the execution happened, but she preferred to tell the story in a fictionalised way. However, her story offers a chilling detailed description of the way the men of the village were shot while handcuffed, giving the number executed as several hundred:

> But Yehonathan continued to yell, and suddenly he turned with his back to Meirke, and walked away furiously, all the time continuing to complain: 'He is out of his mind! Hundreds of people are lying there tied! Go and kill them! Go and waste hundreds of people! A madman kills people bound like this and only a madman wastes all the ammunition on them! ... I don't know who they had in mind, who is coming to inspect them, but I understand it's become urgent, suddenly we have to untie the knots around these POWs' hands and legs, and then I realized they are all dead, 'problem solved'.[63]

According to this account the massacre, as we know from many other mass killings, occurred not only as 'punishment' for 'impertinence' but also because the Hagana had as yet no POW camps for the large numbers of villagers captured. But even after such camps were set up, massacres occurred when large groups of villagers were captured, as in Tantura and Dawaymeh after 15 May 1948.

Oral histories, which provided Elias Khoury with the material for *Bab al-Shams*, also reinforce the impression that the archival material does not tell the full story: it is economical about the methods employed and misleading about the number of people killed on that fateful day in May 1948.

As noted, each village served as a precedent that would become part of a pattern and a model that then facilitated more systematic expulsions. In Ayn al-Zaytun, the villagers were taken to the edge of the village where the Jewish troops then started firing shots over their heads as they ordered them to flee. The routine procedures were followed as well: the people were stripped of all their belongings before being banished from their homeland.

The Palmach later seized the nearby village, Biriyya, and, as in Ayn al-Zaytun, ordered all the houses to be burnt in order to demoralize the Arabs of Safad.[64] Only two villages remained in the area. The Hagana now faced a more complicated task: how to similarly homogenize, or rather 'Judaize', the Marj Ibn Amir region and the vast plains that stretched between the valley and the River Jordan, all the way eastwards to occupied Baysan, and all the way north up to the city of Nazareth, which was still free in those days.

Completing the mission in the East

It was Yigael Yadin who in April demanded a more determined effort to depopulate this vast area. He seemed to suspect the troops of not being enthusiastic enough, and wrote directly to several members of the kibbutzim in the vicinity to check if the troops had indeed occupied and destroyed the villages they had been ordered to eliminate.[65]

However, the soldiers' hesitations were not for lack of motivation or zeal. It was, in fact, the intelligence officers who restricted the operations. In part of the area, especially close to the city of Nazareth, all the way down to Afula, there were large clans who had cooperated – read: 'collaborated' – with them for years. Should they be expelled as well?

Local intelligence officers, such as Palti Sela, were particularly concerned about the fate of one huge clan: the Zu'bis. Palti Sela wanted them to be exempted. In an interview he gave in 2002 he explained that he was not sure how, in the haste of the operation, they would be able to select the right people. It all depended, he remembered, on his ability to tell the difference between them and the others: 'The Zu'bis were always different in their external look from the other villagers. The men, not the females. You could not tell the difference with the females, neither among the old males.' In any case, he later regretted the effort as the Zu'bis in the end proved not that cooperative and after 1948 had reinforced their Palestinian identity. 'Today they are "cholera", (Hebrew colloquial for scum) he told his interviewer, adding that they 'spit into the plate that fed them.'[66]

Eventually, it was decided to leave intact those villages that had a large share of the Zu'biyya clan. The most 'difficult' decision concerned the village of Sirin as it had only a few members of the clan; as we saw, the whole village was eventually expelled. Palti Sela wrote a letter to the heads of the families: 'Although you are part of the seven villages that were allowed to stay, we cannot protect you. I suggest you all leave for Jordan,'[67] which they did.

For many years, his fellow kibbutzniks refused to forgive him for one village that he had 'saved': the village of Zarain. 'Behind my back, people call me traitor, but I am proud,' he told his interviewer many years later.[68]

SUCCUMBING TO A SUPERIOR POWER

One of the major indications that the Jewish forces had the upper hand in 1948, and that the Jewish community in Palestine as a whole was far from facing the fate of extinction and destruction the official Zionist myth paints for us, was the decision of several ethnic minorities in the country to leave the Palestinian camp and join the Jewish forces.

The first and most important of these were the Druze, a religious sect that regards itself as Muslim although Islamic orthodoxy does not accept their claim. The Druze emerged as an offshoot of the Ismailis, themselves a splinter group of Shia Islam. Particularly important in this context are the Druze who had joined the ALA when it entered the country. In the beginning of April 1948, 500 of them deserted the ALA to join the Jewish forces.

How this took place forms one of the more curious chapters in the 1948 war. The deserters first pleaded with the Jewish commanders in the Galilee that before they changed sides, they would participate in a phony battle and be taken captive, and only then would they declare their loyalty to Zionism. Such a battle was duly staged near the town of Shafa'Amr, between the villages of Khirbat al-Kasayir and Hawsha – both later destroyed – and the Druze then signed a pompous-sounding 'treaty of blood'.[69]

Khirbat al-Kasayir and Hawsha were the first two villages Jewish troops attacked and occupied within the area the UN partition resolution had allocated to a Palestinian state. These attacks highlight the determination of the Zionist movement to occupy as much of Palestine as possible, even before the end of the Mandate.

One of the more tragic consequences of their defection was that the Druze troops became the main vehicle for the Jews to carry out the ethnic cleansing of the Galilee. Their alliance with the Zionist movement has inexorably alienated the Druzes from the rest of the Palestinians. Only recently do we find a younger generation seemingly beginning to rebel against this isolation, but also discovering how difficult this proves in a patriarchal society ruled firmly by its elders and spiritual leaders.

Another sect, the Circassians, who had several villages in the north of the country, also decided to show allegiance to the powerful Jewish military presence, and 350 of them joined the Jewish forces in April. This mixture of Druze and Circassians would form the nucleus for the future Border Police of Israel, the main military unit policing, first, the Arab areas in pre-1967 Israel, and then enforcing Israel's occupation of the West Bank and the Gaza Strip after 1967.

ARAB REACTIONS

When the Jewish forces occupied and destroyed the first villages in December 1947, it seemed that Galilee was the only area where there was a chance of stopping these assaults, with the help of Fawzi al-Qawqji. He commanded an army of 2000 men and impressed the local population with a series of attacks he conducted against isolated Jewish settlements (as have other units coming in via today's West Bank). But these were ultimately unsuccessful attempts and never caused any significant change in the balance of power. Al-Qawqji was limited in his ability because of the strategy he followed of dividing his troops into small units and sending them to as many cities, towns and villages as possible, where they then formed inadequate defence forces.

The presence of such an army of volunteers could have caused the situation to deteriorate further, pushing Palestine into a direct confrontation, but this did not happen. On the contrary, having attacked a series of isolated settlements as well as the Jewish convoys that came to assist them, al-Qawqji began seeking a truce in January, and continued this all through February and March 1948. Realising that the Jews enjoyed superiority in every military parameter, he tried to negotiate directly with the Consultancy, some of whose members he knew from the 1930s. At the end of March, he met Yehoshua Palmon, apparently with the blessing of Transjordan's King Abdullah. He offered Palmon a non-aggression pact that would keep the Jewish forces within the designated Jewish state, and would eventually allow negotiations over a cantonised Palestine. His proposals, needless to say, were rejected. Still, al-Qawqji never conducted a significant offensive, nor could he wage one, until the Jewish forces pushed into the areas the UN had allocated to the Arab state.

Al-Qawqji offered not only a cease-fire but also to bring the issue of a Jewish presence in Palestine back to the Arab League to discuss its future. However, Palmon was sent more as a spy than a delegate for negotiations: he was struck by the poor equipment and lack of motivation to fight among the ALA. This was the main piece of information the Consultancy wanted to hear.[70]

Al-Qawqji's appearance was accompanied by the arrival in the southern coastal plain of Muslim Brotherhood volunteers from Egypt. They were full of enthusiasm, but totally ineffective as soldiers or troops, as was quickly proven when the villages they were supposed to defend were occupied, emptied and destroyed in quick succession.

In January 1948, the level of war rhetoric in the Arab world had reached new heights, but the Arab governments by and large never moved beyond talking about the need to salvage Palestine, at the same time that both the local media and dailies, such as *Filastin*, and the foreign press, especially *The New York Times*, were methodically reporting Jewish attacks on Palestinian villages and neighbourhoods.

The Arab League's general secretary, Azzam Pasha, an Egyptian politician, hoped at that point that the UN would re-intervene and absolve the Arab states from direct confrontation in Palestine.[71] But the international organisation was at a loss. Intriguingly, the UN had never posed the question of how it should act if the Palestinians were to decide to reject the partition plan. The UN had left the issue open while its officials, through the good services of countries such as Britain and France, inquired only whether neighbouring Arab countries might annex the areas allocated to the Palestinians, and were basically satisfied to learn that one such neighbour, Jordan, was already negotiating with the Jews a possible takeover of 'Arab' Palestine. The Jordanians eventually did gain control over that area, which became known as the West Bank, most of it annexed without a shot being fired. The other Arab leaders were unwilling to play the game as yet, so they kept up the rhetoric that their intervention was for the sake of helping the Palestinians liberate Palestine, or at least salvage parts of it.

The Arab decision as to how much to intervene and assist was directly affected by developments on the ground. And on the ground they watched – politicians with growing dismay, intellectuals and journalists with horror – the beginning of a depopulation process unfolding in front of their eyes. They had enough representatives in the area to be fully aware of the intent and scope of the Jewish operations. Few of them were in any doubt at that early stage, in the beginning of 1948, of the potential disaster awaiting the Palestinian people. But they procrastinated, and postponed, for as long as they could, the inevitable military intervention, and then were only too happy to terminate it sooner rather than later: they knew full well not only that the Palestinians were defeated, but also that their armies stood no chance against the superior Jewish forces. In fact, they sent troops into a war they knew they had little or no chance of winning.

Many of the Arab leaders were cynical about the looming catastrophe in Palestine, and few were genuinely concerned. But even the latter needed time to assess, not so much the situation as the possible implications of any involvement on their precarious positions back home. Egypt and Iraq were embroiled in the final stages of their own wars of liberation, and Syria and Lebanon were young countries that had just won independence.[72] Only when the Jewish forces intensified their actions and their true intentions became fully exposed did Arab governments design some sort of a coordinated reaction. In order not to be sucked into a whirlwind that could undermine their already shaky standing in their own societies, they transferred the decision to their regional outfit, the Arab League Council, made up, as mentioned above, of the Arab states' foreign ministers. This was an ineffective body as its decisions could be rejected, freely misinterpreted or, if accepted, only partly implemented. This body dragged out its discussions even after the reality in rural and urban Palestine had become too painfully clear to be ignored, and only at the end of April 1948 was it decided that they would send troops into Palestine. By then a quarter of a million Palestinians had already been expelled, two hundred villages destroyed and scores of towns emptied.

It was in many ways al-Qawqji's defeat in Marj Ibn Amir that convinced the Arab leaders they would have to send regular forces. Al-Qawqji had failed to occupy Kibbutz Mishmar Ha-Emeq after ten days of fighting which had begun on April 4, the only Arab offensive action before May 1948.

Before the final decision to enter was taken, on 30 April, responses from the Arab states varied. All were asked by the Council to send arms and volunteers, but not all complied with the request. Saudi Arabia and Egypt pledged small-scale financial help, Lebanon promised a limited number of guns, and it seems that only Syria was willing to engage in proper military preparations, also persuading its Iraqi neighbour to train and send volunteers into Palestine.[73]

There was no lack of volunteers. Many people in the surrounding Arab countries came out and demonstrated against their governments' inaction; thousands of young men were willing to sacrifice their life for the Palestinians. Much has been written about this strong outpouring of sentiment but it remains an enigma – classifying it as pan-Arabism hardly does it justice. Perhaps the best explanation one can offer is that Palestine and Algeria became models for a fierce and bold anti-colonialist struggle, a confrontation that inflamed the national fervour of young Arabs around the Middle East, whereas in the rest of the Arab world national liberation came about through drawn-out diplomatic negotiations, always far less exciting. But I stress again, this is only a partial analysis of the willingness of young Baghdadis or Damascenes to leave everything behind for the sake of what they must have regarded as a sacred, though by no means a religious, mission.

The odd man out in this matrix was King Abdullah of Transjordan. He used the new situation to intensify his negotiations with the Jewish Agency over a joint agreement in post-Mandatory Palestine. While his army had units inside Palestine, and some of them were, here and there, willing to help the villagers protect their houses and lands, they were largely restrained by their commanders. Fawzi al-Qawqji's diary reveals the ALA commander's growing frustration with the unwillingness of the Arab Legion units stationed in Palestine to cooperate with his troops.[74]

During the Jewish operations between January and May 1948, when around 250,000 Palestinians were driven by force from their homes, the Legion stood idly by. In fact, it was in January that the Jordanians and the Jews had cemented their unwritten agreement. In early February 1948 the Jordanian prime minister had flown to London to report on the conclusion of their tacit alliance with the Jewish leadership over the partition of post-Mandatory Palestine between the Jordanians and the Jewish state: the Jordanians were to annex most of the areas allocated to the Arabs in the partition resolution, and in return would not join the military operations against the Jewish state. The British gave the scheme their blessing.[75] The Arab Legion, the Jordanian army, was the best trained in the whole Arab world. It matched, and in some areas was even superior to, the Jewish troops. But it was confined by the King and his British General Chief of Staff, John Glubb Pasha, to act only in those areas the Jordanians deemed theirs: East Jerusalem and the area now known as the West Bank.

The final meeting that determined the limited role the Legion was to play in the rescue of Palestine took place on 2 May 1948. A top-ranking Jewish officer, Shlomo Shamir, met with two senior Legion officers, British, as most of them were: Colonel Goldie and Major Crocker. The Jordanian guests brought a message from their king saying he recognised the Jewish state, but wondered whether the Jews 'wanted to take the whole of Palestine?' Shamir was candid: 'We could, if we wanted to; but this is a political question.' The officers then explained where the Jordanians' main apprehensions lay: they had noticed that the Jewish forces were occupying and cleansing areas that were within the UN-designated Arab state, such as Jaffa. Shamir responded by justifying the Jaffa operation as necessary for safeguarding the road to Jerusalem. Shamir then made it clear to the emissaries from Jordan that, as far as the Zionsts were concerned, the UN designated Arab state had shrunk to include only the West Bank, which the Israelis were willing to 'leave' for the Jordanians.[76]

The meeting ended with an abortive attempt by the Jordanian officers to come to an agreement over the future of Jerusalem. If the Jewish Agency were willing to partition Palestine with the Jordanians, why not apply the same principle to Jerusalem? As Ben-Gurion's faithful proxy, Shamir rejected the offer. Shamir knew the Zionist leader was convinced his army was strong enough to take the city as a whole. An entry in his diary a few days later, on 11 May, shows that Ben-Gurion was aware the Legion would fight fiercely over Jerusalem and, if necessary, for its overall share in post-Mandatory Palestine, that is, the West Bank. This was duly confirmed two days later when Golda Meir met King Abdullah in Amman (on 13 May), where the king seemed more tense than ever before because of the double game he was playing in his effort to come out on top: promising the member states of the League to head the military effort of the Arab countries in Palestine on the one hand, and striving to reach an agreement with the Jewish state on the other.[77]

At the end of the day, the latter became decisive for the course of action he would take. Abdullah did everything he could to be seen to be taking a serious part in the overall Arab effort against the Jewish state, but in practice his main objective was to secure Israeli consent for the Jordanian annexation of the West Bank.

Sir Alec Kirkbride was the British representative in Amman, a position that combined those of Ambassador and High Commissioner. On 13 May 1948, Kirkbride wrote to Ernest Bevin, Britain's foreign secretary:

> There have been negotiations between the Arab Legion and the Hagana which have been conducted by British officers of the Arab Legion. It is understood that the object of these top secret negoti-ations is to define the areas of Palestine to be occupied by the two forces.

Bevin replied:

> I am reluctant to do anything that might prejudice the success of these negotiations, which appear to aim at avoiding hostility between the Arabs and the Jews. The implementation of this agreement depends on the British officers of the Legion. That is why we should not withdraw the Legion officers [from Palestine].[78]

But Ben-Gurion never took for granted that the Jordanians would stick to the limited role he had set aside for them, which reinforces the impression that he felt confident the new state had enough military power to successfully confront even the Legion while simultaneously continuing the ethnic cleansing.

At the end of the day, the Legion had to fight for their annexation, notwithstanding Jordan's collusion with Israel. At first the Jordanians were allowed to take over the areas they wanted without a shot being fired, but a few weeks after the end of the Mandate the Israeli army tried to wrest parts of it back. David Ben-Gurion seemed to regret his decision not to exploit the war more fully in order to enlarge the Jewish state even beyond the seventy-eight per cent he coveted. The general Arab impotence seemed to give the Zionist movement an opportunity that was too good to be missed. However, he underestimated the Jordanian determination. Those parts of Palestine that King Abdullah was adamant were his, the Legion successfully defended until the war was over. In other words, the Jordanian occupation of the West Bank at first came about thanks to a prior agreement with the Jews, but it remained in Hashemite hands thereafter due to the tenacious defensive efforts of the Jordanians and the Iraqi forces that helped repel Israeli attacks. It is possible to see this episode from a different angle: by annexing the West Bank, the Jordanians saved 250,000 Palestinians from being ousted – until, that is, they were occupied by Israel in 1967 and subjected – as they still are – to new waves of expulsion, be they more measured and slow. The actual Jordanian policy in the very last days of the Mandate is detailed in the next chapter.

As for the Palestinian leadership, what remained of it was fragmented and in total disarray. Some of its members left hurriedly and, they hoped in vain, temporarily. Very few of them wished to stay and confront the Jewish aggression in December 1947 and the onset of the cleansing operations in January 1948, but some did stay behind, and remained official members of the national committees. Their activities were supposed to be coordinated and supervised by the Arab Higher Committee, the unofficial government of the Palestinians since the 1930s, but half of its members had by now also left and those remaining found it difficult to cope. For all their failings in the past, however, they stood alongside their communities almost to the bitter end, although they could easily have opted to leave. They were Emil Ghori, Ahmad Hilmi, Rafiq Tamimi, Mu'in al-Madi and Husyan al-Khalidi. Each of them was in contact with several local national committees and with al-Hajj Amin al-Husayni, chairman of the Arab Higher Committee, who followed events with his close associates Shaykh Hasan Abu Su'ud and Ishaq

Darwish, in Cairo, where he now resided. Amin al-Husayni had been exiled in 1937 by the British. Would he have been able to return in those days of chaos and turmoil, given the British presence in the land? He never tried to go back so the point is moot. His relative, Jamal al-Husayni, acting chairman of the Arab Higher Committee in his absence, left in January for the US to try to initiate a belated diplomatic campaign against the UN resolution. The Palestinian community for all intents and purposes was a leaderless nation.

In this context, Abd al-Qadir al-Husayni should be mentioned once more since he tried to organise a paramilitary unit from among the villagers themselves to protect them. His army, the 'Holy War Army', a rather grand name for the shaky outfit he headed, held on until 9 April, when it was defeated and Abd al-Qadir was killed by the Hagana forces that outnumbered them with their superior equipment and military experience.

A similar effort was attempted in the Greater Jaffa area by Hasan Salameh, whom I have already mentioned, and Nimr Hawari (who later surrendered to the Jews and became the first Palestinian judge in 1950s Israel). They tried to transform their scouts' movements into paramilitary units, but these, too, were defeated within a few weeks.[79]

Thus, prior to the end of the Mandate, neither the Arab volunteers from outside Palestine nor the paramilitary troops on the inside put the Jewish community at any serious risk of either losing the battle or being forced to surrender. Far from it; all that these foreign and local forces tried, but were unable, to do was to protect the local Palestinian population against Jewish aggression.

Israeli, and in particular American, public opinion, however, succeeded in perpetuating the myth of potential destruction or a 'second Holocaust' awaiting the future Jewish state. Exploiting this mythology, Israel was later able to secure massive support for the state in Jewish communities around the world, while demonising the Arabs as a whole, and the Palestinians in particular, in the eyes of the general public in the US. The reality on the ground was, of course, almost the complete opposite: Palestinians were facing massive expulsion. The month that Israeli historiography singles out as the 'toughest' actually saw the Palestinians simply attempting to be saved from that fate, rather than being preoccupied with the destruction of the Jewish community. When it was over, nothing stood in the way of the cleansing troops of Israel.

TOWARDS THE 'REAL WAR'

On the face of it, from the Palestinian point of view, the situation seemed to improve towards the second half of April 1948. Abdullah informed his Jewish interlocutors that the Arab League had decided to send regular armies into Palestine: the events in Palestine in the months of March and April left the leaders of the Arab world no other choice. They now began to prepare in earnest for a military intervention. Then from Washington came the unexpected news that the State Department was pushing towards a novel American approach. US representatives on the ground were by now fully aware of the expulsions that were going on and had suggested to their chiefs back home to halt the implementation of the partition plan and try to work towards an alternative solution.

Already by 12 March 1948, the State Department had drafted a new proposal to the UN, which suggested an international trusteeship over Palestine for five years, during which the two sides would negotiate an agreed solution. It has been suggested that this was the most sensible American proposal ever put forward in the history of Palestine, the like of which, alas, was never repeated. In the words of Warren Austin, the US ambassador to the United Nations: 'The USA position is that the partition of Palestine is no longer a viable option.'[80]

Member states of the UN coming together in Flushing Meadows, New York, where the UN was located before it moved to its current high rise in Manhattan, liked the idea. It made a lot of sense to conclude that partition had failed to bring peace to Palestine and, in fact, was breeding more violence and bloodshed. However, while logic was one aspect to take into consideration, the wish not to antagonise a powerful domestic lobby was another, and in this case a superior one. Had it not been for highly effective pressure by the Zionist lobby on President Harry Truman, the course of Palestine's history could have run very differently. Instead, the Zionist sections of the American Jewish community learned an important lesson about their ability to impact American policy in Palestine (and later beyond, in the Middle East as a whole). In a longer process that continued through the 1950s and early 1960s, the Zionist lobby succeeded in sidelining the State Department's experts on the Arab world and left American Middle Eastern policy in the hands of Capitol Hill and the White House, where the Zionists wielded considerable influence.

But the victory on Capitol Hill was not easily won. The 'Arabists' in the State Department, reading more carefully the reports from the *New York Times* than the President's men, desperately tried to convice Truman, if not to substitute partition with trusteeship, at least to allow more time for rethinking the partition plan. They persuaded him to offer the two sides a three month armistice.

On 12 May, a Wednesday afternoon, the ordinary meeting of the *Matkal* and the Consultancy was postponed for a crucial meeting in a new body, the 'People's Board ', which was three days later to become the government of the State of Israel. Ben-Gurion claimed that almost all those present supported the decision to reject the American offer. Historians later claimed he had a difficult time passing the resolution, which meant not only rejecting the American plan but declaring, three days later, a state. This was not such an important meeting after all, as the Consultancy was already pushing ahead with its ethnic cleansing operations, which Ben-Gurion would not have allowed others in the Zionist political elite to halt, who were not privy in the past to the vision and the plan. The White House then went on to recognise the new state and the State Department was pushed again to its back bench on US policy on Palestine.[81]

On the last day of April, the Arab world had appointed the man most of its leaders knew had a secret agreement with the Jews to head the military operations against Palestine. No wonder that Egypt, the largest Arab state, waited until the failure of the last American initiative before deciding to join the military effort, something its leaders knew would end in a fiasco. The decision passed in the Egyptian Senate on 12 May left the Egyptian army with less than three days to prepare for the 'invasion', and its performance on the battlefield testified to this impossibly short period of preparation.[82] The other armies, as we shall see later, did not fare any better. Britain remained the last hope in those days of April and May, but nowhere in its Empire did Albion demonstrate such perfidious behaviour.

British Responsibility

Did the British know about Plan Dalet? One assumes they did, but it is not easy to prove. Highly striking is that after Plan Dalet was adopted, the British announced that they were no longer responsible for law and order in the areas where their troops were still stationed, and limited their activities to protecting these troops. This meant that Haifa and Jaffa and the whole coastal region between them were now one open space where the Zionist leadership could implement Plan Dalet without any fear of being thwarted or even confronted by the British army. Far worse was that the disappearance of the British from the countryside and the towns meant that in Palestine as a whole law and order totally collapsed. The newspapers of the day, such as the daily *Filastin*, reflected the people's anxiety about the rising level of such crimes as theft and burglary in the urban centres and looting around the villages. The withdrawal of British policemen from the cities and towns also meant, for example, that many Palestinians could no longer collect their salaries in the local municipalities: most of the governmental services were located in Jewish neighbourhoods in which they were likely to be assaulted.

No wonder one can still hear Palestinians say today: 'The main responsibility for our catastrophe lies with the British Mandate,' as Jamal Khaddura, a refugee from Suhmata near Acre, put it.[83] He bore this sense of betrayal with him throughout his life and re-articulated it in front of a joint British parliamentary Middle East commission of inquiry on the Palestinian refugees established in 2001. Other refugees who gave testimonies to this commission echoed Khaddura's bitterness and accusations of blame.

Indeed, the British avoided any serious intervention as early as October 1947, and stood idly by in the face of attempts by the Jewish forces to control outposts; nor did they try to stop small-scale infiltration by Arab volunteers. In December, they still had 75,000 troops in Palestine, but these were dedicated solely to safeguard the eviction of the Mandatory soldiers, officers and officials.

The British sometimes assisted in other, more direct, ways in the ethnic cleansing, by providing the Jewish leadership with ownership deeds and other vital data, which they had photocopied before destroying them, as was quite common in their decolonization process. This inventory added to the village files the final details the Zionists needed for the massive depopulation. Military force, and a brutal one at that, is the first requirement for expulsion and occupation, but bureaucracy is no less important for efficiently carrying out a huge cleansing operation that entails not only dispossession of the people but also the repossession of the spoils.

UN Betrayal

According to the Partition Resolution, the UN was to be present on the ground to supervise the implementation of its peace plan: the making of Palestine as a whole into an independent country, with two distinct states that were to form one economic unity. The resolution of 29 November 1947 included very clear imperatives. Among them, the UN pledged to prevent any attempt by either side to confiscate land that belonged to citizens of the other state, or the other national group – be it cultivated or uncultivated land, i.e., land that had lain fallow for about a year.

To the local UN emissaries' credit, it can be said that they at least sensed things were going from bad to worse and were tying to push for a re-evaluation of the partition policy, but they took no action beyond watching and reporting the beginning of the ethnic cleansing. The UN had only limited access to Palestine, since the British authorities forbade an organised UN outfit to be present on the ground, thereby ignoring that part of the Partition Resolution that demanded the presence of a United Nations committee. Britain allowed the cleansing to take place, in front of the eyes of its soldiers and officials, during the Mandate period, which came to an end at midnight on 14 May 1948, and hampered the UN efforts to intervene in a way that might have saved a number of Palestinians. After 15 May, there was no excuse for the way the UN abandoned the people whose land they had divided and whose welfare and lives they had surrendered to the Jews who, since the late nineteenth century, wished to uproot them and take their place in the country they deemed as theirs.

Chapter 6

The Phony War and the Real War Over Palestine: May 1948

I have no doubt a massacre took place in Tantura. I did not go out into the streets and shout it about. It is not exactly something to be proud of. But once the affair was publicized, one should tell the truth. After 52 years, the state of Israel is strong and mature enough to confront its past.

Eli Shimoni, senior officer in the Alexandroni Brigade, *Maariv*, 4 February 2001

Within weeks of the end of the Mandate, the Jewish troops had reached the vast majority of the isolated Jewish settlements. Only two of these were lost to the Arab Legion because they were in the area that both sides, prior to May 1948, had agreed Jordan would occupy and annex, i.e., the West Bank.[1] The Jordanians also insisted they should have at least half of Jerusalem, including the Old City that incorporated the Muslim sanctuaries, but also the Jewish quarter, but since there was no prior agreement on this they had to fight for it. They did so bravely and successfully. It was the only time the two sides were engaged in battle, and stands in complete contrast to the inaction the Arab Legion displayed when their units were stationed near Palestinian villages and towns the Israeli army had begun occupying, cleansing, and destroying.

When Ben-Gurion convened the Consultancy on 11 May he asked his colleagues to assess the possible implications of a more aggressive Jordanian campaign in the future. The bottom line of that meeting can be found in a letter Ben-Gurion sent to the commanders of the Hagana brigades telling them that the Legion's more offensive intentions should not distract their troops from their principal tasks: 'the cleansing of Palestine remained the prime objective of Plan Dalet' (he used the noun *bi'ur*, which means either 'cleansing the leaven' in Passover or 'root out', 'eliminate').[2]

Their calculation proved to be right. Although the Jordanian army was the strongest of the Arab forces and thus would have formed the most formidable foe for the Jewish state, it was neutralised from the very first day of the Palestine war by the tacit alliance King Abdullah had made with the Zionist movement. It is no wonder that the Arab Legion's English Commander-in-Chief, Glubb Pasha, dubbed the 1948 war in Palestine the 'Phony War'. Glubb was not only fully aware of the restrictions Abdullah had imposed on the Legion's actions, he was privy to the general pan-Arab consultations and preparations. Like the British military advisers of the various Arab armies – and there were many of them – he knew that the groundwork of the other Arab armies for a rescue operation in Palestine was quite ineffective – 'pathetic' some of his colleagues called it – and that included the ALA.[3]

The only change we find in the overall Arab conduct once the Mandate had ended was in the rhetoric. The drums of war were now sounding louder and more boisterously than before but they failed to cover the inaction, disarray and confusion that prevailed. The situation may have differed from one Arab capital to the next, but the overall picture was quite uniform. In Cairo, the government only decided to send troops to Palestine at the very last moment, two days before the end of the Mandate. The 10,000 troops it had set aside included a large contingent, almost fifty per cent, of Muslim Brotherhood volunteers. The members of this political movement – vowing to restore Egypt and the Arab world to the Orthodox ways of Islam – regarded Palestine as a crucial battlefield in the struggle against European imperialism. But in the 1940s the Brotherhood also regarded the Egyptian government as a collaborator with this imperialism, and when its more extreme members resorted to violence in their campaign, thousands of them were imprisoned. These were now released in May 1948 so that they could join the Egyptian expedition, but of course they had had no military training and, for all their fervour, were no match for the Jewish forces.[4]

Syrian forces were better trained and their politicians more committed, but only a few years after their own independence, following the French Mandate, the small number of troops the Syrians dispatched to Palestine performed so badly that even before the end of May 1948, the Consultancy had begun to consider expanding the Jewish state's borders on its north-eastern flank into Syria proper by annexing the Golan Heights.[5] Even smaller and less committed were the Lebanese units, which for most of the war were happy to remain on their side of the border with Palestine, where they reluctantly tried to defend the adjacent villages.

The Iraqi troops formed the last and most intriguing component of the all-Arab effort. They numbered a few thousand and had been ordered by their government to accept the Jordanian guideline: that is, not to attack the Jewish state, but just to defend the area allocated to King Abdullah, namely the West Bank. They were stationed in the northern part of the West Bank. However, they defied their politicians' orders and tried to play a more effective role. Because of this, fifteen villages in Wadi Ara, on the road between Afula and Hadera, were able to hold out and thus escape expulsion (they were ceded to Israel by the Jordanian government in the summer of 1949 as part of a bilateral armistice agreement).

For three weeks these Arab units – some provoked into action by their politicians' hypocrisy, others deterred by it – succeeded in entering and holding on to the areas the UN Partition Resolution had allocated to the Arab state. In a few places they were able to encircle isolated Jewish settlements located there and occupy them for a while, only to lose them again within a few days.

The Arab troops that entered Palestine quickly found out they had over-stretched their supply lines, which meant they stopped getting ammunition for their antiquated and quite often malfunctioning arms. Their officers then discovered that there was no coordinating hand between the various national armies, and that even when supply routes were open, the weaponry in their home countries was running out. Weapons were scarce since the Arab armies' main suppliers were Britain and France, who had declared an arms embargo on Palestine. This crippled the Arab armies but hardly affected the Jewish forces, who found a willing furnisher in the Soviet Union and in its new Eastern bloc.[6] As for the lack of coordination, this was the inevitable result of the decision by the Arab League to appoint King Abdullah as the supreme commander of the all-Arab army with an Iraqi general as the acting commander. While the Jordanians never looked back at those days of May, June and July of 1948, when they had done all they could to undermine the general Arab effort, the Iraqi revolutionary rulers who came to power in 1958 brought their generals to trial for their role in the catastrophe.

Still, there were enough Arab troops to engage the Jewish army in battle and provoke some courageous Jewish responses, especially around isolated Jewish communities in the heart of the UN-designated Arab state or at the extreme outer ends of the country, where Ben-Gurion had made a strategic decision to leave vulnerable Jewish outposts to fend for themselves when Arab units started entering Palestine on 15 May. Units of the Syrian army marched along the Damascus–Tiberias road that day and were engaged in battle around the four isolated settlements there: Mishamr Hayarden, Ayelet Hashahar, Haztor and Menahemiya. They succeeded in occupy-ing only Mishmar ha-Yarden, where they remained until the first day of the truce (11 June). In the words of the Israeli intelligence, they 'showed no offensive spirit' when they were later attacked and driven out of Palestine.[7]

Israeli historians later criticised Ben-Gurion for having temporarily abandoned these settlements.[8] From a purely military point of view, Ben-Gurion was right as none of them would ultimately remain in Arab hands anyway, and although the ethnic cleansing operation was obviously far more important and higher up on his agenda, he did care about the fate of these more remote spots.

This also explains why most of the heroic stories that have fed the Israeli mythology and collective memory of the 1948 war have their origin in these first three weeks of hostilities. The real war also included other tests of resilience and resolution on the Israeli side – Tel-Aviv, for instance, was bombarded several times in the first few days of the war by Egyptian airplanes – but these subsided and disappeared over the following weeks. However, the presence of the Arab troops was never enough to stop the ethnic cleansing – none of whose horror stories ever troubled the official and popular Israeli narrative, as they were totally erased from it.

Furthermore, the cleansing operations in the second half of May 1948 were no different from those of April and early May. In other words, the mass evictions were not affected by the end of the Mandate but went ahead uninterrupted. There had been ethnic cleansing on the day before 15 May 1948, and the same ethnic cleansing operations took place the day after. Israel had enough troops both to handle the Arab armies and to continue cleansing the land.

It should be clear by now that the Israeli foundational myth about a voluntary Palestinian flight the moment the war started – in response to a call by Arab leaders to make way for invading armies – holds no water. It is a sheer fabrication that there were Jewish attempts, as Israeli textbooks still insist today, to persuade Palestinians to stay. As we have seen, hundreds of thousands of Palestinians had already been expelled by force before the war began, and tens of thousands more would be expelled in the first week of the war. For most Palestinians, the date of 15 May 1948 was of no special significance at the time: it was just one more day in the horrific calendar of ethnic cleansing that had started more than five months earlier.[9]

DAYS OF TIHUR

Tihur is yet another Hebrew word for cleansing, literally meaning 'purifying'. After the Jewish state was declared on the evening of 14 May, the orders the units in the field received from above used the term frequently and explicitly. It was with this kind of language that the High Command chose to galvanise the Israeli soldiers before sending them on their way to destroy the Palestinian countryside and urban districts. This escalation in rhetoric was the only obvious difference from the previous month – otherwise the cleansing operations continued unabated.[10]

The Consultancy went on meeting, but less regularly as the Jewish state had become a *fait accompli* with a government, cabinet, military command, secret services, etc., all in place. Its members were no longer preoccupied with the master plan of expulsion: ever since Plan Dalet had been put into motion it had been working well, and needed no further coordination and direction. Their attention was now focused on whether they had enough troops to sustain a 'war' on two fronts: against the Arab armies and against the one million Palestinians who, according to international law, had become Israeli citizens on 15 May. By the end of May even these apprehensions had petered out.

If there was anything new about the way the Consultancy now functioned, it was only the physical move to a new building, on a hill top overlooking the evicted village of Shaykh Muwannis. This became the *Matkal*, the headquarters of the general staff of the Israeli army.[11] From this new vantage point, the Consultancy could literally observe the onslaught that had begun on 1 May against the nearby Palestinian villages. By no means the only operation that day, it was conducted simultaneously with identical operations in the east and the north. One brigade, the Alexandroni, was entrusted with the mission of cleansing the villages to the east and north of Tel-Aviv and Jaffa. It was then ordered to move north and, together with other units, start depopulating the Palestine coastline, all the way up to Haifa.

The orders had come on 12 May. 'You must between the 14th and 15th occupy and destroy: Tira, Qalansuwa and Qaqun, Irata, Danba, Iqtaba and Shuweika. Furthermore, you should occupy but not destroy Qalqilya [the city in the occupied West Bank, which Alexandroni failed to take and which today is totally enclosed by the eight-metre-high segregation wall Israel has erected].'[12] Within two days the next order arrived in the Alexandroni headquarters: 'You will attack and cleanse Tirat Haifa, Ayn Ghazal, Ijzim, Kfar Lam, Jaba, Ayn Hawd and Mazar.'[13]

Re-tracing the route the brigade followed, it appears the troops preferred to sweep the area systematically from south to north and accomplish the destruction of the villages in the order that seemed right to them, rather than according to the exact instruction of which village should be hit first. As completing the list was the overall goal, no clear priorities were mentioned. So the Alexandroni began with the villages north and east of Tel-Aviv: Kfar Saba and Qaqun, whose populations were duly expelled. In Qaqun the UN claimed, and testimonies by Jewish troops corroborated, that the takeover had involved a case of rape.

All in all, there were sixty-four villages within the area that stretched between Tel-Aviv and Haifa, a rectangle 100 kilometres long and fifteen to twenty kilometres wide. Only two of these villages were spared in the end: Furaydis and Jisr al-Zarqa. They had been scheduled for expulsion as well, but members of the neighbouring Jewish settlements convinced the army commanders to leave them unharmed, because they claimed they needed the villagers for unskilled labour in their farms and houses.[14] Today this rectangle is bisected by the two main highways that connect these two major cities: highways 2 and 4. Hundred of thousands of Israelis commute daily on these roads, most of them without having the slightest notion of the places they are driving through, let alone of their history. Jewish settlements, pine forests and commercial fishing ponds have replaced the Palestinian communities that once flourished there.

The Alexandroni's pace cleansing the coastal rectangle was horrific – within the second half of the month alone they cleansed the following villages: Manshiyya (in the Tul-Karem area), Butaymat, Khirbat al-Manara, Qannir, Khirbat Qumbaza and Khirbat al-Shuna. A small number of villages courageously put up strong resistance, and the Alexandroni Brigade was unable to take them; nevertheless, they were finally cleansed in July. That is, the ethnic cleansing operations in the central coastal plain developed in two phases: the first in May and the second in July. In the second half of May, the most important 'trophy' was the village of Tantura, which the Alexandroni captured on 21 May 1948.

THE MASSACRE AT TANTURA[15]

Tantura was one of the largest of the coastal villages and for the invading brigade it stuck like 'a bone in the throat', as the official Alexandroni war book puts it. Tantura's day came on 22 May.

Tantura was an ancient Palestinian village on the Mediterranean coast. It was a large village for the time, having around 1500 inhabitants whose livelihood depended on agriculture, fishing and menial jobs in nearby Haifa. On 15 May 1948, a small group of Tantura's notables, including the mukhtar of the village, met the Jewish intelligence officers, who offered them terms of surrender. Suspecting that surrender would lead to the villagers' expulsion, they rejected the offer.

A week later, on 22 May 1948, the village was attacked at night. At first, the Jewish commander in charge wanted to send a van into the village with a loudspeaker calling upon people to capitulate, but this scheme was not carried out.

The offensive came from all four flanks. This was uncommon; the brigade usually closed in on villages from three flanks, tactically creating an 'open gate' on the fourth flank through which they could drive the people out. Lack of coordination meant that the Jewish troops had fully encircled the village and consequently found themselves with a very large number of villagers on their hands.

Tantura's captured villagers were herded at gunpoint down to the beach. The Jewish troops then separated the men from the women and children, and expelled the latter to nearby Furaydis, where some of the men joined them a year and half later. Meanwhile, the hundreds of men collected on the beach were ordered to sit down and await the arrival of an Israeli intelligence officer, Shimshon Mashvitz, who lived in the nearby settlement of Givat Ada and in whose 'district' the village fell.

Mashvitz went along with a local collaborator, hooded as at Ayn al-Zaytun, and picked out individual men – again, in the eyes of the Israeli army, 'men' were all males between the ages of ten and fifty – and took them out in small groups to a spot further away where they were executed. The men were selected according to a pre-prepared list drawn from Tantura's village file, and included everybody who had participated in the 1936 Revolt, in attacks on Jewish traffic, who had contacts with the Mufti, and anyone else who had 'committed' one of the 'crimes' that automatically condemned them.

These were not the only men executed. Before the selection and killing process took place on the coast, the occupying unit had gone on a killing spree inside the houses and in the streets. Joel Skolnik, a sapper in the battalion, had been wounded in this attack, but after his hospitalisation heard from other soldiers that this had been 'one of the most shameful battles the Israeli army had fought.' According to him, sniper shots from within the village as the soldiers entered had caused the Jewish troops to run amok soon after the village was taken and before the scenes on the beach unfolded. The attack happened after the villagers had signaled their surrender by waving a white flag.

Solnik heard that two soldiers in particular had been doing the killing, and that they would have gone on had not some people from the nearby Jewish settlement of Zikhron Yaacov arrived and stopped them. It was the head of the Zikhron Yaacov settlement, Yaacov Epstein, who managed to call a halt to the orgy of killing in Tantura, but 'he came too late', as one survivor commented bitterly.

Most of the killing was done in cold blood on the beach. Some of the victims were first interrogated and asked about a 'huge cache' of weapons that had supposedly been hidden somewhere in the village. As they couldn't tell – there was no such stack of weapons – they were shot dead on the spot. Today, many of the survivors of these horrific events live in the Yarmuk refugee camp in Syria, coping only with great difficulty with life after the trauma of witnessing the executions.

This is how a Jewish officer described the executions at Tantura:

> Prisoners were led in groups to a distance of 200 metres aside and there they were shot. Soldiers would come to the commander-in-chief and say, 'My cousin was killed in the war.' His commander heard that and instructed the troops to take a group of five to seven people aside and execute them. Then a soldier came and said his brother had died in one of the battles. For one brother the retribution was higher. The commander ordered the troops to take a larger group and they were shot, and so on.

In other words, what took place in Tantura was the systematic execution of able-bodied young men by Jewish soldiers and intelligence officers. One eyewitness, Abu Mashaykh, was staying in Tantura with a friend, as he originally came from Qisarya, the village Jewish troops had already destroyed and expelled in February 1948. He saw with his own eyes the execution of eighty-five young men of Tantura, who were taken in groups of ten and then executed in the cemetery and the nearby mosque. He thought even more were executed, and estimated that the total number could have been 110. He saw Shimshon Mashvitz supervising the whole operation: 'He had a "Sten" [sub-machine gun] and killed them.' Later he adds: 'They stood next to the wall, all facing the wall. He came from the back and shot them in the head, all of them.' He further testified how Jewish soldiers were watching the executions with apparent relish.

Fawzi Muhammad Tanj, Abu Khalid, also witnessed the executions. In the account he gives the village men were separated from the women, and then groups of seven to ten were taken and executed. He witnessed the killing of ninety people.

Mahmud Abu Salih of Tantura also reported the killing of ninety people. He was seventeen at the time and his most vivid memory is the killing of a father in front of his children. Abu Salih kept in touch with one of the sons, who went out of his mind seeing his father executed and never recovered. Abu Salih saw the execution of seven male members of his own family.

Mustafa Abu Masri, known as Abu Jamil, was thirteen at the time, but was probably mistaken for being around ten during the selection and thus was sent to the group of women and children, which saved him. A dozen members of his family, aged between ten and thirty, were less fortunate and he witnessed them being shot. The sequence of events he relates makes for chilling reading. His father ran into a Jewish officer whom the family knew and trusted, and so he sent his family away with that officer: he himself was later shot. Abu Jamil recalled 125 people being killed in summary executions. He saw Shimson Mashvitz walking among the people who had been collected on the beach, carrying a whip, lashing out at them 'just for the fun of it'. Anis Ali Jarban told similar horror stories about Mashvitz. He came from the nearby village of Jisr al-Zarqa and had fled with his family to Tantura, thinking the larger village would be safer.

When the rampage in the village was over and the executions had come to an end, two Palestinians were ordered to dig mass graves under the supervision of Mordechai Sokoler, of Zikhron Yaacov, who owned the tractors that had been brought in for the gruesome job. In 1999, he said he remembered burying 230 bodies; the exact number was clear in his mind: 'I lay them one by one in the grave.'

Several more Palestinians who took part in the digging of the mass graves told of the horrific moment when they realised they were about to be killed themselves. They were only saved because Yaacov Epstein, who had intervened in the frenzy of violence in the village, arrived and also stopped the killing on the beach. Abu Fihmi, one of the eldest and most respected members of the village, was one of those recruited to first identify the bodies and then help carry them to the graves: Shimon Mashvitz ordered him to list the bodies, and he counted ninety-five. Jamila Ihsan Shura Khalil saw how these bodies were then put on carts and pushed by the villagers to the burial place.

Most of the interviews with the survivors were done in 1999 by an Israeli research student, Teddy Katz, who 'stumbled upon' the massacre while doing his MA dissertation for Haifa University. When this became public, the University retroactively disqualified his thesis and Alexandroni veterans dragged Katz himself into court, suing him for libel. Katz's most senior interviewee was Shlomo Ambar, later a general in the IDF. Ambar refused to give him details of what he had seen, saying: 'I want to forget what happened there.' When Katz pressed him, all he was willing to say was:

> I connect this to the fact that I went to fight the Germans [he had served with the Jewish Brigade in the Second World War]. The Germans were the worst enemy the Jewish people has had, but when we fought

we fought according to the laws of war dictated by the international community. The Germans did not kill Prisoners of War, they killed Slav Prisoners of War, but not British, not even [when they were] Jewish.

Ambar admitted to hiding things: 'I did not talk then, why should I talk now?' Understandable, given the images that came to his mind when Katz asked him what his comrades had done in Tantura.

In fact the story of Tantura had already been told before, as early as 1950, but then it failed to attract the same attention as the Deir Yassin massacre. It appears in the memoirs of a Haifa notable, Muhammad Nimr al-Khatib, who, a few days after the battle, recorded the testimony of a Palestinian who had told him about summary executions on the beach of dozens of Palestinians. Here it is in full:

> On the night of 22/23 May the Jews attacked from 3 sides and landed in boats from the seaside. We resisted in the streets and houses and in the morning the corpses were seen everywhere. I shall never forget this day all my life. The Jews gathered all women and children in a place, where they dumped all bodies, for them to see their dead husbands, fathers and brothers and terrorize them, but they remained calm.

> They gathered men in another place, took them in groups and shot them dead. When women heard this shooting, they asked their Jewish guard about it. He replied: 'We are taking revenge for our dead.' One officer selected 40 men and took them to the village square. Each four were taken aside. They shot one, and ordered the other three to dump his body in a big pit. Then they shot another and the other two carried his body to the pit and so on.[16]

When they had completed their cleansing operations along the coast, the Alexandroni were instructed to move towards the Upper Galilee:

> You are asked to occupy Qadas, Mayrun, Nabi Yehoshua and Malkiyye; Qadas has to be destroyed; the other two should be given to the Golani Brigade and its commander will decide what to do with them. Mayrun should be occupied and handed over to Golani.[17]

The geographical distance between the various locations is quite considerable, revealing again the ambitious pace the troops were expected to maintain on their journey of destruction.

THE BRIGADES' TRAIL OF BLOOD

The above formed part of the bloody trail the Alexandroni left behind along Palestine's coast. More massacres by other brigades would follow, the worst of which was in the autumn of 1948 when the Palestinians finally succeeded in putting up some resistance against the ethnic cleansing in certain places, and in response the Jewish expellers revealed an ever-increasing callousness in the atrocities they perpetrated.

Meanwhile, the Golani Brigade followed in the footsteps of the Alexandroni. It attacked pockets the other brigades had missed or enclaves that for whatever reason had not yet been taken. One such destination was the village of Umm al-Zinat, which had been spared in the February cleansing operation in the Haifa district. Another was Lajjun near the ruins of ancient Meggido. Controlling the area between Lajjun and Umm al-Zinat meant that the whole western flank of Marj Ibn Amir and Wadi Milk, the canyon leading to the valley from the coastal road, were now in Jewish hands.

By the end of May 1948, some Palestinan enclaves still remaining inside the Jewish state proved harder to occupy than normal and it would take another few months to complete the job. For example, attempts to extend control over the remoter areas of the Upper Galilee that month failed, mainly because Lebanese and local volunteers courageously defended villages such as Sa'sa, which was the primary target of the Jewish forces.

In the order to the Golani Brigade for the second attack on Sa'sa it says: 'The occupation is not for permanent stay but for the destruction of the village, mining of the rubble and the junctures nearby.' Sa'sa, however, was spared for a few more months. Even for the efficient and zealous Golani troops the plan had proved to be too ambitious. Towards the end of May came the following clarification: 'If there is a shortage of soldiers, you are entitled to limit (temporarily) the cleansing operation, take-over and destruction of the enemy's villages in your district.'[18]

The orders the brigades now received were phrased in more explicit language than the vague oral instructions they had been given before. The fate of a village was sealed when the order said either to 'le-taher', to cleanse, meaning leaving the houses intact but expelling the people, or 'le-hashmid', to destroy, meaning to dynamite the houses after the expulsion of the people and lay mines in the rubble to prevent their return. There were no direct orders for massacres, but neither were these fully and genuinely condemned when they took place.

Sometimes the decision to 'cleanse' or 'destroy' was left in the hands of the local commanders: 'The villages in your district you have either to cleanse or destroy, decide for yourself according to consultation with the Arab advisors and the Shai [military intelligence] officers.'[19]

While these two brigades, the Alexandroni and the Golani, applied the methods described in Plan Dalet almost religiously to the coastal area, another brigade, the Carmeli, was sent to the northern areas of Haifa and the western Galilee. Like other brigades at the same time or later, it was also given orders to capture the area of Wadi Ara, the valley that contained fifteen villages and connected the coast, near Hadera, with the eastern corner of Marj Ibn Amir, near Afula. The Carmeli captured two villages nearby – Jalama on 23 April and Kabara soon afterwards, but they did not enter the valley. The Israeli command regarded this route as a crucial lifeline, but never succeeded in occupying it. As mentioned above, it was then given to them by King Abdullah in the summer of 1949, a tragic outcome for a large group of Palestinians who had successfully resisted expulsion.

As in the previous month, the Irgun – its units now part of the newly formed Israeli army – were sent in the second half of May to pockets along the coast to complete what the Hagana had regarded as questionable, or at least undesirable, operations at that particular moment. But even before its official inclusion in the army, the Irgun cooperated with the Hagana in the occupation of the greater Haffa area. It assited the Hagana in launching Operation Hametz ('Leaven') on 29 April, 1948. Three brigades took part in this operation, the Alexandroni, Qiryati and Givati. These brigades captured and cleansed Beit Dajan, Kfar Ana, Abbasiyya, Yahudiyya, Saffuriyya, Khayriyya, Salama and Yazur as well as the Jaffa suburbs of Jabalya and Abu Kabir.

In the second half of May, the Irgun were allocated the greater area of Jaffa to complete the job of the three Hagana brigades. They were regarded as a lesser force, as was the Qiryati Brigade. The Israeli military commanders described it as made up of 'lesser [quality] soldiers', namely Mizrahi Jews. A report of all the brigades submitted by a supervising officer in June 1948 described the Qiryati as a 'most problematic' brigade consisting of 'illiterate people, with no candidates for NCOS and of course none for the post of officers.'[20]

The Irgun and Qiryati were ordered to continue their mopping-up operation south of Jaffa. By the middle of May, their troops helped complete Operation Hametz. The ruins of some of the villages and the suburbs occupied and expelled during that operation lie buried below the 'White City' of Tel-Aviv, that first 'Hebrew' city the Jews had founded in 1909 on sand dunes bought from a local landowner, now spread out into the sprawling metropolis of today.

In the Israeli military archives there is a query from the commander of the Qiryati, dated 22 May 1948, asking whether he could employ bulldozers to destroy the villages instead of using explosives as ordered by Plan Dalet. His request shows how phony 'the war' was: only one week into it, this brigade commander had ample time to allow a slower method for demolishing and erasing the scores of villages on his list.[21]

The Harel Brigade of Yitzhak Rabin showed no hesitation about which method of demolition to employ. Already on 11 May, the day before the final orders for the next stage in the ethnic cleansing were issued, it could report that it had occupied the village of Beit Masir, in what today is Jerusalem's national park, on the western slopes of the mountains, and that 'we are currently blowing up the houses. We have already blown up 60–70 houses.'[22]

Together with Brigade Etzioni, the Harel troops focused on the Greater Jerusalem area. Far away from there, in the north-eastern valleys of the country, the soldiers of the 'Bulgarian' Brigade were so successful in their destruction mission that the High Command thought at the time that they could proceed immediately to occupy parts of the northern West Bank and sections of the upper Galilee. But this proved over-ambitious after all and failed. The 'Bulgarim', as they were called, were unable to push out the Iraqi contingent holding Jenin, and had to wait until October before it could take the upper Galilee. However presumptuous, the belief that this brigade could seize the northern part of the West Bank – despite the agreement with Abdullah – and even conduct invasions into southern Lebanon, while cleansing vast areas of Palestine, reveals once again the cynicism behind the myth that Israel was fighting a 'war of survival'. The brigade, meanwhile, achieved 'enough' as it was and could boast of having destroyed and expelled a larger number of villages than expected.

The two fronts of the 'real' and 'phony' war merged into one in those days in May, as the High Command was now confident enough to dispatch units to the border areas adjacent to the Arab countries, and there to engage the Arab expeditionary forces their governments had sent into Palestine on 15 May 1948. Meanwhile the Golani and Yiftach Brigades concentrated on cleansing operations on the border with Syria and Lebanon. In fact, they were able to carry out their mission unimpeded, following their usual routine for each village they had been ordered to destroy, while nearby Lebanese or Syrian troops stood idly by, looking the other way rather than risking their own men.

CAMPAIGNS OF REVENGE

The sky was not always the limit, however. Inevitably there were hitches in the wild galloping pace of the Israeli operations, and there was a price to be paid for the systematic cleansing of Palestine and simultaneous confrontation with the regular Arab armies that had begun moving into the country. Isolated settlements in the south were left exposed to the Egyptian troops, who occupied several of them – albeit only for a few days – and to Syrian troops, who took over three settlements for a few days as well. Another sacrifice was exacted from the regular practice of sending convoys though densely Arab areas not yet taken: when some of them were successfully attacked, more than two hundred Jewish troops lost their lives.

Following one such attack, on a convoy heading towards the Jewish settlement of Yechiam in the north-western tip of the country, the troops who later carried out operations in its vicinity were particularly vengeful and callous in the way they performed their duties. The settlement of Yechiam was several kilometres south of Palestine's western border with Lebanon. The Jewish troops who attacked the villages in operation 'Ben-Ami' in May 1948 were specifically told that the villages had to be eliminated in revenge for the loss of the convoy. Thus the villages of Sumiriyya, Zib, Bassa, Kabri, Umm al-Faraj and Nahr were subjected to an upgraded, crueler version of the 'destroy-and-expel' drill of the Israeli units: 'Our mission: to attack for the sake of occupation ... to kill the men, destroy and set fire to Kabri, Umm al-Faraj and Nahr.'[23]

The extra zeal thus infused into the troops produced one of the swiftest depopulation operations in one of the densest Arab areas of Palestine. Within twenty-nine hours of the end of the Mandate, almost all the villages in the north-western districts of the Galilee – all within the designated Arab state – had been destroyed, allowing a satisfied Ben-Gurion to announce to the newly assembled parliament: 'The Western Galilee has been liberated' (some of the villages north of Haifa were actually only occupied later). In other words, it took Jewish troops just over a day to turn a district with a population that was ninety-six per cent Palestinian and only four per cent Jewish – with a similar ratio of land ownership – into an area almost exclusively Jewish. Ben-Gurion was particularly satisfied with the ease with which the populations of the larger villages had been driven out, such as those of Kabri with 1500, Zib with 2000, and the largest, Bassa, with its 3000 inhabitants.

It took more than a day to defeat Bassa, because of the resistance from the village militiamen and some ALA volunteers. If the orders to be extra harsh with the village in revenge for the attack on the Jewish convoy near Yechiam had not been enough, its resistance was seen as another reason to 'punish' the village (that is, beyond simply expelling its people). This pattern would recur: villages that proved hard to subdue had to be 'penalised'. As with all traumatic events in the lives of human beings, some of the worst atrocities remain deeply engraved in the survivors' memories. The victims' family members guarded those recollections and passed them down through the generations. Nizar al-Hanna belonged to such a family, whose memories are based on the traumatic events witnessed by his grandmother:

> My maternal grandmother was a teenager when Israeli troops entered Bassa and ordered all the young men to be lined up and executed in front of one of the churches. My grandmother watched as two of her brothers, one 21, the other 22 and recently married, were executed by the Hagana.[24]

The total destruction that followed the massacre spared a church in which the village's Greek Orthodox Christians prayed, and a domed Muslim shrine that served the other half of the population. Today, one can still spot a few houses fenced off with barbed wire standing in an uncultivated field now expropriated by Jewish citizens. The village was so vast (25,000 dunam out of which 17,000 were cultivated) that its territory today includes a military airport, a kibbutz, and a development town. The more observant visitor cannot fail to notice the remains of an elaborate water system, which was the pride of the villagers and had been completed just before the place was wiped out.

Plate 1. Irgun troops march through the streets of Tel-Aviv in a show of strength on the eve of the declaration of the State of Israel

Plate 2. Jewish forces occupy a village near Safad, probably Biriyya

Plate 3. Jewish forces entering Malkiyya

Plate 4. Arab men of military age are rounded up and marched to a holding point in Tel-Aviv

Plate 5. The Red House in Tel-Aviv, headquarters of the Hagana from 1947, where many of the Consultancy meetings took place

Plate 6. Refugee women, children and the elderly are expelled from their homes. Males between the ages of ten and fifty were sent to POW camps.

200 ARABS KILLED, STRONGHOLD TAKEN

Irgun and Stern Groups Unite to Win Deir Yasin—Kastel Is Recaptured by Haganah

By DANA ADAMS SCHMIDT
Special to The New York Times.

JERUSALEM, April 9—A combined force of Irgun Zvai Leumi and the Stern group, Jewish extremist underground forces, captured the Arab village of Deir Yasin on the western outskirts of Jerusalem today. In house-to-house fighting the Jews killed more than 200 Arabs, half of them women and children.

At the same time a Haganah counter-attack three miles away drove an Arab force, estimated by the Haganah at 2,500 men, out of the strategic village of Kastel on a hill overlooking the Jerusalem-Tel Aviv convoy road. This village was captured after a six-hour fight during which it repeatedly changed hands. The Jews, who first seized Kastel last Saturday, had been forced out yesterday.

Tonight Fawzi el-Kawukji, commander of the Arab "Liberation Army," was reported, although without confirmation, to be leading large forces of Syrians, Iraqis and Palestinians in an attempt to retake Kastel. The Arabs were equipped with several French 75-mm field guns, many mortars and at least eight armored cars.

On the scene of this, the greatest Arab-Jewish battle to date, the Arabs claimed that 110 Jews had been killed yesterday. On the other hand, Jews said that Arab casualties ran into the hundreds.

3 Galilee Points Seized

In southern Galilee units of the Haganah in the besieged settlement of Mishmar Haemek, a model colony of Jewish Socialists, ended a two-day truce by breaking out and occupying three Arab villages, Abu Shusha, Abu Zureik and Naaieh.

Still other forces of the Haganah were reported to have evacuated Khulda and Deir Muheisan, villages just west of Latrun on the Jerusalem-Jaffa road, yesterday, and to have driven 600 Iraqis out of the near-by Wadi Sarrar camp this morning.

The capture of Deir Yasin, situated on a hill overlooking the birthplace of John the Baptist, marked the first cooperative effort since 1942 between the Irgun and Stern groups, although the Jewish Agency for Palestine does not recognize these terrorist groups. Twenty men of the gency's Haganah militia reinforced fifty-five Irgunists and forty-five Sternists who seized the village.

This engagement marked the formal entry of the Irgunists and Sternists into the battle against the Arabs. Previously both groups had concentrated against the British.

In addition to killing more than 200 Arabs, they took forty prisoners.

The Jews carried off some seventy women and children who were turned over later to the British Army in Jerusalem.

Victors Describe Battle

The Irgunists and Sternists escorted a party of United States correspondents to a house at Givat Shaul, near Deir Yasin, tonight and offered them tea and cookies and amplified details of the operation.

The spokesman said that the village had become a concentration point for Arabs, including Syrians and Iraqi, planning to attack the western suburbs of Jerusalem. If, as he expected, the Haganah took over occupation of the village, it would help to cover the convoy route from the coast.

The spokesman said he regretted the casualties among the women and children at Deir Yasin but asserted that they were inevitable because almost every house had to be reduced by force. Ten houses were blown up. At others the attackers blew open the doors and threw in hand grenades.

One hundred men in four groups attacked at 4:30 o'clock in the morning, the spokesman said. The Irgunists wore uniforms of a secret design and they used automatic weapons and rifles.

An Arabic-speaking Jew, the spokesman said, shouted over a loudspeaker from an armored car used in the attack, that Arab women and children should take refuge in the caves. Some of them, he said, did so.

Plate 7. *The New York Times*, 10 April 1948, reports the massacre in Deir Yassin by the Irgun and Stern Gang

Plate 8. Thousands of Palestinians throng the beaches in an attempt to flee heavy shelling, many of whom drowned in the mass exodus

Plate 9. Thousands of refugees fled on foot

Plate 10. Palestinian villagers load their belongings onto trucks as Jewish forces occupy their village

Plate 11. Many refugees were forced to walk hundreds of miles

Plate 12. Palestinian refugees scramble onto fishing boats, fleeing to Gaza and Egypt in the south, and Lebanon in the north

Plate 13. Thousands flock to the port city of Haifa to welcome the arrival of 1,500 Jewish immigrants, refugees from Europe, January 31, 1949

Plate 14. The village of Iqrit in 1935, before its destruction. The majority of its residents were expelled in November 1948

Plate 15. This derelict church is the only building left standing in the village of Iqrit, 1990

Plate 16. A theme park now covers the village of Tantura, near Haifa, site of a massacre in 1948

Plate 17. The cemetery of Salama, now lying under a park near Jaffa

Plate 18. Nahr al-Barid refugee camp in northern Lebanon, winter 1948, one of the first camps set up for the displaced Palestinians

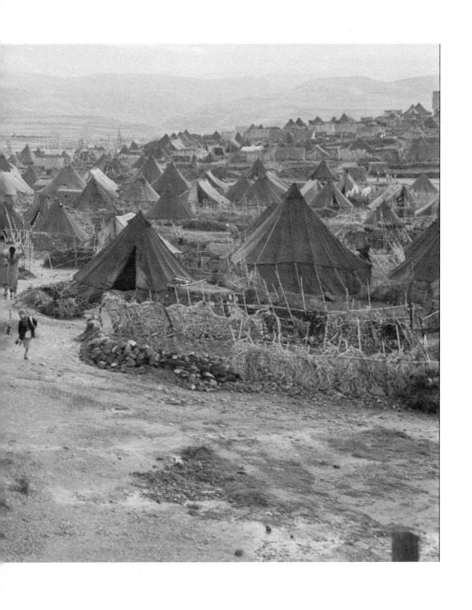

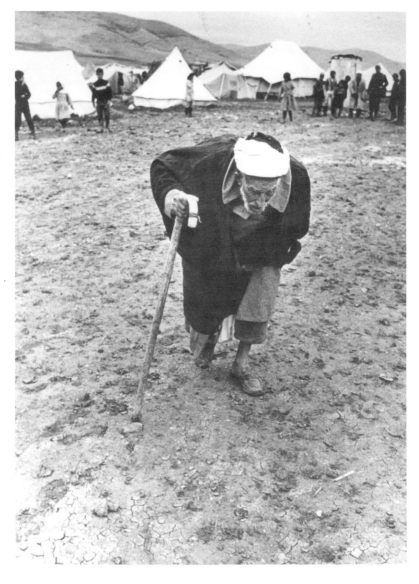

Plate 19. An elderly refugee, Baqa'a refugee camp, Jordan

The expulsion of so many villagers – whom the UN Partition Resolution had just transformed from citizens of the British Mandate into either citizens of the UN-designated Arab state or citizens of the Jewish state – went unnoticed by the UN. Consequently, despite the drama of the British withdrawal and the potential hitch of the Arab world sending units into Palestine, the business of ethnic cleansing continued without interruption. The leaders of the newly created State of Israel – still in the making – and its military commanders knew they had sufficient forces at their disposal to halt the incoming Arab units while continuing their relentless cleansing of the land. It was also obvious that in the following month, the capacity of the Jewish forces would reach new heights: in early June the orders sent down to the troops were even more far-reaching in both their geographical span and the ambitious quota of villages each brigade was now assigned to capture and destroy.

The Arab General Command, on the other hand, was quickly losing its grip. The Egyptian military generals had pinned their hopes on their airforce, but the aircraft they had sent in the crucial second half of May failed in most of their missions, apart from a few raids on Tel-Aviv. In June, the Egyptian and other Arab air forces were preoccupied elsewhere, their main mission limited to protecting the Arab regimes, rather than helping to rescue parts of Palestine.

I am not an expert in military history, nor is this the place to tackle the purely military aspects of the war, since the focus of this book is not on military strategies but on their outcomes, i.e., war crimes. Significantly, many military historians summing up the month of May have been particularly impressed with the performance of the Syrian army, which began its campaign in May 1948 and kept it up intermittently until December 1948. In fact, it did quite poorly. Only for three days, between 15 and 18 May, did Syrian artillery, tanks and infantry, with the occasional help of their air force, constitute any kind of threat to the Israeli forces. A few days later their efforts had already become more sporadic and less effective. After the first truce, they were on their way back home.

By the end of May 1948, the ethnic cleansing of Palestine was progressing according to plan. Assessing the potential strength of the forces eventually sent by the Arab League into Palestine, Ben-Gurion and his advisers concluded – as they had already predicted a week after the Arab armies had moved into Palestine – that the all-Arab force could attack isolated Jewish settlements marginally more effectively than the volunteers' army could ever have done, but apart from this it was as ineffective and weak as the irregular and paramilitary troops that had come first.

This realisation created a euphoric mood, which is clearly reflected in the orders to the twelve brigades of the Israeli army to start considering the occupation of the West Bank, the Golan Heights and southern Lebanon. On 24 May, after Ben-Gurion had met with his advisers, in his diary entry he sounds triumphant and more power-hungry than ever before:

> We will establish a Christian state in Lebanon, the southern border of which will be the Litani River. We will break Transjordan, bomb Amman and destroy its army, and then Syria falls, and if Egypt will still continue to fight – we will bombard Port Said, Alexandria and Cairo. This will be in revenge for what they (the Egyptians, the Aramis and Assyrians) did to our forefathers during Biblical times.[25]

On that same day, the Israeli army had received a large shipment of modern, brand new 0.45-calibre cannons from the Communist Eastern bloc. Israel now possessed artillery unmatched not only by the Arab troops inside Palestine, but by all the Arab armies put together. It should be noted that the Israeli Communist Party was instrumental in arranging this deal.

This meant the Consultancy could now put aside the initial worries it had had at the beginning of the 'real war' about the overall capacity of its army to manage both fronts effectively and comprehensively. Its members were now free to turn their attention to other issues more in line with the qualifications of the Orientalist section of the Consultancy, such as advising the leader on what to do with the small communities of Palestinians that had been left in the mixed towns. The solution they came up with was to have all these people moved into one particular neighbourhood in each town, deprive them of their freedom of movement, and put them under a military regime.

Finally, it may be useful to add that, during the month of May, the definitive infrastructure of the IDF was decided upon and, within it, the central place of the military regime (referred to in Hebrew as *Ha-Mimshal Ha-Tzvai*) and Israel's internal security services, the Shabak. The Consultancy was no longer needed. The machinery of ethnic cleansing was working on its own, propelled by its own momentum.

On the last day of May, Arab volunteers and some regular units made one final attempt to retake some of the villages that lay within the designated Arab state, but failed. The military power that confronted them was such that, except when challenged by a well-trained professional army like the Legion, it had no match. The Legion defended those parts of the West Bank that King Abdullah thought should be his trophy for not having entered the areas the Zionist movement had set its mind on for their Jewish state – a promise he kept until the end of the war. However, his army did pay a heavy price for the two sides' failure to agree on the fate of Jerusalem, as most of the Jordanian soldiers killed in the war fell during the Legion's successful bid for the eastern parts of the Holy City.

Chapter 7

The Escalation of the Cleansing Operations: June–September 1948

Article 9: No one shall be subjected to arbitrary arrest, detention or exile.

Article 13/2: Everyone has the right to leave any country, including his own, and to return to his country.

Article 17/2: No one shall be arbitrarily deprived of his property.

> From the Universal Declaration of Human Rights, adopted as General Assembly Resolution 217 A (III), 10 December 1948, the day before Resolution 194 declared the unconditional right of the Palestinian refugees to return to their homes.

By the beginning of June, the list of villages obliterated included many that had until then been protected by nearby kibbutzim. This was the fate of several villages in the Gaza district: Najd, Burayr, Simsim, Kawfakha, Muharraqa and Huj. Their destruction appeared to have come as a genuine shock to nearby kibbutzim when they learned how these friendly villages had been savagely assaulted, their houses destroyed and all their people expelled.[1] On the land of Huj, Ariel Sharon built his private residence, Havat Hashikmim, a ranch that covers 5000 dunam of the village's fields.

Despite the ongoing negotiations by the UN mediator, Count Folke Bernadotte, to broker a truce, the ethnic cleansing moved on unhindered.

With obvious satisfaction Ben-Gurion wrote in his diary on 5 June 1948, 'We occupied today Yibneh (there was no serious resistance) and Qaqun. Here the cleansing [*tihur*] operation continues; have not heard from the other fronts.' Indeed, by the end of May his diary had reflected a renewed interest in the ethnic cleansing. With the help of Yossef Weitz, he compiled a list of the names of the villages taken, the size of their lands and the number of people expelled, which he meticulously entered in his diary. The language is no longer guarded: 'This is the list of the occupied and evicted [*mefunim*] villages.' Two days later, he convened a meeting in his own house to assess how much money had meanwhile been looted from the banks of the 'Arabs', and how many citrus groves and other assets had been confiscated. Eliezer Kaplan, his minister of finance, persuaded him to authorise the confiscation of all Palestinian properties already taken in order to prevent the frenzied wrangling that was already threatening to break out between the predators who were waiting to swoop down on the spoils.

Dividing the booty was one matter that preoccupied the Prime Minister. Ben-Gurion was both an autocrat and a stickler for details, and was obsessive about questions of security, and his diary reflects other, miniscule problems that accompanied the systematic destruction of Palestine. In several entries he records conversations he had had with army officers about the shortage of TNT, created by the large number of individual houses the army was ordered to blow up under Plan D.[4]

Like a ferocious storm gathering force, the Israeli troops no longer spared anyone in their destructive zeal. All means became legitimate, including burning down houses where dynamite had become scarce and torching the fields and remains of a Palestinian village they had attacked.[2] The escalation of the Israeli army's cleansing operation was the outcome of a meeting of the new, reduced Consultancy, whose members had met on 1 June without Ben-Gurion. They later reported to the Prime Minister that villagers were trying to return to their homes, so they had decided to instruct the army to prevent this at all costs. To make sure that the more liberal-minded among his government members would not object to this policy, Ben-Gurion demanded prior approval, and was duly given *carte blanche* to proceed on 16 June 1948.[3]

Increased callousness was also part of the Israeli response to a brief spurt of activity by the Arab armies in early June. The latter's artillery bombarded whatever was in range, and the Egyptian air force attacked Tel Aviv four or five times, scoring a direct hit on Ben-Gurion's home on 4 June that caused only limited damage. The Israeli air force retaliated by shelling the Arab capitals, resulting in a considerable number of casualties, but the Arab effort to salvage Palestine was already running out of steam, mainly due to the Legion's insistence that East Jerusalem should remain part of Jordan. The war lingered on: the division of labour between the Israeli forces on the different fronts, determined solely by Ben-Gurion, meant that the military effort on the Jewish side fell short of the impact it needed to gain the upper hand over the Jordanians. The fighting also persisted because of the tenacity the Egyptian volunteers displayed, especially the Muslim Brotherhood, who despite their poor equipment and lack of training succeeded in holding their lines in the Negev. The Egyptians were also able to hold on to the Palestinian town of Isdud on the coast and some inner enclaves in the Naqab (the Negev), as well as the villages south-west of Jerusalem, for quite some time. Realising they might have bitten off more than they could chew for the moment, the Israelis now accepted the offer by the UN mediator, Count Folke Bernadotte, for a truce.

THE FIRST TRUCE

Demolition was a core part of the Israeli activities from the moment the truce went into effect (officially declared on 8 June, but in practice beginning on 11 June 1948, and to last four weeks). During the truce, the army embarked on the massive destruction of a number of expelled villages: Mazar in the south, Fayja near Petah Tikva, Biyar 'Adas, Misea, Hawsha, Sumiriyya and Manshiyya near Acre. Huge villages such as Daliyat al-Rawha, Butaymat and Sabbarin were destroyed in one day; many others were erased from the face of the earth by the time the truce ended on 8 July 1948.

All in all, the level of preparation the military command was engaged in during June for the next stages showed a growing confidence in the Israeli Army's ability to continue not only its ethnic cleansing operations, but also its extension of the Jewish state beyond the seventy-eight per cent of Mandatory Palestine it had already occupied. Part of this confidence was due to the significant reinforcement of its air force. At the end of May, the

Israelis were only disadvantaged in one area: air power. In June, however, they received a sizable shipment of new aeroplanes to supplement their rather primitive machines.

Operation 'Yitzhak' was launched on 1 June 1948 to attack and occupy Jenin, Tul-Karem and Qalqilya and capture the bridges on the Jordan River. As we saw, Jenin was attacked the previous month, but the Iraqi contingent guarding the city and its environs had successfully defended the area.[5] Although Israeli air operations were primarily limited to raids along the state's borders at this time, in the military archives one can find orders for the arial bombardment of Jenin and Tul-Karem, as well as other villages on the Palestine's border. From July onwards, aeroplanes were used remorselessly in the cleansing operations, helping to force the villagers into a mass exodus – and indiscriminately targeting anyone unable to take cover in time.

At the beginning of June, Ben-Gurion was content to focus on the long march into the upper Galilee, driving his troops up to the border with Lebanon. The Lebanese army was 5000 strong, of which 2000 were stationed on the border. They were supported by 2000 ALA volunteers, most of them stationed around the city of Nazareth and the rest scattered in small groups among the dozens of villages in the area. Under the charismatic command of Fawzi al-Qawqji, the volunteers continued as best they could to defend the villages and show some resilience in the face of the looming Israeli offensive. But they were hampered not only numerically and by their inferior military skill , but also by the poor quality of their weapons and lack of ammunition.

One of the ALA battalions was the Hittin battalion. The commander at one point sent the following message to al-Qawqji: 'The battalion's equipment is not usable because of the amount of dirt in it. This includes rifles, machine guns and vehicles.' The commander also complained that there was only one logistic supply line from Syria, which was often blocked, and even when the supply lines happened to be open, there were other problems to overcome. At one point he received the following telegram: 'In reply to your telegram asking for cars to remove supply from Tarshiha to Rama, we have no fuel for the cars so we cannot reach you' (sent on 29 June and intercepted by the Israeli military intelligence).

Thus, in the absence of any regular Arab troops the Galilee lay wide open for an Israeli assault. But as early as June, and increasingly over the following months, the villages themselves were beginning to offer the advancing troops more resistance, which is one reason there are still

Palestinian villages in the Galilee today, unlike Marj Ibn Amir, the coast, the inner plains and the northern Negev.

The desperate courage of the Palestinian villages, however, also accounts for the brutality of the front. As they progressed, the Israeli troops were more determined than ever to resort to summary executions and any other means that might speed up the expulsions. One of the first villages to fall prey to this strategy was the village of Mi'ar, today the location of several Jewish settlements built in the 1970s: Segev, Yaad and Manof. The irony is that part of the land taken by force in 1948 remained uninhabited for decades, and was even cultivated by Palestinians living nearby until it was re-confiscated in the 1970s, as part of what Israel calls 'the Judaization of the Galilee', a brutal attempt by the government to de-Arabise the Galilee, which was still, in some areas, equally divided demographically between Jews and Arabs. It would appear that Israel intends to re-activate this scheme with the billions of dollars it hopes to extract from the US government following the pull-out from Gaza in August 2005.

The writer Muhammad Ali Taha was a boy of seventeen when, on 20 June 1948, the Israeli soldiers entered the village of Mi'ar. He was born in nearby Saffuriyya, but much of his poetry and prose today, as an Israeli citizen, is inspired by the traumatic events he saw unfolding in Mi'ar. That June, he stood watching, at sunset, the approaching Israeli troops shooting indiscriminately at the villagers still busy in the fields collecting their dura. When they got tired of the killing spree, the soldiers then began destroying the houses. People later returned to Mi'ar and continued living there until mid-July when Israeli troops re-occupied it and expelled them for good. Forty people were killed in the Israeli attack on 20 June, part of the few thousand Palestinians who perished in the massacres that accompanied the ethnic cleansing operation.[6]

The pace of occupying and cleansing villages in the lower and eastern Galilee was faster than in any phase of the operations that had gone before. By 29 June, large villages with a significant presence of ALA troops, such as Kuwaykat, Amqa, Tel-Qisan, Lubya, Tarbikha, Majd al-Krum, Mghar, Itarun, Malkiyya, Saffuriyya, Kfar Yassif, Abu Sinan, Judeida and Tabash appeared on the lists of future targets the troops were given. Within less than ten days they had all been taken – some villages were expelled but others were not, for reasons that varied from one village to the another.

Majd al-Krum and Mghar are still there today. In Majd al-Krum, the occupying forces had started a mass eviction of the village when a row suddenly erupted between the intelligence officers, resulting in half of the village being allowed to return from the trail of forced exile.[7] 'Most Glorious Olive Groves' is the literal translation of this village name, and it still lies amidst vast vineyards and olive groves, adjacent to the northern slopes of Galilee's highest mountains, not far from Acre. In ancient times the place was known as Majd Allah, 'The Glory of God', but the name was changed when the vineyards that began developing around the village became famous. At the centre of the village was a well whose water explains the abundance of plantations and orchards around it. Some of the houses looked indeed as if they had been there from time immemorial: stone-built and reinforced by clay, surrounded by the olive trees on the south and vast tracts of cultivated land on the east and west.

Today Majd al-Krum is strangulated by Israel's discriminatory policy, which does not allow Palestinian villages to expand naturally, but at the same time continues building new Jewish settlements around it. This is why ever since 1948 the village has had a strong political cadre of nationalist and communist resistance, which the government then punished further by demolishing houses, the rubble of which the villagers have left in place in commemoration of their past resilience and heroism, and which is still visible today from the Acre–Safad highway.

Mghar is also still there, spread out within a scenic canyon in the descending valley that connects the lower Galilee with the Lake of Tiberias. Here the Jewish occupying force was faced with a village where Christians, Muslims and Druze had coexisted for centuries. The military commander interpreted Plan Dalet as calling for the expulsion of only the Muslims. To make sure this was done swiftly, he executed several Muslims on the village's piazza in front of all the villagers, which effectively 'persuaded' the rest to flee.[8]

Many other villages in the Galilee were like Mghar in that they had mixed populations. Hence, from now on, the military commanders were given strict orders to leave the selection process that was to determine who could stay and who could not to the intelligence officers.[9] The Druze were now fully collaborating with the Jews, and in villages that were partly Druze, Christians were generally spared expulsion.

Saffuriyya was less fortunate. All its inhabitants were evicted, with soldiers shooting over their heads to hasten their departure. Al-Hajj Abu Salim was twenty-seven, and the father of one beloved daughter, when the village was taken. His wife was expecting another baby and he recalls the warm family home with his father, a kind and generous man, one of the richest peasants in the village. For Abul Salim, the Nakba began with the news of other villages surrendering. 'When your neighbour's house is on fire, you begin to worry' is a well-known Arab saying that captures the emotions and confusion of the villagers caught in the midst of the catastrophe.

Saffuriyya was one of the first villages Israeli forces bombarded from the air. In July many more would be terrorised in this way, but back in June this was a rarity. Terrified, the women took their children and hastily sought shelter in the ancient caves nearby. The young men prepared their primitive rifles for the inevitable attack, but the volunteers from the Arab countries took fright and escaped from the girls' school where they had been stationed. Abu Salim stayed on with the men to fight although, as he remembered many years later, 'The officer of the ALA advised me and others to run away,' which, he admits, seemed to make sense. But he stayed put and so became a crucial eyewitness to the events that followed.

After the air bombardment came the ground attack, not only on the village but also on the caves. 'The women and children were quickly exposed by the Jews and my mother was killed by the troops,' he told a newspaper fifty-three years later. 'She was trying to enter the Church of Annunciation, and the Jews dropped a bomb that hit her in the stomach.' His father took Abu Salim's wife and fled to Reina, a village that had already surrendered. There they took refuge with a Christian family for a few months, who shared their food and clothing with them. They worked in the family's orchards and were well treated. As they had been forced to leave their own clothes behind in the village, villagers tried to return in the dead of the night to smuggle them out. Israeli troops caught several of them and shot them on the spot. In 2001, Abu Salim, now eighty years old, concluded his story by stating that he was still willing, as he had been in the past, to buy his old house back with good money. What he cannot rebuild is his family. He has lost all contact with his brother, whom he thinks has children somewhere in the diaspora, but he has been unable to track any of them down.

Like many villagers in the vicinity of Nazareth, the people of Saffuriyya fled to the city. Today sixty per cent of Nazareth's residents are internal refugees. The decision of the local Israeli commander who occupied

Nazareth the following month not to drive out its inhabitants meant that many of the expelled villagers around Nazareth were spared the fate of a second eviction. Along with many of the survivors of the other villages, the people of Saffuriyya put up new homes in a neighbourhood that faced their old village, today called Safafra. This meant another traumatic life experience: they actually watched as the Jewish settlers began emptying their houses, occupied them and slowly turned their beloved village into an Israeli moshav – a collective agricultural settlement – that they called Zippori, which Israeli archeologists quickly claimed was the name of the original Talmudic city.

In other neighbourhoods in the city of Nazareth today you can come across survivors of Malul and Mujaydil, who settled in the southern part of the city as near as they could to the Israeli development town of Migdal Ha-Emeq, built on the ruins of their villages after their occupation in July. Malul is gone without a trace; in Mejadyal two churches and a mosque were the only remnants until recently of the Palestinian presence. The mosque was destroyed in 2003 to make room for a shopping mall, and only the churches survive.

The village of Mujaydil had 2000 inhabitants, most of whom fled to Nazareth before the soldiers reached their houses. For some reason the army left these intact. In 1950, after the intervention of the Pope in Rome, the Christians were offered the opportunity to move back but refused to do so without their Muslim neighbours.[10] Israel then destroyed half the houses and one of the village's mosques. Mujaydil's al-Huda Mosque had been built in 1930 and was twelve metres high and eight metres wide. A *kuttab* – an elementary Quranic school – was nearby. The site was famous for the elaborate system it used to collect the rainfall from the mosque's roof into a well. A tall impressive minaret was added to the edifice in the 1940s.

The Christian sites were equally picturesque. Part of the Russian Orthodox Church is still there today, though its walls are long gone. It was built in honour of the brother of the Russian Czar, Serjei Alexandrov, who had visited the place in 1882 and who donated the money for its construction in the hope that local Christians of other denominations could be converted to Orthodox Christianity. But after he had left, the local representative of the Orthodox Church in Palestine, Patriarch Nikodim, proved less insistent on the missionary task he had been entrusted with and more genuinely concerned about education for all: he opened the church to all the denominations in the village and ensured it functioned most of the time as the local school.

The village also had a Roman Catholic church, built in 1903, which housed on its first floor a trilingual school for boys and girls (teaching was in Arabic, Italian and French). It also had a local clinic for the benefit of all the villagers. This church is still there and an old family who decided to come back from Nazareth to take care of the site, the Abu Hani family, now looks after the lovely orchard and the school.

As in other places in Palestine, it is worthwhile to dwell a little on the local history of the village as it demonstrates how not only houses or fields were destroyed in the Nakba but a whole community disappeared, with all its intricate social networks and cultural achievements. Thus in Mujaydil the Israeli army obliterated a piece of history that included some fine architectural specimens and a series of significant social developments. Just twenty years before the Nakba, the proud villagers decided to transform, actually modernise, the old traditional system that placed the mukhtar at the head of the village community. Already in 1925 they had elected a local council, whose first project was to provide lighting along the village's roads.

Mujaydil was a unique place in many other aspects. Apart from its religious buildings and modern infrastructure it had a relatively large number of schools. In addition to the two schools associated with the churches, there was also a state school, the Banin School, known for the magnificent trees that provided shade for the pupils during their breaks, for the well situated in the middle of the school yard and for the fruit trees that surrounded it. The village's main source of collective wealth, which supported all these impressive constructions, was a mill, built in the eighteenth century, that served the villages in the vicinity, including the people of the 'veteran' Jewish settlement of Nahalal (Moshe Dayan, who came from Nahalal, mentions his father's reliance on this mill).

OPERATION PALM TREE

Mujaydil was taken in the military operation to take over Nazareth and the villages around it, which was codenamed '*Dekel*', Hebrew for palm tree. It is actually pine trees and not palms that today cover many of the destroyed Palestinian villages, hiding their remains under vast 'green lungs' planted by the Jewish National Fund for the purpose of 'recreation and tourism'. Such a forest of pine trees, was planted over the destroyed village of Lubya. Only the diligent and meticulous work of later generations, spearheaded by historian Mahmoud Issa, now living in Denmark, has enabled visitors today to trace the vestiges of the village and join in the commemorations of the sixty people who lost their lives there. The village lay near a main junction (today called the 'Golani Junction'), the last main crossroads on the Nazareth–Tiberias road before it starts its steep descent towards the Sea of Galilee.

In those days of June 1948, when Israeli forces were on the whole able to occupy and cleanse Palestinian villages with relative ease, tenacious pockets of resistance sometimes held on for a little longer, though never for too long. These were usually locations where ALA volunteers or Arab regular troops, especially Iraqis, helped in the attempt to repel the attacks. One such village was Qaqun: it was first attacked and occupied in May by the Alexandroni, but had been retaken by Iraqi troops. The Israeli headquarters ordered a special operation codenamed '*Kippa*' ('summit', 'dome', but also 'skullcap' in Hebrew) on 3 June in order to re-occupy the village where Israeli military intelligence estimated 200 Iraqis and ALA volunteers were entrenched. Even this proved an exaggeration: when the Alexandroni once again took it over they found a much smaller number of defenders.

The order for Operation Kippa introduces yet another Hebrew synonym for cleansing. We have already encountered *tihur* and *biur,* and now Platoon D of the Alexandroni Brigade was ordered to execute a 'cleaning' operation (*nikkuy*),[11] all terms that fit the accepted international definitions of ethnic cleansing.

The assault on Qaqun was also the first in which the new state's Military Police were ordered to play an integral role in the occupation. Well before the attack, they had set up prison camps nearby for the expelled villagers. This was done to avoid the problem they had encountered in Tantura and before that in Ayn al-Zaytun, where the occupying forces had ended up with too many men of 'military age' (between ten and fifty) on their hands, many of whom they therefore killed.

In July the Israeli troops took many of the 'pockets' that had been left in the previous two months. Several villages on the coastal road that had held out courageously, Ayn Ghazal, Jaba, Ayn Hawd, Tirat Haifa, Kfar Lam and Ijzim, now fell, as did the city of Nazareth and a number of the villages around it.

IN BETWEEN TRUCES

By 8 July 1948 the first truce had come to an end. It took the UN mediator, Count Folke Bernadotte, ten days to negotiate another one, which came into effect on 18 July. As we have seen, 15 May 1948 may have been a very significant date for the 'real war' between Israel and the Arab armies, but it was totally insignificant for the ethnic cleansing operations. The same goes for the two periods of truce – they were notable landmarks for the former but irrelevant for the latter, with one qualification, perhaps: it proved easier during the actual fighting to conduct large-scale cleansing operations as the Israelis did between the two truces, when they expelled the populations of the two towns of Lydd and Ramla, altogether 70,000 people, and again after the second truce, when they resumed the large-scale ethnic cleansing of Palestine with huge operations of uprooting, deportation and depopulation in both the south and the north of the country.

From 9 July, the day after the first truce ended, the sporadic fighting between the Israeli army and the Arab units from Jordan, Iraq, Syria and Lebanon continued for another ten days. In less than two weeks, hundreds of thousands of Palestinians had been expelled from their villages, towns and cities. The UN 'peace' plan had resulted in people being intimidated and terrorised by psychological warfare, heavy shelling of civilian populations, expulsions, seeing relatives being executed, and wives and daughters abused, robbed and in several cases, raped. By July, most of their houses had gone, dynamited by Israeli sappers. There was no international intervention the Palestinians could hope for in 1948, nor could they count on outside concern about the atrocious reality evolving in Palestine. Neither did help come from the UN observers, scores of whom roamed the country at close hand 'observing' the barbarisation and killings, but were unwilling, or unable, to do anything about them.

One United Nations emissary was different. Count Folke Bernadotte had arrived in Palestine on 20 May and stayed there until Jewish terrorists murdered him in September for having 'dared' to put forward a proposal to re-divide the country in half, and to demand the unconditional return of all the refugees. He had already called for the refugees' repatriation during the first truce, which had been ignored, and when he repeated his recommendation in the final report he submitted to the UN, he was assassinated. Still, it is thanks to Bernadotte that in December 1948, the UN General Assembly posthumously adopted his legacy and recommended the unqualified return of all the refugees Israel had expelled, one of a host of UN resolutions Israel has systematically ignored. As president of the Swedish Red Cross, Bernadotte had been instrumental in saving Jews from the Nazis during the Second World War and this was why the Israeli government had agreed to his appointment as a UN mediator: they had not expected him to try to do for the Palestinians what he had done for the Jews only a few years before.

Bernadotte succeeded in focusing international pressure of some kind on Israel, or he had at least produced the potential for such pressure. In order to counteract this, the Israeli architects of the ethnic cleansing programme realised they would need to involve the state's diplomats and the Foreign Ministry more directly. By July the political apparatus, the diplomatic corps and the military organisations within the new State of Israel were already working harmoniously together. Prior to July, it is not clear how much of the ethnic cleansing plan had been shared with Israeli diplomats and senior officials. However, when the results gradually became visible the government needed a public relations campaign to stymie adverse international responses, and began to involve and inform those officials responsible for producing the right image abroad – that of a liberal democracy in the making. Officials in the Foreign Ministry worked closely with the country's intelligence officers, who would warn them in advance of the next stages in the cleansing operation, so as to ensure they would be kept hidden from the public eye.

Yaacov Shimoni functioned as a liaison between the two branches of the government. As both an Orientalist and a European Jew, Shimoni was pre-eminently suited to help propagate Israel's case abroad. In July he was eager to see a more accelerated pace on the ground: he believed there was a window of opportunity for completing the uprooting and occupation before the world turned its attention once more to Palestine.[12] Shimoni would later become one of the doyens of Orientalism in Israeli academia due to his expertise on Palestine and the Arab world, expertise he and many of his colleagues in Israel's universities had gained during the ethnic cleansing and de-Arabisation of Palestine.

The first targets of the Israeli forces in the ten days between the two truces were the pockets within the Galilee around Acre, and Nazareth. 'Cleanse totally the enemy from the villages' was the order that three brigades received on July 6, two days before the Israeli troops – straining at their leashes to continue the cleansing operations – were ordered to violate the first truce. Jewish soldiers automatically understood that 'enemy' meant defenceless Palestinian villagers and their families. The brigades they belonged to were the Carmeli, the Golani and Brigade Seven, the three brigades of the north that would also be responsible for the final cleansing operations in the upper Galilee in October. The inventive people whose job it was to come up with the names for operations of this kind had now switched from 'cleansing' synonyms ('Broom', 'Scissors') to trees: 'Palm' (*Dekel*) for the Nazareth area and 'Cypress' (*Brosh*) for the Jordan Valley area.[13]

The operation in and around Nazareth was executed at a fast pace, and large villages not taken in May were now quickly captured: Amqa, Birwa (the village where the famous contemporary Palestinian poet Mahmoud Darwish was born), Damun, Khirbat Jiddin and Kuwaykat each had more than 1500 inhabitants and yet they were easily forced out.

It was Brigade Seven that supervised the execution of Operation Palm Tree, with auxiliary forces coming from the Carmeli and the Golani. In many of the Palestinian oral histories that have now come to the fore, few brigade names appear. However, Brigade Seven is mentioned again and again, together with such adjectives as 'terrorists' and 'barbarous'.[14]

The first village to be attacked was Amqa, which like so many villages on the coastal plain from south to north had a long history going back to at least the sixth century. Amqa was also typical because it was a mixed Muslim and Druze community who had been living together in harmony before the Israeli policy of divide and rule forced a wedge between them, deporting the Muslims and allowing the Druze to join other Druze villages in the area.[15]

Today some of the remains of Amqa are still visible despite the massive destruction that occurred almost sixty years ago. In the midst of the wild grass that covers the area, one can clearly see the remnants of the school and the village mosque. Though now dilapidated, the mosque reveals even today the exquisite masonry the villagers produced for its construction.

it cannot be entered, as its current Jewish 'owner' uses it as a storehouse, but its size and unique structure are visible from the outside.

Operation Palm Tree completed the take-over of the Western Galilee. Some of the villages were left intact: Kfar Yassif, Iblin and the town of Shafa'Amr. These were mixed villages, with Christians, Muslims and Druze. Still, many of their inhabitants who proved of the 'wrong' origin or affiliation were deported. Actually, many families had deserted the villages before the occupation, as they knew what was in store for them. Some villages, in fact, were totally emptied, but they are there today because the Israelis allowed them to be repopulated by refugees from other villages they had destroyed. Such policies created confusion and havoc – as orders were followed by counter-orders, they disoriented even the expellers. In some of the mixed villages the Israelis ordered the frenzied expulsion of half of the population, mostly the Muslims, and then permitted Christian refugees from nearby emptied villages to resettle in the newly evacuated places, as happened in the cases of the villages of Kfar Yassif and Iblin, and the town of Shafa'Amr.

As a result of these population movements inside the Galilee, Shafa'Amr became a huge town, swollen by the streams of refugees entering it in the wake of the May-to-July operations in the surrounding area. It was occupied on 16 July but was basically left alone: that is, nobody was expelled. This was an exceptional decision that would recur in Nazareth – in both cases it was local commanders who took the initiative.

Yigael Yadin, the Acting Chief of Staff, visited Shafa'Amr later that month and was clearly taken aback to find an Arab town with all its inhabitants still there: 'The people of the town roam about freely,' he reported in his bewilderment to Ben-Gurion. Yadin immediately ordered the imposition of a curfew and a search-and-arrest campaign, but gave particular instructions to leave the Druze of Shafa'Amr alone.[16]

Operation Policeman

One pocket of resistance held out for so long that some of the villages in the area endured ten days of fighting. This happened along the coast south of Haifa. Of the six villages there, three fell before the second truce was announced; the other three succumbed *after* the truce had taken effect.

The first three were Tirat Haifa, Kfar Lam and Ayn Hawd. The largest of them was Tirat Haifa, only a few kilometres south of Haifa, with a population of 5000. Today it is a dismal Jewish development town – with almost the same name, Tirat Hacarmel – clinging to the lower western slopes of the Carmel, at the bottom of Haifa's wealthiest neighbourhood, Denya, which has gradually been expanding downwards from the crest of Mount Carmel (where Haifa University is located) but with Haifa's municipality studiously avoiding connecting the two with a road system.

It was the district's most populous village and the second largest in terms of area. It was called St Yohan de Tire during the time of the Crusaders, when it became a significant site for both Christian pilgrims and the local churches. Since then, with its Muslim majority, Tirat Haifa had always had a small community of Christians, both groups respecting the village's Christian heritage and its overall Muslim character. In 1596, when it was included in the sub-district of Lajjun, it had no more than 286 inhabitants. Three hundreds years later it was on the way to becoming a town but then fell prey to new centralisation policies in the late Ottoman period and the massive conscription of its younger people into the Ottoman army, most of whom chose not to return.

Tirat Haifa was another village that at the end of the Second World War emerged from tough and difficult times into the dawn of a new era. Signs of recovery were visible everywhere: new stone and mud brick houses were being built and the two village schools, one for boys and one for girls, were renovated. The village's economy was based on the cultivation of arable crops, vegetables and fruit. It was richer than most villages because it was endowed with an excellent water supply from the nearby springs. Its pride was its almonds, famous throughout the area. Tirat al-Lawz, the 'Tira of the almonds', was a household name in Palestine. An additional source of income was tourism, centred mainly around visits to the ruins of the monastery of St Brocardus, still there today.

Throughout my childhood, the remains of the village's old stone houses lay scattered around the cubic grey apartment blocks of the Jewish development town that had been built on the village site. After 1967 the local municipality demolished most of them, more out of profit-seeking real-estate zeal than as part of the ideological memoricide that had remained a priority for the Israelis.

Like so many other villages in the Greater Haifa area, Tirat Haifa was exposed, prior to its final depopulation, to constant attacks and onslaughts by Jewish forces. The Irgun bombarded it as early as December 1947, killing thirteen people, mainly children and the elderly. After the shelling a raiding party of twenty Irgun members approached and began firing at an isolated house on the edge of the village. Between 23 April and 3 May every woman and child of Tirat Haifa was taken out of the village as part of the over-all British 'mediation' effort that enabled the Jewish forces to cleanse the greater Haifa area unhampered by any external pressure. Tirat Haifa's women and children were transferred by buses to the West Bank while the men stayed behind. A unit of special forces consisting of the combined elite troops from several brigades were brought in to bring Tirat Haifa down on 16 July.

Later that same day came the turn of Kfar Lam. South of Tirat Haifa, this village was less wealthy, although it, too, enjoyed a good source of water – about fifteen springs flowed near the northern boundaries of the village. A dusty, unpaved road, off the main asphalt road between Haifa and Tel-Aviv led to the village. Its houses were made of hewn stone, the roofs of cement and the traditional arches of wood. It had no fences or guarding towers, not even in July.

The relative poverty of this village was due to its unusual system of land ownership, quite different from the villages around it. Half of the cultivated fields belonged to Ali Bek al-Khalil and his brother from Haifa, who leased the land for a share in the crops. A small number of families were not included in this leasing agreement and were forced to commute to Haifa for their livelihood. The village as a whole was closely connected to Haifa as most of its agricultural products were sold there. And here, too, three years before the Nakba, life looked brighter and more promising.

Kfar Lam was a particularly apolitical village, which might explain its relative complacency in the face of the destruction already wreaked on the surrounding area since February 1948. The Hagana intelligence file described the village as 'moderate', but already back in the early 1940s an ominous detail had been inserted into the file that hinted at its future fate. The file stated that the village had some Samaritans in it who may originally have been Jews, but who, in the 1940s, had converted to Islam. For the Zionist historian and leading politician of the Zionist movement, Yitzhak Ben-Zvi, this was enough to show that there had been continuity of Jewish presence along Palestine's coast.

This search for continuity was one of the main obsessions of the Zionist academia at the time. Ben-Zvi himself had published a book (in Yiddish) with Ben-Gurion as early as 1918 in which they claimed that the Arab fallahin (peasant farmers) were the descendents of Jewish peasants who had stayed behind in Palestine after the Roman Exile. Ben-Zvi continued to develop this argument in the 1930s and 40s. In his *Sha'ar ha-Yishuv* ('Gate to the Jewish Settlement'), he similarly argued that villagers in the Hebron mountains were actually Jews who had converted to Islam.

In July 1948, proof of continuity did not mean that the *people* of Kfar Lam were entitled to remain as citizens of the new Jewish state, only that their *village* was now 'rightfully returned' to the Jewish people. Neither the relatively low yield of its harvests nor the political indifference of its people could save the village, and only its proximity to the more resilient villages on the coast allowed it to survive into July.

While Kafr Lam has disappeared, the village of Ayn Hawd, occupied at the same time, is still almost intact. Adjectives such as 'beautiful', 'attractive' and other synonyms were used to describe certain villages, and many of them were indeed recognised as such by contemporary visitors and by the inhabitants themselves, who often gave their villages names that clearly expressed the particular charm, beauty and serenity they knew their location exuded, as for instance the people of Khayriyya – literally in Arabic 'The Blessing of the Land' – which Israel demolished and turned into the city of Tel-Aviv's garbage dump.

Ayn Hawd was indeed unusual. It captured a special place in the hearts of many in the area. The main hamulla in the village, the Abu al-Hija, were thought to have special healing powers and therefore many people frequented the village, making their way up from the coast towards the Carmel mountains on a winding road, fifteen kilometres south of Haifa. The village lay partly hidden in one of the many river valleys flowing from the mountain to the sea in the west. This particularly exquisite place was left intact due to the presence of some Bohemian types in the unit that occupied it: they immediately recognised the potential of the village and decided to leave it as they found it before coming back later to settle there and turn it into an artists' colony. For many years it hosted some of Israel's best-known artists, musicians and writers, often affiliated with the country's 'peace camp'. Houses that survived the ravages in the Old Cities of Safad and Jaffa were similarly turned into special artists' enclaves.

Ayn Hawd had already been attacked once in May and the five families making up the Abu al-Hija clan had successfully repelled the offensive, but on 16 July they succumbed. The original villagers were expelled and the governmental 'naming committee', a body in charge of replacing Palestinian names with Hebrew ones decided to call the occupied village Ein Hod. One of the five families of the Abu al-Hija clan found refuge in the countryside nearby a few miles to the east and settled there. Stubbornly and courageously refusing to move, they gradually created a new village under the old name of Ayn Hawd.

The success of this branch of the Abu al-Hija clan is quite remarkable. They looked for refuge first in the nearby village of Tirat Haifa, only to discover that that village had been occupied the day before. They were chased into the canyons near their own village but managed to hold out there. The Israeli commander reported that 'the operations to cleanse the pockets of resistance of refugees in the Wadi east of the village continue',[17] but they failed in their attempts to drive the family away. The rest of the people of Ayn Hawd were scattered, some as distant as Iraq and others as near as the Druze villages overlooking Ayn Hawd from the top of Mount Carmel.

In the 1950s the Abu al-Hija built new cement houses inside the forest that now envelops their village. The Israeli government refused to recognise them as a legal settlement and the threat of expulsion constantly hovered over their heads. In 1986 the government wanted to demolish the new village, but heroically, and against all odds, the Abu al-Hija succeeded in halting attempts to expel them. Finally, in 2005, a relatively liberal-minded Minister of the Interior granted the village semi-recognition.

The Jewish artist community, on the other hand, has gone into decline and seems less 'attractive' in the twenty-first century than it was in its heyday. The colony's coffee bar' 'Bonanza', located in the original village mosque, is generally empty these days. Marcel Janko, the artist founder of Jewish Ein Hod, wanted it to become the centre of Dadaism, the anti-establishment art movement that emerged in the early twentieth century and valued the 'primitive' as a counter to the classical Graeco-Roman tradition. Driven by a wish to preserve the 'primitive' essence of art, Janko was keen to save part of Ayn Hawd's original stone houses from brutal renovation. Soon, however, the original Ayn Hawd village dwellings were turned into modern abodes for European Jewish artists, and the magnificent old village school building became the setting for art exhibitions, carnivals and other tourist attractions.

Janko's own works fittingly represent the racism shown by the contemporary Israeli Left in its approach towards Arab culture in general and towards the Palestinians in particular, a covert and at times even nuanced, but nonetheless pervasive, racism in their writings, artistic works and political activity. Janko's paintings, for instance, incorporate Arab figures, but always fading into the background of occupied Ayn Hawd. In this way, Janko's works are forerunners of the paintings you can find today on the Apartheid wall Israel has planted deep in the West Bank: where it runs near Israeli highways, Israeli artists were asked to decorate parts of this 8-metre high concrete monster with panoramas of the scenic landscape that lies behind the Wall, but always making sure to eliminate the Palestinian villages that lie on the other side and the people who live in them.

Only three villages remained in the coastal area just south of Haifa, and throughout those ten days of fighting between the first and second truces a massive Jewish force tried but failed to capture them. Ben-Gurion appeared to have become obsessed with the three, and ordered the occupation effort to continue even after the second truce had come into effect; the High Command reported to the UN truce observers that the operation against the three villages was a policing activity, even choosing Operation Policeman as the codename for the whole assault.

The largest of the three was the village of Ijzim, which had 3000 inhabitants. It was also the one that resisted the attackers the longest. On its ruins the Jewish settlement of Kerem Maharal was erected. A few picturesque houses are still left, and in one of them lives the former head of the Israeli Secret Service and founder of the 'peace' proposal he recently concocted, together with a Palestinian professor, that abolishes the Palestinian refugees' right of return in exchange for a total withdrawal by Israel from the areas it occupied in 1967.

Operation Policeman (*Shoter*, in Hebrew) began on 25 July, exactly one week into the 'truce', but Ijzim survived another three days of fierce fighting in which a small number of armed villagers courageously held out against hundreds of Israeli soldiers. Israel brought in its air force to break the resistance. When the fighting was over, the population as a whole was expelled to Jenin. One hundred and thirty villagers died in the battle according to the recollection of the survivors. The Israeli intelligence officers of the northern front reported upon entering the village of Ijzim on July 28 that 'our forces collected 200 corpses, many of them civilians killed by our bombardment.'[18]

Ayn Ghazal fell earlier on. It had 3000 inhabitants and, like Kfar Lam, life was harder here than in other places. The houses of this village were mainly made of concrete, atypical of the architecture in the area, and many of them had special wells and holes – sometimes three metres deep – in which people kept wheat. This tradition and its unique construction style may have been the result of the village's ethnic origins. Ayn Ghazal was relatively new, 'only' 250 years old (by comparison, when we talk of relatively 'old' Jewish settlements, they might have been built only thirty to thirty-five years earlier, although a tiny minority were established at the end of the nineteenth century). The people of Ayn Ghazal had come from the Sudan, looking for jobs in Syria and Lebanon, and put down roots here (nearby villages such as Furaydis, Tantura, and Daliyat al-Rawha had been there for centuries).

Ayn Ghazal was a popular destination for many Muslims as it hosted a maqam, the burial place of a religious holy man called Shaykh Shehadeh. Some of the people who had left the village before it was attacked had taken refuge in the only two villages that were left intact on the coast out of the original sixty-four – Furaydis and Jisr al-Zarqa. Elderly members of these villages, ever since 1948, had been trying to maintain the maqam of Shaykh Shehadeh. Aware of these efforts and in an attempt to stop this journey of memory and worship, the Israeli authorities declared the maqam a holy Jewish site. One of the refugees from the village, Ali Hamuda, almost single-handedly safeguarded the maqam and kept its Muslim character alive. Although he was fined and threatened with arrest for having renovated it in 1985, he persisted in keeping the place of his worship sacred and the memory of his village alive.

The people of Ayn Ghazal who had stayed put rejoiced when they heard a second truce had come into effect. Even those who had been guarding the village since May thought they could now relax their guard. These were also the days of the annual Ramadan fast and on 26 July most of the villagers had come out onto the street in the afternoon to break the fast and were gathering at the few coffeehouses in the village centre when an aeroplane appeared and dropped a bomb that scored a direct hit on the crowd. The women and children fled in panic while the men stayed behind and, soon enough, saw the Jewish troops entering the village.[19]

The 'men' were ordered by the occupying forces to gather in one place, as was the routine throughout rural Palestine on such occasions. The informer, always hooded, and the intelligence officer soon appeared. The people watched as seventeen of them were selected, largely for having taken part in the 1936 Revolt, and killed on the spot. The rest were expelled.[20] On the same day, a similar fate befell the sixth village in this pocket of resistance, Jaba.

Operation Dani

Operation 'Dani' was the innocent-sounding codename for the attack on the two Palestinian towns of Lydd and Ramla, located roughly halfway between Jaffa and Jerusalem.

Lydd lies fifty metres above sea level on the inner plains of Palestine. In the local popular memory it is engraved as the 'city of the mosques', some of which were famous around the Arab world. For example, the Big Mosque, al-Umari, which still stands today, was built during the time of the Mamluks by Sultan Rukn al-Din Baybars, who took the city from the Crusaders. Another well-known mosque is the Dahamish Mosque, which could host 800 worshippers and had six shops adjacent to it. Today, Lyyd is the Jewish development town of Lod – one of the belt towns encircling Tel-Aviv housing the poorest and most underprivileged of the metropolis. Lod was also once the name for many years of Israel's only international airport, today called Ben-Gurion Airport.

On 10 July 1948 David Ben-Gurion appointed Yigal Allon as the commander of the attack and Yitzhak Rabin as his second in command. Allon first ordered al-Lydd to be bombarded from the air, the first city to be attacked in this way. This was followed by a direct attack on the city's centre, which caused all the remaining ALA volunteers to leave: some had fled their positions earlier on learning that the Jordanian Legion units, stationed near the city, had been instructed by their British chief, Glubb Pasha, to withdraw. As both Lydd and Ramla were clearly within the designated Arab state, both the residents and the defendants had assumed that the Legion would resist the Israeli occupation by force, as they did in East Jerusalem and in the Latrun area, west of the city (not far from Lydd and Ramla), but they were wrong. For his decision to retreat, Glubb Pasha later lost his position and had to return to Britain.

Deserted by both the volunteers and the Legionaries, the men of Lydd, armed with some old rifles, took shelter in the Dahamish Mosque in the city centre. After a few hours of fighting they surrendered, only to be massacred inside the mosque by the Israeli forces. Palestinian sources recount that in the mosque and in the streets nearby, where the Jewish troops went on yet another rampage of murder and pillage, 426 men, women and children were killed (176 bodies were found in the mosque). The following day, 14 July, the Jewish soldiers went from house to house taking the people outside and marching about 50,000 of them out of the city towards the West Bank (more than half of them were already refugees from nearby villages).[21]

One of the most detailed accounts on what unfolded in al-Lydd was published in the summer of 1998 by the sociologist Salim Tamari in the *Journal of Palestine Studies*. It drew on interviews with Spiro Munayar, who had lived all his life in Lydd and was an eyewitness to the events on that terrible day in July. He saw the occupation, the massacre in the mosque, the way Israeli troops barged into the houses and dragged out the families – sparing not a single house. He watched as the houses were then looted and the refugees robbed before they were told to start marching towards the West Bank, in one of the warmest months of the year, in one of the hottest places in Palestine.

He was working as a young physician in the local hospital, alongside the dedicated Dr George Habash, the future founder and leader of the Popular Front for the Liberation of Palestine. He recalls the endless numbers of corpses and the wounded who were brought in from the scene of the slaughter, and these were the same horrible experiences that were to haunt Habash and drive him to take the road of guerilla warfare in order to redeem his town and homeland from those who had devastated it in 1948.

Munayar also recounted the anguished scenes of expulsion he witnessed:

> During the night the soldiers began going into the houses in areas they had occupied, rounding up the population and expelling them from the city. Some were told to go to Kharruba and Barfilyya, while other soldiers said: 'Go to King Abdullah, to Ramallah'. The streets filled with people setting out for indeterminate destinations.

The same sights were observed by the few foreign journalists who were in the town that day. Two of them were Americans apparently invited by the Israeli forces to accompany them in the attack, what today we would call 'embedded' correspondents. Keith Wheeler of *The Chicago Sun Times* was one of the two. He wrote: 'Practically everything in their [the Israeli forces'] way died. Riddled corpses lay by the roadside.' The other, Kenneth Bilby of *The New York Herald Tribune*, reported seeing 'the corpses of Arab men, women and even children strewn about in the wake of the ruthlessly brilliant charge.' Bilby also wrote a book on these events, *New Star in the Near East*, published two years later.

One might wonder why newspaper reports of a massacre on this scale did not provoke an outcry in the United States. For those who have been shocked by the callousness and inhumanity that US troops have sometimes displayed towards Arabs in the operation in Iraq, the reports from Lydd may seem strangely familiar. At the time, American reporters like Wheeler were astonished by what ironically he called the Israeli '*Blitzkrieg*', and by the resoluteness of the Jewish troops. Like Bilby's description ('ruthlessly brilliant'), Wheeler's account of the Israeli army's campaign sadly neglected to provide a similarly probing report on the number of Palestinians killed, wounded, or expelled from their villages. The correspondents' reports were totally one-sided.

More sensitive and less biased was the *London Economist* as it described for its readers the horrific scenes that took place when inhabitants were forced to start marching after their houses had been looted, their family members murdered, and their city wrecked: 'The Arab refugees were systematically stripped of all their belongings before they were sent on their trek to the frontier. Household belongings, stores, clothing, all had to be left behind.'

This systematic robbery was also recollected by Munayar:

> The occupying soldiers had set up roadblocks on all the roads leading east and were searching the refugees, particularly the women, stealing their gold jewelry from their necks, wrists, and fingers and whatever was hidden in their clothes, as well as money and everything else that was precious and light enough to carry.

Ramla, or Ramleh as is it is known today, the home town of one of the PLO's most respected leaders, the late Khalil al-Wazir, Abu Jihad, lay nearby. The attack on this town with its 17,000 inhabitants had started two days earlier on

12 July 1948, but the final occupation was only completed after the Israelis had taken al-Lydd. The city had been the target of terrorist attacks by Jewish forces in the past; the first one had taken place on 18 February 1948, when the Irgun had planted a bomb in one of its markets that killed several people.

Terrified by the news coming from Lydd, the city notables reached an agreement with the Israeli army that ostensibly allowed the people to stay. The Israeli units entered the city on 14 July and immediately began a search-and-arrest operation in which they rounded up 3000 people who they transferred to a prison camp nearby, and on the same day they started looting the city. The commander on the spot was Yitzhak Rabin. He recalled how Ben-Gurion had first called him in to his office to discuss the fate of both Lydd and Ramla: 'Yigal Alon asked: what is to be done with the population [in Lydd and Ramla]? Ben-Gurion waved his hand in a gesture that said: 'Drive them out!'[22]

The people of both cities were forced to march, without food and water, to the West Bank, many of them dying from thirst and hunger on the way. As only a few hundred were allowed to stay in both towns, and given that people from nearby villages had fled there for refuge, Rabin estimated that a total of 50,000 people had been 'transferred' in this inhuman way. Again, the inevitable question present itself: three years after the Holocaust, what went through the minds of those Jews who watched these wretched people pass by?

Further to the west, the Arab Legion, which had abandoned the two Palestinian towns, defended the Latrun area so tenaciously that the battle here would be engraved in the collective memory of the Israeli armed forces as its biggest defeat in the war. The bitter memory of this fiasco provoked feelings of revenge; the opportunity surfaced in June 1967 when Israel occupied the area. Retaliation then was directed not towards the Jordanians, but towards the Palestinians: three of the villages in the Latrun valley – Biddu, Yalu and Imwas – were expelled and wiped out. The mass deportation of the villagers was the beginning of a new wave of ethnic cleansing.

The Legion also successfully repelled Israeli attacks on the eastern neighbourhoods of Jerusalem in July, especially on Shaykh Jarrah. 'Occupy and destroy', a vengeful Ben-Gurion demanded from the army with this charming neighbourhood in mind.[23] Thanks to the defiance of the Legion, today one can still find among its many treasures the American Colony Hotel – originally one of the first houses built outside the walls in the late nineteenth century by Rabah al-Husayni, a leading member of the local nobility.

Operation Palm Tree continues

On 11 July, the entry in Ben-Gurion's diary reflects considerable confidence in Israel's military strength against the combined might of its Arab neighbours: '[I ordered them] to occupy Nablus, [to inflict] heavy bombardment on Cairo, Alexandria, Damascus and Beirut'[24] Nablus, however, was not captured, despite Ben-Gurion's instructions, but that was to be the fate of another Palestinian city in the ten days of frantic activity between the two truces: the city of Nazareth. Its story forms one of the most exceptional episodes in the urbicide campaign. This relatively large city had only 500 ALA volunteers who, under the command of Madlul Bek, were meant to protect not only the indigenous population but also the thousands of refugees from nearby villages who were flooding into the crowded city and its environs.

The attack on Nazareth started 9 July, the day after the first truce ended. When the mortar bombardment on the city began, the people anticipated forced eviction and decided they would prefer to leave. However, Madlul Bek ordered them to stay. Telegrams between him and commanders of the Arab armies that Israel intercepted reveal that he, and other ALA officers, were ordered to try to stop expulsions by all means: the Arab governments wanted to prevent more refugees streaming into their countries. Thus we find Madlul turning back some people who were already making their way out of the city. When the shelling intensified, however, he saw no point in trying to stand up to the overwhelmingly superior Jewish forces, and encouraged people to leave. He himself surrendered the city at 10 pm on 16 July.

Ben-Gurion did not wish the city of Nazareth to be depopulated for the simple reason that he knew the eyes of the Christian world were fixed on the city. But a senior general and the supreme commander of the operation, Moshe Karmil, ordered the total eviction of all the people who had stayed behind ('16,000,' noted Ben-Gurion, '10,000 of whom were Christians').[25] Ben-Gurion now instructed Karmil to retract his order and let the people stay. He agreed with Ben Donkelman, the military commander of the operations: 'Here the world is watching us,' which meant that Nazareth was luckier than any other city in Palestine.[26] Today Nazareth is still the only Arab city in pre-1967 Israel.

Once again, however, not all those allowed to stay were spared. Some of the people were expelled or arrested on the first day of the occupation, as the intelligence officers began searching the city from house to house and seizing people according to a pre-prepared list of suspects and 'undesirables'. Palti Sela was going around with a well-known Arab personality from Nazareth, carrying with them seven notebooks filled with the names of people who could stay, either because they belonged to clans that had been collaborating with the Israelis, or for some other reason.

A similar process took place in the villages around Nazareth, and in 2002 Palti Sela claimed that thanks to his efforts 1600 people had been allowed to stay, a decision for which, again, he was later criticised. 'The notebooks are lost,' he told his interviewer. He recalled he had refused to write down the name of a single Bedouin: 'They are all thieves,' he had told his partners in the operation.[27]

But nobody was really safe, not even the Arab notable – who will remain anonymous – who accompanied Palti Sela. The first military governor installed after the war did not, for some reason, like this person and wanted to deport him. Palti Sela then stepped in and saved him by promising to move him, his close family and friends to Haifa. He admitted that actually quite a few of those listed in his 'good' notebooks were eventually forced out of the country after all.

One more village in the area between Nazareth and Tiberias was targeted for occupation after attempts to take it over in previous months had failed, and this was the village of Hittin. A 1937 photograph of the village could have come straight from a tourist brochure of today's Tuscany or Greece. Clinging to the mountain slopes, eight kilometres northwest of Tiberias, at an elevation of 125 metres above sea level, but seemingly much higher as it overlooks the Sea of Galilee which is under sea level, the spot is breathtaking. The black-and-white picture clearly shows Hittin's stone-built houses covered by roofs made of arched wood and surrounded by orchards and cactus fences. Cars had easy access to the village, but in 1948 it proved a hard site to take as it put up strong resistance, even though no more than 25 people, all poorly equipped volunteers, defended the village.

The village's history goes all the way back to the famous battle between

Salah al-Din and the Crusaders in 1187. Its fame also rested on the presence of the grave of Nabi Shu'ayb, the holy prophet of the Palestinian Druze, who identify him with Jethro, Moses's father-in-law, and for whom his maqam is a place of worship and pilgrimage. The fact that the Druze had already gone over to the other side and allied themselves with the Israeli army spurred the Israelis in their ambition to capture the village. Today a website for Hittin refugees contains the following reference to the Druze: 'Whether they [the Druze] like it or not, they are still Palestinian Arabs,' a clear reference to the fact that the Druze showed little solidarity or affinity with their fellow Palestinians, let alone compassion. On the contrary, many of them joined in the destruction of rural Palestine, to which – tragically – they, of course, also belonged.[28]

As with so many of the villages mentioned, the Nakba hit when prosperity had just arrived. A new school and a new irrigation system were the signs of its recently won affluence, but these were all lost to the Hittin residents after 17 July 1948, when a unit of Brigade Seven entered the village and began cleansing it in a particularly brutal manner. Many people escaped to nearby villages that would be occupied in October, when they would be uprooted a second time. This brought to an end Operation Palm Tree, which expelled all the villages around Nazareth.

The troops on the ground could now count on the embryonic Israeli air force for assistance. Two of the villages, Saffuriyya and Mujaydil, were shelled from the air, as were several villages on the coast: Jaba, Ijzim and Ayn Ghazal were bombarded into submission well into the second truce. In fact, what developed in July was ethnic cleansing from the air, as air attacks became a major tool for sowing panic and wreaking destruction in Palestine's larger villages in order to force people to flee before the actual occupation of the village. This new tactic would come into its own in October.

But already, in the second half of July, Israeli pilots could tell from the spectacle unfolding before their eyes how effective their sorties were: throngs of refugees, carrying a few hastily collected possessions, flooded out of the villages onto the main roads and slowly made their way towards what they thought would be safer havens. For some troops on the ground this was too good a target to miss. A report from 17 July 1948 of the Northern Command reads as follows: 'Our forces began harassing the only road leading out of Sejra where a throb of refugees were making their way.'[29] Sejra was a village near Mount Tabor, which had maintained an uneasy relationship with the 'veteran' Zionist colonies that had taken in Ben-Gurion when he first arrived in Palestine.

In the summer of 1948, however, Ben-Gurion was less interested in the north, where he had begun his career, and was focusing on the south, where he would end it. In July, the ethnic cleansing operations for the first time extended to the Naqab (the Negev) as well. The Negev Bedouin had inhabited the region since the Byzantine period, and had been following their semi-nomadic away of life since at least 1500. There were 90,000 Bedouin in 1948, divided between 96 tribes, already in the process of establishing a land-ownership system, grazing rights and water access. Jewish troops immediately expelled eleven tribes, while they forced another nineteen into reservations that Israel defined as closed military areas, which meant they were allowed to leave only with a special permit. The expulsion of Negev Bedouin continued until 1959.[30]

The first tribe that was targeted was the Jubarat. Part of the tribe was expelled in July; the tribe as a whole was then forcibly transferred in mid-October, when the second truce was officially over, the majority of them to Hebron and the rest to the Gaza Strip. In 1967, Israel uprooted them once more, this time expelling them to the eastern bank of the River Jordan. Most of the other tribes were driven away towards the end of 1948.

THE TRUCE THAT WASN'T

The news of an impending second truce to come into effect on 18 July 1948 came at an inconvenient moment for the ethnic cleansing operation. Some operations were sped up and thus completed before the truce began, which was the case with the occupation of the villages Qula and Khirbat Shaykh Meisar. By then, the Israelis had added two towns, Lydd and Ramla, and another sixty-eight villages to the 290 they had already occupied and cleansed.

The second truce was violated the moment it came into effect. In its first ten days Israeli forces occupied key villages north of Haifa, another pocket they had left alone for a while, as they had to the villages south of the city along the coast. Damun, Imwas, Tamra, Qabul and Mi'ar were thus taken. This completed the occupation of the Western Galilee.

Fighting also continued in the south during the second truce, as the

Israelis found it difficult to defeat the Egyptian forces that had been caught in the so-called Faluja pocket. Egypt's main military effort was directed towards the coast where their advance was halted at the end of the first week of the official war. Since that debacle they found themselves gradually being pushed back to the border. A second expeditionary force had been sent to southern Jerusalem, where its troops had some initial successes. By the middle of July, however, a third Egyptian contingent in the northern Negev had been cut off from both the forces on the coast and those in southern Jerusalem, and now counted in vain on the Jordanian reinforcements that were scheduled to meet up with them in the original Arab war scheme.

By the end of July, the Israelis started strengthening the siege around this pocket to force it to surrender. The Egyptians, however, held on until the end of the year. The disintegration of the Egyptian forces left the northern Negev, from the slopes of Mt Hebron to the Mediterranean Sea near Gaza, at the mercy of the Israeli troops. The belt of villages that had been settled centuries ago on the edge of the arid Negev desert were now stormed, occupied and expelled in quick succession. Only the Gaza Strip and the West Bank were successfully protected by Egyptian and Jordanian troops respectively, who thereby prevented many more refugees from being added to the thousands of Palestinians already expelled since December 1947.

Sensing that their violation of the truce would go uncensored as long as it was directed towards the remaining 'Arab' pockets within the Jewish state as designated by UN Resolution 181, the Zionist leadership also continued their operations in August and beyond. They now clearly envisaged this 'Jewish state' as stretching over most of Palestine – in fact, all of it – had it not been for the Egyptian and, crucially, Jordanian steadfastness. Consequently, villages that had gradually been isolated were now easily cleansed while the UN observers, who had been sent in to supervise the truce, watched nearby.

Also in August, the Jewish forces took the opportunity of the truce to make some modifications to areas they had already occupied. These might have been on the orders of a local commander, for which he did not need authorisation from above, or, occasionally, at the request of a particular group, which may have collaborated with the Zionists and now wanted to take part in the division of the spoils. One such place was the Druze village of Isfiya on the Carmel. The Druze notables of Isfiya asked for the Bedouin living in their town to be expelled, claiming they were thieves and generally 'incompatible'. The commander in charge said he did not have the time to deal with expulsions of people who were not in any case totally alien to the village. The Bedouins of Isfiya are still there today, discriminated against as 'lesser' members of the local community, but fortunate that the Israeli army was too busy to follow up on the request of the Druze.[31] These internal skirmishes show that in the relative calm that had descended on the fronts with the Arab armies, Israel had decided the time had come to institutionalise the occupation.

The Zionist leadership seemed most pressured to determine the status of the lands it had occupied but that were legally within the UN-designated Arab state. In August, Ben-Gurion still referred to these territories as 'administered areas', not part of the state as yet but governed by a military judicial system. The Israeli government wanted to obfuscate the legal status of these areas, which had originally been granted to the Palestinians, because of its apprehension that the UN would demand an explanation for their occupation, an apprehension that proved totally unfounded. Inexplicably, the issue of Israel's legal (read: 'illegal') status in UN-designated Arab Palestine was never raised during the momentary interest the international community briefly displayed in the fate of post-mandatory Palestine and that of its indigenous population. Until Israel was accepted as a full member of the UN, in May 1949, the designation of these areas alternated between 'administered' and 'occupied'. In May 1949, all distinctions disappeared, along with the villages, the fields and the houses – all 'dissolved' into the Jewish State of Israel.

The Collapse of the Second Truce

The second truce was extended through the summer of 1948, although due to continuing hostilities on both sides, it seemed a truce in name only. However, the UN did succeed in averting an Israeli attack on the Golan Heights and the only proper town there, Qunaitra, the order for which arrived in the forces' headquarters on the day the truce ended. Even at a distance of almost sixty years, it makes chilling reading: 'Your orders,' wrote Yigael Yadin to the commander in charge, 'are to destroy the city'.[32] The city would remain relatively unscathed until 1967, when it was ethnically cleansed by Israeli troops occupying the Golan Heights. In 1974, Yadin's terse order was implemented literally when the Israeli forces destroyed the town of Qunaitra, before returning it to the Syrians a complete ghost town, as part of a disengagement settlement.

In 1948 Israel's determination to take the Golan Heights was fed by the gradual withdrawal of the Syrian troops, first to the slopes of the Golan and then further into the Syrian hinterland, but most of the leaders of the Jewish state coveted Palestine, not Syria. In August there were still three main areas of Palestine that Israel had not yet taken but that Ben-Gurion saw as essential to would-be Israel: Wadi Ara, the western part of the upper Galilee, and the southern Negev. The first two were heavily populated Palestinian areas and thus became the inevitable targets of the ethnic cleansing campaign, wholly outside the theatre of war with the regular Arab armies that had in any case petered out in August due to the truce.

September 1948 looked very much like August 1948: real fighting with the regular Arab armies had dwindled, leaving Israeli troops trying to complete the job they had started in December 1947. Some of them were sent on impossible missions to go beyond the occupation of the seventy-eight per cent of Palestine that had already proven to be within Israel's grasp. One of these assignments in September was for the troops to try for a third time to occupy Wadi Ara and the northern tip of the West Bank, with special orders to capture Qalqilya and Tul-Karem. This was Operation Autumn. The attempt to invade the Wadi Ara area was again repelled. This part would be annexed by Israel when King Abdullah of Jordan decided to cede it in the spring of 1949 as part of the armistice agreement between the two countries. It is one of the ironies of history that many Israelis today, frightened by a potential adverse shift in the 'demographic balance', favour the transfer of this area back to the Palestinian Authority's West Bank. The option between being imprisoned in a locked Bantustan on the West Bank or 'enjoying' second-class citizenship in Israel holds no exciting prospects either way, to say the least, but the people of the Wadi understandably go for the latter, as they rightly suspect that, as in the past, the Israelis want the territory without the people. Israel has already dislocated 200,000 people since it started erecting its Segregation Wall in an area very near to the Wadi and also heavily populated by Palestinians.

In September 1948, every single one of the fifteen villages that make up Wadi Ara showed resilience and bravery in repelling the attackers, aided by Iraqi officers from the nearby contingent that the Arab League had dispatched to protect the northern West Bank when the war started. These

Iraqis were among the few of Palestine's neighbours who actually fought and succeeded in rescuing whole Palestinian villages. Captain Abu Rauf Abd al-Raziq was one such Iraqi officer who helped defend the villages of Taytaba and Qalansuwa. He had chivalrously decided to stay behind when all the other Iraqi soldiers had received orders to leave a few weeks before Operation Autumn. Major Abd al-Karim and Captain Farhan from the Iraqi army led the fortified opposition in Zayta and Jat, and Sargent Khalid Abu Hamud supervised the resistance in Attil. Captain Najib and Muhammad Sulayman did the same in Baqa al-Gharbiyya, Khalil Bek in the village of Ara and Mamduh Miara in Arara. The list of Iraqi junior officers mounting the guard and taking the lead is impressively long.

September also saw the preparations for Operation Snir, in another effort to take over the Golan Heights, including once more the town of Qunaitra, with 14 September set as D-day. The first stage was delayed to the 26th and eventually trimmed down to a mini-operation codenamed '*Bereshit*' (Genesis), involving the attempt to take a Syrian stronghold that, according to the UN map, was inside the Jewish state (Outpost 223). The Syrian defence forces repelled one Israeli attack after another. As part of their preparations, the Israelis tried to contact Circassian and Druze soldiers in the Syrian army to persuade them to collaborate. Israel's military action on the Syrian line continued well into the spring of 1949 and included orders not only to occupy outposts but also villages. On 1 April 1949 the orders were then revised, confining the forces to offensives against military outposts only.[33]

In September the ethnic cleansing operation continued in the central Galilee, where Israeli troops wiped out Palestinian pockets ahead of the last big operation that was to come a month later in the upper Galilee and in the south of Palestine. Local volunteers and the ALA put up some tough resistance in several villages, most notably Ilabun. A report by the Israeli forces describes their abortive assault: 'Tonight our forces raided Ilabun. After overcoming the enemy's resistance, we found the village deserted; after inflicting damage and slaughtering a herd, our forces withdrew while constantly exchanging fire with the enemy.'[34] In other words, although Ilabun had not yet been taken, it had already been emptied of most of its inhabitants. In the village of Tarshiha, on the other hand, mostly Christian Palestinians defended the village while the majority of the people were still there. With hindsight, it would seem that it was their decision to stay that saved them from expulsion, although, had most of them been Muslim, their fate could have been very different. Tarshiha was eventually occupied in October, but was not subsequently evacuated. Had it been taken in September, this outcome, too, might have been very different, since the orders for Operation *Alef Ayn*, from 19 September 1948, read: 'Tarshiha has to be evicted to the north.'[35]

But such moments of grace were few and far between and were certainly not bestowed upon the final group of villages that were depopulated in the western part of the upper Galilee and in the southern parts of the Hebron area, Beersheba, and along the southern coast line.

Chapter 8

Completing the Job: October 1948–January 1949

Over 1.5 million ethnic Albanians – at least 90% of the Kosovo population of the province had been forcibly expelled from their homes. At least a million left the province and half a million appear to be internally displaced persons. This is a campaign on a scale not seen in Europe since the Second World War.

State Department Report on Kosovo, 1999.

In 1948, 85% of the Palestinians living in the areas that became the state of Israel became refugees.

It is estimated that there were more than 7 million Palestinian refugees and displaced persons at the beginning of 2003.

Badil Resource Centre: Facts and figures.

The month of October began rather frustratingly for the Israeli cleansing forces. The Galilee, especially in its upper parts, was still controlled by Palestinian volunteers reinforced by al-Qawqji's ALA units. The latter could still be found in many villages in the northern Galilee – all part of the UN-designated Arab state – where they tried to wage a mini-guerilla warfare against the armed Jewish forces, mainly in the form of sniper fire at convoys and troops. But theirs was an ineffective kind of resistance, largely in vain. October also saw the final futile attempt by regular forces from Lebanon to add their firepower in a last pathetic gesture of Arab solidarity as they shelled one Jewish settlement, Manara, high up in the Galilee. Down south in the lower Galilee the Arab volunteers were left with one artillery gun in Ilabun. It symbolised their imminent and total collapse.

Whatever resistance may still have existed was wiped out during the onslaught of Operation Hiram in the middle of the month. Hiram was the name of the biblical king of Tyre, which was one of the targets of this ambitious and expansionist scheme: Israel's takeover of the upper Galilee and Southern Lebanon. With intensive artillery and air force attacks, Jewish troops captured both in a matter of two weeks.

OPERATION HIRAM

These two weeks now rank, together with the heroic struggle to save Wadi Ara, as one of the most impressive chapters in the history of the Palestinian resistance during the Nakba. The Israeli air force dropped about 10,000 leaflets calling upon the villagers to surrender, although not promising them any immunity from expulsion. None of the villages did and, almost as a whole, came out to confront the Israeli forces.

Thus, for a brief period, in courageous defiance of the vastly superior Israeli military power, Palestinian villages, for the first time since the ethnic cleansing started, turned themselves into strongholds, standing up to the besieging Israeli troops. A mixture of local youth and the remnants of the ALA were entrenched for a week or two, holding out with what meagre arms they had before being overpowered by the assailants. Fifty such brave men defended Ramaysh; others could be found in Deir al-Qasi, most of them in fact not locals but refugees from Saffuriyya, vowing not to be displaced again. They were commanded by a man called Abu Hammud from the ALA. Unfortunately, we only have the names of a few officers from the Israeli intelligence files and oral histories, such as Abu Ibrahim who defended Kfar Manda, but, like the Iraqi officers mentioned in the Wadi Ara campaign, they should all be written into the Palestinian, and universal, book of heroes who did everything they could to try to prevent ethnic cleansing from taking place. Israel, and the West in general, refers to them anonymously and collectively as Arab insurgents or terrorists – as they have done with the

Palestinians who fought within the PLO until the 1980s, and others who led the two uprisings against the Israeli occupation in the West Bank and the Gaza Strip in 1987 and 2000. I have no illusion that it will take more than this book to reverse a reality that demonises a people who have been colonised, expelled and occupied, and glorifies the very people who colonised, expelled and occupied them.

This handful of warriors of a sort were inevitably defeated, subjected to heavy bombardments from the air and fierce ground attacks. The ALA volunteers withdrew first, after which the local villagers decided to surrender, quite often through UN mediation. But a distingushing feature of this phase in the Nakba was that the withdrawal of the volunteers, who by now had already spent ten months in Palestine, only came about after they had desperately fought to defend the villages, quite often disobeying orders from their headquarters to leave: four hundred such volunteers lost their lives in those days in October.

The Israeli air bombardments were massive and caused a considerable amount of 'collateral damage' to the Palestinian villages. Some villages suffered more than others from heavy pounding: Rama, Suhmata, Malkiyya and Kfar Bir'im. Only Rama was left intact; the other three were occupied and destroyed.

Most of the villages in the upper Galilee were seized in a single day at the end of October: Deir Hanna, Ilabun, Arraba, Iqrit, Farradiyya, Mi'ilya, Khirbat Irribin, Kfar Inan, Tarbikha, Tarshiha, Mayrun, Safsaf, Sa'sa, Jish, Fassuta, and Qaddita. The list is long and includes another ten villages. Some villagers were evicted, some were allowed to stay.

The main question about those days is no longer why villages were expelled, but rather why some were allowed to remain, obviously almost always as a result of the decision made by a local commander. Why was Jish left intact and nearby Qaddita and Mayrun expelled by force? And why was Rama spared, while nearby Safsaf was totally demolished? It is hard to tell and much of what follows is based on speculation.

Located on the well-travelled road between Acre and Safad, the village of Rama was already overcrowded, having earlier taken in a large number of refugees from other villages. The size of the village, but quite possibly its large Druze community, were two factors that probably influenced the local decision not to expel its population. However, even for villages that were allowed to stay, scores, sometimes hundreds, of their inhabitants were imprisoned in POW camps or expelled to Lebanon. In fact, the Hebrew noun *tihur*, 'cleansing', assumed new meanings in October. It still described, as before, the total expulsion and destruction of a village, but it could now also represent other activities, such as selective search-and-expulsion operations.

While Israel's divide-and-rule policy proved effective in the case of the Druze, to whom it promised not only immunity but also arms as rewards for their collaboration, the Christian communities were less 'cooperative'. Israeli troops at first routinely deported them together with the Muslims, but then started transferring them to transit camps in the central coastal areas. In October, Muslims rarely remained long in these camps but were 'transported' – in the language of the Israeli army – to Lebanon. But Christians were now offered a different deal. In return for a vow of allegiance to the Jewish state, they were allowed to return to their villages for a short time. To their credit, most of the Christians refused to participate willingly in such a selection process. As a result, the army soon meted out the same treatment to Christian as to Muslim villages where they did not have a Druze population.

Instead of waiting to be deported, imprisoned or killed, many villagers simply ran away. Heavy bombardments in advance of the occupation pre-cipitated the flight of many villagers, varying in numbers from case to case. But in most instances, the majority of the people bravely stayed put until they were forcibly uprooted. Additionally, it would appear that during the very last days of October the 'cleansing' stamina of the Israeli troops was beginning to wane, because villages with large populations were eventually allowed to stay. This may help explain why Tarshiha, Deir Hanna and Ilabun are still intact today.

Or rather, half of the people of Ilabun are still with us today: the other half of the original population live in refugee camps in Lebanon. Those who were allowed to resettle in the village went through horrific experi-ences. During the occupation, the villagers had taken refuge in Ilabun's two churches. The frightened community crowded inside the small church buildings, cowering at the entrances as they were forced to listen to a long 'speech' by the Israeli commander of the operation. A sadistic and capricious person, he told the besieged villagers that he blamed them for the mutilation of two Jewish bodies, for which he instantly retali-ated by mowing down several young men in front of the horrified congregation. The rest of the people were then forcibly evicted, apart from the men between the ages of ten and fifty who were led away as prisoners of war.[1]

At first, everyone the village was expelled, and started making their way in a long column marching towards the Lebanese border, several of the villagers dying on the way. Then the Israeli commander changed his mind and ordered the Christians, who made up half the deportees, to turn back along the same painful and arduous route they had just taken through the rocky mountains of the Galilee. Seven hundred and fifty people were thus allowed to return to their village.

The question of why certain villages were allowed to remain is perplexing, but equally hard to understand is why the Israeli forces subjected certain villages and not others to treatment that proved exceptionally savage. Why, for example, from all the villages conquered in the final days of October were Sa'sa and Safsaf exposed to such barbarity while others were exempted from it?

War Crimes During the Operation

As mentioned earlier, in February 1948 Jewish troops had perpetrated a massacre in the village of Sa'sa that ended in the killing of fifteen villagers, including five children. Sa'sa is located on the main road to Mount Myarun (today Meron), the highest mountain peak in Palestine. After it had been occupied, the soldiers of Brigade Seven ran amok, firing randomly at anyone in the houses and on the streets. Besides the fifteen villagers killed, they left behind them a large number of wounded. The troops then demolished all the houses, apart from a few that the members of Kibbutz Sasa, built on the ruins of the village, took over for themselves after the forced eviction of their original owners. The chronicle of what happened in Sa'sa in 1948 cannot easily be constructed from the archival material, but there is a highly active community of survivors bent on preserving their testimonies for posterity. Most of the refugees live in Naher al-Barid, a refugee camp near Tripoli, Lebanon; some are in Rashidiyya camp near Tyre, and others, mostly from a single clan, live in Ghazzawiyya. A smaller community also resides in the Ayn Hilwa refugee camp in southern Lebanon, while I met a few of the survivors now living in the village of Jish, in the Galilee.[2] They find it difficult to revisit the horrible events surrounding the occupation of their village. Though more information needs to be gathered before we can reconstruct exactly how events unfolded in Sa'sa, the story they tell does indicate, as in the case of the survivors of Tantura, that the Israeli troops perpetrated a massacre in the village.

We know more about Safsaf. Muhammad Abdullah Edghaim was born 15 years before the Nakba. He had attended elementary school in the village until the seventh grade and had completed his first year in Safad's high school when the city fell into Jewish hands in May. No longer able to attend school, he was at home when a mixed unit of Jewish and Druze soldiers entered his village on 29 October 1948.

Their arrival had been preceded by heavy bombardment that had killed, among others, one of Galilee's best known singers, Muhammad Mahmnud Nasir Zaghmout. He died when a shell hit a group of villagers working in the vineyards to the west of the village. The young boy witnessed the singer's family trying to carry his body to the village, but they had to abandon the attempt due to the heavy shelling.

Every one of the defenders of Safsaf, among them ALA volunteers, was waiting, for some reason, for a Jewish attack to arrive from the east, but it came from the west and the village was quickly overrun. The following morning the people were ordered to assemble in the village square. The familiar procedure for identifying 'suspects' now took place, this time also involving the Druze soldiers, and a large number were picked out from the captured population. Seventy of the unfortunate men were taken out, blindfolded and then moved to a remote spot and summarily shot. Israeli archival documents confirm this case.[3] The rest of the villagers were then ordered to leave. Unable to collect even their most meagre personal possessions, they were driven out, with the Israeli troops firing shots above their heads, towards the nearby border with Lebanon.

The oral testimonies, unlike the Israeli military archives, tell of even worse atrocities. There is very little reason to doubt these eyewitness accounts, as so many of them have been corroborated by other sources for other cases. Survivors recall how four women and a girl were raped in front of the other villagers and how one pregnant woman was bayoneted.[4]

A few people were left behind, as in Tantura, to collect and bury the dead – several elderly men and five boys. Safsaf in Arabic means 'weeping willow'. Mahmoud Abdulah Edghaim, our main source for the atrocities, is today an old man, still living in the refugee camp of Ayn Hilwah. His little hut is surrounded by the many weeping willows he planted when he first arrived there almost sixty years ago. This is all that remains of Safsaf.

Bulayda was the last village taken during Operation Hiram. It was left until the end as its people proved steadfast in their determination to protect their homes. It was very close to the Lebanese border and Lebanese soldiers crossed the fence and fought alongside the villagers – probably the only significant Lebanese contribution to the defence of the Galilee. For ten days, the village withstood repeated assaults and raids. In the end, realising the hopelessness of their situation, the population fled even before the Israeli soldiers moved in: they did not want to undergo the horrors the people of Safsaf had experienced.

By 31 October, the Galilee, once an area almost exclusively Palestinian, was occupied in its entirety by the Israeli army.

Mopping-Up Operations

In November and December, some cleansing activity continued in the Galilee, but it took the form of what the Israelis called 'mopping up operations'. These were in essence 'second-thought' operations to cleanse villages that had not originally been targeted. They were added to the list of villages to be evicted because Israel's political elite wanted to eradicate the unmistakably 'Arabic' character of the Galilee. But today, despite all of Israel's efforts to 'Judaize' the Galilee – beginning with direct expulsions in the 1940s, military occupation in the 1960s, massive confiscation of land in the 1970s, and a huge official Judaization settlement effort in the 1980s – it is still the only area in Palestine that has retained its natural beauty, its Middle Eastern flavour and its Palestinian culture. Since half the population is Palestinian, the 'demographic balance' prevents many Israeli Jews from thinking of the region as their 'own', even at the beginning of the twenty-first century.

Back in the winter of 1948, Israeli attempts to tip this 'balance' in their favour included the expulsion of additional small villages such as Arab al-Samniyya near Acre with its 200 inhabitants, and the large village of Deir al-Qasi with a population of 2500.[5] In addition, there is the unique story of the three villages of Iqrit, Kfar Bir'im and Ghabisiyya, which began in October 1948 but has still not ended. The tale of Iqrit is fairly representative of what also happened to the other two villages.

The village was close to the Lebanese border, perched high in the mountains, about thirty kilometres east of the coast. An Israeli battalion occupied it on 31 October 1948. The people surrendered without a fight – Iqrit was a Maronite community and they expected to be welcome in the new Jewish state. The commander of the battalion ordered the people to leave on the grounds that it was dangerous for them to stay, but promised them they would be able to return in two weeks time, after the military operations were over. On 6 November, the people of Iqrit were evicted from their houses and transported by army trucks to Rama. Fifty people, including the local priest, were allowed to stay behind to keep an eye on the houses and property but six months later, the Israeli army came back and drove them out as well.[6]

This is another example of how the methodology of cleansing varied. The case of Iqrit and the neighbouring village of Kfar Bir'im is one of the few publicised instances where, in a long drawn-out process, the indigenous people decided to seek redress through the Israeli courts. The villagers, being Christians, were allowed to stay in the country, but not in their village. They did not capitulate, however, and began a protracted legal struggle for their right to return home, demanding that the army keep its promise. Almost sixty years later, the struggle to regain their stolen lives is still not over.

On 26 September 1949, the Minister of Defence announced that Emergency Regulations (dating from the British Mandate) applied to Iqrit, in order to prevent the repatriation the occupying officer had promised earlier. Almost a year and a half later, on 28 May 1951, the people of Iqrit decided to take their case to the Israeli Supreme Court, which on 31 July declared that the eviction was illegal and ordered the army to allow the people of Iqrit to resettle in their original village. To bypass the Supreme Court ruling, the army needed to show that it had issued a formal order of expulsion during the 1948 war, which would have turned Iqrit into just another depopulated village, like the other 530 Palestinian villages whose expulsion the Israeli courts had condoned retrospectively. The IDF subsequently fabricated this formal order without hesitation or scruples. And in September 1951, the former residents of Iqrit, now refugees living in the village of Rama were bewildered to receive the official military order for their 'formal' expulsion showing the date of 6 November 1948, but sent almost three years later.

In order to settle the matter once and for all, on Christmas Eve 1951 the Israeli army completely demolished all the houses in Iqrit, sparing only the church and the cemetery. That same year, similar destruction was carried out on nearby villages, among them Qaddita, Deir Hanna, Kfar Bir'im and Ghabisiyya, to prevent repatriation.[7] The people of Kfar Bir'im and Ghabisiyya had also managed to secure a categorical ruling from the Israeli courts. As with Iqrit the army had immediately 'retaliated' by destroying their villages, offering the cynical excuse that they had been conducting a military exercise in the area involving an air bombardment, somehow leaving the village in ruins – and uninhabitable.

The destruction was part of an ongoing Israeli battle against the 'Arabisation' of the Galilee, as Israel sees it. In 1976, the highest official in the Ministry of Interior, Israel Koening, called the Palestinians in the Galilee a 'cancer in the state's body' and the Israeli Chief of Staff, Raphael Eitan, openly spoke of them as 'cockroaches'. An intensified process of 'Judaization' has so far failed to make the Galilee 'Jewish', but since so many Israelis today, politicians as well as academics, have come to accept and justify the ethnic cleansing that took place and to recommend it to future policy makers, the danger of additional expulsions still hovers above the Palestinian people in this part of Palestine.

The 'mopping-up' operations actually continued well into April 1949, and sometimes resulted in further massacres. This happened in the village of Khirbat Wara al-Sawda, where the Bedouin tribe al-Mawassi resided. This small village in the eastern Galilee had held out against repeated assaults during Operation Hiram and had then been left alone. After one of the attacks, several of the villagers had severed the heads of the dead Israeli soldiers. After the overall hostilities had finally come to an end, in November 1948, revenge followed. The report of the commanding officer from Battalion 103, which committed the crime, describes it graphically. The men of the village were gathered in one place while the troops set fire to all the houses. Fourteen people were then executed on the spot, and the rest moved to a prison camp.[8]

ISRAEL'S ANTI-REPATRIATION POLICY

The major activities towards the end of the 1948 ethnic cleansing operation now focused on implementing Israel's anti-repatriation policy on two levels.

The first level was national, introduced in August 1948 by an Israeli govern-mental decision to destroy all the evicted villages and transform them into new Jewish settlements or 'natural' forests. The second level was diplomatic, whereby strenuous efforts were made to avert the growing international pres-sure on Israel to allow the return of the refugees. The two were closely inter-connected: the pace of demolition was deliberately accelerated with the specific aim of invalidating any discussion on the subject of refugees return-ing to their houses, since those houses would no longer be there.

The major international endeavour to facilitate the return of the refugees was led by the UN Palestine Conciliation Commission (the PCC). This was a small committee with only three members, one each from France, Turkey and the United States. The PCC called for the unconditional return of the refugees to their homes, which the assassinated UN mediator, Count Folke Bernadotte, had demanded. They turned their position into a UN General Assembly resolution that was overwhelmingly supported by most of the member states and adopted on 11 December 1948. This resolution, UN Resolution 194, gave the refugees the option to decide between uncondi-tional return to their homes and/or accepting compensation.

There was a third anti-repatriation effort, and that was to control the demographic distribution of Palestinians both within the villages that had not been cleansed and in the previously mixed towns of Palestine, at that point already totally 'de-Arabised'. For this purpose, the Israeli army estab-lished, on 12 January 1949, a new unit, the Minority Unit. It was made up of Druze, Circassians and Bedouin who were recruited to it for one specific job only: to prevent Palestinian villagers and town dwellers from returning to their original homes. Some of their methods for achieving this objective can be seen in the summary report of Operation Number 10, submitted by the Minority Unit on 25 February 1949:

> A report on the search and identification of the villages of Arraba and Deir Hanna. In Deir Hanna, shots were fired above the heads of the cit-izens (ezrahim) that were gathered for the identification. Eighty of them were taken to prison. There were cases of 'unbecoming' behav-iour of the military police towards the local citizens in this operation.[9]

As we shall see, 'unbecoming' behaviour usually meant physical and mental harassment of all kinds. In other reports these cases were detailed, yet here we find them obfuscated by vague terminology.

Those who were arrested were deported to Lebanon; but if they found refuge in the area Israel continued to occupy until the spring of 1949, they were likely to be expelled again. Only on 16 January 1949 did the order came to stop the selective deportations from southern Lebanon, and the Minority Unit was instructed to confine its activity solely to the Galilee and the former mixed towns and cities. The mission there was clear: to prevent any attempt – and there were quite a few – by refugees to try to smuggle their way back home, no matter whether they tried to return to a village or a house to live, or just wanted to retrieve some of their personal possessions. The 'infiltrators', as the Israeli army called them, were in many cases farmers who sought surreptitiously to harvest their fields or pick the fruit from their now unattended trees. Refugees who tried to slip past the army lines quite often met their death at the hands of Israeli army patrols. In the language of Israeli intelligence reports, they were 'successfully shot at'. A quote from such a report dated 4 December 1948 records: 'successful shooting at Palestinians trying to return to the village of Blahmiyya and who attempted to retrieve their belongings.' [10]

The 'main problem', complained one intelligence unit, was that 'the Syrians are shooting at the refugees [from their side], so we are shooting back at them to enable the refugees to cross the River Jordan.'[11] Those who tried to cross the river to Jordan were often turned back by the Hashemite Kingdom as it began to feel the burden of an ever-growing refugee community on its territory, which had already doubled the size of the Jordanian population. The same report commended the Lebanese for 'allowing' free passage of refugees into their country.

But even when they were not subjected to 'arrest-and-deport' operations or fired at as 'infiltrators' or returnees, those villagers who were allowed to remain (around fifty villages out of 400 within the borders Israel had established for itself, as yet excluding the Wadi Ara) were still in danger of being forcibly evicted or transferred to other places because of the greed of Jewish farmers, especially kibbutzniks, who coveted their lands or their location.

This happened on 5 November to a small village, Dalhamiyya, near Kibbutz Ashdot Yaacov in the Jordan Valley area, which was evicted so that the kibbutz could expand its arable land.[12] Even worse was the fate of the village of Raml Zayta, near the city of Hadera. It was moved once in April 1949, closer to the West Bank, and then a second time, when in 1953 a new Jewish settlement made up of the younger generation of older kibbutzim decided to move near the new location of Zayta. Upon arrival, the young kibbutzniks were not content with merely grabbing the land, but demanded the government move the houses of the Palestinian village out of their sight.[13]

The crudeness of the kibbutzim's demands was matched by the overall transformation of the language of the expellers. For Operation Hiram, the operative commands read as follows:

> Prisoners: cars will be ready to transport the refugees (plitim) to points on the Lebanese and Syrian borders. POW camps will be built in Safad and Haifa, and a transit camp in Acre; all the Muslim inhabitants have to be moved out.[14]

Under the watchful eyes of UN observers who were patrolling the skies of the Galilee, the final stage of the ethnic cleansing operation, begun in October 1948, continued until the summer of 1949. Whether from the sky or on the ground, no one could fail to spot the hordes of men, women and children streaming north every day. Ragged women and children were conspicuously dominant in these human convoys: the young men were gone – executed, arrested or missing. By this time UN observers from above and Jewish eyewitnesses on the ground must have become desensitised towards the plight of the people passing by in front of them: how else to explain the silent acquiescence in the face of the massive deportation unfolding before their eyes?

UN observers did draw some conclusions in October, writing to the Secretary General – who did not publish their report – that Israeli policy was that of 'uprooting Arabs from their native villages in Palestine by force or threat'.[15] Arab member states attempted to bring the report on Palestine to the attention of the Security Council, but to no avail. For almost thirty years the UN uncritically adopted the rhetorical obfuscations of Abba Eban, Israel's ambassador to the UN, who referred to the refugees as constituting a 'humane problem' for which no one could be held accountable or responsible. UN observers were also shocked by the scope of the looting that went on, which by October 1948 had reached every village and town in Palestine. After so overwhelmingly endorsing a partition resolution, almost a year earlier, the UN could have passed another resolution condemning the ethnic cleansing, but it never did. And worse was to come.

A MINI EMPIRE IN THE MAKING

So successful was Israel during this final phase that dreams re-emerged of creating a mini-empire. The Israeli forces were once again put on the alert to expand the Jewish state into the West Bank and southern Lebanon. The difference with these orders was that the allusions to the West Bank (called Samariyya or the Arab Triangle in those days) were clearer, actually forming the first transparent and official breach of the tacit Israeli–Transjordanian understanding. The order was to try to take the areas around Jenin in the northern part of today's West Bank and, if they were successful, to proceed to Nablus. Although the attack was postponed, in the months to come the military High Command remained obsessed with the areas the army had not yet occupied, especially the West Bank. We have the names that were given to the different operations Israel had planned to implement there between December 1948 and March 1949, the best known of which was Operation 'Snir'; when Israel and Jordan finally signed an armistice agreement, they had to be set aside.

These last operations were cancelled because of concerns over the military alliance Britain had with Jordan, which at least officially obliged His Majesty's government to resist with force an Israeli invasion into Jordanian territory. What the Israeli ministers did not know was that the British government did not regard the West Bank as falling under the terms of this Anglo-Jordanian treaty. Interestingly, Ben-Gurion reports at one point to his government that he had secured French approval for such an operation, but that he was apprehensive of a possible British retaliation.[16] As we know, these plans were eventually reactivated in June 1967, when the Israeli government exploited Gamal Abdel Nasser's brinkmanship policies to wage an attack on the West Bank as a whole.

Ben-Gurion took the discussion of future plans, including the need to occupy Southern Lebanon, to a committee of five (all veterans of the Consultancy) whom he invited to the Israeli army's new headquarters, called the 'Hill'. They met several times through October and November, which must have made Ben-Gurion nostalgic about the cabals of earlier days. Ben-Gurion now consulted this five-man body of decision-makers about a future occupation of the West Bank. His comrades brought to the fore another argument against the occupation of the West Bank. In the words of one of the participants, Yitzhak Greenbaum,

Israel's Minister of the Interior: 'It would be impossible to do there what was done in the rest of Palestine,' i.e., ethnic cleansing. Greenbaum continued: 'If we take places such as Nablus, the Jewish world will demand of us to keep it' [and hence we would have not only Nablus but also the Nabulsians].[17] Only in 1967 did Ben-Gurion recognise the difficulties of re-enacting the 1948 mass expulsions in the areas Israel occupied in the June war. Ironically, it may have been he who dissuaded the then Chief of Staff, Yitzhak Rabin, to refrain from such a massive operation, and be content with the deportation of 'only' 200,000 people. Consequently, he recommended withdrawing the Israeli army from the West Bank immediately. Rabin, supported by the rest of the government at that time, insisted instead on annexing the territories to Israel.

Plans to seize southern Lebanon were based on intelligence reports that the Lebanese had no offensive, but only defensive plans. Thirteen villages were captured in southern Lebanon, which left the Israelis with a larger number of what they called 'prisoners of war' – a mixture of villagers and regular soldiers – than they could handle. Consequently, executions took place here as well. On 31 October 1948, the Jewish forces executed more than eighty villagers in the village of Hula alone, while in the village of Saliha Israeli troops butchered more than 100 people. One person, Shmuel Lahis, later to become Director-General of the Jewish Agency, was brought before a military court at the time for single-handedly executing thirty-five people. Dov Yirmiya, a commander who had himself participated in ethnic cleansing operations between May and July, was one of the few IDF officers who was genuinely appalled when he realised what the operations were leading to. He began protesting vociferously against any atrocities he witnessed or heard about. It was Yirmiya who brought Lahis to trial. Lahis received a seven-year prison term, but was almost immediately pardoned and exonerated by Israel's president, and subsequently rose to high positions in government.[18]

When Israel re-invaded Southern Lebanon in 1978, and again in 1982, the POW 'problem' was solved: the IDF built a network of prisons to interrogate and quite often torture the people it held captive there, with the help of the South Lebanese Army. The prison at Khiyam has become a byword for Israeli cruelty.

Back in 1948, another pattern appeared, inevitable in the repertoire of an occupying army, which would reoccur in the 1982–2001 occupation, and this was the exploitative and abusive conduct towards the occupied population. A complaint from 14 December 1948 by the commander of the Israeli forces in Lebanon to the High Command notes: 'The soldiers in southern Lebanon order the villagers to provide and prepare food for them.'[19] In the light of the Israeli disposition in later years in the West Bank and the Gaza Strip, one can only imagine this was just the tip of the iceberg of abuse and humiliation. The Israeli forces withdrew from southern Lebanon in April 1949, but, as happened in 1978 and once more in 1982, their occupation had created a lot of bad blood and stirred up feelings of revenge as it extended the practices of the 1948 ethnic cleansing in Palestine to the south of Lebanon.

The whole of the Galilee was now in Jewish hands. The Red Cross was allowed to go in and examine the conditions of the people who had been left, or rather allowed to remain, in the region, as Israel knew that barring the Red Cross from such inspections would stand in the way of its application to become a full member of the UN. The toll of siege, bombardment and expulsion could be seen everywhere. In November 1948 the organisation's representatives reported a scene of devastation: in every village they visited, the able men had been imprisoned, leaving behind women and children without their traditional breadwinners and creating total disarray; crops were not harvested and were left to rot in the fields, and diseases were spreading in the rural areas at an alarming pace. The Red Cross reported malaria as being the main problem, but also found numerous cases of typhoid, rickets, diphtheria and scurvy.[20]

FINAL CLEANSING OF THE SOUTH AND THE EAST

The last front was the southern Negev, which the Israelis reached in November 1948. Driving out the remaining Egyptian forces, they continued south and arrived in March 1949 at a fishing village near the Red Sea, Umm Rashrash, today the city of Eilat.

Yigal Allon, aware that the best brigades were being used for the ethnic cleansing operations in the populated areas, now wished to redirect them to the occupation of the Negev: 'I need to replace the Negev Brigade with Brigade Harel and I wish to have Brigade Eight. The enemy is strong, fortified and well equipped and will wage stubborn war but we can win.'[21]

The main worry, however was a British counter-attack, since the

Israelis wrongly believed this area was coveted by Britain or that His Majesty's Government would activate its defense treaty with Egypt, as some of the Israeli forces were about to move into Egyptian territories proper. In the event, the British did neither, although they did clash here and there with the Israeli air force that mercilessly and, perhaps, pointlessly bombarded Rafah, Gaza and El-Arish.[22] As a result, the Gazans, refugees and veteran population alike, have had the longest history as victims of Israeli air bombardment – from 1948 until the present.

On the ethnic cleansing front, the final operations in the south provided, unsurprisingly, an opportunity for further depopulation and expulsions. The two southern coastal towns of Isdud and Majdal were taken in November 1948 and their populations expelled to the Gaza Strip. Several thousands of people who had remained in Majdal were expelled in December 1949, shocking some left-wing Israelis as this was done during a 'time of peace'.[23]

The month of December 1948 was devoted to cleansing the Negev of many of the Bedouin tribes that resided there. A huge tribe, the Tarabins, was expelled to Gaza; the army only allowed 1,000 of its members to remain. Another tribe, the Tayaha, was split into two: half of them were deported to Gaza and the other half forcibly evicted in the direction of Jordan. The al-Hajajre, whose land straddled the railway line, were pushed into Gaza by December. Only the al-Azazmeh succeeded in returning, but they were driven out again between 1950 and 1954, when they became the favourite target of a special Israeli commando force, Unit 101, led by a young ambitious officer called Ariel Sharon. In December the Israeli units also completed the depopulation of the Bersheba district that they had started in the autumn of 1948. When they had finished, ninety per cent of the people who had lived for centuries in this, the most southern inhabited region of Palestine, were gone.[24]

In November and December, Israeli troops attacked Wadi Ara again, but the presence of volunteers, Iraqi units and local villagers both deterred and in several cases defeated this plan yet again. Villages that are familiar names to Israelis travelling on the busy Route 65 that connects Afula and Hadera succeeded in protecting themselves against a far superior military force: Mushayrifa, Musmus, Mu'awiya, Arara, Barta'a, Shuweika and many others. The largest of these villages has grown into the town we know today as Umm al-Fahm. There, with some training from the Iraqi soldiers, the villagers themselves had organised a force that they called the 'Army of Honour'. This fifth Israeli attempt to occupy these villages was called '*Hidush Yameinu ke-Kedem*', that is 'Restoring our Glorious Past', possibly in the hope that such a charged codename would imbue the attacking forces with particular zeal, but it was destined to fail once again.

Another ominous-sounding name was given to the operation in the Beersheba–Hebron area: 'Python'. Apart from the small town of Beersheba, which with its 5,000 inhabitants was occupied on 21 October, two large villages, Qubayba and Dawaymeh were taken. Habib Jarada, who today lives in the city of Gaza, remembered the people of Beersheba being driven out at gunpoint to Hebron. His most vivid image is that of the town's mayor beseeching the occupying officer not to deport the people. 'We need land, not slaves,' was the blunt answer.[25]

The town of Beersheba was protected mainly by Egyptian volunteers from the Muslim Brotherhood's movement under the command of a Libyan officer, Ramadan al-Sanusi. When the fighting was over, the captive soldiers and all local people the Israeli troops suspected of holding arms were rounded up and randomly fired at. Jarada remembers to this day many of the names of the people killed, which included his cousin Yussuf Jarada and his grandfather Ali Jarada. Jarada was taken to a prison camp and was released only in the summer of 1949 in a prisoner exchange following Israel's armistice with Jordan.

THE MASSACRE IN DAWAYMEH

Then there was the village of Dawaymeh, between Beersheba and Hebron. The events that unfolded in Dawaymeh are probably the worst in the annals of Nakba atrocities. The village was occupied by Battalion 89 of Brigade Eight.

The UN's Palestine Conciliation Commission, mentioned before as replacing Count Bernadotte in the UN mediation efforts, convened a special session to investigate what happened in this village on 28 October 1948, less than three miles west of the city of Hebron. The original population was 2,000, but an additional 4,000 refugees had tripled that.

The UN report from 14 June 1949 (accessible today on the Internet by simply searching for the village name) says the following:

> The reason why so little is known about this massacre which, in many respects, was more brutal than the Deir Yassin massacre, is because the Arab Legion (the army in control of that area) feared that if the news was allowed to spread, it would have the same effect on the moral of the peasantry that Deir Yassin had, namely to cause another flow of Arab refugees.

More likely, the Jordanians feared accusations being rightly leveled against them for their impotence and lack of action. The report to the PCC was based mainly on the mukhtar's testimony. He was Hassan Mahmoud Ihdeib and much of what he says was corroborated by the reports that lie in the Israeli military archives. A well-known Israeli writer, Amos Keinan, who participated in the massacre, confirmed its existence in an interview he gave in the late 1990s to the Palestinian actor and film maker Muhammad Bakri, for Bakri's documentary '1948'.

Half an hour after the midday prayer on 28 October, recalled the mukhtar, twenty armoured cars entered the village from Qubayba while soldiers attacked simultaneously from the opposite flank. The twenty people guarding the village were immediately paralysed with fear. The soldiers on the armoured cars opened fire with automatic weapons and mortars, making their way into the village in a semi-circular movement. Following the established routine, they surrounded the village from three flanks, leaving open the eastern flank with the aim of driving out 6,000 people in one hour. When this failed to happen, the troops jumped out of their vehicles and started shooting at the people indiscriminately, many of whom ran to the mosque to seek shelter or fled to a nearby holy cave, called Iraq al-Zagh. Venturing back into the village the next day, the mukhtar beheld with horror the piles of dead bodies in the mosque – with many more strewn about in the street – men, women and children, among them his own father. When he went to the cave, he found the entrance blocked by dozens of corpses. The count the mukhtar carried out told him that 455 people were missing, among them around 170 children and women.

The Jewish soldiers who took part in the massacre also reported horrific scenes: babies whose skulls were cracked open, women raped or burned alive in houses, and men stabbed to death. These were not reports delivered years later, but eye-witness accounts sent to the High Command within a few days of the event.[26] The brutality they describe reinforces my faith in the accuracy of the descriptions, mentioned earlier on, of the hideous crimes Israeli soldiers committed in Tantura, Safsaf and Sa'sa, all reconstructed mainly with the help of Palestinian testimonies and oral histories.

This was the end result of the order that the commander of Battalion 89 of Brigade Eight had received from the Chief of Staff, Yigael Yadin: 'Your preparations should include psychological warfare and "treatment" (*tipul*) of citizens as an integral part of the operation.'[27]

The massacre at Dawaymeh was the last large massacre Israeli troops perpetrated until 1956, when forty-nine villagers of Kfar Qassim, a village transferred to Israel in the armistice agreement with Jordan, were butchered.

Ethnic cleansing is not genocide, but it does carry with it atrocious acts of mass killing and butchering. Thousands of Palestinians were killed ruthlessly and savagely by Israeli troops of all backgrounds, ranks and ages. None of these Israelis was ever tried for war crimes, in spite of the overwhelming evidence.

And if, here and there, in 1948, some remorse was to be found, as in a poem by Natan Alterman – the same Alterman who had in 1945 compared the Palestinians to the Nazis – it was no more than another show of 'shoot and cry', a typically righteous Israeli way of seeking self-absolution. When he first heard of the brutal slaughtering of innocent civilians in the north in Operation Hiram, Alterman wrote:

On a Jeep he crossed the street
A young man, Prince of Beasts
An old couple cowered to the wall
And with his angelic smile he called:
'The submachine I will try', and he did
Spreading the old man's blood on the lid.

Nor did any contrition such as Alterman's stop the forces from completing their mission of cleansing Palestine, a job to which they now applied increasing levels of ruthlessness and cruelty. Hence, starting in November 1948 and all the way up to the final agreement with Syria and Lebanon in the summer of 1949, another eighty-seven villages were occupied; thirty-six of these were emptied by force, while from the rest a selective number of people were deported. As 1950 began, the energy and purposefulness of the expellers finally began to wane and those Palestinians who were still living in Palestine – by then divided into the State of Israel, a Jordanian West Bank and an Egyptian Gaza Strip – were largely safe from further expulsions. True, they were placed under military rule both in Israel and Egypt, and as such remained vulnerable. But, whatever the hardships they incurred, it was a better fate than they had suffered throughout that year of horrors we now call the Nakba.

Chapter 9

Occupation and its Ugly Face

Refugees have claimed that Serb forces have been systematically separating 'military aged' ethnic Albanian men – those ranging from as young as age 14 up to 59 years old – from the population as they expel the Kosovar Albanians from their homes. The Serbs use the Ferro-Nickel factory in Glogovac as a detention centre for a large number of Kosovar Albanians.

State Department Report on Kosovo 1999

The order is to take captive any suspicious Arab of military age, between the ages of 10 and 50.

IDF Orders, IDF Archives, 5943/49/114, 13 April 1948 General Orders for how to treat POWs.

Since the beginning of the Intifada in September 2000 over 2,500 children have been arrested. Currently there are at least 340 Palestinian children being held in Israeli prisons.

The People's Voice, 15 December 2005

Since 1967, Israel has detained 670,000 Palestinians.

Official Declaration by the Arab League, 9 January 2006

A Child: Every human being under the age of 18.

The Convention on the Rights of the Child. UN Rules for the Protection of Juveniles Deprived of their Liberty.

Although Israel had essentially completed the ethnic cleansing of Palestine by now, the hardships did not end for the Palestinians. About 8,000 spent the whole of 1949 in the prison camps, others suffered physical abuse in the towns, and large numbers of Palestinians were harassed in numerous ways under the military rule that Israel now exerted over them. Their houses continued to be looted, their fields confiscated, their holy places desecrated, and Israel violated such basic rights as their freedom of movement and expression, and of equality before the law.

INHUMAN IMPRISONMENT

A common sight in rural Palestine in the wake of the cleansing operations were huge pens in which male villagers, ranging from children from the age of ten to older men up to the age of fifty, were being held after the Israelis had picked them out in the 'search-and-arrest' operations that had now become routine. They were later moved to centralized prison camps. The Israeli search-and-arrest operations were quite systematic, took place all over the countryside, and usually carried similar generic codenames, such as 'Operation Comb' or even 'Distillation' (*ziquq*).[1]

The first of these operations took place in Haifa, a few weeks after the city was occupied. The Israeli intelligence units were after 'returnees': refugees who, understandably, wanted to come back to their homes after the fighting had subsided and calm and normality seemed to have returned to the cities of Palestine. However, others were also targeted under the category of 'suspicious Arab'. In fact, the order went out to find as many such 'suspicious Arabs' as possible, without actually bothering to define the nature of the suspicion.[2]

In a procedure familiar to most Palestinians in the West Bank and the Gaza Strip today, Israeli troops would first put a place – a city or a village – under a closure order. Then intelligence units would start searching from house to house, pulling people out whom they suspected of being present 'illegally' in that particular location as well as any other 'suspicious Arabs'. Often these would be people residing in their own homes. All people picked up in these raids were then brought to a special headquarters.

In the city of Haifa this headquarters quickly became the dread of the Palestinians in the city. It was located in the Hadar neighbourhood, the quarter above the harbour, higher up the mountainside. The house is still there today at 11 Daniel Street, its grey exterior betraying little of the terrible scenes that took place inside in 1948. All those people picked up and brought in for interrogation in this way were according to international law, citizens of the State of Israel. The worst offence was not being in possession of one of the newly-issued identity cards, which could result in a prison term for as long as a year and a half and immediate transfer to one of the pens to join other 'unauthorised' and 'suspicious' Arabs found in now Jewish-occupied areas. From time to time, even the High Command expressed reservations about the brutality the intelligence people displayed towards the interned Palestinians at the Haifa interrogation centre.[3]

The rural areas were subjected to the same treatment. Often the operations reminded the villagers there of the original attack launched against them just a few months or even weeks earlier. The Israelis now introduced a novel feature, also well known among present-day Israeli practices in the Occupied Territories: roadblocks, where they carried out surprise checks to catch those who did not have the new ID card. But the granting of such an ID card, which allowed people limited freedom of movement in the area where they lived, itself became a means of intimidation: only people vetted and approved by the Israeli Secret Service were given such a card.

Most areas were out of bounds anyway, even if you had the required identification. For these areas you needed another special permit. This included a specific authorisation, for example, for people living in the Galilee to travel along their most common and natural routes to work or to see family and friends, such as the road between Haifa and Nazareth. Here, permits were hardest to get.[4]

Thousands of Palestinians languished throughout 1949 in the prison camps where they had been transferred from the temporary pens. There were five such camps, the largest being the one in Jalil (near today's Herzliya) and a second one in Atlit, south of Haifa. According to Ben-Gurion's diary there were 9,000 prisoners.[5]

Initially, the jailing system was quite chaotic. 'Our problem,' complained one officer towards the end of June 1948, 'is the concentration of large numbers of Arab POWs and civilian prisoners. We need to transfer them to safer places.'[6] By October 1948, under the direct supervision of Yigael Yadin, a network of prison camps had been institutionalised and the disarray was over.

As early as February 1948 we find Hagana guidelines concerning the treatment of POWs stating the following: 'Releasing a captive or eliminating him needs an approval of the intelligence officer.'[7] In other words, there was already a selection process in operation, and summary executions took place. The Israeli intelligence officers who orchestrated them hounded the people continuously from the moment they arrived in these camps. This is why, even after captured Palestinians were moved to 'safer' places, as the army put it, they felt anything but safe in these lockups. To begin with, it was decided to employ mainly ex-Irgun and Stern Gang troops as camp guards,[8] but they were not the only tormentors of the camp inmates. At one point, senior ex-Hagana officer Yisca Shadmi was found guilty of murdering two Palestinian prisoners. His is a familiar name in the history of the Palestinians in Israel: in October 1956 Shadmi was one of the principal per-petrators of the Kfar Qassim massacre in which forty-nine Palestinians lost their lives. He escaped punishment for his part in the massacre, and went on to become a high-ranking official in the governmment apparatus that man-aged the state's relations with its Palestinian minority. He was acquitted eventually in 1958. His case reveals two features of Israel's treatment of Palestinian citizens that continue up to the present day: the first is that people indicted for crimes against Arabs are likely to remain in positions in which they continue to affect the lives of Palestinians and, secondly, that they will never be brought to justice. The most recent illustration of this is the case of the policemen who murdered thirteen unarmed Palestinian citizens in October 2000 and another seventeen since then.

One concerned army officer who happened to visit such a prison camp wrote: 'In recent times there were some very grave cases in the treatment of prisoners. The barbaric and cruel behaviour these cases reveal undermines the army's discipline.'[9] The concern voiced here for the army rather than for the victims will also sound familiar by now in the history of military 'self-criticism' in Israel.

Worse still were the labour camps. The idea of using Palestinian prison-ers as forced labour came from the Israeli military command and was endorsed by the politicians. Three special labour camps were built for the purpose, one in Sarafand, another in Tel-Litwinski (today Tel-Hashomer

Hospital) and a third in Umm Khalid (near Netanya). The authorities used the prisoners in any job that could help strengthen both the Israeli economy and the army's capabilities.[10]

One survivor from Tantura, on his eventual release from such a camp, recalled what he had gone through in an interview with one of Haifa's former notables who, in 1950, published a book on those days. Muhammad Nimr al-Khatib transcribed the following testimony:

> The survivors of the Tantura massacre were imprisoned in a nearby pen; for three days without food, then pushed into lorries, ordered to sit in impossible space, but threatened with being shot. They did not shoot but clubbed them on the head, and blood gushed everywhere, finally taken to Umm Khalid (Netanya).[11]

The witness then describes the routine of forced labour in the camp: working in the quarries and carrying heavy stones; living on one potato in the morning and half a dried fish at noon. There was no point in complaining as disobedience was punished with severe beatings. After fifteen days, 150 men were moved to a second camp in Jalil, where they were exposed to similar treatment: 'We had to remove rubble from destroyed Arab houses.' But then, one day, 'an officer with good English told us that "from now on" we would be treated according to the Geneva Convention. And indeed, conditions improved.'

Five months later, al-Khatib's witness told him, he was back at Umm Khalid where he recalled scenes that could have come straight from another place and time. When the guards discovered that twenty people had escaped, 'We, the people of Tantura, were put in a cage, oil was poured on our clothes and our blankets were taken away.'[12]

After one of their early visits, on 11 November 1948, Red Cross officials reported dryly that POWs were exploited in the general local effort to 'strengthen the Israeli economy'.[13] This guarded language was not accidental. Given its deplorable behaviour during the Holocaust, when it failed to report on what went on in Nazi concentration camps, on which it was well informed, the Red Cross was careful in its reproach and criticism of the Jewish state. But at least their documents do shed some light on the experiences of the Palestinian inmates, some of whom were kept in these camps until 1955.

As previously noted, there was a stark contrast between the Israeli conduct towards Palestinian civilians they had imprisoned and the treatment Israelis received who had been captured by the Arab Legion of Jordan.

Ben-Gurion was angry when the Israeli press reported how well Israeli POWs were treated by the Legion. His diary entry for 18 June 1948 reads: 'It is true but it could encourage surrender of isolated spots.'

ABUSES UNDER OCCUPATION

In 1948 and 1949 life outside prison or the labour camps was not much easier. Here, too, Red Cross representatives crossing the country sent back disturbing reports to their headquarters in Geneva about life under occupation. These depict a collective abuse of basic rights, which began in April 1948 during the Jewish attacks on the mixed towns, and continued well into 1949, the worst of which seemed to be taking place in Jaffa.

Two months after the Israelis had occupied Jaffa, Red Cross representatives discovered a pile of dead bodies. They asked for an urgent meeting with Jaffa's military governor, who admitted to the Red Cross's Mr Gouy that they had probably been shot by Israeli soldiers for not complying with their orders. A curfew was imposed every night between 5 pm and 6 am, he explained, and anyone found outside, the orders stated clearly, 'will be shot'.[14]

Under the cover of curfews and closures the Israelis also committed other crimes in Jaffa, which were representative of much that went on elsewhere. The most common crime was looting, of both the systematic official kind and the sporadic private one. The systematic and official kind was ordered by the Israeli government itself and targeted the wholesale stores of sugar, flour, barley, wheat and rice that the British government kept for the Arab population. The booty taken was sent to Jewish settlements. Such actions had frequently taken place even before 15 May 1948, under the eyes of British soldiers who simply looked away as Jewish troops barged into areas under their legal authority and responsibility. Reporting in July to Ben-Gurion on how the organised confiscation was progressing, the military governor of Jaffa wrote:

> As for your demand, sir, that I will make sure 'that all the commodities required by our army, air force and navy will be handed over to the people in charge and taken out of Jaffa as fast as possible,' I can inform you that as of 15 May, 1948 an average load of 100 trucks a day is taken out of Jaffa. The port is ready for operation. The storehouses were emptied, and the goods were taken out.[15]

The same officials who pillaged these food stores promised the Palestinian population in Haifa and other occupied cities that their community centres, religious sites and secular establishments would not be ransacked or plundered. The people soon discovered that this was a false pledge when their mosques and churches were profaned and their convents and schools vandalised. In growing despair, Captain F. Marschal, one of the UN observers, reported back to the organisation that 'the Jews violated frequently the guarantee given several times by the Jewish authorities to respect all buildings belonging to the religious community.'[16]

Jaffa was also a particular victim of house robberies that took place in broad daylight. The looters took furniture, clothes and anything useful for the Jewish immigrants that were streaming into the country. UN observers were convinced that the plundering was also a means of preventing Palestinian refugees from returning, which fitted the overall rationale of the Israeli High Command that was not afraid to resort cold-bloodedly to brutal punitive action so as to push forward their strategic policies.

As the pretext for their robbery and looting campaigns, the Israeli forces often gave 'search for weapons'. The real or imaginary existence of weapons also triggered worse atrocities, as these inspections were frequently accompanied by beatings and inevitably ended in mass arrests: 'Many people arrested for no reason at all,' Yitzhak Chizik, the military governor of Jaffa, wrote to Ben-Gurion.[17]

The level of ransacking in Jaffa reached such intensity that even the Yitzhak Chizik, felt he had to complain, in a letter on 5 June 1948 to Israel's Minister of Finance, Eliezer Kaplan, that he could no longer control the looting. He would continue to protest, but when in the end of July he sensed his remonstrations were totally ignored, he resigned, stating that he surrendered to the uncontrollable ongoing crusade of pillage and robbery.[18] Most of his reports, which are to be found in the Israeli state archives, are censored, particularly, passages relating to the abuse of the local people by Israeli soldiers. In one of these, not properly removed, we find Chizik clearly taken aback by the unlimited brutality of the troops: 'They do not stop beating people,' he writes.

Chizik was no angel himself. He did order the occasional demolition of houses and instructed his troops to torch a number of Palestinian shops, but these were punitive actions he wanted to control, that would bolster his self-image as sovereign master in the occupied domain he ruled: 'It is regrettable,' he wrote in his letter to Kaplan, but he could no longer tolerate 'the attitude of the soldiers in cases where I have given clear orders not to set fire to a house or a shop; not only do they ignore it, they make fun of me in front of the Arabs.' He also criticised the official pillage that went on under the auspices of two gentlemen, a Mr Yakobson and a Mr Presiz, who allowed 'looting of many things the army does not need.'[19]

The High Command sent Abraham Margalit to check into these complaints, who reported back in June 1948: 'There are many violations of discipline, especially in the attitude to the Arabs (beating and torture) and looting which emanate more from ignorance than malice.' As Margalit explains himself, it was this 'ignorance' that led the soldiers to set aside special locations 'where they kept and tortured Arabs.'[20]

This prompted a visit to Jaffa that same month by Israel's Minister of Minorities, Bechor Shitrit. Born in Tiberias, this relatively dovish Israeli politician had shown an empathy towards the possibility of Jewish–Palestinian co-existence in the new state. He had served as judge in the British Mandatory and years later would become Minister of Justice. Shitrit was a token Mizrahi minister in an overwhelmingly Ashkenazi, i.e., Eastern European, government and as such had been 'promoted' at first to deal with the most undesirable job in the government: the Arabs.

Shitrit developed personal relations with some of the notables who had remained in Jaffa after the occupation and headed the Palestinian community there, such as Nicola Sa'ab and Ahmad Abu Laben. Although he listened attentively in June 1948 when they beseeched him to lift at least the more appalling features of life under military occupation, and admitted to them that their complaints were valid, it took time before anything was done.

The notables told Shitrit that the way Israeli troops broke into individual houses was totally unnecessary as they, as members of the local national committee, had the keys people who had been evacuated had left with them, and they were ready to hand them in to the army; but the soldiers preferred to break in. Little did they know that after Shitrit left, some of the same people were arrested for 'being in possession of illegal property': the same keys to the empty houses they had mentioned.[21] Three weeks later Ahmad Abu Laben protested to Shitrit that not much had changed since they last met: 'There is not one house or shop which was not broken into. The goods were taken from the port and stores. Food commodities were taken from the inhabitants.'[22] Abu Laben had been running a factory in the city together with a Jewish partner, but this did not save him. All the machines were removed and the factory was looted.

Indeed, the scope of both the official confiscation and private looting all over urban Palestine was so widespread that local commanders were unable to control it. On 25 June, the government decided to put some order into the looting and confiscation afflicting Jerusalem. David Abulafya, a local citizen, was made responsible for 'confiscation and appropriation'. His main problem, he reported to Ben-Gurion, was that 'the security forces and the militias continue to confiscate without permission.'[23]

Ghettoising the Palestinians of Haifa

That the Israelis had more than one way to imprison people or abuse their most basic rights can be seen from the experiences of the small community of Palestinians left in Haifa after Jewish troops cleansed the city on 23 April 1948. Their story is unique, but only in its details: in general it exemplifies the trials and tribulations of the Palestinian minority as a whole under occupation.

On 1 July 1948, in the evening, the Israeli military commander of the city summoned the leaders of the Palestinian community in Haifa to his headquarters. The purpose of the meeting was to order these notables, who represented the 3–5,000 Palestinians left behind after the approximately 70,000 of the city's Arab residents had been expelled, to 'facilitate' their transfer from the various parts of the city where they were living into one single neighborhood, the crammed and small quarter of Wadi Nisnas, one of the city's poorest areas. Some of those ordered to leave their residences on the upper slopes of Mt Carmel, or even on top of the mountain itself, had been living there for many years among the Jewish newcomers. The military commander now ordered all of them to make sure the move would be completed by 5 July 1948. The shock among the Palestinian leaders and notables was instant and deep. Many of them belonged to the Communist Party that had supported partition and hoped that now the fighting was over, life would return to normal under the auspices of a Jewish state whose creation they had not opposed.[24]

'I don't understand: is this a military command? Let us look at the conditions of these people. I cannot see any reason, least of all a military one, that justifies such a move,' protested Tawfiq Tubi, later a member of the

Israeli Knesset for the Communist Party. He ended his protestation by saying: 'We demand that the people stay in their homes.'[25] Another participant, Bulus Farah, shouted, 'This is racism,' and called the move, appropriately, 'ghettoising the Palestinians in Haifa.'[26]

Even the dry tone of the document cannot hide the dismissive and indifferent reaction of the Israeli military commander. One can almost hear the clipped sound of his voice as he told them:

> I can see that you are sitting here and [think you can] give me advice, but I invited you in here to hear the orders of the High Command and carry them out! I am not involved in politics and do not deal with it. I am just obeying orders . . . I am fulfilling orders and I have to make sure that this order is executed by the 5th of July . . . If you don't do it, I will do it myself. I am a soldier.[27]

After he had finished his long monologue, another of the Palestinian notables, Shehadeh Shalah asked: 'And if someone owns a house, does he have to leave?' The military commander replied: 'Everyone has to leave.'[28] The notables then learned that the inhabitants would themselves have to cover the cost of their enforced transfer.

Victor Khayat tried to reason with the Israeli commander that it would take more than one day for all the people to be notified which would not leave them much time. The commander replied that four days was 'plenty of time'. The person who transcribed the meeting noted that at that point the Palestinian representatives shouted as one man: 'But this is a very short time,' to which the commander retorted: 'I cannot change it.'[29]

But this was not the end of their troubles. In the area to which they were confined, Wadi Nisnas – where today the municipality of Haifa annually celebrates the convergence of Hanuka, Christmas and Id al-Fitr as 'The Feast of all Feasts for Peace and Coexistence' – people continued to be robbed and abused, mostly by Irgun and Stern Gang members, but the Hagana also took an active part in the assaults. Ben-Gurion condemned their behaviour, but did nothing to stop it: He was content with recording it in his diary.[30]

Rape

We have three kinds of sources that report on rape, and thus know that severe cases of rape did take place. It remains more difficult to form an idea of how many women and young girls were victimised by Jewish troops in this way. Our first source is the international organisations such as the UN and the Red Cross. They never submitted a collective report, but we do have short and concise accounts of individual cases. Thus, for instance, very soon after Jaffa was taken, a Red Cross official, de Meuron, reported how Jewish soldiers had raped a girl and killed her brother. He remarked in general that as Palestinian men were taken away as prisoners, their women were left at the mercy of the Israelis. Yitzhak Chizik wrote to Kaplan in the letter mentioned above: 'And about the rapes, Sir, you probably have already heard.' In an earlier letter to Ben-Gurion, Chizik reported how 'a group of soldiers [had] burst into a house, killed the father, injured the mother and raped the daughter.'

We know of course more about cases in places where outside observers were present, but this does not mean women were not raped elsewhere. Another Red Cross report tells of a horrific incident that began on 9 December 1948 when two Jewish soldiers burst into the house of al-Hajj Suleiman Daud, who had been expelled with his family to Shaqara. The soldiers hit his wife and kidnapped his eighteen-year-old daughter. Seventeen days later the father was able to get hold of an Israeli lieutenant, to whom he protested. The rapists appeared to belong to Brigade Seven. It is impossible to know what exactly happened in those seventeen days before the girl was set free; the worst may be presumed.[31]

The second source is the Israeli archives, which only cover cases in which the rapists were brought to trial. David Ben-Gurion seems to have been informed about each case and entered them into his diary. Every few days he has a sub-section: 'Rape Cases'. One of these records the incident Chizik had reported to him: 'a case in Acre where soldiers wanted to rape a girl. They killed the father and wounded the mother, and the officers covered for them. At least one soldier raped the girl.'[32]

Jaffa seems to have been a hothouse for the cruelty and war crimes of the Israeli troops. One particular battalion, Battalion 3 – commanded by the same person who had been in charge when its soldiers committed massacres in Khisas and Sa'sa, and cleansed Safad and its environs – was so savage in its behaviour that its soldiers were suspected of being involved in most of the rape cases in the city, and the High Command decided it best to withdraw them from the town. However, other units were no less guilty of molesting women in the first three to four months of the occupation. The worst period was towards the end of the first truce (July 8) when even Ben-Gurion became so apprehensive about the pattern of behaviour that emerged among the soldiers in the occupied cities, especially the private looting and the rape cases, that he decided not to allow certain army units to enter Nazareth after his troops had taken the town during the 'ten-day' war.[33]

Our third source is the oral history we have from both the victimisers and the victims. It is very difficult to get the facts in the former case and almost impossible, of course, in the latter. But their stories have already helped shed light on some of the most appalling and inhuman crimes in the war that Israel waged against the Palestinian people.

The perpetrators can only talk, it seems, shielded by the safe distance of years. This is how a particularly appalling case came to light just recently. On 12 August 1949, a platoon of soldiers in the Negev, based in Kibbutz Nirim not far for Beit Hanun, on the northern edge of today's Gaza Strip, captured a twelve-year-old Palestinian girl and locked her up for the night in their military base near the kibbutz. For the next few days she became the platoon's sex slave as the soldiers shaved her head, gang-raped her and in the end murdered her. Ben-Gurion lists this rape too in his diary but it was censored out by his editors. On 29 October 2003, the Israeli newspaper *Ha'aretz* publicised the story based on the testimonies of the rapists: twenty-two soldiers had taken part in the barbaric torture and execution of the girl. When they were then brought to trial, the severest punishment the court handed down was a prison term of two years for the soldier who had done the actual killing.

Oral recollection also exposed cases of rape throughout the occupation of Palestine's villages: from the village of Tantura in May, through the village of Qula in June, and ending with one story after another of abuse and rape in the villages seized during Operation Hiram. Many of the cases were corroborated by UN officials who interviewed a number of women from the villages who were willing to come forward and talk about their experiences. When, many years later, some of these people were interviewed, it was obvious how difficult it still proved for the men and women from the village to talk about names and details in these cases, and the interviewers came away with the impression that they all knew more than they wished or were able to tell.

Eyewitnesses also reported the callous and humiliating way in which women were stripped of all their jewellery, to the very last item. The same women were then harassed physically by the soldiers, which in Tantura ended in rape. Here is how Najiah Ayyub described it: 'I saw that the troops who encircled us tried to touch the women but were rejected by them. When they saw that the women would not surrender, they stopped. When we were on the beach, they took two women and tried to undress them, claiming they had to search the bodies.'[34]

Tradition, shame, and trauma are the cultural and psychological barriers that prevent us from gaining the fuller picture of the rape of Palestinian women within the general plunder Jewish troops wreaked with such ferocity in both rural and urban Palestine during 1948 and 1949. Perhaps in the fulness of time someone will be able to complete this chapter of the chronicle of Israel's ethnic cleansing of Palestine.

DIVIDING THE SPOILS

Once the winds of war had subsided and the newly established State of Israel had signed armistice agreements with its neighbours, the Israeli government relaxed its occupation regime somewhat and gradually put a halt to the looting and ghettoisation of the small groups of urban Palestinians left behind. In August 1948, a new structure was put in place to deal with the consequences of the ethnic cleansing, called 'The Committee for Arab Affairs'. As before, Bechor Shitrit's proved to be the more humane voice among his colleagues on this committee, together with that of Israel's first Foreign Minister, Moshe Sharett, but it also included some former members of the Consultancy. The presence of Yaacov Shimoni, Gad Machnes, Ezra Danin and Yossef Weitz, all people who had helped devise the expulsions, would have been quite alarming for those Palestinians who had remained, had they known.

In August, the new outfit mainly dealt with the growing international pressure on Israel to allow the repatriation of the refugees. The tactic it decided upon was to try to push through a resettlement programme that they envisaged would pre-empt all confrontation on the subject, either because the principal players in the international community would agree to endorse it or, even better, it would persuade them to abandon the issue altogether. The Israeli offer suggested that all Palestinian refugees should be resettled in Syria, Jordan and Lebanon. This is not surprising, since it was discussed at a meeting of the Jewish Agency as early as 1944. Ben-Gurion argued: 'The transfer of Arabs is easier than the transfer of any other [people]. There are Arab states around . . . And it is clear that if the [Palestinian] Arabs are transferred this would improve their situation and not the opposite.' While Moshe Sharett noted: [W]hen the Jewish state is established – it is very possible that the result will be transfer of Arabs.'[35] Although the USA and Britain at the time responded favourably to this policy – which has remained the accepted line of argument for all successive Israeli governments – neither they nor the rest of the world seemed interested in investing too much effort in pushing it forward, or in arguing for the implementation of UN Resolution 194, which called for the unconditional repatriation of Palestinian refugees. As Israel had hoped, the fate of the refugees, not to mention their rights, soon dropped out of sight.

But return or resettlement was not the only issue. There was also the question of the money expropriated from the 1,300,000 Palestinians, the ex-citizens of Mandatory Palestine, whose finances had been invested in banks and institutions that were all seized by the Israeli authorities after May 1948. Neither did Israel's proposed policy of resettlement address the issue of Palestinian property now in Israeli hands. A member of the committee was the first governor of the national bank, David Horowitz, and he estimated the combined value of property 'left by the Arabs' at 100 million pounds. To avoid becoming embroiled in international investigations and scrutiny, he suggested as a solution: 'Maybe we can sell it to American Jews?'[36]

An additional problem was the cultivated land the Palestinians had been forced to abandon, and in the Arab Affairs Committee meeting it was again Bechor Shitrit who naïvely pondered aloud its possible fate: 'The cultivated land is probably 1 million dunam. According to international law, we cannot sell anything, so maybe we should buy from those Arabs who do not want to come back.' Without ceremony, Yossef Weitz cut him short: 'The fate of the cultivated land will be no different from the overall territory on which the villages existed.' The solution, recommended Weitz, had to cover all the territory: all village land, whether cultivated or residential, and the urban areas.[37]

Unlike Shitrit, Weitz was in the know. His official position as the head of the JNF settlement department and his de facto leadership of the ad-hoc 'transfer committee' fused into one once the ethnic cleansing had started. Weitz closely followed every single takeover within the rural areas, either personally or through loyal officials such as his close aide Yossef Nachmani. While the Jewish troops were responsible for the expulsion of the people and the demolition of their homes, Weitz went to work to make sure the villages passed into JNF custody.

This proposal frightened Shitrit even more, as it meant the number of dunam Israel would take possession of, illegally in his mind, was triple the figure of 1 million dunam he had originally thought. Weitz's next suggestion was even more alarming for anyone sensitive to international law or legality: 'All we need', declared the head of the settlement department of the Jewish National Fund, 'is 400 tractors, each tractor can cultivate 3000 dunam – cultivating not just for the purpose of procuring food but in order to prevent anyone from returning to their lands. Land of lesser quality should be sold to private or public sectors.'

Shitrit tried one more time, 'At least, let us say that this confiscation is an exchange for the property the Jews from the Arab world lost when they immigrated to Palestine.' Jewish immigration was quite limited at the time, but the concept of 'exchange' would later appeal to the Israeli Foreign Ministry, whose propaganda machine has frequently used it in abortive attempts to silence the debate on the Palestinian refugees' Right of Return. Shitrit's idea was dropped in August 1948 because it risked implicating Israel in the commission of forced transfer. Yaacov Shimoni warned that such a declaration of mutual expropriation would inevitably direct attention to the expulsions – he termed them 'transfer' – Israel had carried out in Palestine.

By now Ben-Gurion had grown impatient. He realised that sensitive subjects such as creating *faits accomplis* so as to pre-empt the threat of international sanctions – for instance the destruction of houses so that nobody could force Israel to allow their Palestinian owners to return to them – was no job for such a cumbersome body as the Committee for Arab Affairs. Thus he decided to appoint Danin and Weitz to a committee of two that from then on would take all final decisions on Palestinian property and land, the main features of which were destruction and confiscation.

For a short and unique period the American administration showed an interest in the subject. Officials in the State Department, in an atypical move, dominated the policy on the refugee issues, while the White House seemed to stand aloof. The inevitable result was a growing dissatisfaction with the basic Israeli position. The US experts saw no legal alternative to the return of the refugees, and were considerably irritated by Israel's refusal to even discuss the possibility. In May 1949, the State Department conveyed a strong message to the Israeli government that it considered the repatriation of the refugees as a precondition for peace. When the Israeli rejection arrived, the US administration threatened Israel with sanctions, and withheld a promised loan. In response, the Israelis at first suggested taking in 75,000 refugees and allowing the reunification of families for another 25,000. When this was deemed insufficient by Washington, the government suggested taking in the Gaza strip, with its 90,000 indigenous inhabitants and its refugee community of 200,000. Both proposals seemed niggardly but by then, the spring of 1949, a personnel reshuffle in the American State Department reoriented America's Palestine policy onto a different course that completely sidelined, if not altogether ignored, the refugee question.

During this short-lived period of US pressure (April–May 1949), Ben-Gurion's basic response was to intensify the settlement of Jewish immigrants on the confiscated land and in the evicted houses. When Sharett and Kaplan objected, apprehensive of international condemnation of such acts, Ben-Gurion again appointed a more cabal-like body that soon encouraged hundreds of thousands of Jewish immigrants from Europe and the Arab world to seize the Palestinian homes left in the towns and cities and to build settlements on the ruins of the expelled villages.

The appropriation of Palestinian property was supposed to follow a systematic national programme, but by the end of September Ben-Gurion gave up the idea of an orderly takeover in the major cities such as Jaffa, Jerusalem and Haifa. Similarly, it proved impossible to coordinate the onslaught of covetous farmers and governmental agencies on the dispossessed villages and lands. The distribution of land was the responsibility of the Jewish National Fund. After the 1948 war other bodies were given similar authority, the most important of which was the Custodian, mentioned below. The JNF found it had to compete for the job of principal divider of the spoils of war. In the final analysis the JNF came out on top, but it took time. All in all, Israel had taken over 3.5 million dunam of land in rural Palestine. This estimate from 1948 included all houses and fields of the destroyed villages. It took a while before a clear centralised policy emerged of how best to use this land. Ben-Gurion deferred a total takeover by private or public Jewish agencies while the UN was still discussing the fate of the refugees, first in Lausanne in 1949, and after that in a series of futile committees set up to deal with the refugee issue. He knew that in the wake of the UN General Assembly's Resolution 194, 11 December 1948, which demanded the unconditional repatriation of all Palestinian refugees, a formal and legal Israeli takeover would cause problems.

In order to forestall international indignation over collective dispossession, the Israeli government appointed a 'custodian' for the newly acquired properties, pending a final decision over their fate. Typical of previous Zionist conduct, this 'pragmatic' solution became policy until a 'strategic' decision would follow to change it (i.e., by redefining the status of the dispossessed assets). The Custodian was thus a function the Israeli government created in order to fend off any possible fallout from UN Resolution 194 that insisted that all refugees be allowed to return and/or be compensated. By putting all private and collective possessions of the expelled Palestinians under its custody, the government could, and in effect did, sell these properties to public and private Jewish groups and individuals later under the spurious pretext that no claimants had come forward. Moreover, the moment the confiscated lands from Palestinian owners were put under government custodianship they became state lands, which by law belonged to the Jewish nation, which, in turn, meant that none of it could be sold to Arabs.[38]

This legal sleight of hand meant that as long as no final strategic decision on how to divide the lands had been made, 'tactical' interim resolutions could be adopted in order to hand over part of the lands to the IDF, for instance, or to new immigrants or (at cheap rates) to the kibbutzim movements. The JNF faced fierce competition from all these 'clients' in the scramble over the spoils. It did well to begin with, and bought up almost every destroyed village together with all its houses and lands. The Custodian had sold a million dunam out of the total 3.5 million directly to the JNF at a bargain price in December 1948. Another quarter of a million was passed on to the JNF in 1949.

Then lack of funds put a halt to the JNF's seemingly insatiable greed. And what the JNF failed to purchase, the three kibbutzim movements, the moshavim movement and private real-estate dealers were happy to divide among themselves. The most avaricious of these proved to be the leftist kibbutz movement, Hashomer Ha-Tza'ir, that belonged to Mapam, the party to the left of Mapai, Israel's ruling party. Hashomer Ha-Tza'ir members were not content only with lands from which the people had already been expelled, but also wanted the lands whose Palestinian owners had survived the onslaught and who were still clinging onto them. Consequently, they now wanted these people to be driven out too,even though the official ethnic cleansing had come to an end. All these contenders had to make way for the Israeli army's demands to have large tracts of land set aside as training grounds and camps. And yet, by 1950, half of the dispossessed rural lands were still in the hands of the JNF.

In the first week of January 1949, Jewish settlers colonised the villages of Kuwaykat, Ras al-Naqura, Birwa, Safsaf, Sa'sa and Lajjun. On the lands of other villages, such as Malul and Jalama in the north, the IDF built military bases. In many ways, the new settlements did not look much different from the army bases – new fortified bastions where once villagers had led their pastoral and agricultural lives.

The human geography of Palestine as a whole was forceably transformed. The Arab character of the cities was effaced by the destruction of large sections, including the spacious park in Jaffa and community centres in Jerusalem. This transformation was driven by the desire to wipe out one nation's history and culture and replace it with a fabricated version of another, from which all traces of the indegenous population were elided.

Haifa was a case in point. As early as 1 May 1948, (Haifa having been taken on 23 April) Zionist officials had written to David Ben-Gurion that an 'historical opportunity' had fallen into their hands to metamorphose Haifa's Arab character. All that was needed, they explained, was 'the destruction of 227 houses.'[39] Ben-Gurion visited the city to inspect the scene of the intended destruction himself, and also ordered the destruction of the covered marketplace, one of the most beautiful markets of its kind. Similar decisions were taken with regard to Tiberias, where almost 500 houses were demolished, and a similar number in Jaffa and Western Jerusalem.[40] Ben-Gurion's sensitivity here vis-à-vis the mosques was unusual, the exception that proved the rule. Israel's official plunder did not spare holy shrines, least of all mosques, that were part of the newly acquired possessions.

DESECRATION OF HOLY SITES[41]

Until 1948 all Muslim holy sites in Palestine belonged to the Waqf, the Islamic endowment authority recognised by both the Ottoman Empire and the British Mandatory government. They were supervised by the Supreme Muslim Council, a body of local religious dignitaries, at the head of which stood al-Hajj Amin al-Husayni. After 1948 Israel confiscated all these endowments, with all the properties incorporated in them, and transferred them first to the Custodian, then to the state, and eventually sold them to Jewish public bodies and private citizens.[42]

Neither were the Christian churches immune from this land grab. Much of the land that churches owned within destroyed villages was confiscated like the Waqf endowments, although unlike the vast majority of mosques, quite a few of the churches remained intact. Many churches and mosques were never properly destroyed, but left to look like 'ancient' historical ruins – vestiges of the 'past' to remind people of Israel's might of destruction. However, among these holy sites were some of Palestine's most impressive architectural gems, and they disappeared forever: Masjad al-Khayriyya vanished under the city of Givatayim, and the rubble of the church of Birwa now lies beneath the cultivated land of the Jewish settlement of Ahihud. A similar masonry treasure was the mosque in Sarafand on the coast near Haifa (not to be confused with the Sarafand in the heart of Palestine where a huge British base was located). The mosque was a hundred years old when the Israeli government gave the go-ahead to have it bulldozed on 25 July 2000, ignoring a petition addressed to the then prime minister, Ehud Barak, beseeching him not to authorise this official act of state vandalism.

In retrospect, however, it was the abuse of their Islamic holy shrines that proved the most painful to a Palestinian community, the large majority of whose members found solace and comfort in the embrace of tradition and religion. The Israelis turned the mosques of Majdal and Qisarya into restaurants, and the Beersheba mosque into a shop. The Ayn Hawd mosque is used as a bar, and that of Zib is part of a resort village: the mosque is still there but owned by the government agency responsible for maintaining the national parks. Some mosques remained intact until the Israeli authorities believed time had released them from the obligation to protect the sanctity of these places. The remains of the Ayn al-Zaytun mosque, for example, were turned into a milk farm as late as 2004: the Jewish owner removed the stone that indicated the founding date of the mosque and covered the walls with Hebrew graffiti. By contrast, in August 2005 the Israeli media, public and politicians castigated their government for its decision to leave in the hands of the Palestinians the synagogues of the settlements Israel evicted in the Gaza Strip that summer. When the inevitable destruction of these synagogues came about – cement structures from which the settlers themselves had removed all religious items prior to their eviction – the general outcry in Israel reached the skies.

As for the Muslim shrines and Christian churches that survived, these are not always accessible. The church and mosque of Suhmata are still visible today, but if you want to pray there or simply wish to visit these sites you have to cross Jewish farms and risk being reported to the police for trespassing. This is also the case if you attempt to visit the Balad al-Shaykh mosque near Haifa and, equally, Muslims are denied access to the mosque of Khalsa located today in the development town of Qiryat Shemona. The people of Kerem Maharal still refuse to allow access to the beautiful nineteenth-century mosque at the centre of what used to be the village of Ijzim, one of the wealthiest villages in Palestine.

Sometimes access is denied by official manipulation rather than force, as in the case of the Hittin mosque. According to tradition Salah al-Din built this amazing structure in the middle of the village in 1187 to commemorate his victory over the Crusaders. Not too long ago, 73-year-old Abu Jamal from Deir Hanna hoped that through a summer camp for Palestinian children he could help restore the place to its past glory and re-open it for worship. But the Ministry of Education tricked him: its senior officials promised Abu Jamal that if he cancelled the camp, the ministry would donate money for the restoration work. However, when he accepted the offer the ministry sealed the site with barbed wire as if it were a high-security installation. All the stones, including the foundation stone, were then removed by the nearby kibbutzniks who use the land to graze their sheep and cows.

The following is a short registry covering the last decade or so. In 1993 the Nabi Rubin mosque was blown up by Jewish fanatics. In February 2000 the Wadi Hawarith mosque was ruined, two weeks after Muslim volunteers had finished restoring the building. Some restored mosques were the target of sheer vandalism. The Maqam of Shaykh Shehade, in the destroyed village of Ayn Ghazal, was burned down in 2002, and the Araba'in mosque of Baysan was ruined by an arson attack in March 2004. The al-Umari and al-Bahr mosques in Tiberias escaped two similar attacks in June 2004 in which they were badly damaged. The Mosque of Hasan Beik in Jaffa is assaulted regularly by people throwing stones at it, and it was desecrated once when the head of a pig with the name of the prophet written on it was tossed into its yard. In 2003, bulldozers erased out all trace of the al-Salam ('Peace') mosque in Zarughara, half a year after the mosque had been re-erected, while the Maqam of Shaykh Sam'an near Kfar Saba was demolished by unknown assailants in 2005.

Other mosques were turned into Jewish places of worship, as in the iconoclastic days of medieval times. The mosques of Wadi Unayn and Yazur are today synagogues, as is the mosque in the maqam of Samakiyya in Tiberias and in the two villages of Kfar Inan and Daliyya. The mosque of Abassiyya, near Ben-Gurion Airport, was turned into a synagogue, too, but has since been abandoned. It is decorated today with graffiti saying 'Kill the Arabs!' The Lifta mosque at the western entrance to Jerusalem has become a *mikweh* (Jewish ritual bath for women).

Recent targets are the mosques of the so-called 'unrecognised villages' in Israel; this is the most recent aspect of the dispossession that first began during the Nakba. Since, according to Israeli law, most of the land in Israel belongs to the 'Jewish people' from which Palestinian citizens are barred, Palestinian farmers are left with very little space to expand or build new villages. In 1965 the government abolished all infrastructure plans for the urban and rural development of the Palestinian areas. As a result Palestinians, and especially the Bedouin in the south, began to establish 'illegal' villages with, of course, mosques in them. Both houses and mosques in these villages are under constant threat of demolition. The Israeli authorities play a highly cynical game with the residents: they are given the option between their houses or their mosque. In one such village, Husayniyya (named after a 1948 destroyed village), a long battle in court saved the mosque but not the village. In October 2003, the authorities offered to leave 13 houses in Kutaymat standing instead of the mosque, which they demolished.

ENTRENCHING THE OCCUPATION

When the international pressure subsided and Israel had put in place clear rules for dividing the spoils, the Committee for Arab Affairs also formalised the official governmental attitude towards the Palestinians left within the territory of the new state, who were now citizens of Israel. Totalling about 150,000, these became the 'Israeli Arabs' – as if it made sense to talk about

'Syrian Arabs' or 'Iraqi Arabs' and not 'Syrians' or 'Iraqis'. They were put under a military regime, based on the British Mandate's emergency regulations issued in 1945, by none other than Menachem Begin. These regulations, which are comparable to the 1953 'Nuremberg Laws', virtually abolished basic rights of expression, movement, organisation and equality before the law. They left them the right to vote for and be elected to the Israeli parliament, but this too came with severe restrictions. This regime officially lasted until 1966, but, for all intents and purposes, the regulations are still in place.

The Committee for Arab Affairs continued to meet, and as late as 1956 some of its more prominent members seriously advocated plans for the expulsion of the 'Arabs' from Israel. Massive expulsions continued until 1953. The last village to be depopulated at gunpoint was Umm al-Faraj, near Nahariyya. The army went in, drove out all the inhabitants and then destroyed the village. The Bedouin in the Negev were subjected to expulsions up to 1962, when the tribe of al-Hawashli was forced to leave. In the dead of night 750 people were put on trucks and driven away. Their houses were demolished and the 8000 dunam they owned were confiscated and then given to families who were collaborating with the Israeli authorities. Most of the plans the Committee discussed were never implemented for various reasons. They have come to light thanks to the Palestinian historian Nur Masalha.

Had it not been for some liberal-minded Israeli politicians who objected to the schemes, and the Palestinian minority's own steadfastness in several cases where such plans to expel them were set in motion, we would long ago have witnessed the ethnic cleansing of the 'remnant' of the Palestinian people now living within the borders of the Jewish state. But if that final danger seemed to have been averted, the 'price' they paid for living in relative physical safety was incalculable – the loss not only of their land, but with it the soul of Palestine's history and future. The appropriation of Palestinian lands by the government continued from the 1950s onwards under the auspices of the JNF.

The Land Robbery: 1950–2000

It was the Settlement Department in the JNF that decided the fate of the destroyed villages once they had been flattened: whether a Jewish settlement or a Zionist forest would take its place. Back in June 1948, the head of the department, Yossef Weitz, had reported to the Israeli government: 'We have begun the operation of cleansing, removing the rubble and preparing the villages for cultivation and settlement. Some of these will become parks.' As he observed the ongoing destruction, Weitz had proudly reported that he remained unmoved by the sight of tractors destroying whole villages.[43] But to the public at large, a very different picture was portrayed: 'creating' new Jewish settlements was accompanied by such slogans as 'making the desert bloom', while the JNF's forestation activities were marketed as an ecological mission designed to keep the country green.

Forestation was not a first choice. The selection process did not actually rest on any clear strategy but consisted of ad-hoc decisions. First there were the abandoned cultivated lands that could immediately be harvested; then there were tracts of fertile land that could potentially yield crops in the near future that went to 'veteran' Jewish settlements or were set aside for the establishment new ones. As we saw, the JNF had a hard time fending off the competition which came from the kibbutzim movements. They would start cultivating the lands of neigbhouring villages even before they had been given permission to take them over, and then on the basis of the work already carried out would demand ownership. As a rule the feeling in the government was that land first had to be allotted to existing Jewish settlements, then to the building of new ones, and only in the third place be made available for forestation.

In 1950, the Knesset passed the Law for Absentee Property, while the Custodian introduced some order into the way it dealt with the booty, but had not yet made the JNF sole owner. On the way to becoming the exclusive proprietor of Israel's new forests – almost all planted over the ruins of Palestinian villages destroyed in the ethnic cleansing of 1948 – the JNF defeated the Ministry of Agriculture, which naturally sought control over the forestation issue. The state, however, recognised the advantage of giving the JNF a full mandate not only as Israel's forest-keepers but also as the principal custodian of the lands as a whole on 'behalf of the Jewish people'. From now on, even on land it did not own, the JNF was responsible for safeguarding its 'Jewishness' by prohibiting all transactions with non-Jews, namely Palestinians.

This is not the place to expand on the complex trajectory the JNF followed in its struggle to keep its spoils. Its primary tool, however, was the use of government legislation. The JNF Law was passed in 1953 and granted the agency independent status as land-owner on behalf of the Jewish state. This law, and a host of others that followed, such as the Law of the Land of Israel and the Law of the Israel Land Authority (ILA), both passed in 1960, all reinforced this position. These were all constitutional laws determining that the JNF was not allowed to sell or lease land to non-Jews. They finalised the JNF's share in the overall state lands (thirteen per cent) but hid a much more complex reality that enabled the JNF to implement its policy of 'guarding the nation's land' in areas beyond its direct control, simply because it had a decisive role in, and impact on, the directorship of the ILA, which became the owner of eighty per cent of all state lands (the rest being owned by the JNF, the army and the government).

The legislative takeover of the land and the process of turning it into JNF property was completed in 1967 when the Knesset passed a final law, the Law of Agricultural Settlement, that also prohibited the sub-letting of the Jewish-owned land of the JNF to non-Jews (until then only sale and direct lease were prohibited). The law furthermore ensured that water quotas set aside for the JNF lands could not be transferred to non-JNF lands (water is scarce in Israel and hence sufficient quotas are vital for agriculture).

The bottom line of this almost two-decade-long bureaucratic process (1949–1967) was that the legislation regarding the JNF, barring the selling, leasing and sub-letting of land to non-Jews, was put into effect for most of the state lands (more than ninety per cent of Israel's land, seven per cent having been declared as private land). The primary objective of this legislation was to prevent Palestinians in Israel from regaining ownership, through purchase, of their own land or that of their people. This is why Israel never allowed the Palestinian minority to build even one new rural settlement or village, let alone a new town or city (apart from three Bedouin settlements in the early 1960s, which actually represented recognition by the state of the permanent residence sedentary tribes had taken up there). At the same time, Israel's Jewish population, with a much lower natural growth, was able to build on these lands – apart from those destined for forestation – as many settlements, villages and cities as they wished, and wherever they wanted.

The Palestinian minority in Israel, seventeen per cent of the total population after ethnic cleansing, has been forced to make do with just three per cent of the land. They are allowed to build and live on only two per cent of the land; the remaining one per cent was defined as agricultural land which cannot be built upon. In other words, today 1.3 million people live on that two per cent. Even with the privatisation of land that began in the 1990s, the JNF policy remains in place, thus excluding the Palestinians from the benefit that opening up the land market would provide for the public at large; that is, Israel's Jews. However, not only have they been prevented from expanding over the land that was theirs, but also much of the land they owned before the 1948 war was confiscated from them, in the 1970s, for the building of new Jewish settlements in the Galilee and again, in the early 2000s, for the construction of the Segregation Wall and a new highway. One study has estimated that seventy per cent of the land belonging to the Palestinians in Israel has been either confiscated or made inaccessible to them.[44]

The final dispossession in the Galilee – so far – which parallels the confiscation of land in the West Bank – for the two-fold purpose of building Jewish settlements and slowly, but surely, driving the Palestinians out of these areas, began after 1967.

In the early 1960s, before the final division of land between the ILA and the JNF, the latter launched Operation 'Finally' (*Sof-Sof*), which sought to further dispossess the Palestinians of land in the Galilee that was still in the villagers' possession. The JNF offered to buy those lands or exchange them with lesser quality land elsewhere. But the villagers refused – their steadfastness forms one of the truly heroic chapters in the struggle against the Zionist ethnic cleansing operations. The JNF then began erecting special military outposts at the entrances to the 'stubborn' villages in an effort to exert psychological pressure on the inhabitants. Even with such callous means, the JNF only achieved its goal in a few cases. As Arnon Soffer, a professor of geography at Haifa University, who is closely connected with the government, explains:

> We were murderous, but it was not malice for the sake of malice. We acted out of a sense of being exposed to an existential threat. And there were objective reasons for this feeling. We were convinced that without Jewish territorial continuity, especially along the national water carrier [the aqueduct that runs from the Lake of Galilee to the south of the coutry], the Arabs would poison the water.[45]

That there are no fences or guard posts along the entire route of the aqueduct raises doubts about the sincerity of the concern expressed here. The need for 'territorial continuity', on the other hand, does sound sincere: it was, after all, the main inspiration in 1948 for Israel's massive operations of expulsion.

The dispossession of Palestinian lands did not only entail the expulsion of their legal owners and the prevention of their repatriation and regaining ownership. It was compounded by the reinvention of Palestinian villages as purely Jewish or 'Ancient' Hebrew places.

Chapter 10

The Memoricide of the Nakba

Nationalist extremists are also trying to wipe out any physical evidence that could remind future generations that people other than Serbs ever lived together in Bosnia. Historic mosques, churches and synagogues as well as national libraries, archives, and museums have been torched, dynamited and bulldozed ... They want to eliminate the memory of the past as well.

Sevdalinka.net

Over 700,000 olive and orange trees have been destroyed by the Israelis. This is an act of sheer vandalism from a state that claims to practise conservation of the environment. How appalling and shameful.

Address by Ronnie Kasrils, Minister of Water Affairs and Forestry, South Africa, London 30 November, 2002.

THE REINVENTION OF PALESTINE

As the owner of lands in general, along with other agencies that possess state land in Israel such as the Israeli Land Authority, the army and the government, the Jewish National Fund was also involved in establishing new Jewish settlements on the lands of the destroyed Palestinian villages. Here, dispossession was accompanied by the renaming of the places it had seized, destroyed and now recreated. This mission was accomplished with the help of archaeologists and biblical experts who volunteered to serve on an official Naming Committee whose job it was to Hebraize Palestine's geography.

This naming committee was in fact an old outfit, already put in place in 1920, when it acted as an ad-hoc group of scholars that granted Hebrew names to lands and places newly purchased by the Jews, and they continued to do so for lands and places taken by force during the Nakba. It was reconvened by Ben-Gurion in July 1949, who turned it into a sub-division of the JNF. The naming committee was not working in a total vacuum. Some of the Palestinian villages were inevitably built on the ruins of earlier and even ancient civilizations, including the Hebrew one, but this was a limited phenomenon and none of the cases involved was unambiguous. The postulated 'Hebrew' sites date back to such ancient times that there is little chance of establishing their locations properly, but then, of course, the motive for Hebraizing the names of the evicted villages was ideological and not scholarly. The narrative accompanying this expropriation was very simple: 'Throughout the years of foreign occupation of Eretz Israel, the original Hebrew names were erased or became garbled, and sometimes took on an alien form.' The archaeological zeal to reproduce the map of 'Ancient' Israel was in essence none other than a systematic, scholarly, political and military attempt to de-Arabise the terrain – its names and geography, but above all its history.

The JNF, as mentioned before, was busy confiscating land in the 1950s and the 1960s, but it did not end there. It also owned land in the Greater Jerusalem area that it had received from the Custodian of Absentee Lands after the 1967 war. In the early 1980s, this land was passed on by the JNF to Elad, the settlers' NGO that was then and remains today devoted to the 'Judaization' of East Jerusalem. This NGO focused on Silwan and stated openly that it wanted to cleanse that village from its original Palestinian inhabitants. In 2005 it received assistance from the Jerusalem municipality, which ordered the destruction of three dozen houses there under the pretext of 'illegal construction and expansion'.

In the beginning of the twenty-first century, the JNF's main challenges were the government policies of privatisation of land ownership, accelerated under Benjamin Netanyahu (1996–1999) and Ariel Sharon (2001–2003; 2003–2006), which threatened to limit the JNF's control. However, both these right-wing prime ministers were torn between Zionism and Capitalism, and time will tell how much land their successors will allow to remain in the JNF's hands in the future. What is not going to change is the strong hold the JNF has over Israel's forests.

In these forests Nakba denial is so pervasive, and has been achieved so effectively, that they have become a main arena of struggle for Palestinian refugees wishing to commemorate the villages that lie buried beneath them. They are up against an organisation – the JNF – which claims that there is only barren land under the pine and cypress trees it has planted there.

VIRTUAL COLONIALISM AND THE JNF

When it set out to create its national parks on the sites of eradicated Palestinian villages, the decision as to what to plant was totally in the hands of the JNF. Almost from the start the JNF executive opted mainly for conifers instead of the natural flora indigenous to Palestine. In part this was an attempt to make the country look European, although this appears nowhere in any official document as a goal. In addition, however, the choice of planting pine and cypress trees – and this has been overtly stated – was meant to support the country's aspiring wood industry.

The three aims of keeping the country Jewish, European-looking and Green quickly fused into one. This is why forests throughout Israel today include only eleven per cent of indigenous species and why a mere ten per cent of all forests date from before 1948.[1] At times, the original flora manages to return in surprising ways. Pine trees were planted not only over bulldozed houses, but also over fields and olive groves. In the new development town of Migdal Ha-Emek, for example, the JNF did its utmost to try and cover the ruins of the Palestinian village of Mujaydil, at the town's eastern entrance, with rows of pine trees, not a proper forest in this case but just a small wood. Such 'green lungs' can be found in many of Israel's development towns that cover destroyed Palestinian villages (Tirat Hacarmel over Tirat Haifa, Qiryat Shemona over Khalsa, Ashkelon over Majdal, etc.). But this particular species failed to adapt to the local soil and, despite repeated treatment, disease kept afflicting the trees. Later visits by relatives of some of Mujaydial's original villagers, revealed that some of the pine trees had literally split in two and how, in the middle of their broken trunks, olive trees had popped up in defiance of the alien flora planted over them fifty-six years ago.

Within Israel and throughout the Jewish world the JNF is seen as a highly responsible ecological agency whose reputation rests on the way it has been assiduously planting trees, reintroducing local flora and land-scapes, and paving the way for scores of resort and nature parks, complete with picnic facilities and children's playgrounds. Israelis find their way to these spots by clicking on the different icons on the JNF's detailed website, or taking their cues from the material posted on the various information boards located at the entrances to these parks, and at various stations along the way within the recreational grounds themselves. These texts and guide and inform visitors wherever they go, even if all they want to enjoy them-selves and relax.

JNF parks do not only offer parking spaces, picnic areas, playgrounds and access to nature, but also incorporate visible items that tell a particular history: the ruins of a house, a fortress, orchards, cactuses (*sabra*), and so on. There are also many fig and almond trees. Most Israelis think these are 'wild' figs or 'wild' almonds, as they see them in full bloom, towards the end of the winter, heralding the beauty of spring. But these fruit trees were planted and nurtured by human hands. Wherever almond and fig trees, olive groves or clusters of cactuses are found, there once stood a Palestinian village: still blossoming afresh each year, these trees are all that remain. Near the now-uncultivated terraces, and under the swings and picnic tables, and the European pine forests, there lie buried the houses and fields of the Palestinians whom Israeli troops expelled in 1948. However, guided only by these JNF signs, visitors will never realise that people used to live there – the Palestinians who now reside as refugees in the Occupied Territories, as second-rate citizens inside Israel, and as camp dwellers beyond Palestine's border.

The true mission of the JNF, in other words, has been to conceal these visible remnants of Palestine not only by the trees it has planted over them, but also by the narratives it has created to deny their existence. Whether on the JNF website or in the parks themselves, the most sophisticated audio-visual equipment displays the official Zionist story, contextualising any given location within the national meta-narrative of the Jewish people and *Eretz Israel*. This version continues to spout the familiar myths of the narrative – Palestine as an 'empty' and 'arid' land before the arrival of Zionism – that Zionism employs to supplant all history that contradicts its own invented Jewish past.

As Israel's 'green lungs', these recreational sites do not so much commemorate history as seek to totally erase it. Through the literature the JNF attaches to the items that are still visible from before 1948 a local history is intentionally denied. This is not part of a need to tell a different story in its own right, but is designed to annihilate all memory of the Palestinian villages that these 'green lungs' have replaced. In this way, the information provided at these JNF sites is a pre-eminent model for the all-pervading mechanism of denial Israelis activate in the realm of representation. Deeply rooted in the people's psyche, this mechanism works through exactly this replacement of Palestinian sites of trauma and memory by spaces of leisure and entertainment for Israelis. In other words, what the JNF texts represent as an 'ecological concern' is yet one more official Israeli effort to deny the Nakba and conceal the enormity of the Palestinian tragedy.

THE JNF RESORT PARKS IN ISRAEL

The home page of the JNF's official website showcases the agency as being responsible for having made the desert bloom and the historical Arab landscape look European. It proudly proclaims that these forests and parks were built upon 'arid and desert-like areas', and that 'Israel's forests and parks were not always here. The first Jewish settlers in the country, at the end of the 19th century, found a desolate land with not a mite of shade.'

The JNF is not only the creator of Israel's 'green lungs', it is also their preserver. The JNF declares that the forests are there to provide recreation for the benefit of all citizens of Israel and to make them 'ecologically aware'. What visitors are not being told is that in addition the JNF is the principal agency whose job it is to prevent all acts of commemoration at these 'forests', let alone visits of return, by Palestinian refugees whose own houses lie entombed under these trees and playgrounds.

Four of the larger and most popular picnic sites that appear on the JNF website – the Birya Forest, the Ramat Menashe Forest, the Jerusalem Forest, and the Sataf – all epitomise, better than any other space today in Israel, both the Nakba and the denial of the Nakba .

The Forest of Birya

Moving from north to south, the Birya Forest is located in the Safad region and covers a total of 20,000 dunam. It is the largest man-made forest in Israel and a very popular site. It conceals the houses and the lands of at least six Palestinian villages. Reading through the text on the website and simply highlighting what it includes and excludes, none of the villages of Dishon, Alma, Qaddita, Amqa, Ayn al-Zaytun or Biriyya are ever mentioned. They all disappear behind the descriptions the website gives of the forest's wonderful charms and attractions: 'No wonder that in such a huge forest one can find a plethora of interesting and intriguing sites: woods, bustans, springs and an old synagogue [namely a small piece of mosaic that may or may not be an old synagogue, as the area through the ages was frequented by the Orthodox Jews of Safad].' In many of the JNF sites, bustans – the fruit gardens Palestinian farmers would plant around their farm houses – appear as one of the many mysteries the JNF promises the adventurous visitor. These clearly visible remnants of Palestinian villages are referred to as an inherent part of nature and her wonderful secrets. At one of the sites, it actually refers to the terraces you can find almost everywhere there as the proud creation of the JNF. Some of these were in fact rebuilt over the original ones, and go back centuries before the Zionist takeover.

Thus, Palestinian bustans are attributed to nature and Palestine's history transported back to a biblical and Talmudic past. Such is the fate of one of the best known villages, Ayn al-Zaytun, which was emptied in May 1948, during which many of its inhabitants were massacred. Ayn al-Zaytun is mentioned by name, but in the following manner:

> Ein Zeitun has become one of the most attractive spots within the recreational ground as it harbors large picnic tables and ample parking for the disabled. It is located where once stood the settlement Ein Zeitun, where Jews used to live ever since the medieval times and until the 18th century. There were four abortive [Jewish] settlement attempts. The parking lot has biological

toilets and playgrounds. Next to the parking lot, a memorial stands in memory of the soldiers who fell in the Six Day War.

Fancifully meshing history and tourist tips, the text totally erases from Israel's collective memory the thriving Palestinian community Jewish troops wiped out within a few hours.

The pages of the JNF website on the history of Ayn al-Zaytun go into great detail, and the narrative that accompanies a virtual or real journey into the forest takes the reader back to the alleged Talmudic town in the third century, before skipping a whole millennium of Palestinian villages and communities. It finally focuses on the last three years of the Mandatory period, as these same grounds were hiding places where the Jewish underground, trying to escape the watchful eyes of the British, trained its troops and stashed the weapons it was amassing.

The Ramat Menashe Park

South of Biriyya lies Ramat Menashe Park. It covers the ruins of Lajjun, Mansi, Kafrayn, Butaymat, Hubeiza, Daliyat al-Rawha, Sabbarin, Burayka, Sindiyana and Umm al-Zinat. At the very centre of the park lie the remains of the destroyed village of Daliyat al-Rawha, now covered by Kibbutz Ramat Menashe of the socialist movement Hashomer Ha-Tza'ir. The remnants of the blown-up houses[2] of one of the villages, Kafrayn, are still visible. The JNF website highlights the admixture of nature and human habitat in the forest when it tells us that in its midst there are 'six villages'. The website uses the highly atypical Hebrew word for 'village', *kfar*, to refer to the *kibbutzim* in the park, and not the six villages underneath the park – a linguistic ploy that serves to reinforce the metaphorical palimpsest at work here: the erasure of the history of one people in order to write that of another people's over it.[3]

In the words of the JNF website, the beauty and the attraction of this site are 'unmatched'. One of the principal reasons is the countryside itself, with its bustans and its ruins of 'the past', but there is a master design behind all this that strives to maintain the contours of the natural scenery. Here, too, nature has its 'particular appeal' because of the destroyed Palestinian villages the park covers up. Both the JNF's virtual and real tour through the park gently guide the visitor from one recommended spot to another, all carrying Arabic names: thesse are the names of the destroyed villages, but here presented as natural or geographical locations that betray no earlier human presence. The reason one can move from one point to the other so smoothly is attributes by the JNF to a network of roads that were paved in the 'British period'. Why did the British bother to pave roads here? Obviously to better connect (and thus control) *existing* villages, but this fact can only be extracted from the text with great difficulty, if at all.

This system of erasure, however, can never be foolproof. For example, the JNF website tells us something you will not find mentioned on the boards that punctuate the forest paths themselves. Within the many ruins dotting the place the 'Village Spring' (*'Ein ha-Kfar'*) is recommended as 'the quietest part of the site'. Often a village spring would be at the heart of the village, close to the village square, as here in Kafrayn, its ruins now providing not only 'peace of mind' but also serving the cattle of the nearby kibbutz Mishmar Ha-Emek as a resting point on their way to meadows down below.

Greening of Jerusalem

The last two examples come from the Jerusalem area. The western slopes of the city are covered with the 'Jerusalem forest', another brainchild of Yossef Weitz. In 1956 Weitz complained to the mayor of Jerusalem about the barren sight of the western hills of the city. Eight years earlier, they had of course been covered with the houses and the cultivated lands of Palestinian villages bustling with life. In 1967 Weitz's efforts finally bore fruit: The JNF decided to plant one million trees on 4,500 dunam that, in the words of the website, 'encircle Jerusalem with a green belt.' At one of its southern corners, the forest reaches the ruined village of Ayn Karim and covers the destroyed village of Beit Mazmil. Its most western point stretches over the land and houses of the destroyed village of Beit Horish, whose people were expelled as late as 1949. The forest extends further over Deir Yassin, Zuba, Sataf, Jura and Beit Umm al-Meis.

The JNF website here promises its visitors unique sites and special experiences in a forest whose historical remnants 'testify to intensive agricultural activity'. More specifically, it highlights the various terraces one finds carved out along the western slopes: as in all other sites, these terraces are always 'ancient' – even when they were shaped by Palestinian villagers less than two or three generations ago.

The last geographical site is the destroyed Palestinian village of Sataf, located in one of the most beautiful spots high up in the Jerusalem Mountains. The site's greatest attraction, according to the JNF website, is the reconstruction it offers of 'ancient' (*kadum* in Hebrew) agriculture – the adjective 'ancient' is used for every single detail in this site: paths are 'ancient', steps are 'ancient', and so on. Sataf, in fact, was a Palestinian village expelled and mostly destroyed in 1948. For the JNF, the remains of the village are one more station visitors encounter on the intriguing walking tours it has set out for them within this 'ancient site'. The mixture here of Palestinian terraces and the remains of four or five Palestinian buildings almost fully intact inspired the JNF to create a new concept, the 'bustanof' ('bustan' plus '*nof*', the Hebrew word for panorama, the English equivalent for which would probably be something like 'bustanorama' or 'orchard-view'). The concept is wholly original to the JNF.

The bustans overlook some exquisite scenery and are popular with Jerusalem's young professional class who come here to experience 'ancient' and 'biblical' ways of cultivating a plot of land that may even yield some 'biblical' fruits and vegetables. Needless to say, these ancient ways are far from 'biblical' but are Palestinian, as are the plots and the bustans and the place itself.

In Sataf the JNF promises the more adventurous visitors a 'Secret Garden' and an 'Elusive Spring', two gems they can discover among terraces that are a 'testimony to human habitation 6,000 years ago culminating in the period of the Second Temple.' This is not exactly how these terraces were described in 1949 when Jewish immigrants from Arab countries were sent to repopulate the Palestinian village and take over the houses that had remained standing. Only when these new settlers proved unmanageable did the JNF decide to turn the village into a tourist site.

At the time, in 1949, Israel's naming committee searched for a biblical association for the place, but failed to find any connection to Jewish sources. They then hit upon the idea of associating the vineyard that surrounded the village with the vineyards mentioned in the biblical Psalms and Song of Songs. For a while they even invented a name for the place to suit their fancy, 'Bikura' – the early fruit of the summer – but gave it up again as Israelis had already got used to the name Sataf.

The JNF website narrative and the information offered on the various boards set up at the locations themselves is also widely available elsewhere.

There has always been a thriving literature in Israel catering for domestic tourism where ecological awareness, Zionist ideology and erasure of the past often go hand in hand. The encyclopedias, tourist guides and albums generated for the purpose appear even more popular and are in greater demand today than ever before. In this way, the JNF 'ecologises' the crimes of 1948 in order for Israel to tell one narrative and erase another. As Walid Khalidi has put in his forceful style: 'It is a platitude of historiography that the victors in war get away with both the loot and the version of events.'[4]

Despite this deliberate airbrushing of history, the fate of the villages that lie buried under the recreational parks in Israel is intimately linked to the future of the Palestinian families who once lived there and who now, almost sixty years later, still reside in refugee camps and faraway diasporic communities. The solution of the Palestinian refugee problem remains the key to any just and lasting settlement of the conflict in Palestine: for close to sixty years now the Palestinians have remained steadfast as a nation in their demand to have their legal rights acknowledged, above all their Right of Return, originally granted to them by the United Nations in 1948. They continue to confront an official Israeli policy of denial and anti-repatriation that seems only to have hardened over the same period.

There are two factors that have so far succeeded in defeating all chances of an equitable solution to the conflict in Palestine to take root: the Zionist ideology of ethnic supremacy and the 'peace process'. From the former stems Israel's continuing denial of the Nakba; in the latter we see the lack of international will to bring justice to the region – two obstacles that perpetuate the refugee problem and stand in the way of a just and comprehensive peace emerging in the land.

Chapter 11

Nakba Denial and the 'Peace Process'

The UN General Assembly resolves that the refugees wishing to return to their homes and live at peace with their neighbours should be permitted to do so at the earliest practicable date, and that compensation should be paid for the property of those choosing not to return and for the loss of or damage to property which, under the principles of international law and in equity, should be made good by the Governments or authorities responsible.

UN GA resolution 194 (III), 11 December 1948.

The US government supports the return of refugees, democratization, and protection of human rights throughout the country.

Bureau of Democracy, Human Rights and Labor,
US State Department, 2003

While the Palestinians Israel had failed to expel from the country were subjected to the military regime Israel put in place in October 1948, and those in the West Bank and the Gaza Strip were now under foreign Arab occupation, the rest of the Palestinian people were scattered throughout the neighbouring Arab states where they had found shelter in makeshift tent camps provided by international aid organisations.

In mid-1949, the United Nations stepped in to try to deal with the bitter fruits of its 1947 peace plan. One of the UN's first misguided decisions was not to involve the International Refugee Organization (IRO) but to create a special agency for the Palestinian refugees. It was Israel and the Zionist Jewish organisations abroad that were behind the decision to keep the IRO out of the picture: the IRO was the very same body that was assisting the Jewish refugees in Europe following the Second World War, and the Zionist organisations were keen to prevent anyone from making any possible association or even comparison between the two cases. Moreover, the IRO always recommended repatriation as the first option to which refugees were entitled.

This is how the United Nation Relief and Work Agency (UNRWA) came into being in 1950. UNRWA was not committed to the return of the refugees as UN General Assembly Resolution 194, from 11 December 1948, had stipulated, but was set up simply to provide employment and subsidies to the approximately one million Palestinian refugees who had ended up in the camps. It was also entrusted with building more permanent camps for them, constructing schools and opening medical centres. In other words, UNRWA was intended, in general, to look after the refugees' daily concerns.

It did not take long under these circumstances for Palestinian nationalism to re-emerge. It was centred on the Right of Return, but also aimed at replacing UNRWA as an educating agency and even as the provider of social and medical services. Inspired by the drive to try to take their fate into their own hands, this nascent nationalism equipped the people with a new sense of direction and identity, following the exile and destruction they had experienced in 1948. These national emotions were to find their embodiment in 1968 in the PLO, whose leadership was refugee-based and whose ideology was grounded in the demand for the moral and factual redress of the evils Israel had inflicted upon the Palestinian people in 1948.[1]

The PLO, or any other group taking up the Palestinian cause, had to confront two manifestations of denial. The first was the denial exercised by the international peace brokers as they consistently sidelined, if not altogether eliminated, the Palestinian cause and concerns from any future peace arrangement. The second was the categorical refusal of the Israelis to acknowledge the Nakba and their absolute unwillingness to be held accountable, legally and morally, for the ethnic cleansing they committed in 1948.

The Nakba and the refugee issues have been consistently excluded from the peace agenda, and to understand this we must assess how deep the level of denial of the crimes committed in 1948 remains today in Israel and associate it with the existence of a genuinely felt fear on the one hand, and a deeply rooted form of anti-Arab racism on the other, both heavily manipulated.

FIRST ATTEMPTS AT PEACE

Despite the 1948 fiasco, the United Nations still seemed to have some energy left in the first two years after the Nakba to try to come to grips with the question of Palestine. We find the UN initiating a series of diplomatic efforts through which it hoped to bring peace to the country, culminating in a peace conference in Lausanne, Switzerland in the spring of 1949. The Lausanne conference was based on UN Resolution 194 and centred around the call for the refugees' Right of Return. For the UN mediation body, the Palestine Conciliation Commission (PCC), unconditional return of the Palestinian refugees was the basis for peace, together with a two-state solution dividing the country equally between the two sides, and the internationalisation of Jerusalem.

Everyone involved accepted this comprehensive approach: the US, the UN, the Arab world, the Palestinians and Israel's foreign minister, Moshe Sharett. But the endeavour was deliberately torpedoed by Israel's prime minister, David Ben-Gurion, and King Abdullah of Jordan, who had set their minds on partitioning what was left of Palestine between them. An election year in America and the onset of the Cold War in Europe allowed these two to carry the day and make sure the chances for peace were swiftly buried again. They thereby foiled the only attempt we find in the history of the conflict at a comprehensive approach to creating genuine peace in Palestine/Israel.

Towards Pax Americana

After the failure of Lausanne, peace efforts quickly subsided: for nearly two decades, between 1948 and 1967, there was an obvious lull. Only after the war in June 1967 did the world wake up to the plight of the region once again. Or so it seemed. The June war ended with total Israeli control over all of ex-Mandatory Palestine. Peace endeavours started immediately after

Israel's *blitzkrieg* had run its swift but devastating course, and proved at first more overt and intensive than the ones at Lausanne. Early initiatives came from the British, French and Russian delegations at the UN, but soon the reins were handed over to the Americans as part of a successful attempt by the US to exclude the Russians from all Middle-Eastern agendas.

The American effort totally relied on the prevailing balance of power as the main avenue through which to explore possible solutions. Within this balance of power, Israel's superiority after 1948 and even more so after the June war was unquestionable, and thus whatever the Israelis put forward in the form of peace proposals invariably served as the basis for the Pax Americana that now descended on the Middle East. This meant that it was given to the Israeli 'Peace Camp' to produce the 'common' wisdom on which to base the next stages and provide the guidelines for a settlement. All future peace proposals thus catered to this camp, ostensibly the more moderate face of Israel's position towards peace in Palestine.

Israel drafted new guidelines after 1967, taking advantage of the new geopolitical reality its June war had created, but also mirroring the internal political debate that emerged inside Israel itself, following what Israeli PR quickly dubbed the '6-Day War' (purposely invoking biblical overtones), between the right wing, the 'Greater Israel' people, and the left wing, the 'Peace Now' movement. The former were the so-called 'redeemers', people for whom the Palestinian areas Israel had occupied in 1967 were the 'regained heartland' of the Jewish state. The latter were dubbed 'custodians', Israelis who wanted to hold on to the Occupied Palestinian Territories so as to use them as bargaining chips in future peace negotiations. When the Greater Israel camp began establishing Jewish settlements in the Occupied Territories, the 'custodian' peace camp appeared to have no problem with the building of settlements in particular areas that immediately became non-negotiable for peace: the Greater Jerusalem area and certain settlement blocks near the 1967 border. The areas the peace camp initially offered to negotiate over have shrunk gradually since 1967 as Israeli settlement construction progressed incrementally over the years in the consensual areas of 'redemption'.

The moment the American apparatus responsible for shaping US policy in Palestine adopted these guidelines, they were paraded as 'concessions', 'reasonable moves' and 'flexible positions' on the part of Israel. This is the first part of the pincer movement Israel now executed to completely eliminate the Palestinian point of view – of whatever nature and inclination. The second part was to portray that point of view in the West as 'terrorist, unreasonable and inflexible'.

THE EXCLUSION OF 1948 FROM THE PEACE PROCESS

The first of Israel's three guidelines – or rather, axioms – was that the Israeli–Palestinian conflict had its origin in 1967: to solve it, all one needed was an agreement that would determine the future status of the West Bank and the Gaza Strip. In other words, as these areas constitute only twenty-two per cent of Palestine, Israel at one stroke reduced any peace solution to only a small part of the original Palestinian homeland. Not only that, it demanded – and continues to demand today – further territorial compromises, either consonant with the business-like approach the US favoured or as dictated by the map agreed upon by the two political camps in Israel.

Israel's second axiom is that everything visible in these areas, the West Bank and the Gaza Strip, can again be further divided and that this divisibility forms one of the keys to peace. For Israel this division of the visible includes not just the territory, but also people and natural resources.

The third Israeli axiom is that nothing that occurred prior to 1967, including the Nakba and the ethnic cleansing, will ever be negotiable. The implications here are clear: it totally removes the refugee issue from the peace agenda and sidelines the Palestinian Right of Return as a 'non-starter'. This last axiom totally equates the end of Israeli occupation with the end of the conflict, and it follows naturally from the previous two. For the Palestinians, of course, 1948 is the heart of the matter and only addressing the wrongs perpetrated then can bring an end to the conflict in the region.

To activate these axiomatic guidelines that so clearly meant to push the Palestinians out of the picture, Israel needed to find a potential partner. Proposals put forward to that end to King Hussein of Jordan, through the mediation skills of the American secretary of state at the time, Henry Kissinger, read: 'The Israeli peace camp, led by the Labour party, regards the Palestinians as non-existent and prefers to divide the territories Israel occupied in 1967 with the Jordanians.' But Jordan's king deemed the share he was allotted insufficient. Like his grandfather, King Hussein coveted the area as a whole, including East Jerusalem and its Muslim sanctuaries.

This so-called Jordanian option was endorsed by the Americans up to 1987, when the first Intifada, the popular Palestinian uprising, erupted in December of that year against Israel's oppression and occupation. That nothing came of the Jordanian path in the earlier years was due to lack of Israeli generosity, while in later years King Hussein's ambivalence was at fault as well as his inability to negotiate on behalf of the Palestinians, as the PLO enjoyed pan-Arab and global legitimacy.

Egypt's President Anwar Sadat suggested a similar path in his 1977 peace initiative to Israel's right-wing prime minister, Menachem Begin (in power between 1977 and 1982). The idea was to allow Israel to maintain control over the Palestinian territories it held under occupation while granting the Palestinians in them internal autonomy. In essence this was another version of partition as it left Israel in direct possession of eighty per cent of Palestine and in indirect control over the remaining twenty per cent.

The first Palestinian uprising in 1987 squashed all ideas of the autonomy option as it led Jordan to remove itself as a partner from future negotiations. The upshot of these developments was that the Israeli peace camp came around to accepting the Palestinians as partners for a future settlement. At first Israel tried, always with the help of the Americans, to negotiate peace with the Palestinian leadership in the Occupied Territories, which was allowed to take part, as an official peace delegation, in the 1991 Madrid peace conference. This conference was the award the American administration had decided to hand out to the Arab states for backing Washington's military invasion of Iraq in the first Gulf War. Openly stalled by Israel, Madrid led nowhere.

Israel's 'peace' axioms were re-articulated during the days of Yitzhak Rabin, the same Yitzhak Rabin who, as a young officer, had taken an active part in the 1948 cleansing but who had now been elected as prime minister on a platform that promised the resumption of the peace effort. Rabin's death – he was assassinated by one of his own people on 4 November 1995 – came too soon for anyone to assess how much he had really changed from his 1948 days: as recently as 1987, as minister of defence, he had ordered his troops to break the bones of Palestinians who confronted his tanks with stones in the first Intifada; he had deported hundreds of Palestinians as prime minister prior to the Oslo Agreement, and he had pushed for the 1994 Oslo B agreement that effectively caged the Palestinians in the West Bank into several Bantustans.

At the centre of Rabin's peace efforts stood the Oslo Accords that began rolling in September 1993. Again, the concept behind this process was a Zionist one: the Nakba was totally absent. The architects of the Oslo formula were Israeli intellectuals who, of course, belonged to Israel's 'peace camp' and who ever since 1967 had played an important role in the Israeli public scene. Institutionalised in an ex-parliamentary movement called Peace Now, they had several political parties on their side. But Peace Now has always evaded the 1948 issue and sidelined the refugee question. When they did the same in 1993, they seemed to have found a Palestinian partner in Yassir Arafat for a peace that buried 1948 and its victims. The false hopes Israel raised with Oslo were to have dire consequences for the Palestinian people, all the more as Arafat fell into the trap Oslo set for him.

The result was a vicious circle of violence. Desperate Palestinian reactions to Israeli oppression in the form of suicide bomb attackers against both the Israeli army and civilians led to an even harsher Israeli retaliation policy that in turn prompted more young Palestinians – many coming from 1948 refugee families – to join the guerrilla groups advocating suicide attacks as the only means left to them of liberating the Occupied Territories. An easily intimidated Israeli electorate brought a right-wing government back into power, whose policy differed little, at the end of the day, from the previous 'Oslo' government. Netanyahu (1996–1999) failed in every aspect of governance, and Labour was back in power in 1999 and, with it, the 'Peace Camp', this time led by Ehud Barak. When within a year Barak was facing electoral defeat for having been over-ambitious in almost every field of governmental policy, a peace with the Palestinians seemed the only way of safeguarding his political future.

THE RIGHT OF RETURN

What for Barak was no more than a tactical move to save his skin, the Palestinians – erroneously – envisaged as the climax of the Oslo negotiations. And when US president Clinton invited Prime Minister Barak and President Arafat to a summit meeting in Camp David in the summer of 2000, the Palestinians went there in the expectation of genuine negotiations over the conflict's end. Such a promise was indeed embedded in the Oslo rationale: the original document of September 1993 promises the Palestinian leadership that if they were willing to agree to a waiting period of between five to ten years (during which Israel would partially withdraw from the Occupied Territories), the essentials of the conflict as they saw them would be on the table in the final phase of the new peace negotiations. This final phase, they thought, had now come and with it the time to discuss the 'three essentials of the conflict': the Right of Return, Jerusalem, and the future of the Israeli settlements.

A fragmented PLO – the organisation had lost all those who had seen through Oslo, including the more radical Islamic movements that began emerging in the late 1980s – had to come up with a counter peace plan. Tragically, it felt unable to do the job itself and sought advice in such unlikely places as the Adam Smith Institute in London. Under its guidance, naïve Palestinian negotiators put the Nakba and Israel's responsibility for it at the top of the Palestinian agenda.

Of course they had completely misread the tone of the US peace scheme: only Israel was allowed to set the items of a peace agenda, including those for a permanent settlement. And it was exclusively the Israeli plan, totally endorsed by the Americans, that was on the table at Camp David. Israel offered to withdraw from parts of the West Bank and the Gaza Strip, leaving the Palestinians about fifteen per cent of original Palestine. But that fifteen per cent would be in the form of separate cantons bisected by Israeli highways, settlements, army camps and walls.

Crucially, the Israeli plan excluded Jerusalem: there would never be a Palestinian capital in Jerusalem. Nor was there a solution to the refugee problem. In other words, the way the proposal defined the future Palestinian state amounted to a total distortion of the concepts of statehood and independence as we have come to accept them in the wake of the Second World War and as the Jewish state, with international support, had claimed for itself in 1948. Even the now frail Arafat, who until then had seemed happy with the *salata* (perks of power) that had come his way at the expense of the *sulta* (actual power) he never had, realised that the Israeli diktat emptied all Palestinian demands of content, and refused to sign.

For nearly four decades Arafat had embodied a national movement whose main aim was to seek legal and moral recognition of the ethnic cleansing Israel had perpetrated in 1948. The notion of how this might come about changed with time, as did the strategy and, definitely, the tactics, but the overall objective remained the same, especially since the demand for the refugees to be allowed to return had been internationally acknowledged already in 1948 by UN Resolution 194. Signing the 2000 Camp David proposals would have amounted to a betrayal of the achievements, however few, the Palestinians had won for themselves. Arafat refused to do so, and was immediately punished for this by the Americans and the Israelis who quickly moved to depict him as a warmonger.

This humiliation, further compounded by the provocative visit of Ariel Sharon to the Haram al-Sharif in Jerusalem in September 2000, triggered the outbreak of the second Intifada. Like the first Intifada, this was initially a non-militarised popular protest. But the eruption of lethal violence with which Israel decided to respond caused it to escalate into an armed clash, a hugely unequal mini-war that still rages. The world looks on as the strongest military power in the region, with its Apache helicopters, tanks and bulldozers, attacks an unarmed and defenseless population of civilians and impoverished refugees, among whom small groups of poorly equipped militias try to make a brave but ineffective stand.

Baroud's *Searching Jenin* contains eyewitness accounts of the Israeli invasion of the Jenin refugee camp between 3 and 15 April 2002 and the massacre Israeli troops committed there, searing testimony of the cowardice of the international community, the callousness of Israel and the courage of the Palestinian refugees.[2] Rafidia al-Jamal is a 35-year old mother of five; her sister Fadwa was twenty-seven when she was killed:

> When the army first entered they took over the roof tops of high buildings and positioned themselves on the top of mosques. My sister is a nurse. She was assigned to work in one of the field hospitals that were set up in every area being invaded.
>
> Around 4 in the morning, we heard the explosion of a shell. My sister was supposed to go to the hospital right away to help care for the wounded. This is why she left the house – especially after we heard people screaming for help. My sister was wearing her white uniform and I was still in my nightgown. I put a scarf on my head and went to escort her as she crossed the street. Before we left I asked her to wash for prayer. She had so much faith, especially in times like these. When the shell fell we did not feel any fear, we just knew that some people were in need of rescue.
>
> When we went outside, some neighbors were also out. We asked them who was wounded. As we were talking with them, Israeli bullets began

to fall on us like rain. I was wounded in my left shoulder. Israeli soldiers were positioned on the top of the mosque, and that was the direction from which the bullets came. I told my sister Fadwa that I was wounded. We were standing under a light post, so it was very clear who we were from the way we were dressed. But as she tried to help me, her head fell on me. She was showered with bullets. Fadwa fell on my leg and now I was lying on the ground. The bullet broke my leg. With her head resting on me I told her, 'Make your prayers', because I knew she was going to die. I didn't expect her to die so fast, though – she couldn't finish her prayers.[3]

On 20 April the UN Security Council adopted Resolution 1405 to send a fact-finding mission into the Jenin camp. When the Israeli government refused to cooperate, UN General Secretary Kofi Annan decided to abandon the mission.

For the Palestinians, the only positive thing to come out of the Camp David episode was that their leadership succeeded, at least for a brief moment, in bringing the catastrophe of 1948 to the attention of a local, regional and, to a certain extent, global audience. Not only in Israel, but also in the United States, and even in Europe, people genuinely concerned about the Palestine question needed to be reminded that this conflict was not just about the future of the Occupied Territories, but that at its heart are the refugees Israel had cleansed from Palestine in 1948. This was an even more formidable task after Oslo, because then it had seemed that the issue had simply been pushed aside with the agreement of ill-managed Palestinian diplomacy and strategy.

Indeed, the Nakba had been so effectively kept off the agenda of the peace process that when it suddenly appeared on the scene at Camp David, the Israelis felt as if a Pandora's box had been opened in front of them. The worst fear of the Israeli negotiators was the looming possibility that Israel's responsibility for the 1948 catastrophe would become a negotiable issue. Needless to say, this 'danger' was immediately confronted. The Israeli media and parliament, the Knesset, lost no time in formulating a wall-to-wall consensus: no Israeli negotiator would be allowed even to discuss the Right of Return of the Palestinian refugees to the homes that had been theirs before 1948. The Knesset swiftly passed a law to this effect,[4] with Barak publicly committing himself to upholding it as he climbed the steps of the plane that was taking him to Camp David.

Behind these draconian measures on the part of the Israeli government to prevent any discussion of the Right of Return lies a deep-seated fear vis-à-vis any debate over 1948, as Israel's 'treatment' of the Palestinians in that year is bound to raise troubling questions about the moral legitimacy of the Zionist project as a whole. This makes it crucial for Israelis to keep a strong mechanism of denial in place, not only to help them defeat the counter-claims Palestinians were making in the peace process, but – far more importantly – so as to thwart all significant debate on the essence and moral foundations of Zionism.

For Israelis, to recognise the Palestinians as the victims of Israeli actions is deeply distressing, in at least two ways. As this form of acknow-ledgement means facing up to the historical injustice of which Israel is incriminated through the ethnic cleansing of Palestine in 1948, it calls into question the very foundational myths of the State of Israel, and it raises a host of ethical questions that have inescapable implications for the future of the state.

Recognizing Palestinian victimhood ties in with deeply rooted psychological fears because it demands that Israelis question their self perceptions of what 'went on' in 1948. As most Israelis see it – and as mainstream and popular Israeli historiography keeps telling them – in 1948 Israel was able to establish itself as an independent nation-state on part of Mandate Palestine because early Zionists had succeeded in 'settling an empty land' and 'making the desert bloom'.

The inability of Israelis to acknowledge the trauma the Palestinians suffered stands out even more sharply when set against the way the Palestinian national narrative tells the story of the Nakba, a trauma they continue to live with to the present. Had their victimhood been the 'natural' and 'normal' outcome of a long-term and bloody conflict, Israel's fears of allowing the other side to 'become' the victim of the conflict would not have been so intense – both sides would have been 'victims of the circumstances', and here one may substitute any other amorphous, non-committal concept that serves human beings, particularly politicians but also historians, to absolve themselves from the moral responsibility they otherwise would carry. But what the Palestinians are demanding, and what, for many of them, has become a sine qua non, is that they be recognised as the victims of an *ongoing* evil, consciously perpetrated against them by Israel . For Israeli Jews to accept this would naturally mean undermining their own status of victimhood. This would have political implications on an international scale, but also – perhaps far more critically – would trigger moral and existential repercussions for the Israeli Jewish psyche: Israeli Jews would have to recognise that they have become the mirror image of their own worst nightmare.

At Camp David Israel need not have feared. After the attacks on 11 September 2001 in the United States and, the year before, the outbreak of the second Intifada in Palestine and the suicide bombings that Israel's horrific repression helped provoke, any courageous attempt to open the discussion evaporated almost without a trace, and the past practices of denial re-emerged with a vengeance.

Ostensibly, the peace process was revived in 2003 with the introduction of the Road Map, and even a somewhat bolder initiative, that of the Geneva Accord. The Road Map was the political product of the Quartet, the self - appointed body of mediators comprising the US, the UN, Britain and Russia. It offered a blueprint for peace that happily adopted the consensual Israeli position as embodied in the policies of Ariel Sharon (prime minister in 2001 and again from 2003 until his illness and departure from political life in 2006). By turning the Israeli withdrawal from Gaza in August 2005 into a media bonanza, Sharon succeeded in fooling the West that he was a man of good intentions. But the army still controls Gaza from the outside even today (including from the air, as it continues its 'targeted assassinations', Israel's way of applying death squads) and will probably remain in full control of the West Bank even when some Israeli settlers and soldiers in the future are removed from certain areas there. Symptomatic, too, is that the refugees of 1948 are not even mentioned in the Quartet's peace agenda.

The Geneva Accord is more or less the best offer the Israeli Jewish peace camp proved able to come up with in the beginning of the twenty-first century. This is a proposal concocted by people who were no longer in power on either side by the time they presented their programme. It is, therefore, difficult to know how valid it would be as a policy, even though they launched their initiative with a PR fanfare. The Geneva document recognises the Right of Return of the Palestinians provided their 'return' is confined to the West Bank and the Gaza Strip. It does not acknowledge the ethnic cleansing itself, but suggest compensation as an option. However, since the territories the document has set aside for a 'Palestinian state' contain one of the most densely populated areas in the world – the Gaza Strip – it immediately undercuts its own claim of offering a practical recipe for Palestinian return.

As strange as it may sound, from its partner Palestinians the Geneva document secured recognition of Israel as a Jewish state, in other words, an endorsement of all the policies Israel has pursued in the past for maintaining a Jewish majority at all cost – even ethnic cleansing. The good people of the Geneva accord are thus also endorsing Fortress Israel, the most significant obstacle on the road to peace in the land of Palestine.

Chapter 12

Fortress Israel

The significance of the disengagement plan [from Gaza] is the freezing of the peace process. And when you freeze that process, you prevent the establishment of a Palestinian state, and you prevent a discussion on the refugees, the borders and Jerusalem. Effectively, this whole package called the Palestinian state, with all that it entails, has been removed indefinitely from our agenda. All with [US] presidential blessings and the ratification of both houses of Congress.

> Dov Weissglas, spokesperson for Ariel Sharon,
> *Ha'aretz*, 6 October 2004

So, if we want to remain alive, we have to kill and kill and kill. All day, every day. [...] If we don't kill, we will cease to exist. [...] Unilateral separation doesn't guarantee 'peace' – it guarantees a Zionist-Jewish state with an overwhelming majority of Jews.

> Arnon Soffer, professor of geography at Haifa University,
> Israel, *The Jerusalem Post*, 10 May, 2004.

In the dead of night on 24 January 2006, an elite unit of Israel's border police seized the Israeli Palestinian village of Jaljulya. The troops burst into houses, dragging out thirty-six women and eventually deporting eight of them. The eight women were ordered to go back to their old homes in the West Bank. Some of them had been married for years to Palestinian men from Jaljulya, some were pregnant, many had children. They were abruptly cut off from their husbands and children. One Palestinian member of the Knesset protested, but the action was backed by the government, the courts and the media: the soldiers were demonstrating to the Israeli public that when the presence of the Palestinian minority population threatens to change from a 'demographic problem' to a 'demographic danger', the Jewish state will act swiftly and without mercy.

The police raid on Jaljulya was entirely 'legal': on 31 July 2003, the Knesset passed a law prohibiting Palestinians from obtaining citizenship, permanent residency or even temporary residency when they marry Israeli citizens. In Hebrew 'Palestinians' always means Palestinians living in the West Bank, the Gaza Strip and in the diaspora, so as to distinguish them from 'Israeli Arabs', as though they are not all part of the same Palestinian nation. The initiator of the legislation was a liberal Zionist, Avraham Poraz, of the centrist party Shinui, who described the bill as a 'defence measure'. Only twenty-five of the 120 members of the Knesset opposed it and Poraz at the time explained that those 'Palestinians' already married 'to Israeli citizens' and with families 'will have to go back to the West Bank', regardless of how long they had been living in Israel.

The Arab members of the Knesset were among a group of Israelis who appealed to the Israeli Supreme Court against this latest racist law. When the Supreme Court turned the appeal down, their energy petered out.[1] The Supreme Court ruling made clear how irrelevant they were in the eyes of both Israel's parliamentary and judicial systems. It also revealed once again how it prefers to uphold Zionism rather than justice. Israelis enjoy telling Palestinians they should be happy they live in 'the only democracy' in the region where they have the right to vote, but no one is under any illusion that voting comes with any actual political power or influence.

THE 'DEMOGRAPHIC PROBLEM'

The raid on Jaljulya and the law behind it help explain why Israel's Palestinian minority were at the heart of the recent Israeli elections. From left to right, the platforms of all the Zionist parties during the 2006 election campaign highlighted policies that they claimed would effectively counter the 'demographic problem' the Palestinian presence in Israel poses for the state. Ariel Sharon decided the pullout from Gaza was the best solution to it, while the Labour Party endorsed the Segregation Wall as the optimal way of ensuring the number of Palestinians inside Israel remains limited. Extra-parliamentary groups, too – among them the Geneva Accord movement,

Peace Now, the Council for Peace and Security, Ami Ayalon's Census group and the Mizrahi Democratic Rainbow – all had their own favourite recipes for how to tackle the 'demographic problem'.

Apart from the ten members of the Palestinian parties and two eccentric Ashkenazi ultra-Orthodox Jews, all members of Israel's new parliament were sent to the Knesset on the strength of the promise that their magic formulae would solve the 'demographic problem' once and for all. Strategies varied, from reducing Israeli occupation and control over the Occupied Territories – for most of them Israeli withdrawal would never be from more than fifty per cent of these territories – to more drastic and far-reaching action. For example, right-wing parties such as Yisrael Beytenu, the Russian ethnic party of Avigdor Liberman, and the religious parties openly argue for the 'voluntary transfer' – their euphemism for ethnic cleansing – of Palestinians to the West Bank. In other words, the Zionist response seeks to solve the problem of the 'demographic balance' either by giving up territory (that Israel holds illegally under international law) or by 'shrinking' the 'problematic' population group.

None of this is new. Already in the late nineteenth century Zionism had identified the 'population problem' as the major obstacle for the fulfillment of its dream. It had also identified the solution: 'We shall endeavour to expel the poor population across the border unnoticed, procuring employment for it in the transit countries, but denying it any employment in our own country,' Herzl had written in his diary in 1895.[2] And David Ben-Gurion was very clear in December 1947 that 'there can be no stable and strong Jewish state so long as it has a Jewish majority of only 60 per cent.'[3] Israel, he warned on the same occasion, would have to deal with this 'severe' problem with 'a new approach in due course'.

The ethnic cleansing of Palestine Ben-Gurion instigated the following year, his 'new approach', ensured that the number of Palestinians was reduced to less than twenty per cent of the overall population in the new Jewish state. In December 2003, Binyamin Netanyahu recycled Ben-Gurion's 'alarming' statistics: 'If the Arabs in Israel form 40 per cent of the population,' Netanyahu said, 'this is the end of the Jewish state.' 'But 20 per cent is also a problem,' he added. 'If the relationship with these 20 per cent becomes problematic, the state is entitled to employ extreme measures.'[4] He did not elaborate.

Twice in its short history Israel has boosted its population with two massive Jewish immigrations, each of about a million people, in 1949 and again in the 1980s. This has kept the percentage of Palestinians down to nearly twenty per cent of Israel's total population, when we do not include the Occupied Territories. Here lies the crux for today's politicians. Ehud Olmert, now prime minister, knows that if Israel decides to stay in the Occupied Territories and its inhabitants become officially part of Israel's population, Palestinians will outnumber Jews within fifteen years. Thus he has opted for what he calls *hitkansut*, Hebrew for 'convergence' or, better, 'ingathering', a policy that aims at annexing large parts of the West Bank but at the same time leaves several populous Palestinian areas outside direct Israeli control. In other words, *hitkansut* is the core of Zionism in a slightly different garb: to take over as much of Palestine as possible with as few Palestinians as possible. This explains the 670-km long serpentine route of the 8m-high concrete slabs, barbed wire and manned watchtowers that make up the Wall, and why it runs more than twice the length of the 315 km long 'Green Line' (the June 1967 border). But even if Olmert's government should succeed and this 'consolidation' goes ahead, there will still be a large population of Palestinians inside the eighty-eight per cent of Palestine where Olmert envisages he will build his future, stable Jewish state. How many Palestinian citizens exactly we don't know: Israeli demographers belonging to the centre or the left provide a low estimate, which makes 'disengagement' seem a reasonable solution,[5] while those on the right tend to exaggerate the figure. But they all seem to agree that the 'demographic balance' will not stay the same, given the higher birth-rate of Palestinians compared with Jews. Thus, at some point soon, Olmert may well come to the conclusion in the end that pull-outs are not the solution.

By now most mainstream journalists, academics and politicians in Israel have liberated themselves from their earlier inhibitions when it comes to talking about the 'demographic problem'. On the domestic scene, no one feels the need any more to explain what is at the heart of it and who it affects. And abroad, once Israel succeeded, after 9/11, in making the West think of the 'Arabs' in Israel and the Palestinians in the Occupied Territories as 'Muslims', it found it easy to elicit support for its demographic policies there too, certainly where it counted most: on Capitol Hill. On 2 February 2003 the popular daily *Ma'ariv* carried the following headline, typical of the new 'mood': 'A quarter of the children in Israel are Muslims.' The piece went on to describe this fact as Israel's next 'ticking bomb'. The natural increase in the population, no longer Palestinian, but

'Muslim' – 2.4% a year – was not portrayed as a problem any more: it had become a 'danger'.

In the run-up to the 2006 Knesset election, pundits discussed the question of the 'demographic balance' using language akin to that employed by majority populations in Europe and the United States in debates over immigration and how to absorb or deter immigrants. In Palestine, however, it is the immigrant community that decides the future of the indigenous people, not the other way round. As we already saw, on 7 February 1948, after driving to Jerusalem from Tel-Aviv and seeing how Jewish troops had already emptied the first Palestinian villages on the western outskirts of Jerusalem of their inhabitants, a jubilant Ben-Gurion reported to a gathering of Zionist leaders how 'Hebrew' Jerusalem had become.

But despite Zionist 'perseverance', a sizable community of Palestinians survived the ethnic cleansing. Today, their children are students at university where they follow courses by professors of political science or geography who lecture on how severe the problem of 'demographic balance' has become for Israel. Palestinian law students – the lucky ones who constitute an informal quota – at the Hebrew University of Jerusalem may well come across Professor Ruth Gabison, a former head of the Association for Civil Rights and a candidate for the Supreme Court, who has come out recently with strong views on the subject, views that she may well think reflect a broad consensus. 'Israel has the right to control Palestinian natural growth,' she has declared.[6]

Away from university campuses, Palestinians can't escape realising that they are viewed as a problem. From the Zionist left to the extreme right, it is broadcast to them daily that Israel's Jewish society longs to get rid of them. And they worry, and rightly so, each time they hear that they and their families have become a 'danger', because while still only a problem, they may feel protected by the pretence Israel keeps up to the outside world of being a liberal democracy. Once the state officially declares they constitute a danger, however, they know they will be the subject of emergency policies Israel has been happy to keep handy from the time of the British Mandate. Houses could be demolished, newspapers shut down and people expelled under such a regime.

The right of the Palestinian refugees whom Israel expelled in 1948 to return home was acknowledged by the UN General Assembly in December

1948. That right is anchored in international law and is consonant with all notions of universal justice. More surprisingly perhaps, it also makes sense in terms of realpolitik, as shown in Chapter 11: unless Israel acknowledges the cardinal role it has played, and continues to play, in the dispossession of the Palestinian nation, and accepts the consequences this recognition of the ethnic cleansing implies, all attempts to solve the Israel–Palestine conflict are bound to fail, as became clear in 2000 when the Oslo initiative broke down over the Palestinians' Right of Return.

But then, the aim of the Zionist project has always been to construct and then defend a 'white' (Western) fortress in a 'black' (Arab) world. At the heart of the refusal to allow Palestinians the Right to Return is the fear of Jewish Israelis that they will eventually be outnumbered by Arabs. The prospect this calls up – that their fortress may be under threat – arouses such strong feelings that Israelis no longer seem to care that their actions might be condemned by the whole world. The principle of maintaining an over-whelming Jewish majority at all costs supersedes all other political and even civil concerns, and the Jewish religious propensity to seek atonement has been replaced by the arrogant disregard for world public opinion and the self-righteousness with which Israel routinely fends off criticism. This position is not unlike that of the medieval Crusaders whose Latin Kingdom of Jerusalem remained for nearly a century a fortified isolated island as they shielded themselves behind the thick walls of their impenetrable castles against integration with their Muslim surroundings, prisoners of their own warped reality. A more recent example of this same kind of siege mentality we find in the white settlers in South Africa during the heyday of Apartheid rule. The aspiration of the Boers to maintain a racially pure, white enclave, like that of the Crusaders in Palestine, held out only for a brief historical moment before it, too, collapsed.

The Zionist enclave in Palestine, as we saw in the opening pages of this book, was constructed around 1922 by a group of Jewish colonialists from Eastern Europe with considerable help and assistance from the British Empire. The political borders the British decided on for Palestine simultaneously enabled the Zionists to define in concrete geographical terms the Eretz Israel they had in mind for their future Jewish state. The colonialists dreamed of massive Jewish immigration to strengthen their hold, but the Holocaust reduced the number of 'white', European Jews and, disappointingly from a Zionist point of view, those who had survived the Nazi onslaught preferred either to emigrate to the United States or even to remain in Europe itself, despite the recent horrors. Reluctantly, Israel's Ashkenazi leadership then decided to prompt one million Arab Jews from the Middle East and North Africa to join them in the enclave they had carved for themselves in the land of Palestine. Here, another discriminatory side of Zionism comes to the fore, perhaps even more poignant for the fact that it was directed against their own co-religionists. This group of Jewish newcomers from the Arab world, Mizrahim,[7] was put through an invidious process of de-Arabisation that scholars who are part of the second and third generation of these immigrants (notable among them Ella Shohat, Sami Shalom Shitrit and Yehuda Shenhav) have done much to expose in recent years. From a Zionist point of view, this process of dispossession also eventually proved a success story. Never threatened by the presence of a small Palestinian minority inside Israel, the illusion was maintained that the enclave was well built and rested on solid foundations.

When, in the mid-1960s, it became clear that the Arab world and the nascent Palestinian national movement refused to reconcile themselves with the reality Fortress Israel had created for them, Israel decided to extend its territorial grasp and, in June 1967, conquered the rest of Palestine, along with parts of Syria, Egypt and Jordan. Subsequently, after the Sinai had been ceded back to Egypt in 1979 in return for 'peace', in 1982, Israel added southern Lebanon to its mini-empire. An expansionist policy had become necessary to protect the enclave.

The withdrawals in May 2000 from southern Lebanon and, in August 2005, from the Gaza Strip, tell us that the Israeli government has shifted its sights to concentrate on aspects it deems more valuable to keeping the Fortress impenetrable: nuclear capability, unconditional American support, and a strong army. Zionist pragmatism has re-emerged in a policy that will finally define where the enclave's borders will run. According to international law, no state can set its own borders unilaterally, but this is not a notion likely to penetrate the thick walls of the Fortress. The consensus in contemporary Israel is for a state whose borders include about ninety per cent of Palestine, provided that territory will be surrounded by electric fences and visible as well as invisible walls.

As in 1948, when Ben-Gurion led the Consultancy to 'reconcile' themselves with a future state over seventy-eight per cent of Palestine, the problem is no longer how much land to grab, but rather what the future of the indigenous Palestinians who live there will be. In 2006, in the ninety per cent Israel covets there are about 2.5 million Palestinians sharing the state with six million Jews. There are also another 2.5 million Palestinians in the Gaza Strip and in the areas Israel does not want in the West Bank. For most main-stream Israeli politicians and the Jewish public this demographic balance is already a nightmare.

However, Israel's adamant refusal even to contemplate the possibility of negotiating the right of the Palestinians to come back to their homes, for the sake of maintaining a predominantly Jewish majority – even if this would bring about an end to the conflict – rests on very shaky ground. For almost two decades, the State of Israel has been unable to claim an over-whelming Jewish majority, thanks to the influx in the 1980s of Christians from former Soviet Union countries, the increasing number of foreign guest workers and the fact that secular Jews find it more and more difficult to define what their Jewishness amounts to in the 'Jewish' state. These realities are known to the captains of the ship of state, and yet none of this alarms them: their primary goal is to keep the population of the state 'white', that is, non-Arab.[8]

Israeli governments have failed in their attempts both to encourage fur-ther Jewish immigration and to increase Jewish birth rates within the state. And they have not found a solution to the conflict in Palestine that would entail a reduction in the number of Arabs in Israel. On the contrary, all the solutions Israel contemplates lead to an increase in the Arab population since they include the Greater Jerusalem area, the Golan Heights and the large settlement blocs in the West Bank. And while Israeli proposals after 1993 for ending the conflict may have met with the approval of some Arab regimes in the region – such as those of Egypt and Jordan, both securely located in the US sphere of influence – they never convinced the civil soci-eties in those countries. Neither does the way the Americans go about 'democratising' the Middle East, as currently pursued by US troops in Iraq, make life inside the 'white' Fortress any less anxious, as the invasion of Iraq is so closely identified with Israel by the Muslim world. Levels of social vio-lence inside the Fortress are high, and the standard of living of the majority is constantly dropping. None of these concerns is dealt with: they are almost as low on the national agenda as the environment and women's rights.

Rejecting the Palestinian refugees' Right of Return is tantamount to making an unconditional pledge to the continuing defence of the 'white' enclave and to upholding the Fortress. Apartheid is particularly popular among Mizrahi Jews, who today are the Fortress' most vociferous supporters, although few of them, especially since they come from North African countries, will find themselves leading the comfortable lives their Ashkenazi counterparts enjoy. And they know this – betraying their Arabic heritage and culture has not brought the reward of full acceptance.

Still, the solution would appear simple: as the last postcolonial European enclave in the Arab world, Israel has no choice but willingly to transform itself one day into a civic and democratic state.

That this is possible we see from the close social relationships that Palestinians and Jews have created between themselves over these long and troubled years and against all odds, both inside and outside Israel. That we can put an end to the conflict in the torn land of Palestine also becomes obvious if we look at those sections of Jewish society in Israel that have chosen to let themselves be shaped by human considerations rather than Zionist social engineering. That peace is within reach we know, above all, from the majority of the Palestinians who have refused to let themselves be de-humanised by decades of brutal Israeli occupation and who, despite years of expulsion and oppression, still hope for reconciliation.

But the window of opportunity will not stay open forever. Israel may still be doomed to remain a country full of anger, its actions and behaviour dictated by racism and religious fanaticism, the features of its people permanently distorted by the quest for retribution. How long can we go on asking, let alone expecting, our Palestinian brothers and sisters to keep the faith with us, and not to succumb totally to the despair and sorrow into which their lives were transformed the year Israel erected its Fortress over their destroyed villages and towns?

Epilogue

THE GREEN HOUSE

Tel-Aviv University, as are all Israel's universities, is dedicated to upholding the freedom of academic research. The Faculty Club of Tel-Aviv University is called the Green House. Originally this was the house of the mukhtar of the village of Shaykh Muwannis, but you would never be able to tell that if you were ever invited there to have dinner, or to take part in a workshop on the history of the country or even on the city of Tel-Aviv itself. The menu card of the Faculty Club's restaurant mentions that the place was built in the nineteenth century and used to belong to a rich man called 'Shaykh Munis' – a fictitious and faceless person imagined in a fictitious, placeless location, as are all the other 'faceless' people who once lived in the destroyed village of Shaykh Muwannis, on whose ruins Tel-Aviv University built its campus. In other words, the Green House is the epitome of the denial of the Zionists' master plan for the ethnic cleansing of Palestine that was finalised not far away along the beach, in Yarkon Street, on the third floor of the Red House.

Had the campus of Tel-Aviv University been dedicated to proper academic research, you would have thought that its economists, for example, would have assessed by now the extent of the Palestinian properties lost in the 1948 destruction, providing an inventory that could enable future negotiators to start working towards peace and reconciliation. The private businesses, banks, pharmacies, hotels and bus companies Palestinians owned, the coffee houses, restaurants and workshops they ran, and the official positions in government, health and education they held – all confiscated, vanished into thin air, destroyed or transferred to Jewish 'ownership' when the Zionists took over Palestine.

The tenured geographers walking around Tel-Aviv's campus might have given us an objective chart of the amount of refugee land Israel confiscated: millions of dunams of cultivated land and almost another ten million of the territory international law and UN resolutions had set aside for a Palestinian state. And to this they would have added the additional four million dunam the State of Israel has expropriated over the years from its Palestinian citizens.

Campus philosophy professors would by now have contemplated the moral implications of the massacres Jewish troops perpetrated during the Nakba. Palestinian sources, combining Israeli military archives with oral histories, list thirty-one confirmed massacres – beginning with the massacre in Tirat Haifa on 11 December 1947 and ending with Khirbat Ilin in the Hebron area on 19 January 1949 – and there may have been at least another six. We still do not have a systematic Nakba memorial archive that would allow one to trace the names of all those who died in the massacres – an act of painful commemoration that is gradually getting underway as this book goes to press.

Fifteen minutes by car from Tel-Aviv University lies the village of Kfar Qassim where, on 29 October 1956, Israeli troops massacred forty-nine villagers returning from their fields. Then there was Qibya in the 1950s, Samoa in the 1960s, the villages of the Galilee in 1976, Sabra and Shatila in 1982, Kfar Qana in 1999, Wadi Ara in 2000 and the Jenin Refugee Camp in 2002. And in addition there are the numerous killings Betselem, Israel's leading human rights organisation, keeps track of. There has never been an end to Israel's killing of Palestinians.

Historians working at Tel-Aviv University might have supplied us with the fullest picture of the war and the ethnic cleansing: they have privileged access to all the official military and governmental documentation and archival material required. Most of them, however, are more comfortable serving as the mouthpiece for the hegemonic ideology instead: their works describe 1948 as a 'war of independence', glorify the Jewish soldiers and officers who took part in it, conceal their crimes and vilify the victims.

Not all the Jews in Israel are blind to the scenes of carnage that their army left behind in 1948, nor are they deaf to the cries of the expelled, the wounded, the tortured and the raped as they keep reaching us through those who survived, and through their children and grandchildren. In fact, growing numbers of Israelis are aware of the truth of what happened in 1948, and fully comprehend the moral implications of the ethnic cleansing that raged in the country. They also recognise the risk of Israel re-activating the cleansing programme in a desperate attempt to maintain its absolute Jewish majority.

It is among these people that we find the political wisdom that all past and present peace-brokers of the conflict appear to lack so totally: they are fully aware that the refugee problem stands at the heart of the conflict and that the fate of the refugees is pivotal for any solution to have a chance of succeeding.

True, these Israeli Jews who go against the grain are few and far between, but they are there, and given the overall desire of the Palestinians to seek restitution and not demand retribution, together they hold the key to reconciliation and peace in the torn land of Palestine. They are found standing alongside the 'internal' Palestinian refugees today, almost half a million people, in joint annual pilgrimages to the destroyed villages, a journey of Nakba commemoration that takes place each year on the day official Israel celebrates (according to the Jewish calendar) its 'Independence Day'. You can see them in action as members of NGOs such as Zochrot – 'remembering' in Hebrew – who stubbornly make it their mission to put up signs with the names of destroyed Palestinian villages in places where today there are Jewish settlements or a JNF forest. You can hear them speak at the Conferences for the Right of Return and Just Peace that began in 2004, where together with their Palestinian friends, from within and outside the country, they reaffirm their commitment to the refugees' Right of Return, and where they, like this writer, vow to continue the struggle to protect the memory of the Nakba against all attempts to dwarf the horror of its crimes or deny they ever happened, for the sake of a lasting and comprehensive peace to emerge one day in the land of Palestine.

But before these committed few will make a difference, the land of Palestine and its people, Jews and Arabs, will have to face the consequences of the 1948 ethnic cleansing. We end this book as we began: with the bewilderment that this crime was so utterly forgotten and erased from our minds and memories. But we now know the price: the ideology that enabled the depopulation of half of Palestine's native people in 1948 is still alive and continues to drive the inexorable, sometimes indiscernible, cleansing of those Palestinians who live there today.

It has remained a powerful ideology today, not only because the previous stages in Palestine's ethnic cleansing went unnoticed, but mainly because, with time, the Zionist whitewash of words proved so successful in inventing a new language to camouflage the devastating impact of its practices. It begins with obvious euphemisms such as 'pullouts' and 'redeployment' to mask the massive dislocations of Palestinians from the Gaza Strip and the West Bank that have been going on since 2000. It continues with less obvious misnomers such as 'occupation' to describe the direct Israeli military rule on areas within historical Palestine, more or less fifteen per cent of it today, while presenting the rest of the land as 'liberated', 'free' or 'independent'. True, most of Palestine is not under military occupation – some of it is under much worse conditions. Consider the Gaza Strip after the pullout where even human rights lawyers cannot protect its inhabitants because they are not guarded by the international conventions that relate to military occupation. Many of its people enjoy ostensibly superior conditions within the State of Israel; much better if they are Jewish citizens, somewhat better if they are Palestinian citizens of Israel. So much better for the latter if they do not reside in the Greater Jerusalem area where the Israeli policy has been, for the last six years, aimed at transferring them to the occupied part or to the lawless and authority-less areas in the Gaza Strip and the West Bank created by the disastrous Oslo accord in the 1990s.

So there are many Palestinians who are not under occupation, but none of them, and this includes those in the refugee camps, are free from the potential danger of future ethnic cleansing. It seems more a matter of Israeli priority rather than a hierarchy of 'fortunate' and 'less fortunate' Palestinians. Those today in the Greater Jerusalem area are undergoing ethnic cleansing as this book goes to print. Those who live in the vicinity of the apartheid wall Israel is constructing, half completed as this book is written, are likely to be next. Those who live under the greatest illusion of safety, the Palestinians of Israel, may also be targeted in the future. Sixty-eight per cent of the Israeli Jews expressed their wish, in a recent poll, to see them 'transferred'.[1]

Neither Palestinians nor Jews will be saved, from one another or from themselves, if the ideology that still drives the Israeli policy towards the Palestinians is not correctly identified. The problem with Israel was never its Jewishness – Judaism has many faces and many of them provide a solid basis for peace and cohabitation; it is its ethnic Zionist character. Zionism does not have the same margins of pluralism that Judaism offers, especially not for the Palestinians. They can never be part of the Zionist state and space, and will continue to fight - and hopefully their struggle will be peaceful and successful. If not, it will be desperate and vengeful and, like a whirlwind, will suck all up in a huge perpetual sandstorm that will rage not only through the Arab and Muslim worlds, but also within Britain and the United States, the powers which, each in their turn, feed the tempest that threatens to ruin us all.

The Israeli attacks on Gaza and Lebanon in the summer of 2006 indicate that the storm is already raging. Organisations such as Hizbullah and Hamas, which dare to question Israel's right to impose its unilaterial will on Palestine, have faced Israel's military might and, so far (at the time of writing) are managing to withstand the assualt. But it is far from over. The regional patrons of these resistance movements, Iran and Syria, could be targeted in the future; the risk of even more devastating conflict and bloodshed has never been so acute.

Endnotes

PREFACE

1. Central Zionist Archives, minutes of the meeting of Jewish Agency Executive, 12 June 1938.
2. While some are convinced it was painted red at the front as a show of solidarity with Socialism.
3. One historian, Meir Pail, claims the orders were sent a week later (Meir Pail, *From Hagana to the IDF*, p. 307).
4. The documents from the meeting are summarized in the IDF Archives, GHQ/Operations branch, 10 March 1948, File 922/75/595 and in the Hagana Archives, 73/94. The meeting is reported by Israel Galili in the Mapai center meeting, 4 April 1948, which is to be found in the Hagana Archives 80/50/18. The composition of the group and its discussions are the product of a mosaic reconstruction of several documents as will be explained in the next chapters. In chapter four the messages that went out on March 10 and the meetings prior to the finalizing of the plan are also documented. For a similar interpretation of Plan Dalet, which was adopted a few weeks before that meeting, see Uri Ben-Eliezer, *The Emergence of Israeli Militarism, 1936–1956*, p. 253; he writes: 'Plan Dalet aimed at cleansing of villages, expulsion of Arabs from mixed towns'. For the dispatch of the orders see also Meir Pail, p. 307 and Gershon Rivlin and Elhanan Oren, *The War of Independence: Ben-Gurion's Diary*, vol. 1, p. 147. The orders dispatched can be found in the Hagana Archives 73/94, for each of the units: orders to the brigades to move to Position D – *Mazav Dalet* – and from the brigade to the Battalions, 16 April 1948.
5. Simcha Flapan, *The Birth of Israel: Myths and Realities*, p. 93.
6. David Ben-Gurion, in *Rebirth and Destiny of Israel* noted candidly that: "Until the British left [May 15, 1948] no Jewish settlement, however remote, was entered or seized by the Arabs, while the Haganah ... captured many Arab

positions and liberated Tiberia, and Haifa, Jaffa, and Safad ... So on the day of
destiny, that part of Palestine where the Haganah could operate was almost
clear of Arabs." Ben-Gurion, *Rebirth and Destiny of Israel*, p. 530.

7. The Eleven composed what I call in this book the Consultancy – see chapter
   three. It is possible that other people, apart from this caucus of decision-
   makers, were present, but as bystanders. As for the senior officers, there were
   twelve orders sent to twelve Brigades on the ground, see 922/75/595 ibid.
8. Walid Khalidi, *Palestine Reborn*; Michael Palumbo, *The Palestinian
   Catastrophe: The 1948 Expulsion of a People from their Homeland* and Dan
   Kurzman, *Genesis 1948: The First Arab-Israeli War*.
9. Avi Shlaim, 'The Debate about the 1948 War' in Ilan Pappe (ed.), *The
   Israel/Palestine Question*, pp. 171–92.
10. Benny Morris, *The Birth of the Palestinian Refugee Problem, 1947–1949*.
11. He makes this claim in the Hebrew version of the book published by Am Oved,
    Tel-Aviv in 1997, p. 179.
12. Morris in the same place talks about 200–300,000 refugees. There were in fact
    350,000 if one adds all of the population from the 200 towns and villages that
    were destroyed by 15 May 1948.
13. Walid Khalidi (ed.), *All That Remains: The Palestinian Villages Occupied and
    Depopulated by Israel in 1948*.

CHAPTER 1

1. State Department, Special Report on 'Ethnic Cleansing', 10 May 1999.
2. United Nations, Report Following Security Council Resolution 819, 16 April 1993.
3. Drazen Petrovic, 'Ethnic Cleansing – An attempt at Methodology', *European
   Journal of International Law*, 5/3 (1994), pp. 342–60.
4. This is actually taken directly from Petrovic, ibid., p. 10, note 4, who himself
   quotes Andrew Bell-Fialkow's 'A Brief History of Ethnic Cleansing'.
5. The most important meetings are described in chapter 3.
6. Ben-Gurion Archives, The Correspondence Section, 1.01.1948–07.01.48, documents 79–81. From Ben-Gurion to Galili and the members of the committee.
   The document also provides a list of forty Palestinian leaders that have been
   targeted for assassination by the Hagana forces.
7. *Yideot Achronot*, 2 February 1992.
8. *Ha'aretz*, Pundak, 21 May 2004.
9. I will detail how it worked in the following chapters, but the authority to
   destroy is the order sent on 10 March to the troops, and the specific orders
   authorizing executions are in IDF Archives, 49/5943 doc. 114, 13 April 1948.

10. See the sources below.
11. Nur Masalha, *Expulsion of the Palestinians: The Concept of 'Transfer' in Zionist Political Thought, 1882–1948* and *The Politics of Denial: Israel and the Palestinian Refugee Problem.*
12. Alexander Bein (ed.), *The Mozkin Book*, p. 164.
13. Baruch Kimmerling, *Zionism and Territory: The Socio-Territorial Dimensions of Zionist Politics*; Gershon Shafir, *Land, Labour and the Origins of the Israel-Palestinian Conflict, 1882–1914* and Uri Ram, 'The Colonialism Perspective in Israeli Sociology' in Pappe (ed.), *The Israel/Palestine Question*, pp. 55–80.
14. Khalidi (ed.) *All That Remains*, and Samih Farsoun and C. E. Zacharia, *Palestine and the Palestinians.*

CHAPTER 2

1. See, for instance, Haim Arlosarov, *Articles and Essays*, Response to the 1930 Shaw Commission on the concept of strangers in Palestine's history, Jerusalem 1931.
2. A very good description of this myth can be found in Israel Shahak, *Racism de l'état d'Israel*, p. 93.
3. Alexander Schölch, *Palestine in Transformation, 1856–1882: Studies in Social, Economic and Political Development.*
4. Neville Mandel, *Arabs and Zionism before World War I*, p. 233.
5. Reported in Alharam of the same date.
6. The warning came in a story published by Ishaq Musa al-Husayni, *The Memories of a Hen* published in Jerusalem, first as a series of articles in the newspaper *Filastin*, then as a book in 1942.
7. For a general analysis, see Rashid Khalidi, *Palestinian Identity: The Construction of Modern National Consciousness*, and more specifically see *Al-Manar*, vol. 3, issue 6, pp. 107–8 and vol. 1, issue 41, p. 810.
8. See Uri Ram in Pappe (ed.), *The Israel/Palestine Question* and David Lloyd George, *The Truth about the Peace Treaties.*
9. The most notable of these works is Zeev Sternahal, *The Founding Myths of Israel: Nationalism, Socialism, and the Making of the Jewish State.*
10. The Balfour Declaration was a letter dated November 2, 1917, from British Foreign Secretary Arthur James Balfour, to Lord Rothschild, a leader of the British Jewish community. The text of the Balfour Declaration, agreed at a Cabinet meeting on October 31, 1917, set out the position of the British Government:

'His Majesty's Government view with favour the establishment in Palestine of a national home for the Jewish people, and will use their best endeavours to facilitate the achievement of this object, it being clearly understood that nothing shall be done which may prejudice the civil and religious rights of existing non-Jewish communities in Palestine, or the rights and political status enjoyed by Jews in any other country.'

11. Yehosua Porath, *The Emergence of the Palestinian Arab National Movement, 1919–1929*.
12. Eliakim Rubinstein, 'The Treatment of the Arab Question in Palestine in the post-1929 Period' in Ilan Pappe (ed.), *Arabs and Jews in the Mandatory Period – A Fresh View on the Historical Research* (Hebrew).
13. On Peel see Charles D. Smith, *Palestine and the Arab–Israeli Conflict*, pp. 135–7.
14. Barbara Smith, *The Roots of Separatism in Palestine: British Economic Policy, 1920–1929*.
15. This connection is made by Uri Ben-Eliezer, *The Making of Israeli Militarism*.
16. John Bierman and Colin Smith, *Fire in the Night: Wingate of Burma, Ethiopia and Zion*.
17. Hagana Archives, File 0014, 19 June 1938.
18. Ibid.
19. The Bulletin of the Hagana Archives, issues 9–10, (prepared by Shimri Salomon) 'The Intelligence Service and the Village Files, 1940–1948' (2005).
20. For a critical survey of the JNF see Uri Davis, *Apartheid Israel: Possibilities for the Struggle Within*.
21. Kenneth Stein, *The Land Question in Palestine, 1917–1939*.
22. This correspondence is in the Central Zionist Archives and is used in Benny Morris, *Correcting A Mistake*, p. 62, notes 12–15.
23. Ibid.
24. Hagana Archives, File 66.8
25. Hagana Archives, Village Files, File 24/9, testimony of Yoeli Optikman, 16 January 2003.
26. Hagana Archives, File 1/080/451, 1 December 1939.
27. Hagana Archives, File 194/7, pp. 1–3, interview given on 19 December 2002.
28. See note 15.
29. Hagana Archives, S25/4131, 105/224 and 105/227 and many others in this series each dealing with a different village.
30. Hillel Cohen, *The Shadow Army: Palestinian Collaborators in the Service of Zionism*.
31. Interview with Palti Sela in the Hagana Archives, File 205.9, 10 January 1988.
32. See note 27.
33. Hagana Archives, Village Files, 105/255 files from January 1947.
34. IDF Archives, 49/5943/114, orders from 13 April 1948.

35. See note 27.
36. Ibid., File 105.178.
37. Quoted in Harry Sacher, *Israel: The Establishment of Israel*, p. 217.
38. Smith, *Palestine and the Arab–Israeli Conflict*, pp. 167–8.
39. Yossef Weitz, *My Diary*, vol. 2, p. 181, 20 December 1940.
40. Ben-Gurion's *Diary*, 12 July 1937, and in *New Judea*, August–September 1937, p. 220.
41. Shabtai Teveth, *Ben-Gurion and the Palestinian Arabs: From Peace to War*.
42. Hagana Archives, File 003, 13 December 1938.
43. On British policy see Ilan Pappe, *Britain and the Arab–Israeli Conflict, 1948–1951*.
44. Interview of Moshe Sluzki with Moshe Sneh, in Gershon Rivlin (ed.), *Olive-Leaves and Sword: Documents and Studies of the Hagana*, and Ben-Gurion's *Diary*, 10 October 1948.
45. See Yoav Gelber, *The Emergence of a Jewish Army*, pp. 1–73.
46. Michael Bar-Zohar, *Ben-Gurion: A Political Biography*, vol. 2, pp. 639–66 (Hebrew).
47. See Pappe, *Britain and the Arab–Israeli Conflict*.
48. Yehuda Sluzki, *The Hagana Book*, vol. 3, part 3, p. 1942.
49. See chapter four.

CHAPTER 3

1. Palestine was divided into several administrative districts. In 1947 these were the percentages of Jews in them: Safad 12%; Acre 4%; Tiberias 33%; Baysan 30%; Nazareth 16%; Haifa 47%; Jerusalem 40%; Lyyd 72% (this includes Jaffa, Tel-Aviv and Petah Tikva); Ramla 24% and Beersheba 7.5%.
2. See Ilan Pappe, *The Making of the Arab–Israeli Conflict, 1947–1951*, pp. 16–46.
3. See United Nations Archives: The UNSCOP Documents, Box 2.
4. Walid Khalidi, 'Revisiting the UNGA Partition Resolution', *Journal of Palestine Studies*, 105 (Autumn 1997), p. 15. For more on UNSCOP and how, prompted by the Zionists, it maneuvered the UN towards the pro-Zionist solution of the partition of Palestine, see Pappe, *The Making of the Arab–Israeli Conflict*, pp. 16–46.
5. Khalidi, ibid.
6. Ibid.
7. Plenary Meetings of the General Assembly, 126th Meeting, 28 November 1947, *UN Official Record*, vol. 2, pp. 1390–1400.
8. Flapan, *The Birth of Israel*, pp. 13–54.
9. See, for example, David Tal, *War in Palestine, 1948: Strategy and Diplomacy*, pp. 1–145.
10. Bar-Zohar, *Ben-Gurion*, part II, pp. 660–1.

11. See his speech in the Mapai Centre on 3 December, 1947.
12. Private Archives, Middle East Centre, St. Antony's College, Cunningham's Papers, Box 2, File 3.
13. Ibid.
14. For an extensive analysis of the Arab reaction see Eugene L. Rogan and Avi Shlaim (eds.), *The War For Palestine: Rewriting the History of 1948*; see especially Charles Tripp, 'Iraq and the 1948 War: Mirror of Iraq's Disorder'; Fawaz A. Geregs, 'Egypt and the 1948 War: Internal Conflict and Regional Ambition' and Joshua Landis, 'Syria and the Palestine War: Fighting King Abdullah's "Greater Syria" Plan.
15. Ben-Gurion's *Diary*, 7 October, 1947.
16. Only once did Ben-Gurion refer to it by name. In an entry in his diary (1.1.1948) he called it 'a party of experts', *Mesibat Mumhim*. The editors of the published diary added that a party means a meeting of the experts on Arab Affairs. The document of that meeting shows a larger forum that included, in addition to the experts, certain members of the High Command. Indeed when the two groups met together they became what I have called the Consultancy.
17. Ben-Gurion's *Diary* refers to the following meetings: 18 June 1947, 1–3 December 1947, 11 December 1947, 18 December 1947, 24 December 1947 (which was reported in his diary on the 25th and dealt with fortifications in the Negev), 1 January 1948, 7 January 1948 (discussion on the future of Jaffa), 9 January 1948, 14 January 1948, 28 January 1948, 9–10 February 1948, 19 February 1948, 25 February 1948, 28 February 1948, 10 March 1948 and 31 March 1948. Pre and post correspondence of all the meetings mentioned in the diary are to be found in the Ben-Gurion Archives, the correspondence section and the private correspondence section. They fill many gaps in the sketchy diary references.
18. Here is a reconstruction of the individuals who were part of the Consultancy: David Ben-Gurion, Yigael Yadin (Head of Operations), Yohanan Ratner (Strategic Adviser to Ben-Gurion), Yigal Allon (Head of the Palmach and Southern Front), Yitzhak Sadeh (Head of Armoured units), Israel Galili (Head of the High Command), Zvi Ayalon (Deputy to Galili and Commander of the Central Front). Others not part of the *Matkal*, the High Command, were Yossef Weitz (Head of settlement department in the Jewish Agency), Isar Harel (Head of intelligence) and his people: Ezra Danin, Gad Machnes and Yehoshua Palmon. In one or two meetings, Moshe Sharett and Eliahu Sasson were present too, although Ben-Gurion met Sasson almost every Sunday separately with Yaacov Shimoni in Jerusalem, as his diary testifies. Some officers from the field were also alternately called in to join: Dan Even (Commander of the Coastal Front), Moshe Dayan, Shimon Avidan, Moshe Carmel (Commander of the Northern Front), Shlomo Shamir and Yitzhak Rabin.
19. The meeting is also reported in his book *When Israel Fought*, pp. 13–18.

CHAPTER 4

1. We have testimony from the British High Commissioner in Palestine, Sir Alan Cunningham, about how this protest, initially a strike, turned violent: 'The initial Arab outbreaks were spontaneous and unorganized and were more demonstrations of displeasure at the UN decision than determined attacks on Jews. The weapons initially employed were sticks and stones and had it not been for Jewish recourse to firearms, it is not impossible that the excitement would have subsided and little loss of life been caused. This is more probably since there is reliable evidence that the Arab Higher Committee as a whole and the Mufti in particular, although pleased at the strong response to the strike call, were not in favour of serious outbreaks'; quoted in Nathan Krystal, 'The Fall of the New City, 1947–1950,' in Salim Tamari, *Jersualem 1948. The Arab Neighbourhoods and their Fate in the War*, p. 96.
2. This is discussed in detail in the next chapter.
3. Bar-Zohar, *Ben-Gurion*, p. 663.
4. Meir Pail, 'External and Internal Features in the Israeli War of Independence' in Alon Kadish (ed.), *Israel's War of Independence 1948–1949*, pp. 485–7.
5. Smith, *Palestine and the Arab–Israeli Conflict*, pp. 91–108.
6. Avi Shlaim, *Collusion.*
7. Avi Shlaim, 'The Debate about 1948' in Pappe (ed.), *The Israel/Palestine Question*, pp. 171–92.
8. Rivlin and Oren, *The War of Independence*, vol. 1, p. 320, 18 March 1948; p. 397, 7 May 1948; vol. 2, p. 428, 15 May 1948.
9. Ibid., 28 January 1948, p. 187.
10. This included an arms deal worth $12,280,000, which the Hagana concluded with Czechoslovakia, purchasing 24,500 rifles, 5,200 machine guns and 54 million rounds of ammunition.
11. See note 8.
12. The order to the Intelligence Officers will be mentioned again. It can be found in the IDF Archives, File 2315/50/53, 11 January, 1948.y t
13. As can be seen from his letters to Ben-Artzi quoted in Bar-Zohar, *Ben-Gurion*, p. 663 and to Sharett in Ben-Gurion Archives, Correspondence Section, 23.02–1.03.48 document 59, 26 February 1948.
14. Ben-Gurion's letters, ibid.
15. Israeli State Archives Publications, *Political and Diplomatic Documents of the Zionist Central Archives and Israeli State Archives*, December 1947–May 1948, Jerusalem 1979 (Hebrew), Doc. 45, 14 December 47, p. 60.
16. Masalha, *Expulsion of the Palestinians.*
17. Bar-Zohar, *Ben-Gurion*, p. 702.
18. On 12 July, 1937, there is a long entry in Ben-Gurion's *Diary* in which he

expresses the wish that the Jewish leadership would have the will and the power to transfer the Arabs from Palestine.

19. The whole speech was published in his book, David Ben-Gurion, *In the Battle*, pp. 255–72.
20. Central Zionist Archives, 45/1 Protocol, 2 November 1947.
21. Flapan, *The Birth of Israel*, p. 87.
22. Morris, *The Birth of the Palestinian Refugee Problem Revisited*.
23. That this was disconnected was reported to Ben-Gurion. See Ben-Gurion Archives, Correspondence Section, 1.12.47–15.12.47, Doc. 7, Eizenberg to Kaplan, 2 December 1947.
24. Ben-Gurion's *Diary* reports one such meeting on 2 December 1947 when the Orientalists suggested attacking water supplies and transport centres of the Palestinians.
25. See Ben-Gurion's *Diary*, 11 December 1947, for the assessment that most peasants did not wish to be involved in a war.
26. Hagana Archives, 205.9.
27. This meeting was reported in Ben-Gurion's *Diary* a day later, on 11 December 1947; it may have taken place in a more limited forum.
28. IDF Archives, 49/5492/9, 19 January 1948.
29. See the website *www.palestineremembered.com* – an interactive site that invites oral history testimonies.
30. Ben-Gurion's *Diary*, 11 December 1947, and the letter to Moshe Sharett, are from G. Yogev, Documents, December 1947–May 1948, Jerusalem: Israel State Archives 1980, p. 60.
31. Reported in *The New York Times*, 22 December 1947. The Hagana report was sent to Yigael Yadin, on December 14; see the Hagana Archives, 15/80/731.
32. IDF Archives, 51/957, File 16.
33. Central Zionist Archives, Report S25/3569, Danin to Sasson, 23 December 1947.
34. *The New York Times*, 20 December 1947, and speech by Ben-Gurion in the Zionist Executive, 6 April 1948.
35. Ben-Gurion summarized the wednesday meeting in his Diary, 18 December 1947.
36. Yaacov Markiviski, 'The Campaign on Haifa in the Independence War' in Yossi Ben-Artzi (ed.), *The Development of Haifa, 1918–1948*.
37. *Filastin*, 31 December 1947.
38. Milstein, *The History of the Independence War*, vol. 2, p. 78.
39. Benny Morris, *The Birth of the Palestinian Refugee Problem*, p. 156 and Uri Milstein, *The History of the Independence War*, vol. 2, p. 156.
40. National committees were bodies of local notables that were established in various localities throughout Palestine in 1937, to act as a form of emergency leadership for the Palestinian community in each city.

41. Morris, *The Birth of the Palestinian Refugee Problem*, p. 50 and Milstein, *The History of the Independence War*, vol. 3, pp. 74–5.

42. Morris, *The Birth of the Palestinian Refugee Problem*, p. 55, note 11.

43. Political and Diplomatic Documents, Document 274, p. 460.

44. Ibid., Document 245, p. 410.

45. Rivlin and Oren, *The War of Independence*, editorial remark, p. 9.

46. The text of the Protocol for the Long Seminar is in Ha-Kibbutz Ha-Meuchad Archives, Aharon Zisling's private collection.

47. Ben-Gurion's *Diary*, 31 December 1947.

48. Weitz, *My Diary*, vol. 2, p. 181.

49. Morris, *The Birth of the Palestinian Refugee Problem*, p. 62.

50. Ben-Gurion Archives, The Galili papers, Protocol of the meeting.

51. Danin testimony for Bar-Zohar, p. 680, note 60.

52. Ben-Gurion Archives, Correspondence Section, 16.1.48–22.1.48, Document 42, 26 January 1948.

53. Ben-Gurion's *Diary*, 7 January 1948.

54. Ben-Gurion's *Diary*, 25 January 1948.

55. Rivlin and Oren, *The War of Independence*, p. 229, 10 February 1948.

56. Ben-Gurion Archives, Correspondence Section, 1.1.48–31.1.48, Doc. 101, 26 January 1948.

57. These were Yohanan Ratner, Yaacov Dori, Israeli Galili, Yigael Yadin, Zvi Leschiner (Ayalon) and Yitzhak Sadeh.

58. Ben-Gurion's *Diary*, 9 January 1948.

59. This appeared in their publication *Mivrak*.

60. Ben-Gurion's *Diary*, 31 January 1948.

61. Rivlin and Oren, *The War of Independence*, pp. 210–11.

62. Ben-Gurion's *Diary*, 1 January 1948.

63. See note 52.

64. Bar-Zohar, *Ben-Gurion*, p. 681.

65. Ben-Gurion's *Diary*, 30 January 1948.

66. Ibid., 14 January 1948, 2 February 1948, and 1 June 1948.

67. Information on the meetings in February is drawn from Ben-Gurion's *Diary*.

68. Ben-Gurion's *Diary*, 9 and 10 February 1948 and *Haganah Book*, pp. 1416–18.

69. *Hashomer Ha-Tza'ir* Archives, Files 66.10, meeting with Galili 5 February 1948 (reporting a day after the *Matkal* meeting on 4 February Wed.).

70. Zvi Sinai and Gershon Rivlin (eds), *The Alexandroni Brigade in the War of Independence*, p. 220 (Hebrew).

71. Morris, *The Birth of the Palestinian Refugee Problem*, pp. 53–4.

72. Weitz, *My Diary*, vol. 3, p. 223, 11 January 1948.

73. The figures listed in the official report were more modest, detailing the blowing

up of forty houses, the killing of eleven villagers, and the wounding of another eighty.

74. Israel Even Nur (ed.), *The Yiftach-Palmach Story*.
75. Ben-Gurion's *Diary*, 19 February 1948.
76. Ibid.
77. Khalidi (ed.), *All That Remains*, pp. 181–2.
78. Weitz, *My Diary*, vol. 3, p. 223, 11 January 1947.
79. Ibid, 239–40.
80. Morris, *The Birth of the Palestinian Refugee Problem*, pp. 84–86.
81. Pail, *From the Hagana to the IDF*, p. 307. See discussion of State D, next chapter.
82. The English translation is in Walid Khalidi, 'Plan Dalet: Master Plan for the Conquest of Palestine', *Journal of Palestine Studies*, 18/69 (Autumn 1988), pp. 4–20.
83. See chapter five.
84. The Plan distributed to the soldiers and the first direct commands are in IDF Archives, 1950/2315 File 47, 11 May 1948.
85. Yadin to Sasson IDF Archives, 16/69/261 The Nachshon Operations Files.

CHAPTER 5

1. Rivlin and Oren, *The War of Independence*, vol. 1, p. 332.
2. Speech to the Executive Committee of the Mapai party, 6 April 1948.
3. Quoted directly from the orders to the Carmeli Brigade, Zvi Sinai (ed.), *The Carmeli Brigade in the War of Independence*, p. 29.
4. Binyamin Etzioni (ed.), *The Golani Brigade in the Fighting*, p. 10.
5. Zerubavel Gilad, *The Palmach Book*, vol. 2, pp. 924–5. Daniel McGowan and Matthew C. Hogan, *The Saga of the Deir Yassin Massacre, Revisionism and Reality*.
6. The descriptions and testimonies about what happened in Deir Yassin are taken from Daniel McGowan and Matthew C. Hogan, *The Saga of the Deir Yassin Massacre, Revisionism and Reality*.
7. Ibid.
8. Contemporary accounts put the number of victims of the Deir Yassin massacre at 254, a figure endorsed at the time by the Jewish Agency, a Red Cross official, *The New York Times*, and Dr Hussein al-Khalidi, spokesperson for the Jerusalem-based Arab Higher Committee. It is likely this figure was deliberately inflated in order to sow fear among the Palestinians and thereby panic them into a mass exodus. Certainly, loudspeakers were later used in villages about to be cleansed to warn the people of the terrible consequences if they did

not leave voluntarily, to generate panic and encourage them to flee for their lives before the ground troops moved in.

Menachem Begin, the leader of the Irgun, described the effect the spreading of such rumours had on the Palestinians in *The Revolt*, 'Arabs throughout the country, induced to believe wild tales of "Irgun butchery" were seized with limitless panic and started to flee for their lives. This mass flight soon developed into a maddened, uncontrolled stampede. Of the almost 800,000 who lived on the present territory of the State of Israel, only some 165,000 are still there. The political and economic significance of this development can hardly be overestimated.' Begin, *The Revolt*, p. 164.

Albert Einstein, along with 27 prominent Jews in New York, condemned the massacre of Deir Yassin in a letter published 4 December 1948 in *The New York Times*, noting 'terrorist bands [i.e. Begin's Irgun] attacked this peaceful village, which was not a military objective in the fighting, killed most of its inhabitants – 240 men, women, and children – and kept a few of them alive to parade as captives through the streets of Jerusalem. Most of the Jewish community was horrified at the deed, and the Jewish Agency sent a telegram of apology to King Abdullah of Transjordan (sic). But the terrorists, far from being ashamed of their act, were proud of this massacre, publicized it widely, and invited all the foreign correspondents present in the country to view the heaped corpses and the general havoc at Deir Yassin.'

9. Uri Ben-Ari, *Follow Me.*
10. Of particular interest is the way Geula Cohen, today an extreme rightwing activist, and a leading member of the Stern Gang, saved Abu-Ghawsh, because a member of the villages helped her escape the British prison in 1946. See her story in Geula Cohen, *Woman of Violence; Memories of a Young Terrorist, 1945–1948.*
11. *Filastin*, 14 April 1948.
12. Palumbo, *The Palestinian Catastrophe*, pp. 107–8.
13. Ibid., p. 107.
14. See a summary in Flapan, *The Birth of Israel*, pp. 89–92.
15. This telegraph was intercepted by the Israeli intelligence and is quoted in Ben-Gurion's *Diary*, 12 January 1948.
16. See Rees Williams, the Under Secretary of States statement to Parliament, *Hansard*, House of Commons Debates, vol. 461, p. 2050, 24 February 1950.
17. Arnan Azariahu, who was Israel Galili's assistant, recalled that when the new *Matkal* was moved to Ramat Gan, Yigael Yadin demanded that the Qiryati people not be put in charge of protecting the site. *Maqor Rishon*, interview, 21 May 2006.
18. Walid Khalidi, 'Selected Documents on the 1948 War', *Journal of Palestine Studies*, 107, Vol. 27/3 (Spring 1998), pp. 60–105, uses the British as well as the Arab committee's correspondence.
19. Hagana Archives, 69/72, 22 April 1948.

20. Central Zionist Archives, 45/2 Protocol.
21. Zadok Eshel (ed.), *The Carmeli Brigade in the War of Independence*, p. 147
22. Walid Khalidi, 'Selected Documents on the 1948 War'.
23. Montgomery of Alamein, *Memoirs*, pp. 4534.
24. Walid Khalidi, 'The Fall of Haifa', *Middle East Forum*, XXXV, 10 (December 1959), letter by Khayat, Saad, Mu'ammar and Koussa from 21 April 1948.
25. The information on the Palestinian side is taken from Mustafa Abasi, *Safad During the British Mandate Period: A Social and Political Study*, Jerusalem: Institute for Palestine Studies, 2005 (Arabic); a version of it appeared as 'The Battle for Safad in the War of 1948: A Revised Study, *International Journal for Middle East Studies*, 36 (2004), pp. 21–47.
26. Ibid.
27. Ibid.
28. Ben-Gurion's *Diary*, 7 June 1948.
29. Salim Tamari, *Jerusalem 1948*.
30. The reconstruction of the orders was done by Itzhak Levy, the head of the Hagana intelligence in Jerusalem in 1948, in his book *Jerusalem in the War of Independence*, p. 207 (these interviews were later incorporated into the IDF archives).
31. Fourteen of these telegrams are quoted by Ben-Gurion in his diary, see Rivlin and Oren, *The War of Independence*, pp. 12, 14, 27, 63, 64, 112, 113, 134, 141, 156, 169, 170, 283.
32. Mentioned in Ben-Gurion's *Diary*, 15 January 1948.
33. Levy, *Jerusalem*, p. 219.
34. Red Cross Archives, Geneva, Files G59/1/GC, G3/82 sent by the international Committee of the Red Cross (ICRC) delegate de Meuron on 6–19 May 1948 describe a sudden typhoid epidemic.
35. All the information is based on the Red Cross sources and on Salman Abu Sitta, 'Israel Biological and Chemical Weapons: Past and Present', *Between the Lines*, 15–19 March 2003. Abu Sitta also quotes Sara Leibovitz-Dar's article in *Hadashot*, 13 August 1993, where she traces, from a clue from the historian Uri Milstein, 'those who were responsible for the Acre operation, but who refused to answer her questions. She concluded her article by saying: 'What was done then with deep conviction and zealotry is now concealed with shame'.
36. Ben-Gurion's *Diary*, 27 May 1948.
37. Ibid., 31 January 1948 and his notes on the history of HEMED.
38. Levy, *Jerusalem*, p. 113, although he does accuse the Legion of joining earlier in attacks on those who had already surrendered. See pp. 109–12.
39. Interview with Sela (see chapter 2, note 31).
40. Evidence given by Hanna Abuied, on the website *www.palestineremembered.com*.

41. Morris, *The Birth of the Palestinian Refugee Problem*, p. 118.
42. Morris in the Hebrew version refers to the meeting on p. 95, Ben-Gurion mentions it in his *Diary*.
43. Most of these operations are mentioned in Morris, ibid., pp. 137–67.
44. The most detailed information on numbers, methods and maps are in Salman Abu Sitta's *Atlas of the Nakbah*.
45. Interview with Sela, (see chapter 2, note 31).
46. The information taken from Khalidi (ed.), *All That Remains*, pp. 60–1 and, the Hagana's Village Files, and Ben-Zion Dinur *et al.*, *The History of the Hagana*, p. 1420.
47. Ha-Kibbutz Ha-Meuchad Archives, Aharon Zisling Archives, Ben-Gurion letters.
48. Almost every expulsion and destruction of the villages was described in *The New York Times*, which is our main source, together with Khalidi (ed.), *All That Remains*, Morris, *The Birth of the Palestinian Refugee Problem*, and Ben-Zion Dinur *et al.*, *The History of the Hagana*.
49. Morris, ibid., pp. 243–4.
50. Palmach Archives, Givat Haviva, G/146, 19 April 1948.
51. Nafez Nazzal, *The Palestinian Exodus from the Galilee 1948*, Beirut: the Institute for Palestinian Studies, 1978, pp. 30–3 and Morris, *The Birth of the Palestinian Refugee Problem Revisited*, p. 130.
52. Khalidi uses this source very extensively in *All That Remains*.
53. This provided the main sources for Morris, *The Birth of the Palestinian Refugee Problem Revisited*.
54. Weitz, *My Diary*, vol. 3, 21 April 1948.
55. See the orders in IDF Archives, 51/967 particularly in Files 16, 24 and 42, and 51/128/50
56. Ben-Gurion Archives, Correspondence Section, 23.02–30.1 doc. 113.
57. Nazzal, *The Palestinian Exodus*, p. 29.
58. Netiva Ben-Yehuda, *Between the Knots*.
59. For a review on the film, see *Al-Ahram Weekly*, 725, 13–19 January 2005.
60. See the synthesis of the available sources in Khalidi (ed.), *All That Remains*, p. 437.
61. Hans Lebrecht, *The Palestinians, History and Present*, pp. 176–7.
62. This is an openly available publication, *The Palmach Book*, vol. 2, p. 304.
63. Ben-Yehuda, *Between the Knots*, pp. 245–6.
64. *The Palmach Book*.
65. Interview with Sela (see chapter 2, note 31).
66. Ibid.
67. Ibid.
68. Ibid.
69. Laila Parsons, 'The Druze and the Birth of Israel' in Eugene Rogan and Avi Shlaim (eds), *The War for Palestine: Rewriting the History of 1948*.

70. Ben-Gurion Archives, Correspondence, 23.02–1.03.48, doc. 70.

71. See the discussion in the Arab League in Pappe, *The Making of the Arab–Israeli Conflict*, pp. 102–34.

72. Walid Khalidi, 'The Arab Perspective' in W. Roger Louis and Robert S. Stookey (eds), *The End of the Palestine Mandate*.

73. Pappe, *The Making of the Arab–Israeli Conflict*.

74. Qasimya Khairiya, *Fawzi al-Qawuqji's Memoirs, 1936–1948*

75. See Shlaim, *Collusion*.

76. Ben-Gurion's *Diary*, 2 May 1948.

77. As much was also conveyed by the Hagana senior officers in a meeting on 8 May 1948 and to Golda Meir by King Abdullah, on May 10. Meir did report to the Zionist leadership that Abdullah would not sign a treaty with the Jews and would have to go to war. But Moshe Dayan affirmed in 1975 what the British suspected, that in fact he promised that the Iraqi and Jordanian troops would invade the Jewish state. See Dayan in *Yeidot Acharonot*, 28 February 1975 and see Rivlin and Oren, *The War of Independence*, pp. 409–10 about the 8 May meetings.

78. PRO, FO 800,477, FS 46/7 13 May 1948.

79. Nimr Hawari wrote a war memoir called *The Secret of the Nakba*, which he published in Nazareth in Arabic in 1955.

80. Quoted in Flapan, *The Birth of Israel*, p. 157.

81. Recently there was an interesting debate between Israeli historians on Ben-Gurion's position. See *Ha'aretz*, 12 and 14 May 2006 'The Big Wednesday'.

82. Wahid al-Daly, *The Secrets of the Arab League and Abd al-Rahman Azzam*.

83. In front of the Joint Parliamentary Middle East Councils, Commission of Enquiry – Palestinian Refugees, London: Labour Middle East Council and others, 2001.

CHAPTER 6

1. Levy, *Jerusalem*, criticized the decision to try and defend these enclaves as a strategic mistake which did not serve the overall strategy; Levy, *Jerusalem*, p. 114.

2. For all meetings I quote from Ben-Gurion's *Diary*.

3. Interview with Glubb, and see Glubb, *A Soldier with the Arabs*, p. 82.

4. Yehuda Sluzky, *Summary of the Hagana Book*, pp. 486–7.

5. This was in the 'operative orders to the Brigades according to Plan Dalet', IDF Archives, 22/79/1303.

6. Amitzur Ilan, *The Origins of the Arab–Israeli Arms Race: Arms, Embargo, Military Power and Decision in the 1948 Palestine War*.

7. IDF Archives, 51/665, File 1, May 1948.

8. Pail, 'External'.

9. In fact some of the books we have mentioned, notably Khalidi (ed.), *All That Remains*, Flapan, *The Birth of Israel*, Palumbo, *The Catastrophe* and Morris, *Revisited* prove this point very convincingly.
10. The orders can be found in the IDF archives, 51/957, File 16, 7 April 1948, and see 49/4858, File 495 to 15 October 1948 [hence IDF Archives, orders].
11. See Maqor Rishon. The reason quoted was direct hits on the Red House and Ben-Gurion's flat by Egyptian airplanes.
12. IDF Archives, 1951/957, File 24, 28 January 1948 to 7 July 1948.
13. Ibid.
14. See Ilan Pappe, 'The Tantura Case in Israel: The Katz Research and Trial', *Journal of Palestine Studies*, 30(3), Spring 2001, pp. 19–39.
15. Based on Pappe, ibid., p. 3 and also Pappe, 'Historical Truth, Modern Historiography, and Ethical Obligations: The Challenge of the Tantura Case,' *Holy Land Studies*, vol. 3/2 November 2004.
16. Nimr al-Khatib, *Palestine's Nakbah*, p. 116.
17. Sinai and Rivlin, *The Alexandroni Brigade*.
18. IDF Archives, 49/6127, File 117, 13 April to 27 September 1948.
19. Ibid.
20. Hagana Archives, 8/27/domestic, 1 June 1948.
21. See note 8.
22. Report to Yadin, 11 May 1948 in Hagana Archives, 25/97.
23. Eshel (ed.), *The Carmeli Brigade in the War of Independence*, p. 172.
24. Posted on *www.palestineremembered.com*, 1 July 2000.
25. Ben-Gurion's *Diary*, 24 May 1948.

CHAPTER 7

1. Morris, *The Birth of the Palestinian Refugee Problem*, p. 128.
2. Four such villages – Beit Tima, Huj, Biriyya, and Simsim – are reported in Ben-Gurion's *Diary*, 1 June 1948; the Israeli State Archives report setting fire to villages, in 2564/9 from August 1948.
3. As reported in his diary.
4. Ben-Gurion's *Diary*, 2 June 1948.
5. Ibid.
6. Naji Makhul, *Acre and its Villages since Ancient Times*, p. 28.
7. Interview by Teddy Katz with Tuvia Lishanski, see Pappe, *Tantura*.
8. The recollections of eyewitnesses were presented in Salman Natur, *Anta al-Qatil, ya- Shaykh*, 1976 (no publishing house); Michael Palumbo, who scrutinized the UN archives, reports that the UN was aware of Israel's method of summary execution, *The Palestinian Catastrophe*, pp. 163–74.

9. IDF Archives, 49/5205/58n, 1 June 1948
10. Israeli State Archives, 2750/11 a report of the intelligence officer to Ezra Danin, 29 July 1948.
11. IDF Archives, 49/6127, File 117, 3 June 1948.
12. Israeli State Archives, 2566/15, various reports by Shimoni.
13. Orders, for instance, to the Carmeli Brigade in the Hagana Archives, 100/29/B.
14. See oral history evidence on the website *www.palestineremembered.com.*
15. Morris, *The Birth of the Palestinian Refugee Problem*, pp. 198–9.
16. Ben-Gurion's *Diary*, 16 July 1948.
17. IDF Archives, 49/6127, File 516.
18. Report by the Intelligence Officer of the Northern Front to the HQ, 1 August 1948 in IDF Archives, 1851/957, File 16.
19. *The New York Times*, 26 and 27 July 1948.
20. Khalidi (ed.), *All That Remains*, p. 148.
21. Lydda in *The Encyclopedia of Palestine.*
22. Dan Kurzman, *Soldier of Peace*, pp. 140–1.
23. Ben-Gurion's *Diary*, 11, 16 and 17 July 1948 (this was a real obsession).
24. Ibid., 11 July 1948.
25. Ben-Gurion's *Diary*, 18 July 1948.
26. Ibid.
27. Interview with Sela (see chapter 2, note 31).
28. Nazzal, *The Palestine Exodus*, pp. 83–5.
29. IDF Archives, 49/6127, File 516.
30. A detailed description of the expulsion of the Bedouin can be found in Nur Masalha, *A Land Without a People: Israel, Transfer and the Palestinians.*
31. IDF Archives, File 572/4, a report from 7 August 1948.
32. Ibid. 51/937, Box 5, File 42, 21 August 1948.
33. Ibid.
34. IDF Archives, 549/715, File 9.
35. Ibid. 51/957, File 42, Operation Alef Ayn, 19 June 1948.

CHAPTER 8

1. Morris, *The Birth of the Palestinian Refugee Problem*, pp. 305–6.
2. Detailed information on the current location of refugees and their original villages may be found in Salman Abu Sitta's *Atlas of Palestine 1948.*
3. Nazzal, *The Palestinian Exodus*, pp. 95–6 and Morris, *The Birth of the Palestinian Refugee Problem*, pp. 230–1 and Khalidi, (ed.), *All That Remains*, p. 497.
4. The oral history evidence was posted on *www.palestineremembered.com* by

Mohammad Abdallah Edghaim on 25 April, 2001, and the archival evidence can be found in the Hashomer Ha-Tza'ir Archives, Aharon Cohen, private collection, a memo from 11 November, 1948.

5. Appears in the testimony of Edghaim, who interviewed Salim and Shehadeh Shraydeh.

6. Morris, *The Birth of the Palestinian Refugee Problem*, pp. 194–5.

7. Iqrit has an official website with a succinct report about the events: *www.iqrit.org*

8. Daud Bader (ed.), *Al-Ghabsiyya; Always in our Heart*, Center of the Defence of the Displaced Persons' Right, May 2002 (Nazareth, in Arabic).

9. IDF Archives, 51/957, File 1683, Battalion 103, company C.

10. Ibid. 50/2433, File 7.

11. Ibid. 51/957, File 28/4.

12. Ibid. 51/1957, File 20/4, 11 November 1948.

13. Morris, *The Birth of the Palestinian Refugee Problem*, p. 182.

14. IDF Archives, 51/957, File 42, Hiram Operative Commands and 49/715, File 9.

15. United Nation Archives, 13/3.3.1 Box 11, Atrocities September–November.

16. IDF Archives, The Committee of Five Meetings, 11 November 1948.

17. Ibid.

18. *Ha-Olam ha-Ze*, 1 March 1978 and testimony of Dov Yirmiya, the Israeli commander on the spot, published in *Journal of Palestine Studies*, vol. 7/4 (Summer 1978), no. 28, pp. 143–5. Yirmiya does not mention numbers, but the Lebanese website of the association of these villages does; see Issah Nakhleh, The *Encyclopedia of the Palestine Problem*, Chapter 15.

19. IDF Archives, 50/121, File 226, 14 December 1948.

20. Michael Palumbo, *Catastrophe*, pp. 173–4.

21. Hagana Archives, 69/95, Doc. 2230, 7 October 1948.

22. IDF Archives, 51/957, File 42, 24 March 1948 to 12 March 1949.

23. *The New York Times*, 19 October 1948.

24. 'Between Hope and Fear: Bedouin of the Negev', Refugees International's report 10 February, 2003 and Nakhleh, ibid., Chapter 11, parts 2–7.

25. Habib Jarada was interviewed in Gaza by Yasser al-Banna and was published in *Islam On Line* on 15 May 2002.

26. All mentioned by Morris, *The Birth of the Palestinian Refugee Problem*, pp. 222–3.

27. A range of strategies that could only be described as psychological warfare was used by the Jewish forces to terrorize and demoralize the Arab population in a deliberate attempt to provoke a mass exodus. Radio broadcasts in Arabic warned of traitors in the Arabs' midst, describing the Palestinians as having been deserted by their leaders, and accusing Arab militias of committing crimes against Arab civilians. They also spread fears of disease. Another, less subtle, tactic involved the use of loudspeaker trucks. These would be used in the

villages and towns to urge the Palestinians to flee before they were all killed, to warn that the Jews were using poison gas and atomic weapons, or to play recorded 'horror sounds' – shrieking and moaning, the wail of sirens, and the clang of fire-alarm bells. See Erskine Childers, 'The Wordless Wish: From Citizens to Refugees', in Ibrahim Abu-Lughod (ed.), *The Transformation of Palestine*, pp. 186–8, and Palumbo, *The Palestinian Catastrophe: The 1948 Expulsion of a People from Their Homeland*, pp. 61–2, 64, 97–8).

CHAPTER 9

1. IDF Archives, 50/2433, File 7, Minorities Unit, Report no. 10, 25 February 1949.
2. The order was already given in one form in January 1948. IDF Archives, 50/2315, File 35, 11 January 1948.
3. IDF Archives, 50/2433, File 7, Operation Comb, undated.
4. IDF Archives, 50/121, File 226, Orders to the Military Governors, 16 November 1948.
5. Ben-Gurion's *Diary*, 17 November, vol. 3, p. 829.
6. IDF Archives, 51/957, File 42, report to HQ, 29 June 1948.
7. IDF Archives, 50/2315 File 35, 11 January 1948; emphasis added.
8. See Aharon Klien, 'The Arab POWs in the War of Independence' in Alon Kadish (ed.), *Israel's War of Independence 1948–9*, pp. 573–4.
9. IDF Archives, 54/410, File 107, 4 April 1948.
10. I wish to thank Salman Abu Sitta for providing me with the Red Cross Documents: G59/I/GG 6 February 1949.
11. Al-Khatib, *Palestine's Nakbah*, p. 116.
12. Ibid.
13. See note 10.
14. See note 4.
15. It appears also in Yossef Ulizki, *From Events to A War*, p. 53.
16. Palumbo, *The Palestinian Catastrophe*, p. 108.
17. See note 4.
18. Dan Yahav, *Purity of Arms: Ethos, Myth and Reality, 1936–1956*, p. 226.
19. See note 15.
20. See note 4.
21. Ibid.
22. Interview with Abu Laben, in Dan Yahav, *Purity of Arms: Ethos, Myth and Reality, 1936–1954*, Tel-Aviv: Tamuz 2002, pp. 223–30
23. Ben-Gurion's *Diary*, 25 June 1948.
24. The protocol of the meeting was published in full by Tom Segev in his book, *1949 – The First Israelis*, and can be found in the State Archives.

25. For the full transcript of the meeting, see Tom Segev, *1949–The First Israelis*, Jerusalem Domino, 1984, pp. 69–73.
26. Ibid.
27. Ibid.
28. Ibid.
29. Ibid.
30. See Ben-Gurion's *Diary*, 5 July 1948.
31. IDF Archives, 50/121, File 226, report by Menahem Ben-Yossef, Platoon commander, Battalion 102, 26 December 1948.
32. Ben-Gurion's *Diary*, 5 July 1948.
33. Ibid., 15 July 1948.
34. Pappe, 'Tantura'.
35. Ben-Gurion, *As Israel Fights*, pp. 68–9.
36. Ben-Gurion's *Diary*, 18 August 1948.
37. Ibid.
38. David Kretzmer, *The Legal Status of Arabs in Israel*.
39. Tamir Goren, *From Independence to Integration: The Israeli Authority and the Arabs of Haifa, 1948–1950*, p. 337, and Ben-Gurion's *Diary*, 30 June 1948.
40. Ben-Gurion's *Diary*, 16 June 1948.
41. All the information in this section is based on an article by Nael Nakhle in *Al-Awda*, 14 September 2005 (published in Arabic in London).
42. Benvenisti, *Sacred Landscape*, p. 298.
43. Weitz, *My Diary*, vol. 3, p. 294, 30 May 1948.
44. Hussein Abu Hussein and Fiona Makay, *Access Denied: Palestinian Access to Land in Israel*.
45. *Ha'aretz*, 4 February 2005.

CHAPTER 10

1. The website address of the JNF is *www.kkl.org.il*; a limited English version can be found at *www.jnf.org.il* from which most of the information in this chapter is taken.
2. Khalidi (ed.), *All That Remains*, p. 169.
3. In Israeli Hebrew, '*kfar*' normally means '*Palestinian* village', i.e., there are no 'Jewish' villages as Hebrew uses instead *yishuvim* (settlements), *kibbutzim, moshavim,* etc.
4. Khalidi (ed.), *All That Remains*, p. 169.

CHAPTER 11

1. For the years 1964–1968, which I have called the 'bogus PLO', see Ilan Pappe, *A History of Modern Palestine: One Land, Two Peoples*.

2. Ramzy Baroud (ed.), *Searching Jenin: Eyewitness Accounts of the Israeli Invasion 2002.*
3. Ibid., p. 53–5.
4. Literally called 'The Law for Safeguarding the Rejection of the Right of Return, 2001'.

CHAPTER 12

1. The Arab members come from three parties: the Communist Party (Hadash), the National Party of Azmi Bishara (Balad) and the United Arab List drawn up by the more pragmatic branch of the Islamic movement.
2. Entry for 12 June 1895, where Herzl discusses his proposal for a shift from building a Jewish *society* in Palestine to forming a *state* for Jews, as translated by Michael Prior from the original German; see Michael Prior, 'Zionism and the Challenge of Historical truth and Morality,' in Prior (ed.), *Speaking the Truth about Zionism and Israel*, p. 27.
3. From a speech in front of the Mapai Centre, 3 December 1947, reproduced in full in Ben-Gurion, *As Israel Fights*, p. 255.
4. Quoted in *Yediot Achrinot*, 17 December 2003.
5. 'Disengagement' is, of course, Zionist newspeak, and was invented to circumvent the use of such terms as 'end of occupation' and to sidestep the obligations incumbent upon Israel, according to international law, as the occupying power in the West Bank and the Gaza Strip.
6. Ruth Gabison, *Ha'aretz*, 1 December, where she literally says: 'Le-Israel yesh zkhut le-fakeah al ha-gidul ha-tivi shel ha-'Aravim.'
7. The term Mizrahim for Arab Jews in Israel came into use in the early 1990s. As Ella Shohat explains, while retaining its implicit opposite, 'Ashkenazim', it 'condenses a number of connotations: it celebrates the past in the Eastern world; it affirms the pan-oriental communities [that] developed in Israel itself; and *it invokes a future of revived cohabitation with the Arab-Muslim East*'; Ella Shohat, 'Rupture and Return: A Mizrahi Perspective on the Zionist Discourse', MIT Electronic Journal of Middle East Studies 1 [2001] (my italics).
8. The 'black' Jews Israel brought over from Ethiopia in the 1980s were immediately relegated to the poor areas of the periphery and are almost invisible in Israeli society today; discrimination against them is high, as is the suicide rate among them.

EPILOGUE

1. *Ha'aretz*, 9 May 2006.

Chronology of Key Dates

1878	First Zionist agricultural colony in Palestine (Petah Tikva)
1882	25,000 Jewish immigrants begin to settle in Palestine, mainly from eastern Europe
1891	Baron Maurice de Hirsch, a German, founds the Jewish Colonization Association in London to aid Zionist settlers in Palestine
1896	*Der Judenstaat*, a book advocating the establishment of a Jewish state, is published by Austro-Hungarian Jewish writer Theodor Herzl
	Jewish Colonization Association (JCA) begins operations in Palestine
1897	Zionist Congress calls for a home for Jewish people in Palestine
	Pamphlet by founder of socialist Zionism, Nahman Syrkin, says Palestine "must be evacuated for the Jews".
	First Zionist Congress in Switzerland sets up the World Zionist Association (WZO) and petitions for "a home for the Jewish people in Palestine".
1901	Jewish National Fund (JNF) set up to acquire land in Palestine for the WZO; the land is to be used and worked solely by Jews.
1904	Tensions between Zionists and Palestinian farmers in Tiberias area
1904–1914	40,000 Zionist immigrants arrive in Palestine; Jews now total 6% of the population.
1905	Israel Zangwill states Jews must drive out the Arabs or "grapple with the problem of a large alien population ..."

1907	First kibbutz established
1909	Tel Aviv founded north of Jaffa
1911	Memo to Zionist Executive speaks of "limited population transfer".
1914	World War I starts
1917	Balfour Declaration; British Secretary of State pledges support for "a Jewish national home in Palestine".
	Ottoman forces in Jerusalem surrender to British General Allenby
1918	Palestine occupied by Allies under Allenby
	World War 1 over, Ottoman rule in Palestine ends
1919	First Palestinian National Congress in Jerusalem rejects Balfour declaration, demands independence
	Chaim Weizmann, of the Zionist Commission at the Paris Peace Conference calls for a Palestine "as Jewish as England is English"
	Other Commission members say "as many Arabs as possible should be persuaded to emigrate".
	Winston Churchill wrote "there are Jews, whom we are pledged to introduce into Palestine, and who take it for granted that the local population will be cleared out to suit their convenience".
1919–1933	35,000 Zionists immigrate to Palestine. Jews now total 12% of the population and hold 3% of the land
1920	Founding of Hagana, Zionist underground military organisation
	Britain is assigned the Palestinian Mandate by the Supreme Council of San Remo Peace Conference
1921	Protests in Jaffa against large-scale Zionist immigration
1922	League of Nations Council approves Britain's Mandate for Palestine
	British census of Palestine: 78% Muslim, 11% Jewish, 9.6% Christian, total population 757,182
1923	British Mandate for Palestine officially comes into force
1924–28	67,000 Zionist immigrants come to Palestine, half of whom are from Poland, raising Jewish population to 16%. Jews now own 4% of land
1925	In Paris the Revisionist Party is founded, which insists on the founding of a Jewish state in Palestine and Transjordan

1929	Riots in Palestine over claims to the Wailing Wall, with 133 Jews and 116 Arabs killed, mainly by British
1930	International Commission founded by the League of Nations to establish the legal status of Jews and Arabs at the Wailing Wall.
1931	Irgun (IZL) founded to support more militancy against Arabs
	Census shows total population of 1.03 million, 16.9% Jewish
	British director of development for Palestine publishes report on "landless Arabs" caused by Zionist colonization
1932	First regularly constituted Palestinian political party, the Istliqlal (Independence) Party, founded
1935	Arms smuggling by Zionist groups discovered at Jaffa port
1936	A conference of Palestinian National Committees demands "no taxation without representation".
1937	Peel Commission recommends partition of Palestine, with 33% of the country to become a Jewish state. Part of the Palestinian population is to be transferred from this state.
	British dissolve all Palestinian political organisations, deport five leaders, establish military courts against rebellion by Palestinians
1938	Irgun bombings kill 119 Palestinians. Palestinian bombs and mines kill 8 Jews
	British bring reinforcements to help suppress rebellion
1939	Zionist leader Jabotinsky writes: "... the Arabs must make room for the Jews in Eretz Israel. If it was possible to transfer the Baltic peoples, it is also possible to move the Palestinian Arabs."
	British House of Commons votes in approval of a White Paper which plans conditional independence of Palestine after 10 years and the immigration of 15,000 Jews into Palestine each year for the next 5 years
	World War II begins
1940	Land Transfer Regulations come into force, protecting Palestinian land against Zionist acquisition
1943	Five-year limit planned in White Paper of 1939 extended
1945	World War II ends

1947   Britain tells newly formed UN that it will withdraw from Palestine
UN appoints committee (UNSCOP) on Palestine
UNSCOP recommends partition
November 29: UN adopts Resolution 181 on partition of Palestine
Mass expulsion by the Jews of the indigenous Palestinian Arabs begins

1948
January
'Abd al-Qadir al-Husayni returns to Palestine after ten-year exile to form a group to resist partition
20   Britain plans to hand over areas of land to whichever group is predominant in the region

February
War breaks out between Jews and Arabs
18   Hagana announces military service and calls up 25–35 year old men and women
24   US delegate to UN announces that the role of the Security Council is peacekeeping rather than enforcing partition

March
6   Hagana announces mobilization
10   Plan Dalet, the Zionist blueprint for the cleansing of Palestine, finalised
18   President Truman pledges support to the Zionist cause
19–20   Arab leaders decide to accept a truce and limited trusteeship rather than partition, as suggested by UN Security Council. Jews reject the truce
30 March–15 May
Coastal "clearing" operation undertaken by Hagana, expelling Palestinians from the coastal area between Haifa and Jaffa

April

1	First delivery of Czech arms arrives for Hagana; includes 4,500 rifles, 200 light machine guns, 5 million rounds of ammunition
4	Plan Dalet launched by Hagana. Villages along the Tel-Aviv-Jerusalem road captured and residents expelled
9	The massacre of Deir Yassin
17	Security Council resolution demands a truce
20	Palestine trusteeship plan submitted to UN by US
22	Haifa cleansed of its Palestinian population
26–30	Hagana attacks an area of East Jerusalem, and are forced to hand it over to the British. Hagana captures an area of West Jerusalem. All Palestinians in West Jerusalem expelled by the Jewish forces

May

3	Report claims that between 175,000 and 250,000 Palestinians have been forced from their homes
12–14	Czech arms arrive for Hagana
13	Arab Legion attacks Jewish communities in retaliation for Jewish military action
13	Jaffa surrenders to Hagana
14	Israel declares independence as British Mandate ends. President Truman recognizes State of Israel
20	Count Bernadotte appointed as UN mediator in Palestine
22	UN Security resolution demands ceasefire

11 June–8 July   First Truce established

July

8–18	Fighting breaks out anew as IDF capture Lydd and Ramla
17	IDF launch an offensive but fail to capture Old City of Jerusalem
18 July–15 Oct	Second Truce established, broken by the capture of several villages by IDF

September

17   UN mediator Count Bernadotte assassinated by Jewish terrorists in Jerusalem. New UN mediator is Ralph Bunche

October

29–31   Thousands of Palestinians are expelled during Operation Hiram

November

4   UN Security Council calls for immediate truce and withdrawal of forces.
UN adopts Resolution 194 on Palestinian refugee right of return
Israel blocks return

November – 1949   IDF begins to expel villagers from settlements inside the Lebanese border

1949

24 February   Israeli–Egyptian Armistice

end February   Between 2000 and 3000 villagers expelled from the Faluja pocket by IDF

23 March   Israeli–Lebanese Armistice

3 April   Israeli–Jordanian Armistice

20 July   Syrian–Israeli Armistice

This map, showing the area of Palestine claimed by the World Zionist
Organisation, was officially presented to the Paris Peace Conference, 1919

LEBANON

SYRIA

Acre
Safad
Haifa
Lake Tiberias
Nazareth

Mediterranean Sea

Jenin
Nablus
Tel Aviv
Jaffa
Jerusalem
Amman

Jordan R.

Hebron
Gaza
Dead Sea
Rafah
Beersheba

TRANSJORDAN

EGYPT

Jewish State
Arab State
Mandated Territory

0   20   40
Miles

Aqaba

The Peel Commission Partition Plan, 1937. This became the Palestine
Partition Commission Plan A the following year

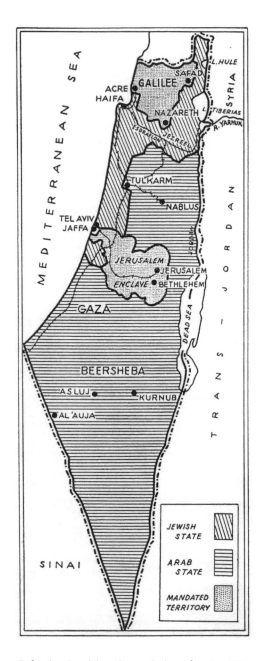

Palestine Partition Commission Plan B, 1938

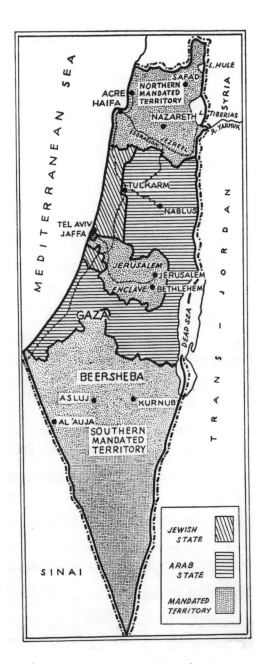

Palestine Partition Commission Plan C, 1938

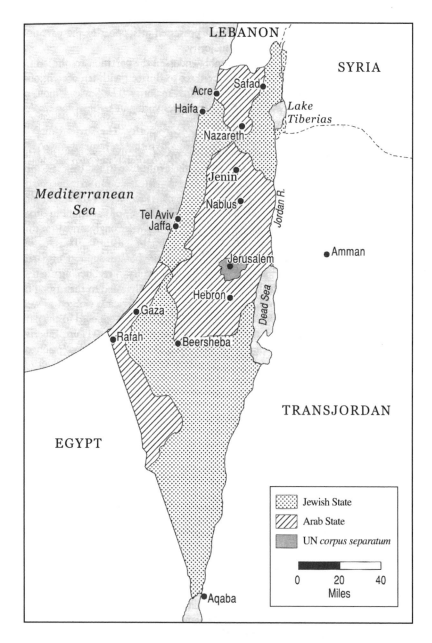

United Nations Partition Plan, adopted as General Assembly
Resolution 181 (29 November 1947)

1949 Armistice Agreement

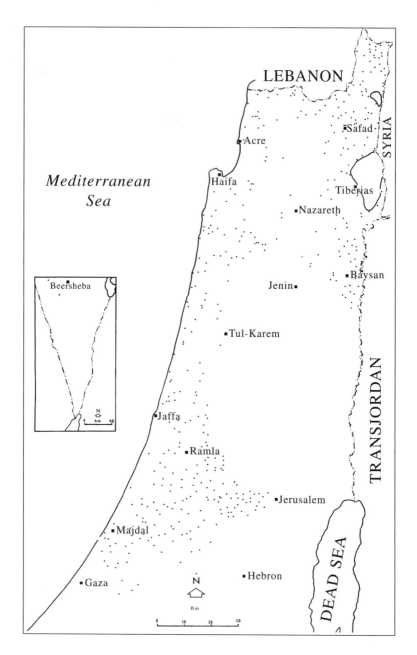

Palestinian villages depopulated, 1947–1949

TABLE 1: PALESTINE: PALESTINIAN AND JEWISH LAND OWNERSHIP
IN PERCENTAGES BY DISTRICT, 1945[1]

DISTRICT	PALESTINIAN	JEWISH	PUBLIC & OTHER[2]
ACRE	87	3	10
BAYSAN	44	34	22
BEERSHEBA	15	<1	85
GAZA	75	4	21
HAIFA	42	35	23
HEBRON	96	<1	4
JAFFA	47	39	14
JERUSALEM	84	2	14
JENIN	84	<1	16
NABLUS	87	<1	13
NAZARETH	52	28	20
RAMLA	77	14	9
RAMALLAH	99	<1	1
SAFAD	68	18	14
TIBERIAS	51	38	11
TUL-KAREM	78	17	5

TABLE 2: PALESTINE: DISTRIBUTION OF POPULATION BY DISTRICT SHOWING
PERCENTAGES OF PALESTINIANS AND JEWS, 1946[3]

DISTRICT	PALESTINIAN	JEWISH
ACRE	96	4
BAYSAN	70	30
BEERSHEBA	99	<1
GAZA	98	2
HAIFA	53	47
HEBRON	99	<1
JAFFA	29	71
JERUSALEM	62	38
JENIN	100	0
NABLUS	100	0
NAZARETH	84	16
RAMLA	78	22
RAMALLAH	100	0
SAFAD	87	13
TIBERIAS	67	33
TUL-KAREM	83	17

[1] The source for this table is *Village Statistics* (Jerusalem: Palestine Government, 1945).
[2] The category of "public ownership" under the British Mandate derived from the Ottoman system of land tenure, which included state domain, & private and communal leasehold.
[3] The source for this table is the *Supplement to a Survey of Palestine* (Jerusalem: Government Printer, June 1947).

Bibliography

Baroud, Ramzy (ed.), *Searching Jenin: Eyewitness Accounts of the Israeli Invasion 2002* (Seattle: Cune Press, 2003)

Bar-Zohar, Michael, *Ben-Gurion: A Political Biography* (Tel-Aviv: Am-Oved, 1977) (Hebrew)

Begin, Menachem, *The Revolt: Story of the Irgun* (New York: Henry Schuman, 1951)

Bein, Alexander (ed.), *The Mozkin Book* (Jerusalem: World Zionist Organization Publications, 1939)

Ben-Ari, Uri, *Follow Me* (Tel-Aviv: Maariv, 1994) (Hebrew)

Ben-Artzi, Yossi (ed.), *The Development of Haifa, 1918–1948* (Jerusalem: Yad Yitzhak Ben-Zvi Institute Publications, 1988) (Hebrew)

Ben-Eliezer, Uri, *The Emergence of Israeli Militarism, 1936–1956* (Tel-Aviv: Dvir, 1995)

——*The Making of Israeli Militarism* (Bloomington: Indiana University Press, 1998)

Ben-Gurion, David, *Diary*, Ben-Gurion Archives

——*In the Battle* (Tel-Aviv: Am Oved, 1949) (Hebrew)

——*Rebirth and Destiny of Israel* (New York: Philosophical Library, 1954) (ed. & trans. from Hebrew by Mordekhai Nurock)

Ben-Yehuda, Netiva, *Between the Knots* (Jerusalem: Domino, 1985) (Hebrew)

Bierman, John and Colin Smith, *Fire in the Night: Wingate of Burma, Ethiopia and Zion* (New York: Random House, 1999)

Cohen, Geula, *Woman of Violence: Memories of a Young Terrorist, 1945–1948* (New York: Holt, Rinehart and Winston, 1966)

Cohen, Hillel, *The Shadow Army: Palestinian Collaborators in the Service of Zionism* (Jerusalem: Hozata Ivrit, 2004) (Hebrew)

al-Daly, Wahid, *The Secrets of the Arab League and Abd al-Rahman Azzam* (Cairo: no publishing house, 1978) (Arabic)

Davis, Uri, *Apartheid Israel: Possibilities for the Struggle Within* (London: Zed Books, 2004)

Dinur, Ben-Zion *et al.*, *The History of the Hagana* (Tel-Aviv: Am Oved 1972) (Hebrew)

Eshel, Zadok (ed.), *The Carmeli Brigade in the War of Independence* (Tel-Aviv: Ministry of Defence Publications, 1973) (Hebrew)

Etzioni, Binyamin (ed.), *The Golani Brigade in the Fighting* (Tel-Aviv: Ministry of Defence Publications, no date) (Hebrew)

Even Nur, Israel (ed.), *The Yiftach-Palmach Story* (Bat-Yam: Palmach Publications, no date) (Hebrew)

Farsoun, Samih and C. E. Zacharia, *Palestine and the Palestinians* (Boulder: Westview Press, 1997)

Flapan, Simcha, *The Birth of Israel: Myths and Realities* (New York: Pantheon Books, 1987)

Gelber, Yoav, *The Emergence of a Jewish Army* (Jerusalem: Yad Ithak Ben-Zvi Institute Publications, 1996) (Hebrew)

Gilad, Zerubavel, *The Palmach Book* (Tel-Aviv: Kibbutz Meuhad, 1955) (Hebrew)

Glubb, John Bagot, *A Soldier with the Arabs* (London: Hodder and Stoughton, 1957)

Goren, Tamir, *From Independence to Integration: The Israeli Authority and the Arabs of Haifa, 1948–1950* (Haifa: The Arab-Jewish Centre of the University of Haifa, 1996) (Hebrew)

Hussein, Hussein Abu and Fiona Makay, *Access Denied: Palestinian Access to Land in Israel* (London: Zed Books, 2003)

Ilan, Amitzur, *The Origins of the Arab-Israeli Arms Race: Arms, Embargo, Military Power and Decision in the 1948 Palestine War* (New York: New York University Press, 1996)

Kadish, Alon (ed.), *Israel's War of Independence 1948–1949* (Tel-Aviv, Ministry of Defence Publications, 2004) (Hebrew)

Khairiya, Qasimya, *Fawzi al-Qawuqji's Memoirs, 1936–1948* (Beirut: PLO Publications, 1975) (Arabic)

Khalidi, Rashid, *Palestinian Identity: The Construction of Modern National Consciousness* (New York: Columbia University Press, 1997)

Khalidi, Walid (ed.), *All That Remains: The Palestinian Villages Occupied and Depopulated by Israel in 1948* (Washington: Institute for Palestine Studies, 1992)

——*Palestine Reborn* (London: I.B. Tauris, 1992)

al-Khatib, Nimr, *Palestine's Nakba* (Damascus: no publishing house, 1950)

Kimmerling, Baruch, *Zionism and Territory: The Socio-Territorial Dimensions of Zionist Politics* (Berkeley: University of California, Institute of International Studies, Research Series, No. 51, 1983)

Kretzmer, David, *The Legal Status of Arabs in Israel* (Boulder: Westview Press, 1990)

Kurzman, Dan, *Genesis 1948: The First Arab-Israeli War*, with a new introduction by Yitzhak Rabin (New York: Da Capo Press, 1992)

——*Soldier of Peace* (London: Harper Collins, 1998)

Lebrecht, Hans, *The Palestinians, History and Present* (Tel-Aviv: Zoo Ha-Derech, 1987) (Hebrew)

Levy, Itzhak, *Jerusalem in the War of Independence* (Tel-Aviv: Ministry of Defence Publications, 1986) (Hebrew)

Lloyd George, David, *The Truth about the Peace Treaties* (New York: Fertig, 1972)

Louis, W. Roger and Robert S. Stookey (eds), *The End of the Palestine Mandate* (London: I. B. Tauris, 1985)

Makhul, Naji, *Acre and its Villages since Ancient Times* (Acre: Al-Aswar, 1977)

Mandel, Neville, *Arabs and Zionism before World War I* (Berkeley: California University Press, 1976)

Masalha, Nur, *Expulsion of the Palestinians: The Concept of 'Transfer' in Zionist Political Thought, 1882–1948* (Washington: Institute for Palestine Studies, 1992)

——*A Land Without People: Israel, Transfer and the Palestinians* (London: Faber and Faber, 1997)

——*The Politics of Denial: Israel and the Palestinian Refugee Problem* (London: Pluto, 2003)

Mattar, Philip (ed.), *The Encyclopedia of Palestine* (Washington: Institute of Palestine Studies, 2000)

McGowan, Daniel and Matthew C. Hogan, *The Saga of the Deir Yassin Massacre, Revisionism and Reality* (New York: Deir Yassin Remembered, 1999)

Milstein, Uri, *The History of the Independence War* (Tel-Aviv: Zemora Bitan, 1989) (Hebrew)

Montgomery of Alamein, *Memoirs* (London: Collins, 1958)

Morris, Benny, *The Birth of the Palestinian Refugee Problem, 1947–1949* (Cambridge: Cambridge University Press, 1987)

——*The Birth of the Palestinian Refugee Problem Revisited* (Cambridge: Cambridge University Press, 2004)

——*Correcting A Mistake* (Tel-Aviv: Am Oved 2000) (Hebrew)

Nakhleh, Issah, *The Encyclopedia of the Palestine Problem* (New York: Intercontinental books, 1991)

Natur, Salman, *Anta al-Qatil, ya- Shaykh* (no publishing house, 1976)

Pail, Meir, *From Hagana to the IDF* (Tel-Aviv, Zemora Bitan Modan) (Hebrew)

Palumbo, Michael, *The Palestinian Catastrophe: The 1948 Expulsion of a People from their Homeland* (London: Faber & Faber, 1987)

Pappe, Ilan (ed.), *Arabs and Jews in the Mandatory Period – A Fresh View on the Historical Research* (Givat Haviva: Institute for Peace Research, 1992) (Hebrew)

——*Britain and the Arab-Israeli Conflict, 1948–1951* (London: St. Antony's/ Macmillan Press, 1984)

——*A History of Modern Palestine: One Land, Two Peoples* (Cambridge: Cambridge University Press, 2004)

——*The Israel/Palestine Question* (London and New York: Routledge, 1999)

——*The Making of the Arab-Israeli Conflict, 1947–1951* (London: I.B. Tauris, 1992)

Porath, Yehosua, *The Emergence of the Palestinian Arab National Movement, 1919–1929* (London and New York: Frank Cass, 1974)

Prior, Michael (ed.), *Speaking the Truth about Zionism and Israel* (London: Melisende, 2004)

Rivlin, Gershon and Elhanan Oren, *The War of Independence: Ben-Gurion's Diary* (Tel-Aviv: Ministry of Defence, 1982)

Rivlin, Gershon (ed.), *Olive-Leaves and Sword: Documents and Studies of the Hagana* (Tel-Aviv: IDF Publication, 1990) (Hebrew)

Rogan, Eugene and Avi Shlaim (eds), *The War for Palestine: Rewriting the History of 1948* (Cambridge: Cambridge University Press, 2002)

Sacher, Harry, *Israel: The Establishment of Israel* (London: Weidenfeld and Nicolson, no date)

Schölch, Alexander, *Palestine in Transformation, 1856–1882: Studies in Social, Economic and Political Development* (Washington: Institute for Palestine Studies, 1993)

Segev, Tom, *1949–The First Israelis* (Jerusalem: Domino Press, 1984)

Shafir, Gershon, *Land, Labour and the Origins of the Israel–Palestinian Conflict, 1882–1914* (Cambridge: Cambridge University Press, 1989)

Shahak, Israel, *Racism de l'état d'Israel* (Paris: Authier, 1975)

Sinai, Zvi and Gershon Rivlin (eds), *The Alexandroni Brigade in the War of Independence* (Tel-Aviv: Ministry of Defence Publications, 1964) (Hebrew)

Sitta, Salman Abu, *Atlas of the Nakbah* (London: Palestine Land Society, 2005)

Sluzki, Yehuda, *The Hagana Book* (Tel-Aviv: IDF Publications, 1964) (Hebrew)

——*Summary of the Hagana Book* (Tel-Aviv: Ministry of Defence Publications, 1978) (Hebrew)

Smith, Barbara, *The Roots of Separatism in Palestine: British Economic Policy, 1920–1929* (Syracuse: Syracuse University Press, 1984)

Smith, Charles D., *Palestine and the Arab–Israeli Conflict* (Boston and New York: Beford/St. Martin's, 2004)

Stein, Kenneth, *The Land Question in Palestine, 1917–1939* (Atlanta: University of North Carolina Press, 1984)

Sternahal, Zeev, *The Founding Myths of Israel: Nationalism, Socialism, and the Making of the Jewish State* (Princeton: Princeton University Press, 1998)

Tal, David, *War in Palestine, 1948: Strategy and Diplomacy*, (London and New York: Routledge, 2004)

Tamari, Salim, *Jerusalem 1948: The Arab Neighbourhoods and their Fate in the War* (Jerusalem: The Institute of Jerusalem Studies, 1999)

Teveth, Shabtai, *Ben-Gurion and the Palestinian Arabs: From Peace to War* (New York: Oxford University Press, 1985)

Ulizki, Yossef, *From Events to A War* (Tel-Aviv: Hagana Publication of Documents, 1951) (Hebrew)

Weitz, Yossef, *My Diary*, manuscript in *Central Zionist Archives*, A246

Yahav, Dan, *Purity of Arms: Ethos, Myth and Reality, 1936–1956* (Tel-Aviv, Tamuz, 2002) (Hebrew)

Index